Decolonizing Nature

D0781715

Decolonizing Nature

Strategies for Conservation in a Post-colonial Era

Edited by

William M Adams and Martin Mulligan

Earthscan Publications Ltd
London • Sterling, VA

First published in the UK and USA in 2003
by Earthscan Publications Ltd

Copyright © William Adams and Martin Mulligan, 2003

All rights reserved

ISBN: 1 85383 749 0 paperback
     1 85383 750 4 hardback

Typesetting by PCS Mapping & DTP, Gateshead
Printed and bound in the UK by Creative Print and Design (Wales), Ebbw Vale
Cover design by Andrew Corbett

For a full list of publications please contact:

Earthscan Publications Ltd
120 Pentonville Road, London, N1 9JN, UK
Tel: +44 (0)20 7278 0433
Fax: +44 (0)20 7278 1142
Email: earthinfo@earthscan.co.uk
Web: **www.earthscan.co.uk**

22883 Quicksilver Drive, Sterling, VA 20166-2012, USA

Earthscan is an editorially independent subsidiary of Kogan Page Ltd and publishes in association with WWF-UK and the International Institute for Environment and Development

A catalogue record for this book is available from the British Library

Library of Congress Cataloging-in-Publication Data

Decolonizing nature : strategies for conservation in a postcolonial era / edited by William M. Adams and Martin Mulligan.
      p. cm.
   Includes bibliographical references and index.
   ISBN 1-85383-749-0 (pbk.) – ISBN 1-85383-750-4 (hardback)
    1. Nature conservation–Great Britain–Colonies–Africa–Philosophy. 2. Nature conservation–Australia–Philosophy. 3. Colonization–Environmental aspects–Great Britain–Colonies–Africa–History. 4. Colonization–Environmental aspects–Australia–History. I. Adams, W. M. (William Mark), 1955- II. Mulligan, Martin.

QH77.G7 D43 2002
333.7'2'0994–dc21

                                                                    2002152952

This book is printed on elemental chlorine-free paper

Contents

List of figures and tables

FIGURES

TABLES

List of authors

Adams, William H (Bill)
Bill Adams is Reader in the Geography of Conservation and Development at the Department of Geography, University of Cambridge, UK. He has written several books, including *Future Nature: A Vision for Conservation* (Earthscan, 1996) and *Green Development: Environment and Sustainability in the Third World* (Routledge, 2001). He is interested in conservation and rural change, especially in Africa and the UK, and has served on the councils of the Cambridgeshire Wildlife Trust, the British Association for Nature Conservationists and Fauna and Flora International.

Cameron, John
John Cameron is a Senior Lecturer and coordinator of the postgraduate research programme in the School of Social Ecology and Lifelong Learning at the University of Western Sydney (UWS). He initiated a series of national Australian colloquia on sense of place (held in the Blue Mountains, central Australia, outside Melbourne, and in Canberra), and has edited a volume of papers arising from those gatherings. Before joining UWS, he was employed by the Australian Conservation Foundation as a resource economist for research and consultancy on national forest policy and land management.

Colston, Adrian
Adrian Colston is the National Trust Property Manager for Wicken Fen, Cambridgeshire, UK. He has worked as a professional nature conservationist for 20 years for the Wildlife Trusts, the Royal Society for the Protection of Birds (RSPB) and the National Trust. He has written several books, including *The Nature of Northamptonshire*, with Franklyn Perring (Barracuda Books, 1989) and *Cambridgeshire's Red Data Book*, with Chris Gerrard and Rosemary Parslow (Wildlife Trust for Cambridgeshire, 1997).

Figgis, Penelope
Penelope Figgis is currently Vice President of the Australian Conservation Foundation (first elected in 1985), Director of the Australian Bush Heritage Fund and a member of the World Commission on Protected Areas. She was previously a member of the boards of management of the Environment Protection Authority of New South Wales, Uluru/Kata Tjuta National Park, the Great Barrier Reef Consultative Committee and Landcare Australia, and a

director of the Australian Tourism Commission. Her major publications include *Rainforests of Australia* (Weldon, 1985), *Australia's Wilderness Heritage: World Heritage Areas*, co-authored with J G Mosley (Weldon, 1988) and *Australia's National Parks and Protected Areas: Future Directions* (Occasional Paper No 8, published by the Australian Committee for International Union for the Conservation of Nature, 1999). In 1994 she was made a Member of the Order of Australia (AM) for her services to conservation and the environment.

Langton, Marcia

Marcia Langton holds the Chair of Indigenous Studies at the University of Melbourne. She was the Ranger Professor at the Northern Territory University and Founding Director of the university's Centre for Indigenous, Natural and Cultural Management. She is a well-known public figure in Australia, appearing regularly in the media and in documentary films concerned with indigenous issues. She is the author of *Burning Questions: Emerging Environmental Issues for Indigenous Peoples in Northern Australia* (Centre for Indigenous, Natural and Cultural Resource Management, Northern Territory University, 1998).

Magome, Hector

Hector Magome is Director of Conservation Services at South African National Parks, where he is responsible for developing biodiversity and livelihoods related practices. This includes developing management plans for national parks and managing scientific programmes for biodiversity research and monitoring. Before joining South African National Parks, Hector was responsible for implementing community wildlife extension programmes for the North West Parks and Tourism Board of South Africa.

Mulligan, Martin

Martin Mulligan is a Senior Lecturer in the School of Social Ecology and Lifelong Learning at the University of Western Sydney. He is co-author (with Stuart Hill) of *Ecological Pioneers: A Social History of Australian Ecological Thought and Action* (Cambridge University Press, 2001) and is general editor of the Australasian journal *Ecopolitics: Thought and Action* (Pluto Press Australia). He has been an environmental activist and active supporter of Aboriginal people and communities since the early 1970s.

Murombedzi, James

James Murombedzi is the Environment and Development Officer for Southern Africa for the Ford Foundation. He was previously a lecturer in political and social ecology at the Centre for Applied Social Sciences, University of Zimbabwe. His research has focused on the micro-political dynamics of natural resources management in the communal tenure regimes of Southern Africa. He has consulted for various organizations, including the World Conservation Union (IUCN), the Global Environmental Facility and the Food and Agriculture Organization of the UN.

Plumwood, Val

Val Plumwood is Australian Research Council Fellow at the Australian National University, Canberra. She has published over 100 papers and four books, including *The Fight for the Forests* (as Val Routley, Australian National University Canberra, 1973), *Feminism and the Mastery of Nature* (Routledge, 1993) and *Environmental Culture: The Ecological Crisis of Reason* (Routledge, 2002). She is an international pioneer of environmental philosophy, a forest activist and the survivor of an encounter with a saltwater crocodile in Kakadu National Park in 1985, which delivered a strong message about human vulnerability and the power and agency of nature.

Toogood, Mark

Mark Toogood teaches geography at the University of Central Lancashire and is an Honorary Research Fellow at the Centre for the Study of Environmental Change, Lancaster University. His research interests concern the political and cultural dimensions of ecological knowledge and nature conservation.

List of acronyms and abbreviations

ABC	Australian Broadcasting Corporation
ACF	Australian Conservation Foundation
AONB	Area of Outstanding Natural Beauty (UK)
AWC	Australian Wildlife Conservancy
CAMPFIRE	Communal Area Management Programme for Indigenous Resources (Zimbabwe)
CAP	Common Agricultural Policy (EU)
CAP	Caracas Action Plan
CAR	comprehensive, adequate and representative reserve system (Australia)
CBD	Convention on Biological Diversity
CBNRM	community-based natural resource management
CCAGS	Crofting Counties Agricultural Grants Scheme (Scotland)
CDI	conservation and development initiative
CI	Conservation International
CITES	Convention on International Trade in Endangered Species of Wild Flora and Fauna
CMN	Conservation Management Networks (Australia)
CNP	contract national park
CNPPA	Commission on National Parks and Protected Areas (now the WCPA)
DEFRA	Department for the Environment, Food and Rural Affairs (UK)
EA	Environment Agency (UK)
ESA	Environmentally Sensitive Area (UK)
EU	European Union
FATE	Future of Australia's Threatened Ecosystems
FAO	Food and Agriculture Organization (UN)
FOM	Friends of Makuleke
GABMP	Great Australian Bight Marine Park
GATT	General Agreement on Tariffs and Trade
GKG	Gaza-Kruger-Gonarezhou
GKG TFCA	Gaza-Kruger-Gonarezhou Trans-Frontier Conservation Area
GLTP	Great Limpopo Trans-Frontier Park
HLF	Heritage Lottery Fund (UK)
IBP	International Biological Programme
IBRA	Interim Biogeographic Regionalization for Australia

IDB	Internal Drainage Boards (UK)
IMCRA	Interim Marine and Coastal Regionalization for Australia
IPA	Indigenous Protected Areas programme (Australia)
IRA	Irish Republican Army
IRSAC	Institut pour la Récherche Scientifique en Afrique Central
IUCN	International Union for the Conservation of Nature and Natural Resources (World Conservation Union)
KNP	Kruger National Park
KTP	Kgalagadi Trans-Frontier Park
LIFE	Living in a Finite Environment programme (Namibia)
MAB	Man and the Biosphere programme (UNESCO)
MOMPA	multiple-objective marine-protected area
MoU	memorandum of understanding
MSP	Member of the Scottish Parliament
NGO	non-governmental organization
NHMF	National Heritage Memorial Fund (Scotland)
NNR	National Nature Reserve (UK)
NPWS	National Parks and Wildlife Service
NRE	new range economics
NRS	National Reserve System (Australia)
NRSMPA	National Representative System of Marine Protected Areas (Australia)
NSW	New South Wales
OLD	operations likely to damage Sites of Special Scientific Interest (UK)
ORSTOM	Office de Récherche Scientifique et Technique d'Outre Mer
PA	protected area
PPF	Peace Parks Foundation
RA TFCA	Richtersveld Ai-Ais Trans-Frontier Conservation Area
RDC	rural district council (Zimbabwe)
RFA	Regional Forest Agreement (Australia)
RNP	Richtersveld National Park
RSPB	Royal Society for the Protection of Birds (UK)
SAC	special area of conservation (UK)
SADC	Southern African Development Community
SANParks	South African National Parks
SEERAD	Scottish Executive Environment and Rural Affairs Department
SLOSS	single large or several small principle
SNH	Scottish Natural Heritage
SPWFE	Society for the Preservation of the Wild Fauna of the Empire
SSSI	Site of Special Scientific Interest (UK)
TFCA	trans-frontier conservation area
TWINSPAN	Two-Way Indicator Species Analysis
UN	United Nations
UNESCO	United Nations Educational, Scientific and Cultural

	Organization
UWS	University of Western Sydney
VIDCO	village development committee (Zimbabwe)
WADCO	ward development committee (Zimbabwe)
WCPA	World Commission on Protected Areas

Chapter 1

Introduction

William M Adams and Martin Mulligan

CONSERVATION AND DECOLONIZATION

At its height, the British Empire was the most impressive example of colonialism ever constructed. Its global reach was unparalleled, its legacy enduring. It transformed political relations, economies, ethnicities and social relations, sometimes quickly and almost everywhere profoundly. It also transformed nature, creating new landscapes, new ecologies and new relations between humans and non-human nature; in the process, it created new ideologies of those relationships (Shiva, 1989).

In time, conservation also struck root in the colonial world, both in colonized territories and in industrializing metropolitan countries in Europe and North America. By the 19th century, ideas about nature, whether as an economic resource that needed conserving and exploiting, or as a precious reservoir of unchanged wildness, were an important element in colonial ideology, at home and abroad. Through the 20th century, those ideas flowered and seeded widely. Conservation became a global concern, the subject of major investment by states, and of urgent concern to growing environmental movements.

At the start of the third millennium, the British Empire has long since been swept away, but colonial conservation ideas remain. In some cases they have changed; but many are remarkably intact. Does decolonization have any significance for conservation? If so, how does conservation thinking and practice need to change to take account of a post-colonial world? Have ideas about nature been allowed to shift, or are they still the subject of some kind of neo-colonial domination by Northern urban environmentalists? What kind of conservation is needed in a post-colonial world? These are among the questions addressed by this book.

ORIGINS OF THIS BOOK

This book had its genesis in a meeting between the editors at Cambridge in July 1998. Martin Mulligan had already used Bill Adams' book on conservation in the UK, *Future Nature* (1996), in teaching a subject related to environmental values and conservation strategies at the University of Western Sydney. He suggested the possibility of working together on a book that would develop some of the themes introduced in *Future Nature* with reference to both Australian and UK experiences. Having a long-standing interest in the post-colonial experiences of southern Africa, and knowing that Bill was involved in a range of conservation-oriented projects in the region, Martin decided to travel to the UK via Zimbabwe. By the time they met, Martin had gained a taste of 'wild' Africa and had spent a couple of days in the carefully manicured gardens of central London, noting in his travel diary that:

> ...*all the monuments to the colonial era make me feel uneasy, more acutely because I have come here from Africa... [I]t strikes me even more strongly that highly structured gardens represent an attempt to control nature by making it into an ornament or trophy, and we have inherited that attitude in Australia... I look forward to visiting a part of England where nature is less subdued.*

Reflecting on this 'enhanced' culture shock, Martin suggested the title *Decolonizing Nature* to Bill and we quickly agreed that we should draw on some African experiences, as well as those of Australia and the UK. Instead of simply building on ideas already outlined in *Future Nature*, we began to explore the common ground and contrasts involved in decolonizing attitudes towards nature in different parts of the old British Empire. The idea was born of seeking contributions to a book from writers and practitioners already engaged in trying to overcome the legacy of colonialism in thinking about nature conservation, or in conservation work.

It is important to stress that we come to this project with an active commitment to conservation. In highlighting a need to rethink conservation strategies, we have no desire to decry the important work of conservation pioneers and the movements they were able to build, or to dismiss conservationists' present-day aspirations. We take it as self-evident that without the legacy of conservation work that has been built in countries such as the UK, Australia, Zimbabwe and South Africa, there would be little or no basis to work from – no thinking to be rethought. However, we do believe that the current discourse about nature conservation needs to become much more inclusive (particularly of the peoples who were colonized) and more dynamic in the face of complex global socio-political changes. Some of the contributions to this book (see, for example, Chapters 5 and 6 by Magome and Murombedzi on southern Africa; Chapter 9 by Figgis on Australia; or Chapter 11 by Colston on the UK) make it clear that there is broad agreement about the need to rethink conservation strategies, even if the debates about preferred strategies are, not surprisingly, vigorous and sometimes heated. It is also clear that many new strategies are already being implemented and refined. What this book attempts to do is bring to such strategic discussions a much stronger focus on the complex, contradictory and difficult processes of decolonization and, at the same time, create opportunities for a cross-fertilization of ideas and experiences between the UK, Australia and southern Africa. The book seeks both to discuss conservation in these three regions, and also to address more general themes.

EMPIRE AND NATURE

The importance of empire to the shape of modern conservation cannot be in doubt. British imperialism grew with the emergence of capitalism. As capitalism grew most strongly in Britain, the British Empire came to overshadow the empires of other European powers, and many British scientists were recruited to the service of empire in order to improve the technologies of 'resource utilization' and trade (Mackay, 1985). However, alongside this mercantile agenda, the British imperial project also reflected the values of the broader European Enlightenment that had unfolded during the 18th century. Ushering in the Age of Reason, with its direct challenge to religious dogmatism, the European Enlightenment placed faith in the capacity of the rational human mind to order and conquer all – suggesting a superiority of mind over matter and of humans over 'non-rational' nature. In its imperialist vision, 'civilized' Europe, bearing the torch of reason, had a duty to enlighten the rest of the world, conquering wildness and bringing order and rationality to 'uncivilized' peoples and nature. The mission of British colonialism was not only to enrich the imperial metropole, but also, in so doing, to 'improve' the world. In the name of the imperial endeavour, peoples and nature were subjected to conquest and control, harnessed and transformed to serve projects of agricultural improvement, industrialization and trade (MacKenzie, 1990a; Grove, 1995; Drayton, 2000).

During the 19th century, European colonialism became intertwined with the international growth of capitalism. By the end of that century, Britain was being challenged in its industrial might and its domination of world trade by both Germany and the US, a recently colonized land whose settlers had achieved independence from Britain a century earlier. At the dawning of the 20th century, Victorian Britain's faith in bureaucracy as a measure of stability was proving to be cumbersome for the administration of the colonies, and simmering resistance grew into more overt anti-colonial revolts. Although it was a war against Britain by non-British European settlers in southern Africa, the Boer War of 1899–1902 ushered in a century in which direct and indirect forms of colonial rule would be overtly challenged. If the long reign of Queen Victoria (1837–1901) marked the height of British imperial power, it also marked the end of one era of colonialism and its replacement with a more complex interplay between neo-colonialism and decolonization that continued throughout the 20th century.

However, the legacy of 19th-century British colonialism would not simply fade away with the ending of direct and indirect rule from London. If European colonialism had begun in the 17th century with the extraction of 'surplus' commodities (such as gold, ivory, skins, spices and slaves), the version of colonialism that was taken furthest by Britain in the 19th century meant that the economies of the colonies were captured and re-ordered to serve the interests of the colonial power. European colonizers had moved from trade to territorial annexation, and they dug in for a long stay.

In some places (for example North America, Argentina, Australia and New Zealand), the Europeans created settler societies. These were stocked with various cadres of European society, from convicts to yeoman farmers, who brought with them an array of diseases and economically productive organisms that formed the basis for 'neo-Europes' (Crosby, 1986). In others (for example, West Africa or India) the colonial powers inserted political managers into pre-existing, or merely imagined, indigenous governance systems, and exerted control by indirect rule (see, for example, Shenton, 1986). Colonized peoples were variously coerced and taxed into engagement in the formal economy, often as migrant labourers in mines or plantations.

As Val Plumwood explains in Chapter 3, European colonial power came to be based upon a series of separations and exclusions that cast colonized peoples and nature as being outside the 'ideals' of 'civilized' Europe and, therefore, inferior. The colonized were denied their individuality and diversity and treated as belonging to stereotyped classes; they were both marginalized by, and incorporated within, the colonial project, which was, in turn, driven by an overriding desire for order and control. Increasingly, the biological sciences were recruited to the task of rationalizing nature to make it more amenable to human exploitation. Not surprisingly, the experience of colonialism abroad entrenched the separation between people and nature at home, and further undermined the possibility of diverse development paths within the UK itself. Despite the diversity of colonial experiences, colonialism – a precursor to globalization – created the illusion that a particular model of development could be recreated in all parts of the world, and the powerful (and so often destructive) homogenization of 'Modernism' began. As the chain of events initiated by the terrorist attacks on the US on 11 September 2001 have reminded us so painfully, efforts to impose uniform models of development across natural and cultural diversity have failed to deliver peace and prosperity, or freedom from tension, conflict and insecurity.

The engagements between colonizer and colonized, between metropolitan and peripheral economies, and between modern technology and nature, were not only direct and material, but also discursive. Knowledge of the colonized world, and its increasingly transformed nature, was intrinsic to colonial domination (Pratt, 1992; Drayton, 2000). The production of knowledge was an integral part of the exercise of colonial power (Loomba, 1998). The 'Orientalist' discourses of colonialism (Said, 1978; Moore-Gilbert, 1997) took as their subjects both people and nature. Indeed, the two were commonly linked in loosely theorized (and deeply racist) discourses that dismissed as unordered, undisciplined, worthless and uncivilized the 'wildness' of exotic and remote peoples and landscapes. For indigenous peoples, colonialism reached 'into our heads' (Smith, 1999), and it did the same (with very different implications) for the colonizer: colonization changed the very categories within which nature and society were conceived.

Richard Grove (1995) and other environmental historians (see, for example, Griffiths and Robbins, 1997) have made the point that experiences of colonialism with regard to exploiting nature have been far from uniform, and that an impetus to conserve nature began when colonial authorities grew alarmed at the speed of environmental degradation in colonized lands. Somewhat paradoxically, while ideas about the exploitation of nature moved with the colonizers from the centre to the periphery of old empires, ideas about the conservation of nature circulating in the periphery were brought back to the centre. However, it is important to recognize that both the exploitation of nature in the colonies and the impetus to conserve nature for longer-term human use were a product of the colonial mindset, which was shaped by the interaction between colonial experiences in the centre and periphery. The colonial mindset can only be understood by looking at this interaction; but it was fundamentally rooted in European values, which constructed nature as nothing more than a resource for human use and wildness as a challenge for the rational mind to conquer. As Tom Griffiths (1996) has pointed out, even those settlers who were most enamoured of the flora and fauna in their adopted homelands saw themselves as either hunters or collectors, and wanted to assert their mastery over the wildness that they simultaneously admired and feared, or to collect specimens that could be named and safely deposited in museums. Early colonial ideas about the conservation of nature essentially grew out of a broader desire to 'tame' the wild.

DECOLONIZATION AND CONSERVATION

In terms of direct political control by European powers, colonial rule was finally brought to an end in much of the world in the third quarter of the 20th century, especially as the result of a string of anti-colonial struggles that emerged in former European colonies in the wake of World War II. In South Asia and sub-Saharan Africa, new post-colonial political structures emerged. The end of direct political control might have been expected to open the way for more independent thinking about the relations between society and nature, perhaps based on non-Western traditions and cultural fusions. This did not happen. From the late 19th century onwards, the decolonization process had involved the creation of 'modern' nation states that were built, essentially, on European models and traditions, and the deep ideological legacy of colonialism endured. Smith (1999) comments that indigenous people have been subjected to 'the colonization of their lands and cultures, and the denial of their sovereignty, by a society that has come to dominate the shape and quality of their lives, even after it has formally pulled out' (p7).

Modern European colonialism was not monolithic, and the diverse experiences of decolonization were complicated. In parts of the world where European settlement and land occupation was either complete or very extensive (for example, Australia, New Zealand, South Africa, the US, Canada and South America), direct imperial control by European political powers ended as the settler societies progressively assumed administrative control (in a relatively painless form of decolonization). But such settler societies had established their own, internal, forms of colonialism in order to dominate indigenous minorities (for example, in Australia; see Chapter 4), or profoundly suppressed majorities (as in the case of South Africa or Rhodesia [Zimbabwe] before majority rule). In many settler societies, indigenous peoples were herded into isolated fragments of their former terrain, on 'reservations', 'missions' or 'tribal lands', administered with a complex mix of brute exploitation, paternalistic exhortation and racist disdain. In such contexts decolonization has often been piecemeal and is still far from complete.

As decolonization reached its peak in terms of the political independence of nation states, new forms of trans-national and global colonization – in the form of cultural and economic engagement – began to gather force, accelerating rapidly during the last part of the 20th century. The process of political decolonization was therefore overtaken by globalization and neo-colonialism, making the transition to post-colonial societies complex and messy. Even in the post-colonial era, dominant global development strategies are still rooted in European or Western values, and in familiar ideologies of nature. Through the 'development decades' of the third quarter of the 20th century, nature was treated either as the fuel for modernist economic growth, or as something precious, needing absolute preservation. The adoption of the language of 'sustainable development' at the end of the 20th century (especially in the 1987 Brundtland Report [World Commission on Environment and Development, 1987] and the outputs of the 1992 Earth Summit in Rio) maintained a view of nature as an economic resource, to be managed in ways that yield sustainable economic benefits (Adams, 2001). This may have created new frameworks for 'natural resource management', but it did not challenge the colonial legacy of imperial, anthropocentric and utilitarian attitudes towards nature.

In trying to make some sense of the implications for conservation of the complex transition to the post-colonial era, this book focuses on the legacy of colonial mindsets in specific regions that were in the periphery and centre of the former British Empire. This is partly because we felt a need to narrow the focus to parts of the world within which we felt confident we could identify key issues and important contributors to the discussion. However, given the size and power of the British Empire, and the weight in contemporary global affairs of settler societies originally set up by the British (most notably, of course, in the US), the focus on the British Empire seems fortuitous. The ideologies fostered by British imperialism, especially during the 19th century, were important not only in the colonial world that Britain came to dominate, but also in the colonized world, more generally. Furthermore, this focus enabled us to explore the legacy of colonialism inside the pre-eminent colonial power: Britain. The experience of being at the centre of a vast empire obviously influenced the ways in which British people (especially the English) came to think of themselves and their relationships with other peoples and places (MacKenzie, 1986).

While no set of experiences can be deemed to be representative, we have been able to take a significant cross-section of the British colonial experience by comparing post-colonial experiences in two parts of the old empire: one in which a white settler society largely displaced the indigenous people (Australia), and the other (southern Africa) in which the balance of forces was less favourable for the white settlers and where the indigenous people have eventually been able to reassert a measure of political control. What is relatively unusual about this book is that we also seek to make sense of the post-colonial era by discussing the former imperial metropole. The UK has its own internal colonial history with regard to Ireland, Scotland and Wales. Moreover, it was affected by the cultural backwash and economic profits of British imperialism overseas. The same colonial mindsets created similar damaging illusions about human 'mastery' over nature. Imperial ideologies of nature were important to understandings of nature within the UK, and to the way that ideas about conservation emerged (Sheail, 1976; Evans, 1992; Adams, 2001). Like Richard Grove (1997), we are interested in how complex political, economic and ideological interchanges between the centre and periphery have been important to conservation, both globally and nationally (within the UK, as well as between the UK and the colonies). Organizations that aimed to conserve nature began to emerge in both the centre and periphery of the British Empire during the second half of the 19th century. However, not surprisingly, they reflected ideologies of nature that grew out of utilitarian and reductionist 'natural' sciences. Even the more aesthetic and ecocentric ideologies about nature sought to ground themselves in 'rational' scientific frameworks. Western ideas about conservation were disseminated by state bureaucracies, scientific networks and passionate conservation advocates through colonized and metropolitan societies alike – through Scotland, as well as Africa; the English Lake District, as well as the Australian outback.

Of course, it would be simplistic, even misleading, to suggest that strategies for nature conservation have been uniform in regions as diverse as Australia, southern Africa and the UK. Conservation has been deeply imbued with the European Enlightenment values that drove global colonial development. However, it has also reflected a social reaction against technology, industrialization and growth-oriented 'development'. In all three regions, nature-conservation thinking emerged partially in opposition to the impacts of the excesses of utilitarian resource exploitation. This central paradox has created a diversity of conservation thinking both within and between the regions that were once at the centre or periphery of the British Empire.

In the UK, conservation has inherited both a romantic tradition that has decried the impact of 'modernization', and a scientific rational tradition that seeks to manage nature for human enjoyment and material benefit (see Bate, 1991; Veldman, 1994; Adams, 1996). From romanticism came a celebration of wild nature, from Wordsworth's presentation of the Lake District during the 19th century to the cultural landscape conservation of the Lake District National Park in the 1950s. From scientific rationality came the different tradition of 'nature' (or, later, 'wildlife') conservation, and the establishment of National Nature Reserves (NNRs) and Sites of Special Scientific Interest (SSSIs) (Evans, 1992; Adams, 1996). British conservation has a rich but confused heritage. British imperialism funded aristocratic aspirations and attempts to create controlled, orderly and beautiful landscapes in the UK, as seen in the growing dominance of the 'picturesque movement' in horticulture and landscape art. The resulting idealization of Arcadian rural landscapes had little to do with 'wild' nature (Bunce, 1994). During the 20th century, the maintenance and preservation of these landscapes have been important themes of conservation in the UK – for example, in the work of the National Trust (Bullock and Harvey, 1995). Some of these valued landscapes were cleared of their people for 'improvement' (for example, the Scottish Highland clearances; see Chapter 7), or to create a landscape that fitted an aristocratic aesthetic vision. The landscapes valued by conservationists in the UK include those drastically remodelled using the profits of colonial trade and exploitation, in response to very similar ideologies of 'improvement'.

In North America, by contrast, transcendental concern for nature, epitomized in the ideas of John Muir and his legacy in the Sierra Club, led to a complex concern with 'wilderness' (Nash, 1973; Cronon, 1995). This has long been in conflict with the rational utilitarian tradition of resource conservation – for example, in the US Forest Service or the Bureau of Reclamation (Hays, 1959; Worster, 1994). The construction of 'wildness' (for example, in creating Central Park in New York or the remodelling of Niagara Falls) reveals the hidden synergies between the two (Spirn, 1995). Here, too, conservation draws on both colonial and anti-colonial ideas in its conception and treatment of nature.

Australia shares with the US a mixture of a rational tradition and a preservationist ideology that identifies and seeks to preserve 'pristine' wilderness. The former has underpinned a culture and economy of resource exploitation, the latter an ideology of preservationism that resists human-induced change. Until very recently, the ecocentric beliefs and practices of the indigenous Australians have had no influence on dominant ideas about conservation in Australia. Certainly, there have been conservationists, most notably Judith Wright, who have urged their colleagues to open their hearts and minds to Aboriginal cosmology; but they remained in a minority (see Mulligan and Hill, 2001). Only when Aboriginal communities were able to regain title to significant tracts of land (under land rights legislation and the very late recognition of native title) were they taken more seriously by conservation organizations. This gave indigenous leaders such as Marcia Langton (see Chapter 4) the opportunity to challenge some of the Eurocentric values and ideas that continued to motivate a lot of conservation practice.

In sub-Saharan Africa, indigenous people have, until very recently, also been ignored in both colonial and post-colonial conservation ideas and practices. Close working relationships with non-human nature were ignored, overlain by an elitist conservation aimed initially at the preservation of game for colonial hunters, and latterly at the preservation of exotic species and 'wild' Africa (MacKenzie, 1988; Neumann, 1998). As the contribution by James Murombedzi to this book makes clear (see Chapter 5), recent 'community-based' conservation strategies that involve indigenous communities have been rather half-hearted and easily undermined by political elitism and corruption. Attempts to rehabilitate African ideas about simultaneously catering for the needs of people and nature have been badly compromised.

Like it or not, debates about nature conservation have themselves now been globalized. The Convention on Biological Diversity (CBD) provides a common language for 'scientific' conservation, and the continuing assault of global consumption on non-human nature provides a fertile seedbed for arguments about nature that range from the rational anthropocentrism of sustainable development to the arguments (found, for example, in 'deep ecology') that urge the need to preserve nature for its own sake (Merchant, 1992; Holdgate, 1996; Adams, 2001; Lewis, 1992). In the latter discourse, indigenous and non-Western cosmologies have attracted renewed interest. However, the global discourse on conservation – dominated as it is by people and organizations from nations that benefited most from colonialism – has sometimes been used to justify new forms of colonization (see Chapter 4). Many conservationists have worked hard to adapt their agendas to discourses about dismantling the colonial legacy – for example, in debates about 'community conservation' (Western et al, 1994; Hulme and Murphree, 2001). However, even when conservation action has involved resistance to imperial, utilitarian views of nature, it has rarely been sensitive to local human needs and a diversity of world views. It has often been imposed like a version of the imperial endeavour itself: alien and arbitrary, barring people from their lands and denying their understanding of non-human nature.

In countries such as the UK and Australia, the 'modern' conservation movement reached a high point in social and political influence during the late 1980s (Pepper, 1996). Since that time, concern for nature has waxed and waned along with broader environmental concerns. Meanwhile, in countries such as South Africa and Zimbabwe, conservation and development have become entangled in messy post-colonial transitions. Despite the global reach of conservation concern, widespread popular support for formal conservation measures is confined to industrialized countries, and is hence widely dismissed as a 'Western' (that is, neo-colonial) preoccupation in the context of non-industrialized countries. While organizations such as the International Union for the Conservation of Nature and Natural Resources (IUCN – more commonly known as the World Conservation Union) have shifted further and further towards a view of conservation as sustainable resource use, the dominant Western ideology regarding conservation has remained, paradoxically, preservationist. The language of biodiversity enshrined in the CBD has come to drive a programme of action based upon the identification and protection of critical biodiverse areas – a 'protected area' strategy based largely upon a US model of national parks and wilderness reserves.[1] This tradition tends to foster a conceptual separation between humans and nature, and between nature and culture, which creates both moral and practical dilemmas, especially in poor countries where human needs cannot be set aside in pursuing the 'intrinsic' rights of nature.

If there is a need to revisit the founding ideas of nature conservation in post-colonial societies, that exploration also must take into account the fact that the cherished notion of a 'balance of nature' has now been questioned by ecologists who once popularized the idea. 'Non-equilibrium ecology' (discussed further in Chapter 10), properly understood, creates some opportunities for overcoming the legacy of separating people from nature; yet it also makes our task more ethically complex. During the 1990s, for example, conservationists were challenged to rethink the idea that nature could be preserved by maintaining representative sections of it free from human interference (see, for example, Langton, 1998; Plumwood, 1993; Cronon, 1995). However, if the disengagement of people from nature (for the sake of nature) is impossible, then we must seek new, more ethical, forms of engagement. What this might mean in practice is the central interest of this book.

THE BOOK

In Chapter 2, Bill Adams reviews the ways in which nature was understood and treated in the British Empire. He discusses, in particular, the role of science and ideas of the rational exploitation of nature, the nature of colonial impacts on the environment, colonial fears about environmental degradation, the importance of hunting and the rise of formal conservation. He assesses the significance of this colonial inheritance for conservation. In Chapter 3, Val Plumwood extends this account with a theoretical analysis of the dynamics of European colonialism before turning her attention to language and conservation discourse and practice. Val ends her contribution with a challenging proposal about decolonizing place names in order to begin a more 'dialogical' relationship between people and places.

In Chapter 4, Marcia Langton (writing primarily from the perspective of indigenous Australians) outlines the features of new, globalized forms of colonization before offering some insights on sustainable resource use based upon her research and consultations with Australian indigenous communities. In Chapter 5, Hector Magome and James Murombedzi (writing about conservation in post-apartheid South Africa) discuss negotiations between local people and the state conservation agency over land rights and national parks. In Chapter 6, James Murombedzi then discusses the sometimes half-hearted efforts to incorporate local indigenous communities within resource management strategies in southern Africa, particularly the Zimbabwean CAMPFIRE programme. These chapters both support Langton's contention that indigenous people face new forms of expropriation under the guise of biodiversity management. They suggest a need for the negotiation of localized, diverse conservation strategies that put biodiversity goals alongside human needs – building conservation goals into local, national and international political strategies aimed at eliminating elitism, corruption and gross social inequities.

In Chapter 7, Mark Toogood brings the legacy of British colonialism back 'home' by discussing conservation in Scotland. He explores the nature and significance of colonial thinking within conservation in Scotland, and the significance of local grassroots opposition to conservation by government agencies in the Scottish Highlands. He goes on to consider ways in which a revitalized discourse on Scottish identity and history challenges, and potentially refreshes, the discourse on conservation.

In Chapter 8, John Cameron draws upon his experience of teaching and writing about 'sense of place' in the Australian context to suggest some ways in which conscious attention to the building of place attachments can lead to a more grounded exploration of the colonial legacy, while providing people with a starting point for building more ethical relationships with the environments in which they dwell.

In Chapter 9, Penelope Figgis reviews new and emerging conservation strategies in Australia. Her argument has substantial relevance for other countries grappling with the legacy of colonialism. She explores new global challenges and constraints and new ideas about the dynamic processes involved in the search for sustainability.

In his second contribution to the book, in Chapter 10, Bill Adams explores some of the implications of the growing discourse about non-equilibrium ecology for conservation. He argues that a deeper understanding of the complex processes involved in ecosystem change can give humans a new sense of control over nature, particularly visible in the rise of restoration ecology.

In Chapter 11, Adrian Colston offers a case study of a long-term wetland restoration project at Wicken Fen in the UK. Wicken Fen has been a formal nature reserve for more than a century, containing once-common species in a drained and intensively managed agricultural landscape. But the fen has become increasingly isolated and dry, and its long-term future is insecure. In response, conservation strategy has turned outwards, seeking to acquire and restore reclaimed farmland across the whole river catchment. Attempts to build more complex and resilient ecosystems require a serious allocation of human and material resources and a lot of patience (something that is rarely valued in result-oriented modern societies). These efforts also necessitate a more sophisticated exploration of practical applied ethics in trying to ensure that such endeavours can have optimal outcomes for both people and nature.

In Chapter 12, Martin Mulligan takes up the need to deregulate our very conception of landscapes, arguing for more sensuous and imaginative relationships with 'storied landscapes' and a much more serious attempt to learn from the ways in which Aboriginal people conceive of relationships between people and 'country'. A much deeper dialogue between indigenous and non-indigenous conservationists, Mulligan contends, is one way in which conservation work can be re-enchanted.

Inevitably, this book raises more questions than it answers and some of our starting assumptions have been challenged along the way. There are, of course, no universally appropriate conservation strategies or models. Contradictory ideas are expressed between, and discussed within, some of the chapters in this volume. We are pleased with the way the book has grown out of our initial idea, and with the way that contributors have expanded on our initial themes without losing sight of our central concerns. In the deliberate diversity of the contributions it contains, this book seeks to contribute to the vital, ongoing discussions that are needed in order to revitalize conservation during a period of considerable uncertainty and change. New thinking is urgently needed, and it is to this need that this book is addressed.

A NOTE ON TERMINOLOGY

The enormous gap between living standards in the richer and poorer countries of the world is universally acknowledged. However, there is no consensus about what terms should be used to designate the richer and poorer sectors. The terms 'First World' and 'Third World' are still in use, but are widely seen as dated (with the 'Second World' no longer in existence). The phrases 'developed world' and 'underdeveloped world' are widely used by international organizations, but they imply that the poorer nations ought to develop themselves in the direction and manner of the richer nations. In fact, that 'development' is often seen as being both impossible from the point of view of the global environment and undesirable from the point of view of the cultures and existing lifestyles within the 'underdeveloped world'. The very concept of 'development' is complex and double-edged (see, for example, Sachs, 1992; Cowen and Shenton, 1996; Adams, 2001).

It has become common to use 'developing world' in place of 'underdeveloped world', to avoid the implication of failure to measure up to the rich-world standards and model (see, for example, Edwards, 2000). However, this still implies that the sort of 'development' manifested by richer nations is a necessary goal of poorer nations. Environmentalists have favoured 'industrialized' and 'non-industrialized' worlds, but this tends to focus on just one aspect of the difference between the two worlds; while the terms 'overdeveloped' and 'underdeveloped' shift the blame for the gap but still imply that a convergence is necessary and desirable. The terms 'North' and 'South' are popular in some sectors – particularly in nations of the 'South' – but they don't work for Australia (a nation of the 'North' located in the 'South').

The editors of this volume tend to favour the term 'Third World' because it seems the most neutral of all, and because it was originally coined as an act of political self-definition rather than external 'expert' labelling. However, we have not insisted on a single term, preferring to leave the decision to each author. Perhaps a more widely accepted terminology will emerge at some point in the future but for now it seems wise to respect a diversity of terms used for different purposes.

NOTES

1   For a discussion of competing Western traditions, see 'Local Development and Parks in France' by Andrea Finger-Stich and Krishna B Ghimire in *Social Change and Conservation* (Earthscan, 1997), edited by Krishna B Ghimire and Michel P Pimbert.

REFERENCES

Adams, W M (1996) *Future Nature: A Vision for Conservation.* Earthscan, London

Adams, W M (2001) *Green Development: Environment and Sustainability in the Third World.* Routledge, London

Bate, J (1991) *Romantic Ecology: Wordsworth and the Environmental Tradition.* Routledge, London

Bullock, D J and Harvey, H J (1995) (eds) *The National Trust and Nature Conservation: 100 Years On. Biological Journal of the Linnean Society 56* (Suppl). The Linnean Society, London

Bunce, M (1994) *The Countryside Ideal: Anglo-American Images of Landscape.* Routledge, London

Cowen, M P and Shenton, R W (1996) *Doctrines of Development.* Routledge, London

Cronon, W (1995) 'The trouble with wilderness: or, getting back to the wrong nature', in W Cronon (ed) *Uncommon Ground: Toward Reinventing Nature.* W W Norton and Co, New York, pp69–90

Crosby, A W (1986) *Ecological Imperialism: The Ecological Expansion of Europe 1600–1900.* Cambridge University Press, Cambridge

Drayton, R (2000) *Nature's Government: Science, Imperial Britain and the 'Improvement' of the World.* Yale University Press, New Haven

Edwards, M (2000) *Future Positive: International Co-operation in the 21st Century,* Earthscan, London

Evans, D (1992) *A History of Nature Conservation in Great Britain.* Routledge, London

Griffiths, T (1996) *Hunters and Collectors: The Antiquarian Imagination in Australia.* Cambridge University Press, Cambridge

Griffiths, T and Robbins, L (eds) (1997) *Ecology and Empire: Environmental History of Settler Societies.* Melbourne University Press, Melbourne

Grove, R H (1995) *Green Imperialism: Colonial Expansion, Tropical Island Edens and the Origins of Environmentalism, 1600–1800.* Cambridge University Press, Cambridge

Grove, R H (1997) 'Scotland in South Africa: John Croumbie Brown and the roots of settler environmentalism', in T Griffiths and L Robin (eds) *Ecology and Empire: Environmental History of Settler Societies.* Keele University Press, Keele, pp139–153

Hays, S (1959) *Conservation and the Gospel of Efficiency: The Progressive Conservation Movement, 1890–1920*. Harvard University Press, Cambridge, MA

Holdgate, M (1996) *From Care to Action: Making a Sustainable World*. Earthscan, London

Hulme, D and Murphree, M (2001) (eds) *African Wildlife and Livelihoods: The Promise and Performance of Community Conservation*. James Currey, Oxford and Heinemann, New Hampshire

Langton, M (1998) *Burning Questions: Emerging Environmental Issues for Indigenous People in Northern Australia*. Centre for Indigenous, Natural and Cultural Resource Management, Northern Territory University, Darwin

Lewis, M W (1992) *Green Delusions: An Environmentalist Critique of Radical Environmentalism*. Duke University Press, Durham and London

Loomba, A (1998) *Colonialism/Post-colonialism*. Routledge, London

Mackay, D (1985) *In the Wake of Cook: Exploration, Science and Empire 1780–1801*. Victoria University Press, Wellington

MacKenzie, J (ed) (1986) *Imperialism and Popular Culture*. Manchester University Press, Manchester

MacKenzie, J M (1988) *The Empire of Nature: Hunting, Conservation and British Imperialism*. Manchester University Press, Manchester

MacKenzie, J M (ed) (1990a) *Imperialism and the Natural World*. Manchester University Press, Manchester

MacKenzie, J M (1990b) 'Introduction', in J M MacKenzie (ed) *Imperialism and the Natural World*. Manchester University Press, Manchester

MacKenzie, J M (1997) 'Empire and the ecological apocalypse: the historiography of the imperial environment', in T Griffiths and L Robin (eds) *Ecology and Empire: Environmental History of Settler Societies*. Keele University Press, Keele, pp215–228

Merchant, C (1992) *Radical Ecology: The Search for a Livable World*. Routledge, New York

Moore-Gilbert, B (1997) *Post-colonial Theory: Contexts, Practices, Politics*. Verso, London

Mulligan, M and Hill, S (2001) *Ecological Pioneers: A Social History of Australian Ecological Thought and Action*. Cambridge University Press, Melbourne

Nash, R (1973) *Wilderness and the American Mind*. Yale University Press, New Haven, CT

Neumann, R P (1998) *Imposing Wilderness: Struggles over Livelihood and Nature Preservation in Africa*. University of California Press, Berkeley

Pepper, D (1996) *The Roots of Modern Environmentalism: An Introduction*. Routledge, London and New York

Plumwood, V (1993) *Feminism and the Mastery of Nature*. Routledge, London

Pratt, M L (1992) *Imperial Eyes: Travel Writing and Transculturation*. Routledge, London

Sachs, W (ed) (1992) *The Development Dictionary: A Guide to Knowledge as Power*, Witwatersrand University Press, Johannesburg and Zed Books, London

Said, E (1978) *Orientalism*. Pantheon, New York

Sheail, J (1976) *Nature in Trust: The History of Nature Conservation in Great Britain*. Blackie, Glasgow

Shenton, R W (1986) *The Development of Capitalism in Northern Nigeria*. James Currey, London

Shiva, V (1989) *Staying Alive: Women, Ecology and Development*. Zed Books, London

Smith, L Tuhiwai (1999) *Decolonising Methodologies: Research and Indigenous Peoples*. Zed Books, London

Spirn, A W (1995) 'Constructing nature: the legacy of Frederick Law Olmstead', in W Cronon (ed) *Uncommon Ground: Toward Reinventing Nature*, W W Norton and Co, New York, pp91–113

Veldman, M (1994) *Fantasy, the Bomb and the Greening of Britain: Romantic Protest 1945–1980*. Cambridge University Press, London

Western, D, White, R M and Strum, S C (eds) (1994) *Natural Connections: Perspectives in Community-based Conservation*. Island Press, Washington

World Commission on Environment and Development (1987) *Our Common Future*. Oxford University Press, Oxford

Worster, D (1994) *Nature's Economy: A History of Ecological Ideas*. Cambridge University Press, Cambridge (second edition)

Chapter 2

Nature and the colonial mind

William M Adams

INTRODUCTION

One of the unsung delights of having children is that you get to see films and read books that adults typically disdain. Sometimes these turn out to reveal troubling insights into accepted ways of thinking and doing things. For me, one such was the Disney Corporation's cartoon *The Lion King*. For any conservationist, this film provides a sobering reflection of idealized thinking about nature. For any critic of colonial conservation, it provides the most wonderful ammunition.

Africa, seen through the computers and pens of the great corporate iconographer, is homogenized into a placeless landscape of towering beauty and openness. Nature is synthesized for global consumption and cast within a vision of Eden, a wild yet harmonious place. The film opens at Pride Rock, a mythical land of primitive order, where broad plains teem with wild animals in pairs and small bands – *Bambi* come to Serengeti or Maasai Mara. Up on the rock, Mufasa, the true ruler, presents Simba, the young lion, to his assembled subjects: social relations (age, gender, race and power) are naturalized. There is a hierarchy of species, gender and age. The lions (male, of course) have a stern imperial duty to maintain order for the lesser animals; the female lions live in an imperial court – supportive, intelligent and subservient. Simba has much to learn before he can take his place as a ruler of his world. The core of his learning (beyond the usual challenge of 'becoming a man', to be expected as the values of the American West are celebrated in a cartoon East Africa) is 'the circle of life': the stars look down, Simba looks up, and he tunes in to the principles of ecology and environmentalism. Here is ecological responsibility as preached to the children of the baby-boom generation, a 'naturalizing' of conservation principles within Disney's timeless and placeless (and people-less) world. It is an ecological vision backed by deep religion: there is a bizarre baboon witch doctor who authenticates the wise ruler and endorses the good management of the Pride Lands. Only the lions understand their deep responsibility to work within limits and respect the circle of life. They must therefore govern for those lesser creatures who might otherwise deviate from the necessary balanced path.

Of course, paradise is severely challenged. Governance collapses when Mufasa is killed; Simba wimps out for a while, and degradation stalks the land in the shape of the evil and destructive hyenas. This is a thinly racialized presentation of the threat to the environment of Africa: black actors' voices usher in destruction, a lack of integrity on all sides, unsustainable hunting practices, drought and famine. The new ruler is weak, camp, lazy and violent (and English!). In the end, of course, Simba returns, trained in self-sufficiency (like Mowgli in *The Jungle Book*) by an unlikely combination of a warthog and a meerkat (some very odd ecology here), reminded of his deep duty by the baboon and empowered by a feisty female to do the decent thing. At the last minute, Simba fights, Scar is ousted, the world burns and evil is overturned. The film finally ends where it began, with the lions on Pride Rock and their admiring subjects around them, the world green and fertile once more, ecological order and moral governance restored under the firm but wise paternalism of the new Lion King.

This is an engaging and sweetly told morality tale, and a fantastically successful one; but it is also disturbing. For *The Lion King* reflects dominant ideologies of nature, and of human governance of nature, only too accurately. In Africa, and elsewhere, conservationists do speak like remote rulers, believing that they alone understand how nature works. They call most insistently for management of nature within certain bounds, and the need to respect both 'the circle of life' (even if it is labelled differently – for example, as 'ecological principles for economic development' or 'sustainable development': Farvar and Milton, 1973; Adams, 2001) and lesser creatures (this is called 'biodiversity'). Furthermore, when nature is described, it is often in terms that suggest a vision disturbingly like Disney's Pride Lands: a wilderness, a place of timeless natural rhythms, a place where ecology, not human choice, determines patterns of life and death. Innumerable television wildlife documentaries present nature in intricate and predetermined (if quaintly brutish) harmony, with humans the external and disruptive force.[1]

However, while *The Lion King* reflects ideas that are current today (although by no means universal), it also harks back to the past. Mufasa and Simba are idealized rulers, paternalistic imperialists, selflessly balancing opposing forces and imposing the common good. Today's ideologies of nature and the governance of nature draw directly upon the inheritance of colonialism. The sense of duty that Mufasa attempts to inculcate into Simba reflects Kipling's 'white man's burden'.[2]

The Lion King reveals the specific power of colonial ideologies of nature: they cast a long shadow in thinking about conservation, and in many instances they have been built into the structure of established institutions, from national parks to soil conservation programmes.

This chapter attempts to tease out something of the shape and significance of colonial thinking about nature, particularly in the British Empire. It is necessarily a partial and personal review of a large and rapidly growing literature, embracing Africa, Australia, South Asia and the Caribbean, and, of course, North America.[3] The point of this chapter is to explore the significance of the colonial mind in influencing the cast of our own.

WHOSE COLONIAL MIND?

This chapter's title speaks of 'a colonial mind'; but did such a thing ever exist with respect to conservation? The rapidly growing literature on environmental history suggests not. There has been enormous diversity in the ways nature has been understood, and the ways conservation has been practised, in colonial countries. There is no consistent 'colonial mind', and no simple account to be given of colonial ideologies of nature.

There is, in particular, now recognized to be considerable complexity in the interplay of environmental ideas from the colonial metropole and periphery. The work of Richard Grove, for example (1990; 1992; 1995; 1997) has challenged the conventional wisdom that environmentalism was an Anglo-American concern, merely 'a local response to Western industrialization', that was exported around the colonial world (Grove, 1990, p11). Indeed, he argues that the reverse was the case, with the development of global trade from the 15th century onwards yielding ideas and knowledge that themselves transformed European ideas of nature. The colonized world should be seen as the hearth of ideological innovation, with ideas forged there during the 17th and 18th centuries (in the West Indies, in the islands of the Indian Ocean and in India) being relayed to the metropole through international scientific networks (Grove, 1995; 1997; MacKenzie, 1997).

There is plenty of evidence of diversity in the historical emergence of ideologies of nature and conservation under colonialism. One risk of post-colonial analysis is that it homogenizes this diversity in both space and time, inventing a single discourse without geography or history as a logical source of a hegemonic colonial gaze. It is easy to hypothesize such an ideology, with capitalist market rationality transforming diverse indigenous understandings of, and social engagements with, nature. However, it is clear that such a simplistic writing of history is highly misleading. Place, period, race, class, caste and gender all offer distinct (although inter-linked) circuits for the formation and exchange of ideas about nature in the colonial world. Not all actors have left the same signature in the written archive: there is more recorded about the ideas of governors than governors' wives; more about the attitudes to nature of district commissioners than of engineers running cotton mills. There is more recorded about what all of these individuals thought than about the ideas of their subjects, or their servants, or members of their households. Reflection suggests that there might be sharp distinctions between ideas of nature, even at local scales; between different kinds of actors; and subtle inter-plays between individuals within them. There is every reason to expect colonial ideologies of nature to be as diverse, confused and contested as those of the present day (Norton, 1991). Grove comments: 'the ideological and scientific content of early colonial conservationism as it had developed under early British and French colonial rule amounted, by the 1850s, to a highly heterogeneous mixture of indigenous, romantic, Orientalist and other elements' (Grove, 1995, p12).

However, within this diversity there are common themes in colonial discourse. This chapter tries to demonstrate this, exploring some key themes among the many dimensions of colonial thought about nature. It discusses colonialism's impact on nature and the importance of rationality and science in underpinning colonial ideas about nature. It explores the roles of ecology and applied science in the service of development planning, and the nature of colonial environmentalism. It then considers three particular obsessions of colonial views of nature: the idea of wilderness, the issue of hunting and the desire to separate nature off in protected areas. The chapter's argument is that ideas forged under colonial rule still fly, like a comet's tail of ideological debris, behind contemporary thinking on conservation. They have enduring power.

COLONIALISM'S IMPACT ON NATURE

There has been much debate about the extent of the destructive impact of colonialism on nature. The environmentalism of the last three decades of the 20th century took as its conceptual premise the unprecedented scale and significance of the impacts of industrial technology on nature. The roots of this view lie deep within Western popular consciousness; but romantic opposition to industrialism, to nuclear weapons, to urbanization and to landscape change are all significant (Veldman, 1994; Bunce, 1994). As Meredith Veldman points out, C S Lewis's *The Lion, the Witch and the Wardrobe* is, like *The Lion King*, a tale of balance destroyed and restored; the pastoral world of Tolkein's Middle Earth is threatened by Sauron's dark arts.

Alfred Crosby's *Ecological Imperialism* (1986) gives this rather vague environmentalist oppositionism a geography and a history. He describes the success of 'neo-Europes' in Australasia, and in North and South America, where greedy but marginally competent Europeans were able to gain colonial footholds. In these countries, Europeans became numerically dominant, as did elements of European biota and production systems. European settlers 'used guns, traps and poison to kill the wildlife, steel axes and ploughs to clear the land and turn the soil'; they also placed bounties 'on almost anything that walked, flew, swam or crawled' (Dunlap, 1999, pp49, 51). The reason for the success of this invasion in some places, and its sapping failure in others (notably Africa), was not the limited range of developed technologies (whether domestic livestock or guns). Many of these technologies were, anyway, developed in China or the Middle East (survival and expansion were, in many cases, dependent upon the bold and effective cooption of proven local technologies, such as Arabic sailing technologies in the Indian Ocean, or indigenous crops in North America). Still less did it lie in racial superiority or superior moral fibre, explanations beloved of imperialistic history books. Crosby highlights the influence of pathogens (and particularly human diseases) that decimated local populations and laid lands open to the blind, cruel but ultimately profitable legal fiction of *terra nullius*.[4] The ravages of disease, killings and (more rarely) open warfare served to clear the land in North America, Australia, New Zealand and the South African Cape (Flannery, 1994; Beinart and Coates, 1995), a clearance entrenched by economic competition and legal process. In places like lowland tropical Africa, however, disease culled European colonizers, often on arrival. Outside the salubrious highlands they were restricted to extractive trade, and not occupation. Even in neo-Europes such as Australia, successive attempts to eradicate malaria in the north through the 19th century failed (Flannery, 1994).

MacKenzie (1997) places Crosby firmly in an 'apocalyptic school' of imperial history. In its more extreme forms, this school would portray world history as 'one long free fall, with imperialism as its global accelerator' (MacKenzie, 1997, p220). Famously, Helge Kjekshus (1977) argued that the advent of colonial rule in what is now Tanzania had remarkably destructive environmental impacts, destabilizing established relations between people and nature, particularly over the control of tsetse fly (and sleeping sickness). In doing this, Kjekshus contrasted favourable descriptions of pre-colonial Tanzania, with horrifying accounts of colonial times in a way that failed to take account of the complexities of either situation (Iliffe, 1979; 1995). There was no golden age in pre-colonial Africa. Poverty did not begin in the colonial period, and historians rightly shy away from romantic assumptions about pre-colonial social, economic and ecological equilibrium (Iliffe, 1987; Sutton, 1990). Moreover, as Beinart (2000) argues, although the ideological impacts of colonization were huge, it did not necessarily or immediately cause a breakdown in social constraints on the exploitation of nature.

In Africa, as elsewhere in the colonial world, historians need to understand people as 'one element in complex and evolving ecosystems' (Weiskel, 1988, p142). However, that evolution was often drastic and dramatic at the onset of colonial annexation. Thus, in East Africa, societies were torn apart by multiple catastrophes at the end of the 19th century. In north-east Africa, pastoral people were made destitute in the 1880s and 1890s by a combination of disease (especially rinderpest, introduced from the Indian subcontinent in the 1880s), drought and warfare (Pankhurst and Johnson, 1988; Waller, 1988). The imposition of colonial rule was a significant factor in some of these, and certainly in their significance for future patterns of resource use and rights; but its impact was by no means simple. These political and economic catastrophes, in turn, both reflected and caused environmental change. Thus, when livestock populations crashed and scrub and tsetse fly expanded, Maasai social organization also collapsed. Incoming colonists could imagine a land scantly occupied, its people warlike and turbulent cattle raiders. Rinderpest also drastically reduced populations of wild ungulates (such as buffalo and wildebeest: Sinclair and Norton-Griffiths, 1979), and East Africa's future national parks appeared as unoccupied plains, undergrazed and luxuriant. The ramifications of the biopolitical catastrophes of the 1880s and 1890s for colonial visions of African 'nature' and the role of people within it resonated through the 20th century.

Colonialism and capitalism not only extracted from nature, they also added to it – here, too, with sometimes disastrous effects (Dunlap, 1999). The urge to make colonies self-sufficient, and to supply the food and materials needed to make a global navy self-sufficient, made what Frost (1996) describes as the 'habit of plant transfer' a fundamental feature of British imperialism. The Royal Botanic Gardens at Kew were central to the exchange of knowledge and plants in the name of imperial economic development (Drayton, 2000). In Australia, enthusiasm for introduced species was unmatched, their toughness and fecundity a metaphor for European settlers themselves (Griffiths, 1996). Throughout the 19th century, and indeed for much of the 20th, non-Aboriginal Australians sought not to adapt to the country but to make Australian nature adapt to them, attempting to create a 'second Britain' (Flannery, 1994, p355).

A wide range of temperate and Mediterranean crops and fruits were imported to Australia by naturalization or acclimatization societies, and with them came a wide spectrum of accidental arrivals. Some brought diseases that wiped out local competitors, others ran wild (such as horses, donkeys, cattle, camels and the water buffalo, among domestic livestock alone); some propagated prodigiously, reaching plague proportions (for example, the European rabbit in Australia or the red deer in New Zealand). Indigenous species, particularly island species or those long isolated and ill adapted to competition, became extinct. The fauna and flora of islands and isolated continents such as Australia were drastically simplified.[5]

In the later 20th century, by which time conservation had everywhere become an important element in public concern and government policy, attitudes to the introduction of exotic species changed dramatically. In place of the enthusiastic colonial promotion of the impacts of familiar species on wild nature, conservationists sought to exclude 'aliens' in the name of ecological purity. In a world of global capitalism and culture, local specificity is seen to have cultural and survival value, and there are vigorous calls for the extirpation of cats or rats from oceanic islands, rhododendrons from British woodlands or the ubiquitous Australian eucalyptus from African, South Asian or British landscapes.

Not all colonial introductions led to ecological disaster: in some cases, crops became indigenized, fully integrated within local production systems. Thus, for example, the African slave trade saw the introduction to the Ivory Coast of a host of new crops from the New World (cassava, groundnut, tomato, maize, sweet potato, cocoyam, pineapple, papaya, avocado, hot peppers, tobacco and New World cottons), and from Asia (Asian rice, taro, sweet banana, sugar cane, orange, grapefruit, lemon and mango; Weiskel, 1988). The changes in ecology and economy consequent upon colonization could be rapid and complex. The cultivation of cocoa (introduced from South America to the island of Sao Thomé during the 15th century, but introduced to the West African mainland only in 1878) expanded very rapidly in the Gold Coast and Ivory Coast from the 1880s. Local innovation sought, with considerable success, to recreate some economic autonomy following 'the brutal destruction of pre-colonial forms of manufacture and trade' consequent on military defeat (Weiskel, 1988, p167). In the South African Cape, Merino sheep from Spain transformed grazing husbandry on the dry Karoo, and wool was South Africa's main export from1840 to 1930 (Beinart and Coates, 1995).

COLONIALISM, RATIONALITY AND NATURE

The colonial period saw a distinctive pattern of engagement with nature: a destructive, utilitarian and cornucopian view of the feasibility of yoking nature to economic gain. Where did these ideas come from? The bedrock of colonial ideas about nature was the European Enlightenment, and the fundamental Cartesian dualism between humans and nature. The idea that 'man' and nature were separate formed the world view of the pioneers of imperial trade, and of the annexation of the tropics and the new worlds in Asia, the Americas and Australasia. In his book *Nature's Government* (2000), Richard Drayton traces the idea that knowledge of nature allows the best possible use of resources. This idea emerged in medieval England (as an argument for the enclosure of common land), and was progressively exported to Ireland, to the plantations of the New World, and then worldwide. It was the driving force of imperialism and colonialism, and of the universal ideology of developmentalism that dominated the 20th century as the age of empire waned and died. Drayton argues that these ideas about the ways in which nature might be governed shaped government both in the empire and in the UK.

Colonialism, 'control by one power over a dependent area or people', can be seen as an outworking of bureaucratic rationalization (Murphy, 1994).[6] Rationality has four dimensions. The first is the development of science and technology: 'the calculated, systematic expansion of the means to understand and manipulate nature', and the scientific world view's 'belief in the mastery of nature and of humans through increased scientific and technical knowledge' (Murphy, 1994, p28). The second dimension of rationalization is the expansion of the capitalist economy (with its rationally organized and, in turn, organizing market); the third dimension is formal hierarchical organization (the creation of executive government, translating social action into rationally organized action). The fourth is the elaboration of a formal legal system (to manage social conflict and promote the predictability and calculability of the consequences of social action). All these things were features of colonial states.

Raymond Murphy argues that thought since the Enlightenment has been characterized by 'a radical uncoupling of the cultural and the social from nature, that is, by the assumption that reason has enabled humanity to escape from nature and remake it' (1994, p12). The acquisition of colonies was accompanied by, and to an extent enabled by, a profound belief in the possibility of restructuring nature and re-ordering it to serve human needs and desires.

Colonial enthusiasm for the large-scale re-ordering of nature is seen most clearly in the area of water resources. Mike Heffernan describes the plans of the French topographer and surveyor Élie Roudaire to flood the vast salt depressions of southern Tunisia, (named the Chotts) in the 19th century. He comments that European military and commercial expansion in Africa and Asia during the 19th century was driven by technical self-confidence and 'an almost limitless ambition' (1990, p94). These lands seemed underdeveloped, unmanaged and underexploited, and on the strength of the achievements of the Industrial Revolution, European faith in the power of science to control and manipulate nature found a significant challenge. Roudaire conceived of a project on a scale 'designed consciously to convey the monolithic power and authority of European rule in Africa' (Heffernan, 1990, p109). The Chotts are vast salt pans that lie below sea level, and reach from very close to the Mediterranean coast far into the Sahara. During the 1870s, Roudaire began surveys to investigate whether canals could be built to flood them in order to recreate a vast inland sea ($6700km^2$ in area and up to 30m deep). Roudaire led two survey expeditions. He believed that flooding would transform the climate of the area and provide a route for trade into the interior of Africa. '[F]ertility and life would take the place of sterility and death; the power of civilization would drive back the forces of fatalism' (Heffernan, 1990, p103).

Despite advocacy by Ferdinand de Lesseps (builder of the Suez Canal), the Tunisian scheme was not implemented: there were technical doubts about the canals, the area's geology, evaporation and (by 1879) about whether the area had ever been a sea at all. The theoreticians and intellectuals of the French scientific community were suspicious of 'men of action' such as Roudaire and Lesseps. However, grand plans for the reorganization of water flows continued to be a feature of colonial thinking. In India, colonial engineers annexed and extended vast canal irrigation systems, creating tightly regulated bureaucratic worlds of agricultural production in seasonally arid lands. In Australia, colonial entrepreneurs promoted a similar vision of a desert in bloom: the Grand Victorian North-Western Canal Company proposed a 300km irrigation canal in north-western Victoria in 1871 (Powell, 1997). In Egypt, a series of barrages and dams were built on the Lower Nile, including the original Aswan Dam in 1902. The first technical studies of the Upper Nile (under the Anglo-Egyptian Condominium of the Sudan) were carried out in 1904, and through the 1920s and 1930s a series of further dams were added in the upper basin. In 1946, studies began on a grand canal to carry water past the Sudd wetlands in the White Nile to yield water for irrigation in northern Sudan and Egypt (known as the Equatorial Nile Project). The Jonglei Canal was finally begun (although never finished) in the 1970s, by which time the Aswan High Dam had been completed, and there were also dams on the Niger, the Volta, the Zambezi and many smaller rivers (Collins, 1990; Adams, 1992). At the hands of colonial engineers, wild nature was brought under control, its power harnessed (literally, in the form of hydro-electric power) to serve the grand purposes of colonial development.

NAMING AND CLASSIFYING NATURE

The classification of nature was a critical element in the rationalizing gaze of colonialism: the 'othering' of nature in science, art and society is 'the ideological practice that enables us to plunder it' (Katz and Kirby, 1991, p265). In her book *Imperial Eyes*, Mary Pratt (1992) discusses the significance for imperial consciousness of the work of the Swedish taxonomist Linnaeus during the 18th century. The Linnaean system of classifying organisms not only drew upon biological collections from colonial explorers; it also 'epitomized the continental, transnational aspirations of European science' (Pratt, 1992, p25). Arguably, northern European taxonomic science (of which Linnaeus was the most famous practitioner) – the naming and classifying of unknown organisms – 'created a new kind of Eurocentred planetary consciousness' (Pratt, 1992, p39). More critically, taxonomy both represented and brought into being a new understanding of the world, one that had profound implications for human relations with nature, and with each other. Natural history 'asserted an urban, lettered, male authority over the whole of the planet; it elaborated a rationalizing, extractive, dissociative understanding which overlaid functional, experiential relations among people, plants and animal' (Pratt, 1992, p38). The scientific definition of species locked them into colonial patterns of global exploitation. New knowledge was a catalyst to intellectual enquiry and speculation in the colonial metropole; but it also stimulated imperial ambition. For Joseph Banks, for example, 'new wonders bespoke not only new knowledge, but also, perhaps primarily, new economic and spiritual opportunities' (Miller, 1996, p3).

Colonial scientific discourses about nature drew on pre-existing views of nature in the colonial periphery (Pratt, 1992; Grove, 1995), taking possession, institutionalizing and re-exporting them to the colonized world (Loomba, 1998). Colonialism promoted the naming and classification of both people and places, as well as nature, in each case with the aim of control. Landscapes were renamed, and these names were entrenched through mapping and the formal education system. Linda Tuhiwai Smith comments that 'renaming the landscape was probably as powerful ideologically as changing the land' (Smith, 1999, p51). Colonial states occupied human landscapes whose nature, names and boundaries were to them indistinct; but they conceptualized them as specific entities, with ethnicities 'constructed in their imagination on the model of a bargain-basement nation state' (Bayart, 1993, p51). To achieve these 'specific entities', the colonial state used science and bureaucratic power, including forced settlement (and resettlement), control of migratory movements, artificial fixing of ethnic identity through birth certificates and identity cards, and the restriction of indigenous people to demarcated reservations. As Bayart comments: 'the precipitation of ethnic identities becomes incomprehensible if it is divorced from colonial rule' (Bayart, 1993, p51).

James Scott argues, in *Seeing Like a State*, that legibility and simplification were central to the work of bureaucracy in the modern state. In land tenure, language, legal discourse, urban design, population census and many other areas, 'officials took exceptionally complex, illegible and local social practice … and created a standard grid whereby it could be centrally recorded and monitored' (1998, p2). This social simplification was accompanied by similar views of nature. Simplification allowed 'a high degree of schematic knowledge, control and manipulation' (p11). Scott describes the rise of scientific forestry in Prussia and Saxony during the 18th century. This was developed and exported under colonial rule (for example, to India), and persisted in government forest policy in many countries through the 20th century (see, for example, Fairhead and Leach, 1998).

The 20th century saw a steady expansion in scientific exploration of the living world. This took place under the wing of colonial administrations, and increasingly it served colonial purposes. Ecologists classified nature and charted its boundaries, providing categories for its effective exploitation. In this, colonial attitudes to nature strongly reflect the progressive idea of conservation as controlled or wise use, which developed in the US at the end of the 19th century under President Theodore Roosevelt and the administrator Gifford Pinchot (Hays, 1959). The pattern of scientific knowledge of nature being accumulated at the metropole so that its value could be assessed and amassed continued into the second half of the 20th century. Robin (1997) comments that the International Biological Programme was 'the last great imperial exercise in ecology, with information from the periphery being sent to the metropolitan centre to be converted into "science"' (p72).

Science and conservationism developed hand-in-hand. Colonial conservation allowed resources to be appropriated, both for the use of private capital and as a source of revenue for the state itself. As Grove comments: 'colonial states increasingly found conservation to their taste and economic advantage, particularly in ensuring sustainable timber and water supplies and in using the structure of forest protection to control their unruly and marginal subjects' (1995, p15).

NATURE, ECOLOGY AND DEVELOPMENT

The critical branch of science for colonial development was ecology, the 'science of empire' (Robin, 1997; Dunlap, 1999). Ecology developed at the end of the 19th century in Europe and the US, and became established institutionally during the first decades of the 20th (Worster, 1985; McIntosh, 1985). In its first issue (in 1914), the *Journal of Ecology* reviewed publications on the forests of British Guiana and vegetation in Natal and the eastern Himalayas. Subsequent volumes reviewed work on the vegetation of Aden, North Borneo, Sikkim, The Philippines and Jamaica (Adams, 2001), and the journal soon began to publish substantive papers on the vegetation of the British Empire – for example, in South Africa and the forests of the Garhwal Himalaya. During the late 1920s and 1930s, it reported a series of biological research expeditions from Oxford or Cambridge to British Guiana, Sarawak, the East African lakes and Nigeria (Adams, 2001).

This engagement of ecologists with tropical environments was not simply scholarly: ecology was explicitly presented as a scientific practice that was useful to the wider colonial endeavour. Robin (1997) divides colonial ecology into periods: the science of exploitation during the 19th century, followed, in the 20th century, by the science of settlement and, in due course, the science of development. The Imperial Botanical Conference, held at Imperial College in London in 1924, suggested that science should serve commerce: 'it is our duty as botanists to enlighten the world of commerce, as far as may lie in our power, with regard to plants in their relation to man and their relation to conditions of soil and climate' (Hill, 1925, p198). A 'complete botanical survey of the different parts of the Empire' was proposed (Brooks, 1925, p156). The imperial government had good reason to take a prominent part in such a survey, since it depended so much upon 'the overseas portions of the Empire for the supply of raw materials for manufacture, and of foodstuffs' (Davy, 1925, p215). Drayton (2000) comments that scientists, and particularly botanists, were important partners in imperial administration.

Vegetation analysis and classification could serve 'a most practical purpose', allowing delimitation of natural regions as an input to forestry and agricultural planning (Shantz and Marbut, 1923, p4). In 1931, Phillips proposed a programme of ecological investigation in East, Central and South Africa to help develop natural resources, agriculture ('the rational use of biotic communities'), grazing (the 'wise utilization of natural grazing'), forestry (the development of 'progressive forestry policies'), soil conservation (the 'prevention of soil erosion and its concomitant evils'), catchment water conservation and research into tsetse fly (Phillips, 1931, p474).

The rational management of nature as a natural resource was extensively developed in the colonial world in the context of forests. Forest policy focused on the reservation and commercial exploitation of timber at the expense of other uses of land, tree resources and wildlife, and at the expense of those groups (often indigenous people) who had previously used the forest. In India, the Forest Department was established in 1864, and the Forest Act of 1878 allowed for the closing or reservation of forests to allow 'scientific forestry' to concentrate on efficient timber production (Gadgil and Guha, 1994; Jewitt, 1995). In the Himalayan hills of Kumaon and Garhwal, demand for railway sleepers led to the closure of vast tracts of forests to subsistence use, and practices such as burning and grazing were banned, resulting in a long history of hardship (and protest against state forest policy: Guha, 1989). In Burma, forests were reserved for the production of timber (especially teak), effectively making alternative uses invisible (and illegal). Existing use rights for timber and non-timber forest products were extinguished (Bryant, 1996). In French-controlled Madagascar during the 20th century, a 'rational' approach to forest management included forest reserves and an attempt to suppress indigenous shifting cultivation practices. This effectively removed indigenous institutions that regulated how and where the forest could be cleared; and forest cover fell dramatically due to an uncontrolled mixture of cultivation (especially for coffee), grazing, burning and timber extraction (especially for the railways: Jarosz, 1996).

Above all, agriculture was the most favoured means of organizing 'nature's government', whether in Tudor England, Irish or American plantations, or (during the mid-20th century) in the intricately jumbled fields of African peasant farmers (Drayton, 2000). Under the doctrine of improvement, agriculture could reclaim wastelands and make barbarous peoples civilized. Improvement demanded science and planning, and in its 20th-century guise of 'development' it became an all-powerful ideology for modernization and change: a 'self-conscious or planned construction, mapping and charting [of] both landscapes and mindscapes' (Croll and Parkin, 1992, p31).

In Africa, formal development initiatives by colonial governments following World War II (the 'second colonial occupation': Low and Lonsdale, 1976) drew extensively on scientific ideas. Ecologists found a ready audience in the powerful but scientifically untrained officers of the colonial state who were charged with development, and scientists found new and important roles in applied fields, such as fisheries, livestock management and agriculture. Action to address the 'development problems' of rural Africans demanded knowledge of the ecology of production systems and the ecosystems from which they gained subsistence. The importance of the biology of agriculture, grazing, forestry and disease, and the physical geography of erosion and water supply, were recognized. Scientific expertise in each field won a significant role within colonial government.

In Africa, science flowered following the end of World War II. Empire Scientific Conferences were held in London in 1946 and in Johannesburg in 1949, and new science research organizations were set up in British, French and Belgian colonial territories.[7] In 1953, a conference at Bukavu in the Belgian Congo led to the African Convention on the Conservation of Nature and Natural Resources, adopted by the Organization of African Unity in Addis Ababa in 1968. This convention broadened the definition of conservation to include not only wild fauna and flora, but also soil and water: these resources were to be managed on scientific principles and 'with due regard for the best interests of the people' (McCormick, 1992, p46). Wildlife came to be presented as a critical resource for development. Barton Worthington, then deputy director general of the UK government's Nature Conservancy, wrote in 1961 after a visit to East and Central Africa: 'until recent years there has been little recognition by the governments or people of these countries that wildlife is a large natural resource in its own right, capable of development to big sustained yields by the application of appropriate technical knowledge' (1961, p1). There was a sustained effort to change that perception.

Ecology provided ample contributions to colonial aspirations of power and control over territory and nature. As a science it was able to produce rational stories in the face of novel environmental complexity (for example, the 'useful purpose' served by surveys that 'properly analysed and classified vegetation': Shantz and Marbut, 1923, p4). Ecology also provided a highly applicable model of the wider relevance of the rationalizing and ordering power of science for planning and structuring action.

In Australia, scientific research that addressed limits to settlement and productivity had particular importance, especially agricultural and veterinary science, applied entomology and ecology. Federation (in 1901) brought renewed interest in the development of a scientific approach to agriculture and the problem of pests. Plant ecology began with a visit by R S Adamson to the University of Adelaide. Adamson had worked with the pioneer ecologist Arthur Tansley in the UK, and had published the British Empire Vegetation Committee's first regional monograph, on the vegetation of South Africa, in 1938 (Adamson, 1938; Sheail, 1987). The Department of Botany at Adelaide subsequently developed an applied science tradition, working, in particular, with the Waite Agricultural Research Institute (Robin, 1997). The national Council for Scientific and Industrial Research was founded in 1926, partly funded by the Empire Marketing Board. Its Division of Economic Entomology, under A J Nicholson, developed a research tradition in the ecology of animal populations, subsequently carried on by Andrewartha and Birch (1954; Mulligan and Hill, 2001). Their research on grasshoppers, and that of Francis Ratcliffe on fruit bats and, subsequently, soil erosion, set the tone for an applied ecology harnessed firmly to economic productivity (Robin, 1997; Dunlap, 1997). By the mid-20th century, ecology was offering new insights into sustained environmental management. The hazards of reckless species introductions, drastic bush clearance and rural development that was blind to drought, were by then beginning to be widely recognized (Dunlap, 1999). Australian environmental science had become 'the voice of reason and restraint, of management for a long-term yield' (Robin, 1997, p70).

Science was also a critical element in the development of thinking about sustainability internationally (Adams, 2001). Barton Worthington argued in 1938 in *Science in Africa* (arising from his work with Lord Hailey's African Survey) that science (especially ecology) was useful in promoting human welfare. He wrote much later that 'a key problem was how *Homo sapiens* could himself benefit from this vast ecological complex which was Africa, how he could live and multiply on the income of the natural resources without destroying their capital' (Worthington, 1938, p46). This insight became the basis for ideas of sustainability in the World Conservation Strategy and Agenda 21 during the 1980s and 1990s (Adams, 2001).

COLONIAL ENVIRONMENTALISM AND THE
DEGRADATION OF NATURE

The plundering of nature was a widespread feature of colonization, particularly in its pioneer form. This did not go unnoticed. During the second half of the 19th century, the destructive power of human activities was widely appreciated in North America and Europe, most famously in George Perkins Marsh's *Man and Nature* (1864). Marsh observed:

> *...man is everywhere the disturbing agent. Wherever he plants his foot, the harmonies of nature are turned to discords. The proportions and accommodations which ensured the stability of existing arrangements are overthrown* (Marsh, 1864, p36).

As we have seen, Richard Grove traces such environmentalist sentiments not only to classical Europe but to the colonial periphery, where capitalist and European imperialist expansion engaged with tropical ecosystems and peoples for the first time. During the 16th and 17th centuries, the increasingly intensive exploitation of nature by capitalism and colonialism was accompanied by the idea that tropical regions were akin to Eden (Grove, 1995; Drayton, 2000). Tropical islands, in particular, became the symbolic location for 'the idealized landscapes and aspirations of the Western imagination' (Grove, 1990, p11). The question of a possible geographical location for the Garden of Eden was a subject of serious academic speculation and of exploratory endeavour during the 17th century, at the interface of the Enlightenment's tension between belief and rational understanding (Withers, 1999). Ironically, what capitalism destroys, Western culture personifies as precious: 'romantic constructions of nature accompany its systematic plunder, exoticism serves exploitation; romance and rapacity are familiar partners' (Katz and Kirby, 1991, p265). Imperial exploitation could destroy both natural beauty and bounty. Paradise was both found and lost in the Pacific from 1650 (Withers, 1999). During the mid-17th century, awareness of the environmental impacts of capitalism began to stimulate theories about limits to resources and the need for conservation. Experience of rapid ecological change on islands (for example, on Mauritius between the 1760s and 1810s) was translated into more general fears of environmental destruction on a global scale – for example, the issue of climate change (Grove, 1990; 1997; 1998a).

A sensitivity to the ecological impacts of imperialism and capitalism developed as colonial environmentalists felt the threat of deforestation, climatic change and famine (Grove, 1995; 1998a). There followed a sense that there were limits to nature's capacity to meet human demands, from which grew colonial conservationism. The timing of the expression of this in legislation varied. Scientists employed by trade companies as surgeons and botanists (the French Compagnie des Indes and the Dutch and English East India Companies) developed and disseminated ideas about environmental limits. Forest protection began to be institutionalized in British Caribbean territories from 1764, while during the 19th century environmentalist ideas were developed and disseminated through the coercive bureaucracy of the Indian Forest Service (Rajan, 1998; Rangarajan, 1998). In South Africa, conservation legislation was passed during the 19th century (Grove, 1987; McCormick, 1992). Concern about the depletion of forests led to the appointment of a colonial botanist in 1858; legislation to preserve open land near Cape Town was passed in 1846, and acts were passed concerning the preservation of forests (in 1859) and game (in 1886: Grove, 1987; MacKenzie, 1987).

By contrast, in Australia, settlers struggled through the 19th century to 'tame' and 'civilize' what they saw as wild and primitive nature (Lines, 1991). Few 'allowed themselves to be diverted from the task of chopping down trees long enough to absorb the beauty of what they were destroying' (Mulligan and Hill, 2001, p27). It was predicted in 1847 that it would take five or six centuries to clear the 'Big Scrub' in northern New South Wales; but it was gone within 20 years of clearance starting in 1880 (Flannery, 1994). However, even in settler societies profoundly wedded to the transformation of landscapes in the name of 'civilization', there were early examples of latent conservationist sensibilities. One such was Georgina Molloy, a settler in the 1830s at Flinders Bay, south of Perth, whose enthusiasm for introduced plants was succeeded by an intelligent and sensitive interest in the plants of the local bush (Mulligan and Hill, 2001). A larger-scale conservationist shift in opinion in Australian settler society began much later, in Victoria, during the 1860s and 1870s, as part of a rising interest in 'natural history' (Griffiths, 1996). It was in the middle of the 20th century, on the back of formal environmental science (as described above), that it reached beyond a few stalwart ecological pioneers (Mulligan and Hill, 2001).

In Africa following World War II, some colonial scientists began to pay serious attention to the ways in which ordinary people actually used their environments. Surveys of vegetation and soils in the context of agricultural land use in Northern Rhodesia (contemporary Zambia) during the 1930s (see, for example, Trapnell and Clothier, 1937) led to concepts such as 'carrying capacity' and 'critical population density'. Similar insights arose from research in West Africa (Faulkner and Mackie, 1933). While it is paternalistic and predicated on the superior analytical power of formal science, this work reads now like the first scientific recognition that African farming was ordered, intelligently designed and adapted to local environmental conditions. It seems like a forerunner of the celebration of indigenous knowledge that became fashionable in development studies half a century later.

However, this kind of insight was the exception, not the rule. Conventional colonial scientific wisdom emphasized the risks of local agriculture and stock-keeping. Farmers, pastoralists and forest users were short-sighted and ignorant of the implications of their actions: local systems of resource use threatened nature, for they led almost inevitably to degradation. William Beinart describes the importance to colonial officers in Africa of regulating the ways in which people used the environment (2000). Regulation seemed essential to the efficient and long-term success of natural resource exploitation and agriculture. Both settlers and African peasants were, at various times, perceived to be wasteful and inefficient in their resource use, and the governmental response was to impose environmental and social controls.

Concern about environmental degradation associated with drought and drylands was well established in the African Cape during the 19th century (Grove, 1987). It surfaced again in West Africa during the 1930s, in the writings of the forester E P Stebbing (1935). These are discussed in Chapter 11, as are the concerns about pastoral overgrazing and desertification into which they eventually grew. Stebbing believed that he could detect the physical advance of the Sahara desert into seasonally arid areas further south: essentially, an advance from French West Africa into Nigeria. The second decade of the 20th century had seen a series of droughts in the Sahel (Grove, 1973), and the idea of a spreading desert gained considerable credence among colonial officers in West Africa and more widely, despite early counter-arguments (for example, Jones, 1938). These ideas received an enormous boost with the 'dust bowl' phenomenon in the Great Plains of the US during the 1930s, and became part of global hysteria about soil erosion. The perception of the environmental crisis in the US travelled via newspapers and other routes to feed concern about soil erosion in arid and semi-arid environments worldwide (Jacks and Whyte, 1938). These took firm root in Africa (Beinart, 1984; Anderson, 1984), in Canada (Jones, 1987) and in Australia (Dunlap, 1999), where the disastrous implications of recurrent droughts (for example, during 1864–1866, 1880 and 1896–1902) were acknowledged (Flannery, 1994).

In Kenya, concern about soil erosion during the 1930s was not only a product of fears generated by the US dust bowl, but also of the concurrence of drought, the Great Depression and fears on the part of white settlers at African population growth. The years from the mid-1920s to the mid-1930s were dry in East Africa, and drought created periodic local food shortages and sometimes extensive cattle deaths. Famine relief by the state was expensive, and drought heightened the perception of environmental degradation caused by African husbandry. By the 1930s, the problems of overcrowding and landlessness in the Kikuyu reserves had become a matter of concern to both settlers and the colonial government. Meanwhile, African farmers responded to the slump in agricultural prices caused by the worldwide economic recession by expanding the areas under production of cotton and coffee in Uganda and maize in Kenya and Tanganyika, threatening to out-compete white farmers. Facing bankruptcy, the latter argued that African farming practices were damaging the environment. They did so to such effect that when colonial intervention in African agriculture finally began, its major focus was the prevention of erosion. By 1938, soil conservation had become a major concern of government in the East African colonies, the cutting edge of a policy of state intervention in African agriculture.

Outside Africa, drought and soil erosion were more obviously problems caused by inappropriate agricultural technologies wielded by European settlers.

In Australia, repeated droughts destroyed the hopes of farming settlers, and they, in their turn, drew down soil fertility and left sterile land behind them. Soil conservation authorities were established in New South Wales in 1938 and in Victoria in 1940 (Robin, 1997). In Canada, attempts to boost smallholder settlement to grow wheat in the dry belt of south-east Alberta and south-west Saskatchewan proved disastrous (Jones, 1987).

To the colonial observer, degradation was not limited to soil erosion. James Fairhead and Melissa Leach (1996) describe the persistence in the official mind of misconceptions of environmental change on the forest–savanna boundary in Guinea, West Africa. This landscape is one of forest patches around villages and corridors along streams, set in a matrix of grassland. In 1909, a French colonial botanist, Auguste Chevalier, reached the conclusion that people were clearing the forest at an alarming rate, and that the mosaic landscape was subject to rapid degradation, particularly by fire. Throughout the 20th century (up to the 1990s), a succession of outside experts and administrators reached the same conclusion. These people saw the forest patches around villages and along streams as fragments of a once-continuous forest cover, and they proposed urgent and often draconian measures to conserve them (for example, the prohibition of tree-cutting and fires, and attempts to persuade local people to plant trees in open patches).

Fairhead and Leach show that, in fact, the landscape that greeted the first French intruders was substantially the same as it is today: if anything, forest cover has increased in the last century. The forest islands are not relics of former forest cover that was destroyed by agriculture, but are actually the fruit of agricultural management and settlement that creates the conditions for forest trees to grow. Far from causing degradation, high population densities are necessary to allow the management and control of fire. Kissi people do not see a forest landscape that is progressively losing its trees, but a savanna landscape filling with forest. Policy-makers had managed to read the history of the forest in reverse. In doing so, they had:

> ...*accused people of wanton destruction, criminalized many of their everyday activities, denied the technical validity of their ecological knowledge and research into developing it, denied value and credibility to their cultural forms, expressions and basis of morality, and at times denied even people's consciousness and intelligence* (Fairhead and Leach, 1996, p295).

Wildlife preservation became the subject of trans-imperial concern about environmental degradation by the start of the 20th century. In 1900, the African colonial powers (Germany, France, Britain, Portugal, Spain, Italy and Belgium) met in London and signed a Convention for the Preservation of Animals, Birds and Fish in Africa (although it was never implemented: McCormick, 1992). In 1903, the Society for the Preservation of the Wild Fauna of the Empire (SPWFE) was established to lobby for wildlife conservation with the British Colonial Office. Its membership drew on the British political elite, and its lobbying was persistent and highly specific (Fitter and Scott, 1978; Neumann, 1996). Six years later, an international organization to promote conservation was proposed at an International Congress for the Preservation of Nature, held in Paris in 1909. Such ideas were buried by World War I, but they resurfaced between the wars. In 1928, the Office International de Documentation et de Corrélation pour la Protection de la Nature was established, becoming the International Office for the Protection of Nature in 1934, and eventually the International Union for Conservation of Nature and Natural Resources (IUCN) in 1956 (Holdgate, 1999).

Concern about the threat of extinctions in the tropics, and particularly in Africa, was widespread in Europe and North America during the 1950s and 1960s. By the 1960s, African countries were winning independence from colonial rule and the prospect of poachers turning gamekeepers caused disquiet in Europe and North America. Conservation in Africa was seen by IUCN as a critical challenge, and in 1961 it therefore joined with the United Nations Food and Agriculture Organization (FAO) to launch an African Special Project with the aim of influencing African leaders (Boardman, 1981; Holdgate, 1999). A symposium on the Conservation of Nature and Natural Resources in Modern African States, held in Arusha in Tanzania in 1961, set out the arguments for conservation in independent Africa, reflecting both the ideological and economic importance: 'these wild creatures amid the wild places they inhabit are not only important as a source of wonder and inspiration but are an integral part of our natural resources and of our future livelihood and well-being' (Worthington, 1983, p154).

The idea of a standardized approach to conservation across colonial territories had been proposed to the British government by the SPWFE in 1905 (Neumann, 1996), and by the 1960s it was in place. The central element within it was the idea of national parks. These are discussed below.

WILDERNESS IN THE COLONIAL MIND

Katz and Kirby (1991) argue that myths of nature emerge from the scientific processes of exploration, mapping, documentation, classification and analysis. During the 18th century, 'nature' came to be defined in terms of the absence of human impact, specifically European human impact. 'Nature' came therefore to imply regions and ecosystems that were not dominated by Europeans (Pratt, 1992). As the precursors of modern environmentalism took hold in the industrializing North towards the end of the 19th century, 'nature' came to be understood not purely as something distinct from society, but somehow in opposition to culture, the city and industry, to technology and human work. Nature was wild, unrestricted, magnificently unknown.

One way in which this new Romantic conception of nature was expressed was in the reformulation of the idea of wilderness. The original meaning of this word in Western Europe was a wild place lacking human amenity and civilization: a place beyond settlement, of wild animals and wild people, unused and unusable (Schama, 1995). Over this meaning was laid a new sense of wilderness as a precious, unsullied, natural wonderland, a place of natural balance and wild order, providing a backdrop for human action, and a moral baseline for destructive human engagements with nature (Cronon, 1995). In the sense in which it has been understood in the West during the 20th century (and which has increasingly spread worldwide), wilderness is valuable precisely because it is imagined as being free of human influence, uninhabited (Langton, 1998).[8] Wilderness is 'the Wholly Other opposite from man', such that any human change 'pulls wilderness down from its peak of perfection' (Graber, 1976, p116).

This conception of wilderness was principally forged in the US. In his classic book *Wilderness and the American Mind*, Roderick Nash suggests 'a society must become technological, urban and crowded before a need for wild nature makes economic and intellectual sense' (1982, p343). As the US industrialized and urbanized, as the 'open' frontier of the West was progressively settled and harnessed to agriculture, as forests were progressively fed into the industrial machine, the loss of the wild seemed a threat to American manhood. Ruggedness, self-sufficiency and hardihood were to be found in the wilderness, not in the effete lifestyles or degraded working conditions of the urban and industrial economy. This was the tenor of the arguments of eastern lobby groups, such as the Boone and Crockett Club (formed in 1887), and, in a different way, that of the Romantic conservation movement associated with John Muir (for example the Sierra Club, founded in 1892). Concern to secure wilderness was an important element in the foundation of the first US national parks during the closing decades of the 19th century, and became the leading issue in debates about their management in the 20th (Nash, 1982; Runte, 1987).

For many Europeans, both in the colonial era and after, the open savanna landscapes of Africa have been understood as 'a lost Eden in need of protection and preservation' (Neumann, 1996, p80). The survival of great numbers of large mammals (whose Pleistocene equivalents in Eurasia, the Americas and Australasia had been extirpated) contributed to the sense that Africa was a place apart, where nature persisted in a more complete and damaged state. Critical in this aesthetic reading of African landscapes is the illusion that Africa is more 'natural' than the familiar built urban and industrial cities and the manicured and controlled rural landscapes of Europe and North America: the very naturalness of Africa allows it to be constructed as a wilderness, quite unlike the decadent metropole (Anderson and Grove, 1987; MacKenzie, 1988; Neumann, 1998). The colonial mind found in the nature of Empire something more natural than familiar lands at home – something wilder, conceptually remote from the developed and sown lands of Europe. During the 20th century, parts of the British Empire's scarcely known territories were imagined as wilderness, with all the new positive connotations of that word (Griffiths, 1996; Dunlap, 1999).

The problem with this was (obviously) that people lived in this 'wilderness', and had organized active agricultural, pastoral, manufacturing and trading economies. In some places (particularly the plains of East Africa), the first colonial governments encountered landscapes recently artificially cleared of their populations by disease and war. Elsewhere, slaving and colonial annexation had disrupted economy, society and environment before settled colonial reflection could begin. Such landscapes (like those in North America) perhaps genuinely seemed empty, and were 'running wild' like the garden of an abandoned house. To an extent, people could be airbrushed from the imagined landscape because they were in a sense seen to be 'natural' themselves – close to wildness in their primitive use of technology and 'savage' customs (Neumann, 1998). Africans living 'traditionally' were therefore an acceptable part of nature, at least until the advent of development planning during the middle of the 20th century, when rural population growth began to close around the vast tracts of land set aside by the colonial state in game reserves and national parks. Then those same people began to be seen as unnatural, threatening the natural balance of nature (as discussed above), hunting in unacceptable ways for unacceptable reasons and without a sense of sustainable harvest (see below). In Africa, as in the US, the idea of nature as wilderness made hunters into poachers, wood-cutters into law-breakers, and farmers into the enemies of conservation (Jacoby, 2001).

In colonial neo-Europes, wilderness could be important to emergent national identity (Dunlap, 1999). The existence of vacated (or empty) landscapes, 'new lands' and a frontier between them and settled, sown and developed country was important to the national psyche. Such ideas offered no place for indigenous people, and none at all for the notion that the landscape was the product of their ideas and their labour (Langton, 1998). Pyne (1997) comments: 'its wilderness made America distinctive from Europe; its ineffable bush rendered Australians something more than Europeans in exile; its veld assured African colonists that they could never be subsumed under a strict European order' (p33).

The representation of particular spaces as 'wilderness' by the suppression of knowledge of the extent and scope of human occupation was an integral part of creating ideologically significant landscapes. In *Voices from the Rocks*, Terence Ranger describes the various ways in which the Matopos Hills were understood and represented in colonial and post-colonial Zimbabwe. Colonial conservationists recognized ancient occupation by hunter-gatherers, who left cave paintings in the hills; but they dismissed contemporary agricultural activity, and more or less completely eradicated its traces when they declared the Matopos National Park. Land was first set aside in the name of conservation in 1926; but in 1962 the national park was divided, and part of it was forcibly depopulated. A 'wilderness area' was created that could only be entered by tourists and officials on foot or on horseback, and wildlife was introduced or reintroduced. The Rhodes Matopos National Park had become a white Rhodesian shrine, sacred to the memory of Cecil Rhodes, who was buried there (Ranger, 1999). Some colonial overtones were removed by independence, and some of the other voices from the rocks were heard more loudly. However, the 'wilderness values' of the Matopos National Park (and especially the economic development benefits of tourism) have meant that those evicted have not been allowed to return. The continuity of human occupation and management of the Matopos has been expunged from official (although not local) memory.

Western conceptions of wilderness had, by the end of the 20th century, become global in the sense that they were very widely recognized. They have, however, never been uncontested. They were opposed from both within and outside the colonial governments. Within government, the idea of the preservation of 'wild' nature seemed bizarre to many actors. Thus, during the first decades of this century, nature enthusiasts faced considerable opposition to establishment of game reserves for 'sportsmen' in the Transvaal and KwaZulu-Natal from Boer farmer-hunters, from industrial (mining) interests, and from settlers who saw game reserves as reservoirs of cattle diseases (particularly sleeping sickness: Carruthers, 1995).

Ideas of wilderness as wonderful and valuable also very often found little purchase in the thinking of colonized people, whose thoughts about wild animals and unsettled places were perhaps closer to those of pre-industrial Europeans: namely, fear and mistrust. Burnett and wa Katg'ethe (1994) suggest that a conservation ethic based upon the standard Western transcendental and Romantic idea of wilderness is unappealing to Africans. Analysing published ethnographies of Kikuyu people, they argue that wilderness has never meant an absence of people, but a place of persistent human interaction. It is a place engaged by a frontier of settlement, a place of some danger, to be approached as a group and transformed through a social process of settlement. They make the point that whereas the American idea of wilderness created locations where society plays with transcendentalism, the closure of the Kikuyu frontier (in the name of conservation and to provide land for white settlers) was sudden, and by arbitrary fiat not a communal process: 'whole peoples were denied opportunities as wilderness was converted from social space to the domain of beasts, a tourist's pleasuring ground' (Burnett and wa Katg'ethe, 1994, p155).

Colonial and post-colonial conservationists have tended to imagine that their ideas of wilderness are universal, and are bound to touch somewhere on indigenous ideas of non-human nature. This is, to many people, an attractive assumption (Kemf, 1993), but it has never been a wise one. Sweeping assumptions about the relationship between religious belief and environmental management need to be treated with considerable caution (Mukumuri, 1995).

HUNTING NATURE

A vital element in colonial thinking about nature is the importance of hunting, and in both Africa and Australia hunters were among the first conservationists (MacKenzie, 1987; Griffiths, 1996; Dunlap, 1999). The most important species according to the colonial gaze were large mammals, particularly antelope and deer, buffalo, elephant and large predators (especially lion and tiger). These were classified as 'game', and made subjects of a separate moral universe from other species, one where only white men could engage with them legitimately. Like the pheasants and deer of British estates, they were reserved for the attention of a racial and class elite: white hunters.

In Africa, MacKenzie (1987) identifies three phases in the extension of European hunting. The first was commercial hunting for ivory and skins by white hunters and (from the 1850s) by African rulers who traded with them, gaining guns and seeking power over neighbours in the process. The second phase of hunting saw it serve as a subsidy for the European advance, providing meat for railway construction workers or to feed missionaries and finance trade. The third phase is the most relevant to the subsequent evolution of conservation: the development of a ritualized and idealized practice of 'the hunt' on the part of a white elite, with an obsession with trophies, sportsmanship and other ideals of private British boys' schools (MacKenzie. 1988). Beryl Markham (herself at one time employed in spotting trophy elephants from the air) provides a nice example of the confused psychology of the hunter when she writes:

> *...it is absurd for a man to kill an elephant. It is not brutal, it is not heroic, and certainly it is not easy; it is just one of those preposterous things that men do, like putting a dam across a great river, one tenth of whose volume would engulf the whole of mankind without disturbing the domestic life of a single catfish* (Markham, 1942, p180).

As rifles improved and the number of hunters grew, vast numbers of game animals were killed, their pursuit carefully choreographed, and their deaths lovingly chronicled. By the last decades of the 19th century substantial areas of southern Africa, especially near white population centres and along ox-wagon and rail routes, were more or less emptied of game. This carnage led to the emergence of ideas of controlling hunting, and to ideas of protected areas. In South Africa, the Cape Act for the Preservation of Game of 1886 was extended to the British South African Territories in 1891 (MacKenzie, 1987), and in 1892 the Sabie Game Reserve was established (to become the Kruger National Park in 1926). In Kenya, the Ukamba Game Reserve was created in 1899; the Kenyan Game Ordinance was passed in 1900, effectively banning all hunting except by licence (Graham, 1973).

Colonial conservation tried to end hunting by Africans through control on the possession of firearms, and latterly the establishment of game reserves. Hunting continued, out of sight and illicitly, and 'the poaching problem' became the common lament of game departments throughout Africa (Graham, 1973; Beinart and Coates, 1995). Most commentators condemned African hunting for its barbarity (using traps, spears and bows and arrows, ancient muzzle-loaders or home-made guns, not the high-velocity sporting rifles necessary for the white hunter's ritual 'clean kill'), and for its presumed lack of moderation. This primitive hunting was conventionally contrasted with the careful, considered and clinically humane big game hunter. Hingston, writing a polemic promoting national parks, wrote:

> *What the sportsman wants is a good trophy, almost invariably a male trophy, and the getting of that usually satisfies him... The position is not the same with the native hunter. He cares nothing about species or trophies or sex, nor does he hunt for the fun of the thing* (Hingston, 1931, p404).

Indeed not: they hunted for food and for trade materials, a base obsession with commerce and the belly that demeaned noble wild beasts.

If the expression in conservation policy of colonial ideas about wildness is largely American in origin, the importance of hunting and 'game preservation' bears a strongly British imprint. Rod Neumann argues that just as the Empire was 'a means to extend patrician country life beyond its inevitable demise in England' (1996, p81), ideas about conservation borrowed directly from the world of English aristocratic rural estates. His argument is based on the extraordinary dominance of aristocratic members of the SPWFE during the first half of the 20th century. These reformed big game hunters attempted to build conservation in Africa in the image of the great British sporting estate: 'as wealth, power and prestige drained from the body of the landlord class, hunting and nature protection in the empire was one realm in which patrician norms and standards still held sway' (p88). In 1929, the Earl of Onslow, president of the SPWFE from 1926 to 1945, drew specific comparisons between the importance of the country estate to game preservation in the UK and the system of national parks in Africa. Both needed aristocratic vision and leadership, and support from the state (Neumann, 1996).

Jacoby (2001) describes the mixture of British upper-class tradition and an American desire to recreate the imagined world of the frontier from which ideas about hunting in the Adirondack Park in New York State at the end of the 19th century grew:

> *...out of this peculiar mixture of history, militarism and upper-class pretence, there developed during the late 19th century a sportsman's code in which* how *one hunted was almost as important as* what *one hunted* (p58, emphasis in original).

In Australia, despite the lack of gratifyingly dangerous large beasts, hunting and the freedom of the bush were important to the settler imagination, not least because of the echoes of poaching, transportation and oppressive English landed gentry (Griffiths, 1996).

In Africa, too, the idea of what was 'proper hunting' was constructed and reinforced by an elite within the colonial elite, translating centuries of aristocratic concern with game and the proper rules under which it could be killed, and with 'poachers' and other ne'er-do-wells who threatened sport, game and class barriers by their lawlessness. The mentality of Georgian England, when under the 'Black Act' poachers were transported to penal colonies or hanged, was recreated in Africa (Thompson, 1977). African rural landscapes were conceptually (and sometimes physically) cleared of peasants as unthinkingly as any village moved to enhance the picturesque landscape of an English stately home.

Viceroys and governors (mostly recruited from the aristocracy) hunted, as did the lesser ranks of colonial officials, each (mostly) obeying the written laws of the colony and the unwritten laws of hunting etiquette. The majority of these self-styled sportsmen railed against the poverty, ignorance and canny cruelty of African hunters, except when reformed and recruited as game scouts. In time, a major industry developed in the plains of East and Central Africa, as specialized tour companies, increasingly employing the classic 'white hunter', took wealthy clients into the wilds to claim their trophy (Packer, 1994). The American obsessions with wilderness and hunting made Africa a natural destination for millionaire sportsmen, Hollywood stars and playboys. Roderick Nash comments: 'Africa became the new Mecca for nature tourists like Roosevelt, who were wealthy enough to import from abroad what had become scarce at home' (1982, p343). In practice, big game hunting often lacked the noble qualities of the inheritance it claimed; but it was lucrative, and until the rise of the car-borne tourist in South Africa, and eventually the airliners, package holiday hotels and zebra-striped tour buses of the photo-safari, hunting provided the most visible purpose of conservation.

POLICING NATURE'S LIMITS

The classic feature of colonial approaches to nature was the attempt to separate people and wild non-human nature. Animals were to be confined to reserves and shot as 'problem animals' when they transgressed invisible administrative boundaries and raided crops. People were to be kept at bay by the policing of protected area boundaries and the control of incursions through paramilitary anti-poaching patrols.

By about 1880, a pattern of conservation (derived from a mix of Indian and Cape Colony philosophies) was established in southern Africa. The utilitarian basis of these ideas brought them into conflict with settler interests. Holistic conservation ideas could not be reconciled with 'the driving interests of local European capital' (Grove, 1987, p36). In India these forces were resisted: 30 per cent of non-agricultural land in some provinces was brought under the control of the Forest Department (Grove, 1990). In Africa, a more aesthetic preservationism became of much greater importance. Conservation moved from a concern with the wider environment and its resources to an obsession with big game hunting, with parks to protect game from poaching, and with the need for land alienation to protect nature.

Although hunting and forest reserves have a much longer history in many countries, what has come to be the dominant form of protected area, the national park, began in the US, with the Yosemite Act in 1864 and the Yellowstone Park Act of 1872. Alfred Runte (1987) comments that they were 'born of romanticism and cultural nationalism' (p236): Americans might lack the great artistic and archaeological treasures of Europe; but in the waterfalls and geysers of Yellowstone, and the incomparable mountains of Yosemite, they had natural monuments that were world-beaters. Cultural insecurity was the catalyst for national parks, and only later did they start to be re-imagined as places for tourism.

Where America led, others followed, and national parks were established during the 1880s and 1890s in Canada, Australia and New Zealand; in 1892, the Sabie Game Reserve (later the Kruger National Park) was established in the Transvaal (Fitter and Scott, 1978). In the Canadian Rockies, what became the Banff National Park was first established (in 1885) to regulate commercial exploitation of the hot springs. However, national parks in the Rockies (Banff, Yoho, Jasper, Waterton) soon became vehicles for development, particularly in response to the need of the Canadian Pacific Railway for tourist traffic (McNamee, 1993). Luxurious hotels were built, and the mountains packaged as Alpine resorts, European Alpine guides being recruited to see visitors safely into, and out of, the wild (Sandford, 1990).

In colonial Africa, conservation protected areas predominantly took the form of game reserves for the first half of the 20th century, although in 1925 King Albert of Belgium created the gorilla sanctuary that became the Parc National Albert (now the Virunga National Park: Fitter and Scott, 1978; Boardman, 1981). Kruger National Park was created in South Africa in 1926 (Carruthers, 1995). During the 1940s and 1950s, South Africa provided a model (in many ways a most unhelpful one) for the rest of British colonial Africa. As a whole, Africa was the chief concern of colonial lobbyists for conservation. The SPWFE only began to press for conservation in British colonial Asia in the 1930s, following the 1933 conference (MacKenzie, 1988).

In most of Africa, national parks came somewhat later, with many of the parks that became famous in the last quarter of the century being created following World War II. Thus, in 1948 Nairobi National Park was created in Kenya, with Tsavo following in 1948; in 1951 Wankie was created in Southern Rhodesia and Serengeti in Tanganyika; and in 1952 Murchison Falls and Queen Elizabeth National Parks were created in Uganda (Fitter and Scott, 1978). In many instances, these were created from pre-existing game reserves or similar areas (for example, Amboseli National Park in Kenya was created out of the game reserve established in 1899: Lindsay, 1987).

There was a great deal of international pressure at this time promoting the idea of national parks, and a determination on the part of late colonial governments to set them in place before decolonization, as part of the rapid establishment of systems of governance of all kinds. E B Worthington commented in 1961 that UK and African countries had been less active in planning the conservation and development of wild resources than in fields such as administration, law or social and political development. He concluded:

'there is still opportunity to catch up, and to provide in each of the countries a sound administrative and scientific structure, ready to be taken over at the appropriate time by independent governments' (p23).

The importance of national political identity is well demonstrated by the creation of the Kruger National Park in 1926. Jane Carruthers (1995; 1997) describes how the mostly English-speaking advocates of the park successfully linked the memory of Boer leader Paul Kruger to the history of the game reserves from which the park was created. In fact, he was no enthusiast for preservation; but by implying that the idea was his, the park's future was secured. Indeed, ironically, it became a shrine to Boer nationalism. This may be a special case, but many protected areas in former colonial territories exist because they served a political purpose.

It was the extinction of the large African mammals upon which calls for national parks were founded (Hingston claimed 'it is as certain as night follows day that unless vigorous and adequate precautions be taken, several of the largest mammals of Africa will within the next two or three decades become totally extinct', 1931, p402). The main reason for that extinction was seen by colonial commentators to be hunting by Africans. The irony of this view is considerable, since the most vocal advocates of protected areas that excluded Africans were, of course, themselves hunters: colonial white men, 'penitent butchers', as the members of the SPWFE were labelled (Fitter and Scott, 1978; Neumann, 1996). Their voices (Hingston's is a prime example) dominate contemporary colonial statements about conservation; but, in practice, colonial views of the need for national parks, and especially of the fairness of excluding rural people, were very mixed. The attempts of the SPWFE to apply pressure to the colonial office in London were at times both resented and resisted (Neumann, 1996). There were also awkward relations between the staff of game departments (who had established a low-key *modus operandi*, enjoying a 'Boy's Own' existence, touring remote areas and shooting problem animals such as lion or elephant, and generally attempting to keep the peace between people and wildlife), and the new national park bureaucracies (see Kinloch, 1972). Nonetheless, national parks came to dominate state-run conservation almost everywhere in the former British colonial empire.

Until the 1990s, the establishment of national parks conventionally meant the suppression of resource use by local people and the forced abandonment of established rights and resource-use patterns. The economic impacts of eviction from protected areas can be considerable, as Brockington (2002) demonstrates in the case of pastoralists evicted from the Mkomazi Game Reserve in Tanzania. The exclusion of people by colonial regimes from parks set aside for nature has often had particularly drastic impacts upon indigenous people. In the US, home of the created wilderness concept and wilderness park, these impacts are well known and widely discussed. Jacoby (2001), for example, describes the progressive restriction of the freedom of the Havasupai people to hunt in winter on the plateau above the Colorado River as land was designated first as a forest reserve and (in 1919) as the Grand Canyon National Park. Unable to survive by farming in the tiny canyon reservation, the Havasupai were eventually reduced to working for the Park Service as labourers, building trails and facilities for urban visitors who came to view the wilderness. By the 1920s, the plateau lands above the Havasupais' reservation, which for the tribe had once been an intimate geography of family camping grounds, hunting areas and places for gathering wild foodstuffs, had instead become a symbol of their diminished status as wage-workers in a touristic wilderness (Jacoby, 2001, p191).

In Canada, residents were evicted upon the creation of national parks until 1970 (McNamee, 1993). Two hundred families were evicted from Forillon National Park in Quebec, and 228 households (1200 people) from Kouchibouguac National Park in New Brunswick. However, violence arising from the latter forced removal led to a change in policy and amendment of the National Parks Act. Indigenous people have been particularly affected by evictions for national parks in Canada as elsewhere; but a succession of legal cases and land claims have established indigenous rights to various extents (Berg et al, 1993). In the Arctic, protected areas have been an issue in the Inuvialuit Final Agreement (1984) and the establishment of Nunavut. In Pacific Rim National Park (designated in 1970), there are 28 reserves belonging to seven Indian groups in and near the park; but they have had little influence on its declaration and management. By contrast, in the South Moresby National Park Reserve/Gwai Hanaas on the Haida Gwaii (Queen Charlotte Islands), indigenous people have far more influence (Berg et al, 1993).

COLONIALISM'S LEGACY FOR CONSERVATION

The 'fortress' approach to conservation is a significant and enduring legacy of colonial conservation in the former British Empire. However, contemporary thinking about nature in former colonial territories bears the imprint of colonial ideas in a variety of ways. While the phenomenon of colonialism is, at one level, one of uniformity, experiences are diverse. Nonetheless, the colonial legacy exhibits a series of common features that reflect the ideological ordering of the colonial mind.

Firstly, there is the way knowledge has been acquired, formalized, stored and passed on. Colonialism favoured modern techno-scientific knowledge over folk knowledge, and privileged centralized and formalized ways of knowing nature over localized and informal ways. Those undertaking conservation priority-setting for international conservation organizations based in industrialized countries at the start of the 21st century inherit a rich (if dubious) heritage of colonial expertise and top-down planning of nature and human interactions with it.

Secondly, colonial ideas of nature repeatedly portrayed it as separated from human life and not engaged with it. Nature was a resource to be plundered or preserved, a wilderness to be researched or protected from the ravages of human demands. In the colonial mind, nature was 'out there', never 'in here', and the possibility of knowing human engagement with nature was rarely considered (whether in the form of knowledgeable and sustainable use of farmland, or the hunting of game). White men feared nature in the form of disease and the dark forest, and did their best to overcome it. They venerated nature in the shape of formalized hunting rituals and wilderness preservation; but always the distance between human and non-human was maintained, an apartheid at species level.

Thirdly, the colonial mind proposed an engagement with nature that was regulated by bureaucratic control. Colonial states showed an enthusiasm for the development of nature (and later for its conservation) that made the colonial metropole seem feeble. But behind the pioneer spirit was an instinct for classification and standardization. Nature (and the peoples who subsisted through its direct exploitation) was not treated as diverse and unique, and not engaged with on its own terms. Standardized models of landscape management and social administration were applied wholesale. Haste and arrogance made powerful but often disastrous precursors to the ignorant imposition of uniformity.

Fourthly, colonialism approached its engagement with nature through regulation and coercion. Nature was there to be disciplined and regulated, harnessed to the imperative of imperial development. It was regulation and control that were important, and the disciplining of unruly nature and unruly people was achieved not through self-regulation or self-discipline, but by paternalistic external imposition. The relations between local people and nature were restructured by the colonial state, and made subject to external rules.

Fifthly, while colonial ideas of nature involved a deliberate engagement with the aim of increasing productivity, the resulting strategies rarely worked with nature, but against it. Colonial scientific knowledge was harnessed to production, to the specialization of human benefits from nature (whether through agriculture or, latterly, through conservation). Colonial nature was made productive, but only through drastic restructuring. New species, new systems of production, new forms of social relations were all the out-workings of the colonial mind. Nature was conquered, made productive despite itself. People were dealt with in the same way.

It might seem from this catechism of colonialism's narrow-mindedness that its legacy for conservation is grimly negative. There were, however, compensatory gains and practical achievements. Colonial conservation provided a counterbalance to the megalomania of development planners. By making 'nature' a land use (in the form of protected areas), conservationists reserved a space for it in the economic landscapes being carved up by planners, whose disregard for the ideas and aspirations of ordinary people made conservationists seem models of sensitivity. Protected areas, for all their history of misanthropy, thoughtlessness and often arbitrary cruelty, have served a wider social purpose in buying time for colonized peoples to identify the impacts of modern industrial economies, and make choices about their relations with nature. Ideas such as wilderness, the value of biodiversity and the moral unacceptability of extinction are Western in origin, but no more so than representative democracy, private property in land or the notion that economics is an appropriate way to make decisions about development projects. Like other once-imposed Western ideas, some conventional notions widely accepted in conservation might need to be rejected, while others are accepted as decolonization is worked through.

Conservationists have much to learn about their past, and much of it will be painful. Many ideas that are commonly taken to be intuitive will be seen to be baseless dogma. Many practices will be seen to be dramatically unfair to some groups of people. It will be recognized that many views common in the West seem bizarre to those living alongside wild nature on the ground who are trying to wrest a living from the land. Learning these lessons is vitally important. The challenge of decolonizing the mind is urgent and of huge significance to the future of conservation. However, recognizing these truths is not enough. This new understanding will not necessarily tell conservationists what to suggest in the future. The real work of re-imagining conservation for a post-colonial era is just beginning.

NOTES

1   The importance of ideas of balance in nature is explored further in Chapter 10.
2   The phrase is from the title of a poem that is a reflection on the colonialism of the US; its full title is 'The White Man's Burden 1899 (The United States and the Philippine Islands)'. It is reprinted in *Rudyard Kipling: Selected Verse*, selected by James Cochrane, 1981, Penguin Books, Harmondsworth.
3   For example, see MacKenzie, 1988; Lines, 1991; Gadgil and Guha, 1994; Beinart and Coates, 1995; Grove, 1995; Arnold and Guha, 1995; Grove, Damadoran and Sangwan, 1998; Griffiths and Robin, 1997; Grove, 1998a; Drayton, 2000.
4   Joseph Banks, in Australia with Cook in 1770, concluded that the land had little to excite Europeans, and was 'essentially unoccupied' (Mulligan and Hill, 2001, p27; see also Chapter 4 in this book).
5   Flannery, 1994; Chapters 3 and 4 in this volume.
6   *Longman Dictionary of the English Language*, 1991, Longman, London.
7   These included the British Colonial Research Council (under Lord Hailey), the French Office de Récherche Scientifique et Technique d'Outre Mer (ORSTOM) and the Belgian Institut pour la Récherche Scientifique en Afrique Central (IRSAC): Worthington, 1983.
8   The issue of wilderness is discussed by Val Plumwood in Chapter 3 and Marcia Langton in Chapter 4.

REFERENCES

Adams, W M (1992) *Wasting the Rain: Rivers, People and Planning in Africa*. Earthscan, London
Adams, W M (2001) *Green Development: Environment and Sustainability in the Third World*. Routledge, London (second edition)

Adamson, R S (1938) *The Vegetation of South Africa*. British Empire Vegetation Committee, London

Anderson, D M (1984) 'Depression, dust bowl, demography and drought: the colonial state and soil conservation in East Africa during the 1930s', *African Affairs*, vol 83, pp321–344

Anderson, D M and Grove, R H (1987) 'The scramble for Eden: past, present and future in African conservation' in D M Anderson and R H Grove (eds) *Conservation in Africa: People, Policies and Practice*. Cambridge University Press, Cambridge, pp1–12

Andrewartha, H G and Birch, L C (1954) *The Distribution and Abundance of Animals*. Chicago University Press, Chicago

Arnold, D and Guha, R (1995) (eds) *Nature, Culture, Imperialism: Essays on the Environmental History of South Asia*. Oxford University Press, New Delhi

Bayart, J-F (1993) *The State in Africa: The Politics of the Belly*. Longman, London

Beinart, W (1984) 'Soil erosion, conservation and ideas about development: a Southern African exploration 1900–1960', *Journal of Southern African Studies*, vol 11, pp52–84

Beinart, W (2000) 'African history and environmental history', *African Affairs*, vol 99, pp269–302

Beinart, W and Coates, P (1995) *Environment and History: The Taming of Nature in the USA and South Africa*. Routledge, London

Berg, L, Fenge, T and Dearden, P (1993) 'The role of aboriginal peoples in national park designation, planning and management in Canada' in P Dearden and R Rollins (eds) *Parks and Protected Areas in Canada*. Oxford University Press, Oxford, pp225–252

Boardman, R (1981) *International Organisations and the Conservation of Nature*. Indiana University Press, Bloomington, IN

Brockington, D (2002) *Fortress Conservation: The Preservation of the Mkomazi Game Reserve, Tanzania*. James Currey, Oxford

Brooks, F T (ed) (1925) *Imperial Botanical Conference, London 1924: Report of Proceedings*. Cambridge University Press, Cambridge

Bryant, R L (1996) 'Romancing colonial forestry: the discourse of "forestry as progress" in British Burma', *Geographical Journal*, vol 162, pp169–172

Bunce, M (1994) *The Countryside Ideal: Anglo-American Images of Landscape*. Routledge, London

Burnett, G W and wa Katg'ethe, K (1994) 'Wilderness and the bantu mind', *Environmental Ethics*, vol 16, pp145–160

Carruthers, J (1995) *The Kruger National Park: A Social and Political History*. University of Natal Press, Pietermaritzberg

Carruthers, J (1997) 'Nationhood and national parks: comparative examples from the post-imperial experience' in T Griffiths and L Robin (eds) *Ecology and Empire: Environmental History of Settler Societies*. Keele University Press, Keele, pp125–138

Collins, R O (1990) *The Waters of the Nile: Hydropolitics and the Jonglei Canal 1900–1988*. Clarendon Press, Oxford

Croll, E and Parkin, D (1992) 'Cultural understandings of the environment' in E Croll and D Parkin (eds) *Bush Base: Forest Farm; culture, environment and development*. Routledge, London, pp11–36

Cronon, W (1995) 'The trouble with wilderness, or, getting back to the wrong nature' in W Cronon (ed) *Uncommon Ground: toward reinventing nature*. W W Norton and Co, New York, pp69–90

Crosby, A W (1986) *Ecological Imperialism: the ecological expansion of Europe 1600–1900.* Cambridge University Press, Cambridge

Davy, J B (1925) 'Correlation of taxonomic work in the Dominions and Colonies with work at home' in F T Brooks (ed) *Imperial Botanical Conference, London 1924, Report of Proceedings.* Cambridge University Press, Cambridge, pp214–234

Drayton, R (2000) *Nature's Government: science, imperial Britain and the 'improvement' of the World.* Yale University Press, New Haven

Dunlap, T R (1997) 'Ecology and environmentalism in the Anglo settler colonies' in T Griffiths and L Robin (eds) *Ecology and Empire: environmental history of settler societies.* Keele University Press pp76–86

Dunlap, T R (1999) *Nature and the English Diaspora: environment and history in the United States, Canada, Australia and New Zealand.* Cambridge University Press, Cambridge

Fairhead, J and Leach, M (1996) *Misreading the African landscape: society and ecology in a forest savanna land.* Cambridge University Press, Cambridge

Fairhead, J and Leach, M (1998) *Reframing Deforestation: global analysis and local realities.* Routledge, London

Farvar, M T and Milton, J P (1973) (eds) *The Careless Technology: ecology and international development.* Stacey, London

Faulkner, O T and Mackie, J R (1933) *West African Agriculture.* Cambridge University Press, Cambridge

Fitter, R S R and Scott, P (1978) *The Penitent Butchers: the Fauna Preservation Society, 1903–1978.* Collins, London

Flannery, T (1994) *The Future Eaters: an ecological history of the Australasian lands and people.* Reed Books Australia, Sydney (New Holland edition 1997, Sydney)

Frost, A (1996) 'The Antipodean exchange: European horticulture and Imperial designs' in D H Miller and P H Reill (eds) *Visions of Empire: voyages, botany and representations of nature.* Cambridge University Press, Cambridge, pp58–79

Gadgil, M and Guha, R (1994) *This Fissured Land: an ecological history of India.* Oxford University Press, New Delhi

Graber, L H (1976) *Wilderness as Sacred Space.* Association of American Geographers, Washington

Graham, A (1973) *The Gardeners of Eden.* Allen and Unwin, Hemel Hempstead

Griffiths, T (1996) *Hunters and Collectors: the antiquarian imagination in Australia.* Cambridge University Press, Cambridge

Griffiths, T and Robin, L (1997) (eds) *Ecology and Empire: environmental history of settler societies.* Keele University Press

Grove, A T (1973) 'A note on the remarkably low rainfall of the Sudan Zone in 1913', *Savanna,* vol 2, pp133–138

Grove R H (1987) 'Early themes in African conservation: the Cape in the Nineteenth Century' in D M Anderson and R H Grove (eds) *Conservation in Africa: people, policies and practice.* Cambridge University Press, Cambridge, pp21–40

Grove, R H (1990) 'Colonial conservation, ecological hegemony and popular resistance: towards a global synthesis' in J M MacKenzie (ed) *Imperialism and the Natural World.* Manchester University Press, pp15–50

Grove, R H (1992) 'Origins of western environmentalism', *Scientific American,* vol 267, pp42–47

Grove, R H (1995) *Green Imperialism: colonial expansion, tropical island Edens and the origins of environmentalism, 1600–1800.* Cambridge University Press

Grove, R H (1997) 'Conserving Eden: the (European) East India Companies and their environmental policies on St Helena, Mauritius and in Western India, 1660–1854' in R H Grove (ed) *Ecology, Climate and Empire; colonialism and global environmental history 1400–1940*, White Horse Press, Knapwell, pp37–85

Grove, R H (1998a) 'The East India Company, the Raj and the El Niño: the critical role played by colonial scientists in establishing the mechanisms of global climate teleconnections 1770–1930' in R H Grove, V Damodaran and S Sangwan (eds) *Nature and the Orient: the environmental history of South and Southeast Asia*. Oxford University Press, New Delhi

Grove, R H (1998b) *Ecology, Climate Change and Empire: the Indian legacy in global environmental history 1400–1940*. Oxford University Press, New Delhi

Grove, R H, Damodaran, V and Sangwan, S (1998) (eds) *Nature and the Orient: the environmental history of South and Southeast Asia*. Oxford University Press, New Delhi

Guha, R (1989) *The Unquiet Woods: ecological change and peasant resistance in the Himalaya*. Oxford University Press, New Delhi

Hays, S P (1959) *Conservation and the Gospel of Efficiency: the progressive conservation movement 1890–1920*. Harvard University Press, Cambridge, Mass.

Heffernan, M (1990) 'Bringing the desert to bloom. French ambitions: the Sahara desert during the late 19th century – the strange case of "la mare intérieure"' in D Cosgrove and G Petts (eds) *Water, Engineering and Landscape: water control and landscape transformation in the modern period*. Belhaven Press, pp94–114

Hill, A W (1925) 'The best means of promoting a complete botanical survey of the different parts of the empire' in F T Brooks (ed) *Imperial Botanical Conference, London 1924: report of proceedings*. Cambridge University Press, Cambridge, pp196–204

Hingston, R W G (1931) 'Proposed British National Parks for Africa', *Geographical Journal*, vol 77, pp401–428

Holdgate, M (1999) *The Green Web: a union for world conservation*. Earthscan, London

Iliffe, J (1979) *A Modern History of Tanganyika*. Cambridge University Press

Iliffe, J (1987) *The African Poor: A History*. Cambridge University Press, Cambridge

Iliffe, J (1995) *Africans: the history of a continent*. Cambridge University Press

Jacks, G V and Whyte, R O (1938) *The Rape of the Earth: a world survey of soil erosion*. Faber and Faber, London

Jacoby, K (2001) *Crimes Against Nature: squatters, poachers, thieves, and the hidden history of American conservation*. University of California Press, Berkeley

Jarosz, L (1996) 'Defining deforestation in Madagascar' in R Peet and M Watts (eds) *Liberation Ecologies: environment, development, social movements*. Routledge, London, pp148–164

Jewitt, S (1995) 'Europe's "others"? Forestry policy and practices in colonial and post-colonial India', *Environment and Planning D: Society and Space*, vol 13, pp67–90

Jones, B (1938) 'Desiccation and the West African Colonies', *Geographical Journal*, vol 41, pp401–423

Jones, D C (1987) *Empire of Dust: settling and abandoning the Prairie Dry Belt*. University of Alberta Press, Edmonton

Katz, C and Kirby, A (1991) 'In the nature of things: the environment and everyday life', *Transactions of the Institute of British Geographers*, vol 16, pp259–271

Kemf, E (ed) (1993) *The Law of the Mother: protecting indigenous peoples in protected areas*. Sierra Club Books, San Francisco

Kinloch, B (1972) *The Shamba Raiders: memories of a game warden*. Collins and Harvill Press, London

Kjekshus, H (1977) *Ecology Control and Economic Development in East African History.* University of California Press, California (2nd edition, James Currey, 1996)

Langton, M (1998) *Burning Questions: Emerging environmental issues for indigenous peoples in northern Australia.* Centre for Indigenous Natural and Cultural Resource Management, Northern Territories University, Darwin

Leach, M and Mearns, R (1996) *The Lie of the Land: challenging received wisdom on the African environment.* James Currey/International African Institute, London

Lindsay, W K (1987) 'Integrating parks and pastoralists: some lessons from Amboseli' in D M Anderson and R H Grove (eds) *Conservation in Africa: people, policies and practice,* Cambridge University Press, Cambridge, pp149–168

Lines, W (1991) *Taming the Great South Land: A History of the Conquest of Nature in Australia.* Allen and Unwin, Sydney

Loomba, A (1998) *Colonialism/Post-colonialism.* Routledge, London

Low, D A and Lonsdale, J M (1976) 'Introduction: towards a new order 1945–1963' in D A Low and A Smith (eds) *History of East Africa. Volume III.* Clarendon Press, Oxford, pp1–63

MacKenzie, J M (1987) 'Chivalry, social Darwinism and ritualised killing: the hunting ethos in central Africa up to 1914' in D M Anderson and R H Grove (eds) *Conservation in Africa: people, policies and practice.* Cambridge University Press, Cambridge, pp41–62

MacKenzie, J M (1988) *The empire of nature: hunting, conservation and British imperialism.* University of Manchester Press, Manchester

MacKenzie, J M (1997) 'Empire and the ecological apocalypse: the historiography of the imperial environment' in T Griffiths and L Robin (eds) *Ecology and Empire: environmental history of settler societies.* Keele University Press, pp215–228

Markham, B (1942) *West With the Night* (republished Penguin Books, Hemel Hempstead, 1988)

Marsh, G P (1864) *Man and Nature; or, physical geography as modified by human action.* Scribners, New York; Sampson Low, London (reprinted Harvard University Press, 1965)

McCormick, J S (1992) *The Global Environmental Movement: reclaiming Paradise.* Belhaven, London (first published 1989, Indiana University Press, Bloomington, Indiana)

McIntosh, R P (1985) *The Background of Ecology: concept and theory.* Cambridge University Press, Cambridge

McNamee, K (1993) 'From wild places to endangered spaces: a history of Canada's national parks' in P Dearden and R Rollins (eds) *Parks and Protected Areas in Canada.* Oxford University Press, Oxford, pp17–41

Miller, D H (1996) 'Introduction' in D H Miller and P H Reill (1996) (eds) *Visions of Empire: voyages, botany and representations of nature.* Cambridge University Press, Cambridge, pp1–18

Miller, D H and Reill, P H (1996) (eds.) *Visions of Empire: voyages, botany and representations of nature.* Cambridge University Press, Cambridge

Mukumuri, B B (1995) 'Local environmental conservation strategies: Karanga religion, politics and environmental control', *Environment and History,* vol 1, pp297–311

Mulligan, M and Hill, S (2001) *Ecological Pioneers.* Cambridge University Press, Melbourne

Murphy, R (1994) *Rationality and Nature: a sociological inquiry into a changing relationship.* Westview Press, Boulder, Colorado

Nash, R (1982) *Wilderness and the American mind.* Yale University Press, New Haven, Connecticut (first published 1967)

Neumann, R P (1996) 'Dukes, earls and ersatz Edens: aristocratic nature preservationists in colonial Africa', *Environment and Planning D: Society and Space*, vol 14, pp79–98

Neumann, R P (1998) *Imposing Wilderness: struggles over livelihood and nature preservation in Africa.* University of California Press, Berkeley

Norton, B C (1991) *Toward Unity Among Environmentalists.* Oxford University Press, London

Oates, J F (1999) *Myth and reality in the Rain Forest: how conservation strategies are failing in West Africa.* University of California Press, Berkeley

Packer, C (1994) *Into Africa.* University of Chicago Press, Chicago

Pankhurst, R and Johnson, D H (1988) 'The great drought and famine of 1888–1892 in Northeast Africa' in D Johnson and D Anderson (eds) *The Ecology of Survival.* Lester Crook, London, pp47–70

Phillips, J (1931) 'Ecological investigations in South, Central and East Africa: outline of a progressive scheme' *Journal of Ecology*, vol 14, pp474–482

Powell, J M (1997) 'Enterprise and dependency: water management in Australia' in T Griffiths and L Robin (eds) *Ecology and Empire: environmental history of settler societies.* Keele University Press, pp102–121

Pratt, M L (1992) *Imperial Eyes: travel writing and transculturation.* Routledge, London

Pyne, S J (1997) 'Frontiers of fire' in T Griffiths and L Robin (eds) *Ecology and Empire: environmental history of settler societies.* Keele University Press, pp19–34

Rajan, R (1998) 'Imperial environmentalism or environmental imperialism? European forestry, colonial foresters and the agendas of forest management in British India 1800–1900' in R H Grove, V Damodaran and S Sangwan (1998) (eds) *Nature and the Orient: the environmental history of South and Southeast Asia.* Oxford University Press, New Delhi, pp324–371

Rangarajan, M (1998) 'Production, desiccation and forest management in the Central provinces 1850–1930' in R H Grove, V Damodaran and S Sangwan (eds) *Nature and the Orient: the environmental history of South and Southeast Asia.* Oxford University Press, New Delhi, pp575–595

Ranger, T (1999) *Voices from the Rocks: nature, culture and history in the Matopos Hills of Zimbabwe.* James Currey, Oxford

Robin, L (1997) 'Ecology: a science of empire?' in T Griffiths and L Robin (eds) *Ecology and Empire: environmental history of settler societies,* Keele University Press, pp63–75

Runte, A (1987) *National Parks: the American experience.* University Nebraska Press

Sandford, R W (1990) *The Canadian Alps: the history of mountaineering in Canada, Volume 1.* Altitude Publishing, Banff

Schama, S (1995) *Landscape and Memory.* HarperCollins, London

Scott, J C (1998) *Seeing Like a State: how certain schemes to improve the human condition have failed.* Yale University Press, New Haven

Shantz, H L and Marbut, C F (1923) *The Vegetation and Soils of Africa.* American Geographical Society Research Series 13, American Geographical Society and National Research Council, New York

Sheail, J (1987) *Seventy-five Years of Ecology: the British Ecological Society.* Blackwell Scientific, Oxford

Sinclair, A R E and Norton-Griffiths, M (1979) (eds) *Serengeti: Dynamics of an Ecosystem.* University of Chicago Press, Chicago

Smith, L Tuhiwai (1999) *Decolonising methodologies: research and indigenous peoples.* Zed Press, London

Stebbing, E P (1935) 'The encroaching Sahara: the threat to the West African Colonies', *Geographical Journal*, vol 85, pp506–524

Sutton, J (1990) *A Thousand Years of East Africa.* British Institute in Eastern Africa, Nairobi

Thompson, E P (1977) *Whigs and hunters: the origin of the Black Act.* Penguin, Harmondsworth

Trapnell, C G and Clothier, J N (1937) *The Soils, Vegetation and Agricultural Systems of North-Western Rhodesia.* Government Printer, Lusaka

Veldman, M (1994) *Fantasy, the Bomb and the Greening of Britain: romantic protest 1945–1980.* Cambridge University Press, Cambridge

Waller, R T (1988) 'Emutai: crisis and response in Maasailand 1883–1902' in D Johnson and D Anderson (eds) *The Ecology of Survival.* Lester Crook, London, pp73–112

Weiskel, T (1988) 'Toward an archaeology of colonialism: elements of ecological transformation of the Ivory Coast' in D Worster (ed) *The Ends of the Earth: perspectives on modern environmental history.* Cambridge University Press, Cambridge, pp141–171

Withers, C W J (1999) 'Geography, enlightenment and the paradise question' in D N Livingstone and C W J Withers (eds) *Geography and Enlightenment.* Chicago University Press, Chicago, pp67–92

Worster, D (1985) *Nature's Economy: a history of ecological ideas.* Cambridge University Press, Cambridge

Worthington, E B (1938) *Science in Africa: a review of scientific research relating to tropical and southern Africa.* Royal Institute of International Affairs, London

Worthington, E B (1961) *The Wild Resources of East and Central Africa: a report following a visit to Kenya, Tanganyika, Northern and Southern Rhodesia and Nyasaland in February and March, 1960.* HMSO, London

Worthington, E B (1983) *The Ecological Century: a personal appraisal.* Cambridge University Press, Cambridge

Chapter 3

Decolonizing relationships with nature

Val Plumwood

COLONIZATION, EUROCENTRISM AND ANTHROPOCENTRISM

This chapter begins by giving a general outline of the logical structure of colonial and centrist relationships. This is then used to cast light on several issues. Firstly, at this post-colonial remove, many of us are accustomed to seeing colonial relationships between peoples as oppressive, damaging and limiting for the colonized. Colonial centres, which during the 18th and 19th centuries were typically drawn from European and North American powers, thought of themselves as superior, bringing 'civilization' as an unalloyed benefit to the backward races and regions of the world. Usually, however, the colonial system plundered the wealth and lands of the colonized, whose peoples were either annihilated or left severely damaged – socially, culturally and politically. Colonizers made use of, and often accentuated, divisions between privileged and non-privileged groups in colonized societies, and, for the benefit of the centre, they created boundaries that divided colonized groups from one another and from their lands in ways that guaranteed a legacy of conflict and violence long after the colonial rulers departed.

The Eurocentric colonial system was one of hegemony – a system of power relations in which the interests of the dominant party were disguised as universal and mutual, but in which the colonizer actually prospered at the expense of the colonized. The analysis presented below of the colonizing conceptual structure that justifies all of this (often in the name of bringing reason or enlightenment) is extracted from some of the leading thinkers who have analysed and opposed Eurocentric systems of hegemony. It is also drawn from my own experience of both sides of the colonization relationship, as a member of a colonizing culture (with respect to Australian indigenous people and the Australian land) and as a member of a culture which, in some respects, has also been a colonized one (with respect to 'the mother country', as well as in the contemporary context of global US hegemony). It is a significant, but often insufficiently remarked, feature of such centric relationships that many of us experience them from both sides and that they can mislead, distort and impoverish both the colonized and the centre – not just the obvious losers.

It is usually now acknowledged that in this process of Eurocentric colonization, the lands of the colonized and the non-human populations who inhabit those lands were often plundered and damaged, as an indirect result of the colonization of the people. What we are less accustomed to acknowledging is the idea that the concept of colonization can be applied directly to non-human nature itself, and that the relationship between humans, or certain groups of them, and the more-than-human world might be aptly characterized as one of colonization. This is one of the things that an analysis of the structure of colonization can help to demonstrate. Analysing this structure can cast much light upon our current failures and blind spots in relationships with nature, because we are much more able to see oppression in the past or in contexts where it is not our group who is cast as the oppressor. It is a feature of colonizing and centric thought systems that they can disguise centric relationships in a way that leaves the colonizer (and sometimes even the colonized) blind to their oppressive character.

An analysis of the general structure of centric relationships can therefore help us to transfer insights from particular cases where we are colonized to cases where we are, instead, the colonizers, and thus to transcend the colonizing perspective and its systematic conceptual traps (Plumwood, 2002b). In the case of nature, such analysis can help us to understand why our relationships with nature are currently failing. To make this discussion more concrete, this chapter looks at two contemporary examples of a nature-colonizing system in practice: firstly, the way the conceptual framework of colonization has helped to bring about the mistreatment by the Australian colonizing culture of the land to which it has supposedly brought progress and reason; and, secondly, the way the naming of the land can both reflect and reinforce colonial relationships and also give us powerful opportunities to subvert them.

Although now largely thought of as the non-human sphere, in contrast with the truly or ideally human (identified with reason), the sphere of 'nature' has, in the past, been taken to include what are thought of as less ideal or more primitive forms of the human. This included women and supposedly 'backward' or 'primitive' people, who were seen as exemplifying an earlier and more animal stage of human development. The supposed deficit in rationality of these groups invites rational conquest and reordering by those taken to best exemplify reason – namely, elite white males of European descent and culture (Said, 1978). 'Nature' then encompasses the underside of rationalist dualisms that oppose reason to nature, mind to body, emotional female to rational male, human to animal, and so on. Progress is the progressive overcoming, or control of, this 'barbarian' non-human or semi-human sphere by the rational sphere of European culture and 'modernity'. In this sense, a culture of rational colonization in relation to those aspects of the world, whether human or non-human, that are counted as 'nature' is part of the general cultural inheritance of the West (Plumwood, 1993), underpinning the specific conceptual ideology of European colonization and the bioformation of the neo-Europes (Crosby, 1986).

An encompassing and underlying rationalist ideology applying both to humans and to non-humans is thus brought into play in the specific processes of European colonization. This ideology is applied not only to indigenous peoples but to their land, which was frequently portrayed in colonial justifications as unused, underused or empty – areas of rational deficit. The ideology of colonization, therefore, involves a form of *anthropocentrism* that underlies and justifies the colonization of non-human nature through the imposition of the colonizers' land forms and visions of ideal landscapes in just the same way that *Eurocentrism* underlies and justifies modern forms of European colonization, which see indigenous cultures as 'primitive', less rational and closer to children, animals and nature (Plumwood; 1993; 1996). The resulting Eurocentric form of anthropocentrism draws upon, and parallels, Eurocentric imperialism in its logical structure. It tends to see the human sphere as beyond or outside the sphere of 'nature', construes ethics as confined to the human (allowing the non-human sphere to be treated instrumentally), treats non-human *difference* as inferiority, and understands both non-human agency and value in hegemonic terms that deny and subordinate them to a hyperbolized human agency.

The colonization of nature thus relies upon a range of conceptual strategies that are employed also within the human sphere to support supremacism of nation, gender and race. The construction of non-humans as 'Others' involves both distorted ways of seeing sameness, continuity or commonality with the colonized 'Other', and distorted ways of seeing their difference or independence. The usual distortions of continuity or sameness construct the ethical field in terms of moral dualism, involving a major boundary or gulf between the 'One' and the 'Other' that cannot be bridged or crossed. This can be seen, for example, in the gulf between an elite, morally considerable group and an out-group defined as 'mere resources' for the first group. Such an out-group need not, or cannot, be considered in similar ethical terms as the first group. In the West, especially, this gulf is usually established by constructing non-humans as lacking in the very department that Western rationalist culture has valued above all else and identified with the human – that of mind, rationality, or spirit – and what is often seen as the outward expression of mind in the form of language and communication. The excluded group is conceived, instead, in the reductionist terms established by mind/body or reason/nature dualism: 'mere' bodies, which can thus be servants, slaves, tools or instruments for human needs and projects. Reductionist and dualistic constructions of the non-human remain common today, especially among scientists.

Dualism: exaggerating differences; denying commonality

Centric and reductionistic modes of conceiving nature as Other continue to thrive. Like the conceptual forms that characterize the treatment of human colonies, the forms of 'othering' the non-human that are outlined below are the precursors of many forms of injustice in our relations with non-humans. They prevent the conception of non-human others in ethical terms, distort our distributive relationships with the non-human, and legitimate insensitive commodity and instrumental approaches. My sketch of the chief structural features of hegemonic centrism draws upon some analyses of centrism by the feminists Simone de Beauvoir, Nancy Hartsock and Marilyn Frye, and upon criticisms of Eurocentrism made by people such as Edward Said and Albert Memmi. Analyses framed in terms of colonization models are especially appropriate if we are attracted to thinking of Earth 'others' as *other nations* 'caught with ourselves in the net of life and time', as Henry Beston has expressed it so powerfully (1928). Human-centredness is inflected by its social context, and the model outlined below is drawn from critiques (developed, in particular, by Edward Said) of appropriative colonization. These may be adapted to model the capitalist-scientific appropriation of nature. The model is illustrated with examples drawn from counter-centric theorists and from the colonization experiences of indigenous peoples, especially Australian Aboriginal people, whose oppression combines elements of ethnocentrism and Eurocentrism.

Radical exclusion

Under this heading we meet, first, *hyper-separation* – an emphatic form of separation that involves much more than just recognizing difference. Hyper-separation means defining the dominant identity emphatically against, or in opposition to, the subordinated identity, by exclusion of their real or supposed qualities. The function of hyper-separation is to mark out the Other for separate and inferior treatment. Thus, 'macho' identities emphatically deny continuity with women and try to minimize qualities seen as being appropriate for, or shared with, women. Colonizers exaggerate differences – for example, through emphasizing exaggerated cleanliness, 'civilized' or 'refined' manners, body covering, or alleged physiological differences between what are defined as separate races. They may ignore or deny relationship, conceiving the colonized as less than human. The colonized are described as 'stone age', 'primitive' or as 'beasts of the forest', and this is contrasted with the qualities of civilization and reason that are attributed to the colonizer.

Similarly, the human 'colonizer' treats nature as radically Other, and humans as emphatically separated from nature and animals. From an anthropocentric standpoint, nature is a hyper-separate lower order, lacking any real continuity with the human. This approach stresses heavily those features that make humans different from nature and animals, rather than those we share with them.

Anthropocentric culture often endorses a view of the human as outside, and apart from, a plastic, passive and 'dead' nature, which lacks agency and meaning. A strong ethical discontinuity is felt at the human species boundary, and an anthropocentric culture will tend to adopt concepts of what makes a 'good' human being that reinforce this discontinuity by devaluing those qualities of human selves and human cultures that it associates with nature and animality. Thus, it associates with nature 'inferiorized' social groups and their characteristic activities. Women are, therefore, historically linked to 'nature' as reproductive bodies and through their supposedly greater emotionality, while indigenous people are seen as a primitive, 'earlier stage' of humanity. At the same time, dominant groups associate themselves with the overcoming, or mastery of, nature, both internal and external. For all those classed as nature, as Other, identification and sympathy are blocked by these structures of 'othering'.

Homogenization/stereotyping

The Other is not an individual but a member of a class stereotyped as interchangeable, replaceable, all alike – that is, as homogeneous. Thus, essential female and 'racial' nature is uniform and unalterable (Stepan, 1993). The colonized are stereotyped as 'all the same' in their deficiency, and their social, cultural, religious and personal diversity is discounted. (Memmi, 1965). Their nature is essentially simple and knowable (unless they are devious and deceptive), not outrunning the homogenizing stereotype (Said, 1978). The Other is stereotyped as the homogeneous and complementary polarity to the One. Edward Said writes: 'The Oriental is irrational, depraved (fallen), childlike, "different"; thus, the European is rational, virtuous, mature, "normal"' (Said, 1978, p40). Homogenization is a major feature of pejorative slang – for example, in talk of 'slits', 'gooks' and 'boongs' in the racist case, and in similar terms for women.

Ronald Reagan's famous remark 'You've seen one redwood, you've seen them all' invokes a parallel homogenization of nature. An anthropocentric culture rarely sees nature and animals as individual centres of striving or needs, doing their best in their conditions of life. Instead, nature is conceived in terms of interchangeable and replaceable units (as 'resources'), rather than as infinitely diverse and always in excess of knowledge and classification. Anthropocentric culture conceives nature and animals as all alike in their lack of consciousness, which is assumed to be exclusive to the human. Once nature and animals are viewed as machines or automata, minds are closed to the range and diversity of their mind-like qualities. Human-supremacist models promote insensitivity to the marvellous diversity of nature, since they attend to differences in nature only if they are likely to contribute in some obvious way to human interests, conceived as separate from those of nature. Homogenization leads to a serious underestimation of the complexity and irreplaceability of nature. These two features of human/nature dualism – radical exclusion and homogenization – work together to produce, in anthropocentric culture, a polarized understanding in which the human and non-human spheres correspond to two quite different substances or orders of being in the world.

Polarization

Typically, supremacist classifications use radical exclusion, combined with homogenization, to construct a polarized field. A highly diverse field, in which there may be many forms of continuity, is reconstructed in terms of polarized and internally homogenized 'superior' and 'inferior' racialized, genderized or naturalized classes of 'us' versus 'them'. In post-colonial liberation movements, much effort is put into countering this polarization: thus, the women's movement disrupts this structure (known as 'sex-role stereotyping') to reveal that men can be emotional, bake cakes and do childcare, while women can be rational, scientific and selfish. In the ecological case, these two features of human/nature dualism – radical exclusion and homogenization – work together to produce in anthropocentric culture a polarized understanding in which overlap and continuity between the human and non-human spheres are denied and discouraged.

Human nature and identity are treated as hyper-separated from, or 'outside' of, nature, and are assumed to exist in a hyper-separate sphere of 'culture'. Ecological identity is assumed to be a contingent aspect of human life and human cultural formation. On the other side, nature is only truly nature if it is 'pure', uncontaminated by human influence, as untouched 'wilderness'. Such an account of nature prevents us from recognizing its importance and agency in our lives. In this form, 'nature', instead of constituting the ground of our being, has only a tenuous and elusive hold on existence and can never be known by human beings. Nature and culture represent two quite different orders of being, with nature (especially as pure nature) representing the inferior and inessential one. The human sphere of 'culture' is supposedly an order of ethics and justice, which apply not to the non-human sphere but only within the sphere of culture. Thus, human/nature dualism reconstructs in highly polarized terms a field where it is really essential to recognize overlap and continuity in order to understand our own nature as ecological, nature-dependent beings and to relate more ethically and less arrogantly to the more-than-human world.

The polarized structure itself is often thought of as characterizing dualism; but dualism is usually symptomatic of a wider hegemonic centrism, and involves a further important dynamic of colonizing interaction in the features set out below. This is a dynamic of denial, 'backgrounding', assimilation and reduction, which frames and justifies the processes of colonization and appropriation applied to the radically separated and subordinated party in the logic of the One and the Other.

Denial, backgrounding

Once the Other is marked, in these ways, as part of a radically separated and inferior group, there is a strong motivation to represent them as inessential. Thus, the centre's dependency upon the Other cannot be acknowledged, since to acknowledge dependence upon an inferiorized Other would threaten the

One's sense of superiority and apartness.[1] In an androcentric context, the contribution of women to any collective undertaking is denied, treated as inessential or as not worth noticing. 'Women's tasks' will be 'backgrounded' to the aspects of life considered important or significant, and they are often classified as 'natural' in involving no special skill or care. This feature enables exploitation of the denied class via expropriation of what they help to produce; but it also carries the usual problems and contradictions of denial. Denial is often accomplished through a perceptual politics of what is worth noticing, what can be acknowledged, 'foregrounded' and rewarded as achievement, and what is relegated to the background. Women's traditional tasks in house labour and child-raising are treated as inessential, as the background services that make 'real' work and achievement possible, rather than as achievements or as work themselves. Similarly, the colonized are denied as the unconsidered background to 'civilization'. They become the 'other' whose prior ownership of the land and whose dispossession and murder is never spoken or admitted. Their trace in the land is denied, and they are represented as *inessential* because their land and their labour embodied in it are taken over as 'nature' or as 'wilderness'. Australian Aboriginal people, for example, were not seen as ecological agents, and their land was taken over as unoccupied, *terra nullius* (no-one's land), while the heroic agency of white pioneers in 'discovering', clearing and transforming the land is celebrated.

Nature is represented as inessential and massively denied as the unconsidered background to technological society. Since anthropocentric culture sees non-human nature as a basically inessential constituent of the universe, nature's needs are systematically omitted from account and consideration in decision-making. Dependency upon nature is denied, systematically, so that nature's order, resistance and survival requirements are not perceived as imposing a limit upon human goals or enterprises. For example, crucial biospheric and other services provided by nature, and the limits they might impose upon human projects, are not considered in accounting or decision-making. We only pay attention to them after disaster occurs, and then only to 'fix things up' for a while. Where we cannot quite forget how dependent upon nature we really are, dependency appears as a source of anxiety and threat, or as a further technological problem to be overcome. Accounts of human agency that background nature's 'work' as a collaborative co-agency feed hyperbolized concepts of human autonomy and independence from nature.

Assimilation

This is synonymous with what Mazama (1994) called incorporation. In androcentric culture, the woman is defined in relation to the man as central, often conceived as lacking in relation to him, sometimes crudely (as in Aristotle's account of reproduction), sometimes more subtly. Simone de Beauvoir expressed this well in her classic statement that:

> *...humanity is male and man defines woman not in herself but as relative to him; she is not regarded as an autonomous being...she is defined and differentiated with reference to man and not he with reference to her; she is the incidental, the inessential as opposed to the essential . He is the Subject, he is the Absolute, she is the Other* (de Beauvoir 1965, p8).

His features are set up as culturally universal, making her the exception, negation or lack of the virtue of the One. The Other is marked as deviation from the centrality of the One, as colour is a deviation from the 'normal' condition of whiteness. Her difference, thus represented as a lack and represented as deficiency rather than diversity, becomes the basis of hierarchy and exclusion. The Other's deficiency invites the One 'to control, contain and otherwise govern (through superior knowledge and accommodating power) the Other' (Said, 1978, p 48).

The colonized, too, is judged not as an independent being or culture but as an 'illegitimate and refractory foil' to the colonizer (Parry, 1995, p42), as a lack in relation to the colonizer, and as negativity (Memmi, 1965). The colonized are devalued as having an absence of the colonizer's chief qualities, usually represented in the West as reason. Differences are judged as deficiencies, grounds of inferiority. The order that the colonized possesses is represented as disorder or unreason. The colonized, and their 'disorderly' space, are available for use, without limit, and the assimilating project of the colonizer is to remake the colonized and their space in the image of the colonizer's own self-space, culture or land, which are represented as the paradigm of reason, beauty and order. The speech, voice, projects and religion of the colonized are acknowledged and recognized as valuable only to the extent that they are assimilated to that of the colonizer.

Similarly, rather than according nature the dignity of an independent other or presence, anthropocentric culture treats nature as Other in the sense of being merely a refractory foil to the human. Defined in relation to the human, or as an absence of the human, nature has a conceptual status that leaves it entirely dependent for its meaning upon the 'primary' human term. Thus, nature and animals are judged as lacking in relation to the human colonizer, as negativity, and as devalued in having an absence of those qualities said to be essential for the human condition, such as rationality. We consider non-human animals inferior because they lack, we think, human capacities for abstract thought. But we do not consider as superior those positive capacities that many animals have and which we lack, such as remarkable navigational capacities. Differences are judged as grounds of inferiority, not as welcome and intriguing signs of diversity. The intricate order of nature is perceived as disorder, as unreason, to be replaced, where possible, by human order in development – the assimilating project of colonization. Where the order present in nature is not seen, or seen as representing a constraint on human action, nature is treated as available for use without restriction.

Instrumentalism

Similarly, the colonized Other is reduced to being a means to the colonizer's ends. Their blood and treasure, as Said (1978) notes, are available to the colonizer and used as a means of increasing central power. The colonizer, as the origin and source of 'civilized values', denies the Other's agency, social organization and independence, and subsumes them under his own. The Other is not the agent of their own cultural meanings, but receives these from the home culture of the centre through the knowledgeable manipulations of the One (Said, 1978, p40). The extent to which indigenous people were ecological agents who actively managed the land, for example, is denied, and they are presented as largely passive in the face of nature. In the colonizer's history, their agency is usually disappeared: they do not present any resistance to colonization, and do not fight or win any battles. Since the Other is perceived in terms of inferiority, and their own agency and creation of value are denied, it is appropriate that the colonizer imposes his own value, agency and meaning, and that the colonized be made to serve the colonizer as a means to his ends, (for example, as servants, or 'boys'). The colonized, so conceived, cannot present any moral or prudential limit to appropriation.

In anthropocentric culture, nature's agency and independence are denied, subsumed in, or remade to coincide with human interests, which are thought to be the source of all value in the world. Mechanistic world views especially deny nature any form of agency of its own. Since the non-human sphere is thought to have no agency of its own and to be empty of purpose, it is thought appropriate that the human colonizer impose his own purposes. Human-centred ethics views nature as possessing meaning and value only when it is made to serve the human/colonizer as a means to his or her ends. Thus, we get the split characteristic of modernity in which ethical considerations apply to the human sphere but not to the non-human sphere. Since nature itself is thought to be outside of the ethical sphere, imposing no moral limits on human action, we can deal with nature as an instrumental sphere, provided we do not injure other humans in doing so. Instrumental outlooks distort our sensitivity to, and knowledge of, nature, blocking humility, wonder and openness in approaching the more-than-human, and producing narrow types of understanding that reduce nature to raw materials for human projects.

COUNTERING CENTRIC STRUCTURE

The injustice of colonization does not take place in a conceptual vacuum; rather, it is closely linked to these desensitizing and 'othering' frameworks for identifying self and other. The centric structure imposes a form of rationality, a framework for beliefs, which naturalizes and justifies a certain sort of self-centredness, self-imposition and dispossession. Dispossession is what Eurocentric and ethnocentric colonization ventures accomplish, as do anthropocentric frameworks. The centric structure *achieves* this by promoting insensitivity to the Other's needs, agency and prior claims and by promoting a belief in the colonizer's apartness, superiority and right to conquer or master the Other. This promotion of insensitivity is, in a sense, its function. It provides a highly distorted framework for perception of the Other, and the project of mastery that it gives rise to involves dangerous forms of denial, perception and belief that can put the centric perceiver *out of touch* with reality about the Other. Think, for example, of what the Eurocentric framework led Australian colonizers to believe about Aboriginal people. These highly diverse people, who spoke over 300 languages and whose complex culture revolved around their spiritual relationship to their land, were thought (even 'perceived') to lack all religion, to possess a single 'primitive' or 'stone-age' culture and language, to be ecologically passive 'nomads' with no deep relationship to any specific areas of land, and so on. Frameworks of centrism do not provide a basis for sensitive, sympathetic or reliable understanding and observation of either the Other or of the self. Centrism is (it would be nice to say 'was') a framework of moral and cultural blindness.

To counter the first dynamic of 'us–them' polarization, it is necessary to acknowledge and reclaim continuity and overlap between the polarized groups, as well as internal diversity within them. However, countering the second dynamic of denial, assimilation and instrumentalization requires recognition of the Other's difference, independence and agency. Thus, a double movement or gesture of affirming kinship and also affirming the Other's difference, as an independent presence to be engaged with on its own terms, is required. To counter the 'othering' definition of nature that is outlined above, we need a depolarizing re-conception of non-human nature that recognizes the denied space of our hybridity, continuity and kinship, and which is also able to recognize, in suitable contexts, the difference of the non-human in a non-hierarchical way. Such a nature would be no mere resource or periphery to our centre, but another, and prior, centre of power and need whose satisfaction can and must impose limits upon our conception of ourselves, and on our own actions and needs. The nature we would recognize in a non-reductive model is no mere human absence or conceptually dependent Other, no mere precondition for our own star-stuff of achievement, but is an active collaborative presence capable of agency and other mind-like qualities. Such a biospheric Other is not a background part of our field of action or subjectivity, not a mere precondition for human action, not a refractory foil to self. Rather, biospheric Others can be other ethical and communicative subjects and other actors in the world – others to whom we owe debts of gratitude, generosity and recognition as prior and enabling presences.

The re-conception of nature in the agentic terms that deliver it from construction as background is perhaps the most important aspect of moving to an alternative ethical framework, because 'backgrounding' is perhaps the most hazardous and distorting effect of 'othering' from a human prudential point of view. When the Other's agency is treated as background or denied, we give that Other less credit than is due to them; we can come to take for granted what they provide for us; and we pay attention only when something goes wrong. This is a problem for prudence, as well as for justice. When we are, in fact, dependent upon this Other, we can gain an illusory sense of our own ontological and ecological independence, and it is just such a sense that seems to pervade the dominant culture's contemporary disastrous misperceptions of its economic and ecological relationships.

To counter the features of 'backgrounding' and denial, ecological thinkers and green activists try to puncture the contemporary illusion of human disembeddedness and self-enclosure, raising people's consciousness of how much they depend upon nature, and of how anthropocentric culture's denial of this dependency upon nature is expressed in local, regional or global problems. There are many ways of doing this. Through local education, activists can stress the importance and value of nature in practical daily life, enabling people to keep track of the ways in which they use and impinge upon nature. This can create understandings of the fragility of ecological systems and relationships. Those activists prepared for long-term struggles can work to change systems of distribution, accounting, perception and planning so that these systems reduce remoteness, make our dependency relationships more transparent in our daily lives, and allow for nature's needs and limits. Bringing about such systematic changes is what political action for ecological sustainability is all about.

Countering a hegemonic dualism, such as that between nature and culture, presents many traps for young players. A common temptation among those who mistake a hegemonic dualism for a simple value hierarchy is to attempt a reversal of value that fails to challenge the hegemonic construction of the concepts concerned (see also Langton, 1993, p41). For example, we may decide that traditional devaluations of nature should give way to strong positive evaluations of nature as a way of fixing the environmental problem, but fail to notice the polarized meaning that is commonly given to 'nature'. Dualistic concepts of nature insist that 'true' nature must be entirely free of human influence, ruling out any overlap between nature and culture. This reversal, which suggests that only 'pure' nature (perhaps in the form of 'wilderness') is valuable or has needs that should be recognized and respected, leaves us without adequate ways of recognizing and tracking the agency of the more-than-human sphere in our daily lives, since this rarely appears in a pure or unmixed form. Yet, this is one of the most important things we need to do to counter the widespread and very damaging illusion that modern urban life has 'overcome' the need for nature or has become disconnected from nature.

Polarized concepts of wilderness as the realm of an idealized, pure nature remain popular in the environment movement where they are often employed for protective purposes, to keep, for example, market uses of land at bay. The concept of wilderness has been an important part of the colonial project, and attempts by neo-European conservation movements to press it into service as a means of resisting the continuing colonization of nature must take account of its double face. On the one hand, it represents an attempt to recognize that nature has been colonized and to give it a domain of its own; on the other hand, it continues and extends the colonizing refusal to recognize the prior presence and agency of indigenous people in the land. If we understand wilderness in the traditional way, as designating areas that are purely the province of nature, then to call Australia, or parts of it, wilderness is to imply that no human influence has shaped its development. We imply that it is purely Other, having no element of human culture. However, the idea that the Australian continent, or even substantial parts of it, are pure nature, is insensitive to the claims of indigenous peoples and denies their record as ecological agents who have left their mark upon the land. Indigenous critics such as Marcia Langton have rightly objected that such a strategy colludes with the colonial concept of Australia as *terra nullius* and with the colonial representation of Aboriginal people as merely animal and as 'parasites on nature' (Langton, 1996). To recognize that both nature and indigenous peoples have been colonized, we need to rethink, relocate and redefine our protective concepts for nature within a larger anti-colonial critique.[2]

Attempts by the Green movement to redefine the concept of wilderness in order to meet these objections have often involved minimal rethinking and have not really allayed this important class of objections to the conventional wilderness framework and terminology. Thus, wilderness is often defined, for example, as land that is in, or is capable of being restored to, its pre-settlement condition. However, this strategy is just a conceptual shuffle: it continues to assume implicitly that the pre-settlement condition of the land was 'the pure state of nature', because if the land was not wilderness before settlement, how could restoring it to its pre-settlement condition make it wilderness now? So, this sort of formula seeks to evade, rather than come to terms with, the reality that the pre-settlement condition of the land was rarely pure nature but was a mix of nature and culture and included a substantial human presence and ecological agency. Restorative definitions of wilderness that attempt to harness the colonial mystique along the lines so strongly developed in the US collaborate with discredited colonial narratives of past purity (Cronon, 1983; 1995; Spence, 1999).

Alternative approaches to wilderness that might avoid this collaboration could be performative rather than descriptive, and future oriented rather than past oriented, so that the designation of such areas as, say, 'biodiversity reserves' (Callicott and Nelson, 1998; Preston and Stannard, 1994) would represent a decision to treat the appropriate management and ethical stance as one where non-humans should come first, rather than making a descriptive and historical claim to purity.[3] An alternative protective concept could aim to identify healthy communities of biodiversity in structural terms and specify standards for keeping them healthy, thus providing a basis for deciding what is overuse without appealing to colonial narratives of the past purity of nature (Mackey, 1999; Preston and Stannard, 1994; Whitehouse, 1994).

The framework of colonization that is outlined here and elsewhere, while forming a basis for appropriation and commodification of the land (Plumwood, 2002b), has many disabling and undesirable implications for deeper land relationships. In the present context of crisis in our relationships with nature, colonial and centric relationships of the sort outlined in this chapter are especially dangerous because they are monological rather than dialogical. Humans are seen as the only rational species, the only real subjectivities and agents in the world, and nature is a background substratum that is there to be exploited. This is the rationality of monologue, termed monological because it recognizes the Other only in one-way terms. It is a mode of interaction where the Others must always hear and adapt to the One, and never the other way around. Monological relationships block mutual adaptation and its corollaries in negotiation, accommodation, communication and attention to the Other's needs, limits and agency (see Plumwood, 2002b). The colonizing task is to make the land accommodate to us rather than we to it, leading to the rejection of communicative and negotiated ecological relationships of mutual adaptation in favour of one-way relationships of self-imposition. Thus, the Eurocentric colonization of nature insists that the land be adapted to European models. The general cultural consequences of colonizing relationships with nature then lead to failures of ecological identity and ecological rationality; they include the disabling of communicative and mutually adaptive modes of relationship, and the reduction of land to something to be experienced instrumentally – as resource rather than as ancestral force. For this reason alone we must abandon the centric paradigm that has governed Western civilization for so long and move towards a framework that encourages listening to the other and encountering the land in the active rather than the passive voice.

DISABLING LAND RELATIONSHIPS:
AN EMPTY, SILENT LAND

Colonizing frameworks of the sort outlined above can occupy both a general background role as 'deep structures' regarding nature, in general (these structures are rarely put up for conscious examination), and a more local and specific political role in subordinating colonized areas to places of the centre, or 'home'. For specific, recently colonized countries, such as Australia, we must add to the background level of Western colonizing consciousness (see Plumwood, 1993) further attitudes and practices that are more specifically associated with neo-European and Australian colonial origins. Thus, we can have colonizing frameworks operating at several levels, reflecting both the persistence of the sort of colonial framework that treats the basic land relationship as one of European centre to colonial periphery, and also of the kind of anthropocentric conceptual framework that treats the human homeland of rational modernity as the centre and nature, in general, as a background, periphery or instrument – as a silent emptiness that provides no meaning and imposes no real constraint.[4] Both of these frameworks persist in dominant post-colonial land relationships. Modern Australians are among the most mobile and urbanized of populations in the world, only exceptionally encountering the land in any intense way and conceiving it as largely inessential to their lives as dwellers in the globalized city. For both urban and rural populations, the land exists primarily in instrumental terms, as a resource to be drawn upon to support the economy and to maintain their livelihood or identification with affluent global, urban lifestyles. Yet, this background resource role as adjunct to, and enabler of, 'the Australian way of life' systematically inflicts catastrophes upon the land in the name of economic development.

New arrivals must, of course, learn their land, and can be excused some early mistakes. But this kind of ignorance cannot fully explain the harsh character of Australian land relationships or the persistence of this harshness into recent times. To understand this, we must revert to the framework of colonization. Firstly, in the context of the colonial project, rapid conversion of land into profitable and productive private property is strongly emphasized by ambitious governments anxious to expand their own economic base. There are usually no older or gentler traditions of land relationship for settlers to draw upon (Lines, 1991). Secondly, in the Australian colonial context, Eurocentric projects of assimilation that value land according to its conformity to European agricultural ideals have been especially influential in settler land culture. The imposition of these Eurocentric ideals has been especially damaging for a fragile land whose ecology bears little resemblance to that of Europe. The result in Australia, over the 200 years of colonization, has been damage to the land on an unprecedented scale, damage that is reflected in soil loss, desertification, salination and extinction rates that are among the worst in the world. Almost half of Australia's indigenous species are threatened or vulnerable. Land degradation over areas used as rangeland (75 per cent of the continent) has reached a point where 13 per cent is degraded beyond probable recovery, and over half is in an earlier stage of the same process (Commonwealth of Australia, 1996; Rose, 1996, p.79). These figures are a testament not primarily to ignorance but to the monological land relationships encouraged by colonial frameworks. In many cases, for example the western Australian wheat belt, scientific advice as far back as the 1920s gave clear advance warning that severe land degradation or salination would be the outcome of land opening and clearance projects; but such advice was dismissed and clearing projects went ahead.

Colonial projects of assimilation clearly lie behind the deliberate introduction of feral predators and competitors from Europe, such as the fox and the rabbit, which along with habitat destruction has done much of the damage to native fauna. Assimilative projects continue to insist upon the imposition of Eurocentric agricultural regimes that are inappropriate to fragile and vulnerable environments. The imposition of Eurocentric agricultural models presupposes a quiet, benign and malleable nature that imposes few limits on high-intensity tillage or grazing. It is not only the economic and political drive to develop Eurocentric agriculture but the colonial failure to value the difference of Australian biodiversity, plants and animals that is expressed in the widespread, and often indiscriminate, destruction of indigenous ecosystems in order to create short-term productivity. The ongoing clearance of woodland

and arid-zone vegetation in Australia at the present time has no shreds of justification where long-term consequences in salination, desertification and species extinctions are clearly predictable. Yet, Australians adhere to these colonizing traditions, continuing to destroy indigenous vegetation at one of the highest rates in the world in order to create a standardized 'open' agricultural landscape. Bird care groups have pointed out that the continuation of such a practice is likely to result in the extinction of as many as one third of indigenous bird species, especially those that rely on arid-zone woodland.

Damage to the land is traceable not just to ignorance or to the contemporary economic rationalist subservience to 'the economy', but also to the way colonizing Eurocentric paradigms have imagined the continent as inferior, as silent and empty. Traditional devaluing attitudes associated with colonization encouraged Eurocentric nostalgia for the European homeland, leading to views of the new country as inferior to, or as an extension of, the old, to be experienced and judged primarily in relation to the old, or to be remade in the image of the old, rather than as an independent presence to be engaged with on its own terms. This practice corresponds especially to the dynamic of assimilation discussed above, in which the Other is seen to have worth or virtue only to the extent that it can be seen as an extension of, or as similar to, the centre or the One. So, for example, when British settlers first arrived in Australia, they encountered a highly unfamiliar fauna and flora. For them, the unfamiliar birds and land were silent, so they set about forming acclimatization societies to introduce 'real' (familiar) songbirds to these supposedly barren shores (Marshall, 1966; Bolton, 1981; Lines, 1991).[5] It is amazing to think that they were unable to hear superb and now well-loved indigenous songsters such as the grey shrike thrush, mountain thrush, lyrebird, magpie and butcher bird, as well as the lively songs of countless smaller birds such as the yellow-throated scrub wren and the numerous honey-eaters. These birds, and many others, make up what has come to be recognized as one of the world's most impressive and unique avian communities.

Although an element in what we must construe as the deafness of the settlers was the strangeness and unfamiliarity of the colony, another major part of it was the colonial mindset and Eurocentric conceptual framework that considered Australia as a deficient, empty land, a mere absence of the positive qualities of the homeland. It is not only that the settlers were ignorant and had not yet 'learned their land'; rather, the colonizing framework sets up powerful barriers to such learning. In the colonizing framework, the Other is not a positively-other-than entity in its own right, but an absence of the self, home or centre, something of no value or beauty of its own except to the extent that it can be brought to reflect, or bear the likeness of, home as standard (Plumwood, 2000a). Hence, the colonized land in its original state had to be – could only be – improved by the introduction of the fauna of home, including the fox and the rabbit. To the extent that colonizing conceptual frameworks comprehend or explain experience rather simply, they can have an important filtering effect in blocking the learning of the land.[6]

Frameworks of colonization, of both the local and cultural background variety, breed insensitivity to the land, blocking imaginative and dialogical encounter with the more-than-human-world, and treating it as an inessential constituent of identity. Both distortions of difference, such as assimilation, and distortions of continuity, such as hyper-separation, have a role here. The radical separation of human from non-human and the reduction of the non-human that is part of Western thought means that the more-than-human world is consigned to object status and cannot comfortably occupy the role of narrative subject. The colonizing framework's exclusion of the non-human from subject status and from intentionality marginalizes the non-human as narrative subject and agent, and pushes the more-than-human sphere into a background role as a mere context for human thought and life. Since the non-human world is a very important source of narratives and narrative subjects that define the distinctiveness of place, this exclusion also marginalizes place, in general, as a constituent of human identity and meaning. By contrast, these same elements that are disempowered in modern Western thought systems – place, narrative and non-human agents as narrative subjects and life context – have a central structural place in indigenous land relationships and in environmental philosophies. The recognition of Earth others as fellow agents and narrative subjects is crucial for all ethical, collaborative, communicative and mutualistic projects that involve them, as well as for place sensitivity. Recent ethical theorists have emphasized the importance of narrative for constituting the moral identity of actors and actions (Gare, 1998; Warren, 1990). Legitimating rich narrative description of the non-human sphere is crucial to liberating the narrative moral imagination that 'activates our capacity for thinking of possible narratives and act descriptions' (Benhabib, 1992, p129). This can help us to configure nature as a realm of others who are independent centres of value and need and who demand from us various kinds of response, especially ethical responses of attention, consideration and concern.

Features of the colonizing framework, like radical exclusion, that deny intentionality and subject status to the more-than-human world not only deny and background nature as agent and context but also deny the importance and agency of place. The contrast between this nullification of place and context and the sensitivity to, and recognition of, agency, centrality and specificity of place that is a feature of indigenous life could hardly be greater. In 'backgrounding' particularity, place and narrative as factors in human thought and life, colonizing frameworks make places into mere passive instruments or neutral surfaces for the inscription of human projects. The marginality of land and place for identity in modernist culture contrasts sharply with its centrality for indigenous culture. For indigenous philosopher Bill Neidjie, 'obligations concerning the land are at the centre of social, moral and religious life. The natural world is not, as in our case, the unconsidered background to human life – it is in the foreground' (Plumwood, 1990, p531). Bill Neidjie's statement that 'Our story is in the land/ it is written in those sacred places' (p47) articulates this centrality. If environmental thought and questions about relationships with the natural world are on the margins, at best, within modernist culture, they are surely at the heart of indigenous philosophy and spirituality, where non-human life forms take their place as narrative subjects in a speaking and participating land, full of narratives and mythic voices.[7]

There are a group of factors that combine to explain the especially damaging character of Australian land relationships. The insensitivity and human-centredness of the Western framework of human–nature relationships are amplified in the colonial context. Lifestyle factors collude with symbolic ones to promote relationships with place and land that are primarily instrumental. Sensitivity to the land seems to require a deep acquaintance with a place, or perhaps a group of places. It also requires an ability to relate dialogically to the more-than-human world, a crucial source of narratives and narrative subjects defining the distinctiveness of place. The mobility and urbanism of modernity combines with the ethical and perceptual framework of colonization to dis-empower both place and the more-than-human sphere as major constituents of identity and meaning. Western moderns mostly do not relate dialogically to the non-human sphere and have come to believe that the land is dumb, that culture and meaning are 'exclusively an interaction of man on man' (Thoreau 1862, p655), thus strengthening both 'placelessness' and what David Abram (1996) calls 'the project of human self-enclosure'. As a result, there are several different kinds of reasons why many of us now lack sensitivity to place and land. One reason is that mobile modern urban life-ways do not allow the necessary depth of familiarity; but another, more basic, reason is that our perceptions are screened through a colonizing conceptual sieve that eliminates certain communicative possibilities and dialogical encounters with the more-than-human world. Such an analysis suggests that our main problem lies not in silence, but in a certain kind of (constructed) deafness.

THE COLONIZING POLITICS OF PLACE NAMES: RENAMING AS DECOLONIZATION

A colonial dynamic of seeing Australian land and nature as silent and empty appears clearly in the Australian culture's response to the naming of the continent. However, if colonizing frameworks and relationships are clearly expressed in the naming of the land, as is demonstrated below, then renaming could become a decolonization project aimed at reconciling the culture of the colonizers with the land and with indigenous people and their culture.

Not only do many Australian place names express colonizing world views and naming practices, but these naming practices tend to be both anthropocentric and Eurocentric, registering a monological or non-interactive relationship with a land conceived as passive and silent. What is often expressed in place names is the dynamic of assimilation: the land is defined in terms of colonial relationships that exhibit Eurocentricity and nostalgia for the European homeland. Such naming practices refuse to relate to the land on its own terms, denying it the role of narrative subject in the stories that stand behind its name. Instead of treating the land dialogically as a presence in its own right, colonizing namings speak only of the human, or of what is of use to the human as resource, and of certain kinds of humans at that. The outcome is a reduction and impoverishment of Australian land culture that parallels the extinction and impoverishment of its biodiversity. However, through decolonization strategies, there are possibilities of opening this land culture to change and enrichment – of creating places in our culture so that the empty, silent land can begin to speak in many tongues and reveal some of its many names.

The significance of names and of naming is often underestimated in the modern West. Different cultures have different bases for ownership of the land: these differences can be so radical that they amount to different paradigms of land relationship, which are incomprehensible to those from a different framework. In some cultures, it is the paradigm of expenditure, or mixing in, of human labour that validates the claim to own the land. As we have seen above, this formula – which corresponds to John Locke's criteria for forming property from land conceived as 'wilderness' by adding human labour – validates capitalist and colonial models of appropriation and ownership. It creates a one-way, monological form of relationship in which nature's agency and independence are discounted and the land is conceived as an adjunct to, or raw resource for, human projects. An alternative paradigm of ownership and belonging is communicative, relying upon narrative methods for naming and interpreting the land through telling its story in ways that show a deep and loving acquaintance with it, and a history of dialogical interaction. In terms of this second paradigm, non-indigenous Australians have a long way to go in achieving ownership and belonging. Aboriginal narrative patterns of naming can help to show us possibilities for a richer dialogical relationship.

We can see these different paradigms at work in the naming of the Murray River. The difference between dirt and country, between a muddy irrigation channel and a rich, winding river, includes the difference between being conceived, on the one hand, as a mute medium for another's projects (perhaps as a transparent intermediary between the owner and the investment agent) and, on the other, as an ancestral force, speaker and giver of myth. In the latter, a river such as the Murray can be a narrative subject and agent in a story of its own making, in which its course is created by, and follows, the struggles of its characteristic being, a great Murray cod. The river's name draws upon this narrative. This gives the river's name a solid foundation in evolutionary time: river and fish are made by, and for, each other. Conceived in the other way as a mute medium, however, the river's name can be arrived at by processes that are quite arbitrary and human-centred, having nothing at all to do with the river itself or its characteristics. Its naming can be made to serve the purposes of flattery or influence, by having it bear the name of some august colonial figure, for example. Just so did Charles Sturt on 23 January 1830 name Australia's major river, then as now a profoundly Aboriginal place, in honour of Sir George Murray, Britain's secretary of state for the colonies (Sinclair, 2001, p17).

I made a close acquaintance with the first paradigm, growing up on a small New South Wales farm whose front gate bore the hand-lettered name *Wyeera*. The name, my father told me, meant 'to dig the soil'. He said it was an Aboriginal word, but it was very conveniently detached in his mind from specific tribal languages and locations.[8] If the name of our place did have this meaning, it seems likely that the nature of the digging designated by *wyeera* was very different from the digging we practiced. Digging and the hard work that went with it were venerated on our land, a piece of low-fertility Sydney sandstone my father had to strip of its trees in order to make our farm. Digging was my father's most characteristic exertion, his most memorable pose leaning on his spade, throwing fat, white wichetty grubs to swooping kookaburras. Nobody, least of all the people like us who did the hard clearing work, questioned how far these European regimes and values of cultivation were appropriate for the new land and soils, or how they destroyed the indigenous economy or the forests we felled to make it possible. In our pioneering mythology, it was cultivation (interpreted as digging), and the exemplary hard work of altering the land to fit the Eurocentric formula of cultivation and production, that supposedly made us European settlers superior to other races and species.

However, it is not just the romantic call of another culture that makes me think, now, that digging and sweating in order to force the land into the ideal Lockean form of the European farm is not the best basis for land relationship. The kind of narrative basis for ownership typical of many indigenous cultures seems to me to have much more to offer. A communicative paradigm – the reflexive relationship that Deborah Bird Rose (1992) describes in her classic study of the Yarralin of the Victoria River Downs region and their land relationship, *Dingo Makes Us Human* – makes good sense for non-indigenous Australia, too, in the context of the ecological failure of Eurocentric farming models in Australia.

As we have seen, a narrative project of sensitivity to place requires discarding the mechanistic, reductionist and human-centred conceptual frameworks that strip intentionality (and thereby narrative subjecthood) from the land and from non-humans generally. Human self-enclosure, which denies subject positioning to all but the human, vastly contracts the range of subjects and possible narratives that give meaning and richness to place. Human-centredness reduces the land to a passive and neutral surface for the inscription of human projects. Capitalist versions of human-centredness reduce the agency and value of the land to a mere potentiality for aiding or realizing these projects (such as profit-making). These are monological modes of relating that reduce the land to an instrumentalized Other upon which projects are imposed, rather than an interactive and dialogical relationship that recognizes agency in the land. Monological modes of relating are dysfunctional, especially in the context of the current environmental crisis. They allow no space for two-way adaptation to the Other, or for negotiation, attentiveness or sensitivity.

These contrasting paradigms are reflected in our respective cultures' naming practices. The way in which we name places reflects our land-related spirituality and the depth of our relationship to the land and its narratives. Western philosophy's theories of naming the land illustrate this. Logical positivist philosophers treated names as purely conventional, neutral markers without cultural content, mere pointers or numbered labels. They could not have been more wrong. Names are only conferred in individualistic, and therefore arbitrary, ways when there is no recognition of the importance of community, in whose absence there is no such thing as meaning. Conventionalism reflects the concept of the land as neutral, passive and silent; as such, it is an index of the shallowness of relationships to place. A completely instrumental approach may require only a number as a name because this could represent the shortest distance between two points – that of the namer and his purpose – and would require the least possible investment of attention and effort in understanding the Other. Naming workers are often required to follow positivist practice. A friend who had worked on creating and registering street names told me of the arbitrary lists they used to select from – lists compiled from dictionary words, first names and surnames. These official namers never saw the places they were naming and knew nothing of their histories, but followed conventionalistic rules like 'a short name for a short street'.

There is an important politics embedded in names and naming. Colonizing modes of naming the land are often blatantly incorporative, as well as being monological. Consider Frederick Turner's account of Columbus's naming of the New World:

> *To each bit of land he saw he brought the mental map of Europe with which he had sailed. Anciently…place names arose like rocks or trees out of the contours and colors of the lands themselves…as a group took up residence in an area, that area would be dotted with names commemorating events that took place in it…where one tribal group supplanted another, it too would respond to the land, its shapes, moods, and to tribal experiences had there. Now came these newest arrivals, but the first names by which they designated the islands were in no way appropriate to the islands themselves. Instead, the Admiral scattered the nomenclature of Christianity over these lands, firing his familiar names like cannon balls against the unresisting New World….One group was called Los Santos because the Christ-bearer sailed past them on All Saints' Day…. An armoured Adam in this naked garden, he established dominion by naming* (Turner, 1986, p131).

Several things emerge from this account. Firstly, Columbus's naming was an act of power over the land and those who inhabited it – an act of incorporating the named places into what is thought of as an empire. Secondly, Turner contrasts dialogical indigenous modes of naming with colonial monological modes that are not a response to the character of the land and are 'in no way appropriate' to the lands themselves. Columbus's naming does not record any of the land's features or any real encounter with the land, but merely registers its conquest and incorporation within the empire. Beyond this incorporative meaning, these names invoke no depth of knowledge or narrative, being little more than mnemonic devices holding place for a neutral marker, like the logical positivist labels.

It seems to me that far too many Australian namings are in the Columbian tradition, with the difference that the names of Christian saints were replaced by those of the bigwigs of the British colonial office, many of whom never visited the places that were named after them. Seen in this light, the names of many of Australia's capital cities – such as Sydney, Melbourne, Brisbane, Adelaide and Hobart – are but empty reminders of largely forgotten power plays.[9] Such naming practices overlay the land, conceived as neutral, with a grid of bureaucratic or political power that registers obeisance to the empire, or commemorates those in the surveyor's office in 1903.[10] The names of those cities and many of the suburbs within them sadly locate us in terms of a grid of colonial power that is now largely meaningless.

ASSIMILATION, COLONIAL NOSTALGIA AND FERAL NAMES

Another group of names exhibits the colonial dynamic in a different way from those commemorating major figures of colonial power. These are the names that refer back to the places of a European homeland, usually bearing no resemblance at all to the new place 'named after' them. ('To each bit of land he saw he brought the mental map of Europe with which he had sailed', Turner, 1986, p131.) It is now hard to connect Perth, the commercial capital of a state largely driven by industrial mining, with the small town on the upper reaches of the River Tay in Scotland. Ipswich, Camden and Penrith are places in Britain; these names have no relevance to the places upon which they were imposed in Australia.

For the purpose of introducing the biota of the homeland into the colonies, settler societies formed 'acclimatization societies'. Perhaps we can regard the 'acclimatized' place names as being the equivalent of the feral fauna that the colonists tried (sometimes with unfortunate success) to introduce in their efforts to assimilate the new land to the old; hence we might refer to such place names as feral names. Feral names, like feral biota, register the colonial dynamic of periphery and centre: the assimilation and devaluation of Australian landscapes and biota in comparison to those of 'home'. Feral names such as Perth and Ipswich are pointedly assimilationist in their references to home, and in their longing inscription of the landscape of Britain, and occasionally Europe, on the new 'featureless' land. They invoke no shared narratives and provide no evidence of affection for, attention to, or even interaction with, the land.

A third category of names we should focus upon comprises blatantly monological colonial namings that take no notice of the land when it is nearly impossible to ignore it. ('One group was called Los Santos because the Christ-bearer sailed past them on All Saints' Day', Turner, 1986, p131.) The contrast between the empty egoism or nostalgia of these monological colonial namings and the rich dialogical practice of Aboriginal narrative namings impressed itself upon me strongly in a recent bushwalk in the Mount Brockman area of Arnhem Land. In this region you encounter fully the Kakadu region's extraordinary qualities of beauty, power and prescience. The massif we know as Mount Brockman is part of an extravagantly eroded sandstone plateau weathered to immense, fantastic ruins that bring to mind enigmatic artefacts from some titanic civilization of the past. In the place where my party camped on Baraolba Creek, on the second day of our walk, an inchoate sphinx face and a perfect sarcophagus, both the size of battleships, topped the great towers of the domed red cliffs to the south. Everywhere, strangely humanoid figures of shrouded gods and finely balanced sandstone heads gazed out over country formed by 1000 million years of play between the sandstone and the hyperactive tropical atmosphere. Yet namings such as Mount Brockman take no notice at all of this extraordinary place, or of its power and agency.[11] The puzzling, pointless and Eurocentric naming of this great outlier of the escarpment, marked by remarkable and ancient Aboriginal places and rock art galleries, commemorates a European 'discoverer' finding the place notable only for the accident of its being on the path of a member of the colonial aristocracy who was travelling by. Such monological namings treat the place itself as a vacuum of mind and meaning, to be filled through the power plays of those in favour with the current political equivalent of the old colonial office.

In what I call 'deep naming', names connect with a narrative, as they so often do in Aboriginal patterns of naming. In deep naming, a narrative gives depth, meaning and a voice to the land and its non-human inhabitants. Walking in the upper stretches of Baraolba Creek during Yegge (the early dry season), I encountered the *kunbak*, a small waterplant whose fine green fronds represent the hair of the Yawk Yawk sisters (Nawakadj Nganjmirra, 1997, p172). The Yawk Yawks live in the slowly moving water along the edges of this little stream, which drains a huge area of the stone country. In the narratives of the Kunwinkju people of the western part of Kakadu, these sisters are little spirit mermaids with fish tails instead of legs. They dwell in the holes beneath the banks and come out to sing and play where the pandanus plants grow. From underneath the water, they watch women swimming, ever on the lookout for one ready to become their mother, to birth them as human. For a *balanda* woman like myself, the Yawk Yawks offer welcome sisterly and *binitj* (Aboriginal) travelling companions in the landscape, enticing Westerners across the high wall we have tried to build between the human and non-human worlds.[12] Many *binitj* namings invoke narratives such as those of the Yawk Yawks. These striking stories function to cunningly and irresistibly impress their meanings within memory, and to bind together botanical, experiential, practical and philosophical knowledge. They build community identity and spiritual practice in a rich and satisfying integration of what we in the West usually treat as opposites: life and theory. *Binitj* stories and namings envelop a journey in their land within a web of narrative, so that one travels as a communicative partner through a speaking land that is encountered deeply in dialogical mode.

DECOLONIZING THE NAMING RELATIONSHIP

The deeply colonized and colonizing naming practices discussed above still figure too prominently on the Australian map. Neither they nor their underlying narratives of Eurocentrism and of colonial power are in any way challenged by formal and superficial decolonization exercises, like recent efforts to move from our monarchical political model to that of a republic. Since, in my view, it is a much more important decolonizing project to work on these cultural modes of naming than to tinker with the way a head of state is appointed, I am tempted to call the project of cultural change suggested here 'deep republicanism'. It is precisely such cultural practices that we have to take on if we Australians are ever to belong culturally to this land and to develop a mode of exchange that attends to, and respects, the uniqueness and power of place, while recognizing its prior naming and occupation by Aboriginal people. A renaming project of this kind must recognize the double-sidedness of the Australian colonial relationship, in which non-indigenous Australians were historically positioned both as colonizers of indigenous Australians and as colonized themselves (in relation to the British).

An empty and highly conventionalized naming practice is both a symptom and a partial cause of an empty relationship to the land. If we want a meaningful relationship with the land that expresses a healthier pattern than the colonial one, we have to look to naming it in meaningful terms that acknowledge its agency and narrative depth. This chapter therefore proposes the renaming project as a project of cultural convergence, cross-fertilization, reconciliation and decolonization. It might be helpful to start the cultural decolonization project from locations, and based upon issues, that offer the possibility of generating some common culture through involving and engaging indigenous and non-indigenous communities. This might create some possibilities for developing shared spiritual meaning and ritual observance, not just an individual search for privatized spiritual meaning. A shared renaming project might enable indigenous and non-indigenous communities to come together in order to rework their relationship with each other and with the land. This chapter proposes that we start a joint renaming project that is part of 're-mythologizing' the land and that prioritizes for replacement the categories of names discussed above, as well as others that are particularly disrespectful of indigenous people. At the very top of the list might be those names that commemorate and honour the makers of massacres against indigenous people, such as the name for the major highway that runs right through the middle of Perth – the Stirling Highway. We might better call it the Jack Davis Highway, to honour the great Aboriginal poet and activist, another kind of hero who surely better deserves our commendation.

In terms of encounters with the land, however, such a renaming appears to remain monological. Where nature is dominant over culture, as in Kakadu, we could hope that a dialogical naming practice might engage with the land. However, where culture is highly dominant over nature, as in the city, it might be reasonable to begin with naming practices that draw more upon human cultural engagements and elements. Even so, these urbanized namings could be much more adventurous, witty and less colonial than the 'neutral marker' suburban place names we often have now, and they could connect with real or imaginary narratives of events that have occurred there or with people worth remembering. For example, it might be worth renaming Germaine Greer's birthplace (Mentone) after her.

Of course, it can be objected that names that honour the colonial office are now a genuine part of our history, a story that might be lost if they were eliminated. They are a part of history, it's true, but not everyone's history, and not for all time. We don't have to passively remain in the mindset that created them. We can take charge of how our land is named and make it relevant to today. I do not suggest that colonial names should be just thrown away and forgotten; they may have something important to tell us about where we have come from. But that is not necessarily who we are now, and I believe we need alternatives that do not force us to honour slayers of Aboriginal people and others responsible for similar atrocities. If we are a dynamic and evolving society, we should be able to democratize, de-bureaucratize and put our processes of naming places up for community cultural engagement and debate. This will be a long-term process, but one that we should get started on now. To allow for cultural difference, I think we should aim for the formal possibility of multiple naming, and also for names that are worked through communities as part of a democratic cultural process in which a broad range of groups can participate.[13]

It might surprise some individuals to hear that, in my view, we should also reconsider the many Aboriginal place names that appear on our maps. These names were primarily imposed upon places by non-indigenous namers, and are treated by the dominant non-indigenous population in logical positivist style as neutral markers. What is most important, now, is that non-indigenous communities should make an effort to understand their historical and narrative significance. Where these names correctly acknowledge Aboriginal presence, commemorate tribal land, or have other appropriate meanings, then non-indigenous communities should learn about them, in cooperation with the relevant indigenous communities. However, many of these names reflect the larger cultural practice in which features of Aboriginal culture are appropriated by settler culture in order to create the air of a distinctive national identity, a colonizing practice that often leads to inappropriate or paradoxical use of Aboriginal words and symbols. To overseas visitors, these names are part of what makes Australia interesting; they mark out our unique 'Australianness'. But where we use them shamelessly for this purpose, without understanding or respect, we should think of them as stolen names. We must develop a critique of this practice if Aboriginal place names are to become part of our precious cultural heritage.

In summary, recovering a popular naming practice that decolonizes the mind and generates meaningful dialogical names is part of recovering a meaningful relationship with the land. We need to construct new naming practices to replace, or at least provide alternatives for, the problem categories of power names, feral names and monological names, and we need to rethink our relationship to stolen names. In this decolonizing project, indigenous patterns, models and practices have much to teach non-indigenous culture; but we need an active, dynamic practice of naming and narrating that can also incorporate elements from non-indigenous Australian cultures – not a slavish imitation or colonizing assimilation, or incorporation, of indigenous naming and narrative.[14] Such a dynamic outcome could only be possible if we make the project of renaming the land one of cultural cooperation and convergence between indigenous and non-indigenous communities.

NOTES

1   This is also for the more general reasons that appear in Hegel's master-slave dialectic.
2   As a centric position, Eurocentric anthropocentrism equates the absence of the centre, the lack of a (rational) European human presence, with emptiness or, in some versions, with wilderness. This wilderness concept plays a key role in colonization because it justifies a system of appropriation based upon the way the lands of others are represented as pure nature, as *terra nullius*, containing neither any European-style labour that needed to be recognized, nor any other trace of culture. This is especially clear with respect to the Lockean model of land acquisition, which requires that the appropriated land was originally wilderness, bearing no trace of human labour. This model provides the mythological basis for the recipe for property formation, which founded contemporary capitalism. In the context of the 'New World', it also provided, as Deloria (1970) notes, the basis for erasing the ownership of indigenous people and for appropriating their lands. Locke's recipe for property formation allows the colonist to appropriate that into which he has mixed his own labour, as part of the self. He thus transfers his ownership of self to what is laboured on, on condition that it falls under the category of 'nature' and is not under any prior ownership – that is, as *terra nullius*. But since the colonist was not able, or not disposed, to recognize either the prior ownership of indigenous Others or their different expression of labour and agency, the formula aided the large-scale appropriation of indigenous lands by those individuals who imposed highly transforming and destructive European-style agricultural labour.

Applying the formula retrospectively led to a regress, a failure to recognize as conferring ownership indigenous hunting and gathering activities that did not transform the land significantly in ways European colonists recognized as sufficient 'labour' to qualify for past or present property ownership. (Even until very recently, as Deloria notes, it was held that the failure of indigenous people to make properly individualistic and maximally transformative use of their land was a sufficient reason for taking it away from them.) To the extent that indigenous people were seen as 'nature', 'nomads' or 'parasites on nature', who were incapable of effective ecological agency or the kind of agricultural labour that was considered, according to the European model, to be the true mark of humanity, the Lockean formula helped to erase their claim to prior ownership. In the context of the hyperbolized autonomy and hegemonic conceptions of agency associated with Western individualism and colonial property formation, the Lockean formula (including the assumption that the land is wilderness) is virtually an invitation to appropriate what others have made their own, often in much deeper and less exploitative ways than the Western method of converting land to resource and market-based uses.

3   This might be appropriate for some areas; but for others, non-humans might be the beneficiaries, together with some specified group of indigenous people. See Robinson and Robinson (1994) and Preston and Stannard (1994). It can be argued that a future-oriented performative is already what the designation 'wilderness' represents in practical terms, since many areas that the environment movement wants to protect are well known to no longer be 'untouched' nature. The focus on purity works at least as strongly against conservation as for it. See Callicott and Nelson (1998) and Gomez-Pompa and Kraus (1992).

4   For a discussion of 'the great Australian silence', see Stanner (1979).

5   Even poets who extolled the land, such as Adam Lindsay Gordon, wrote of its 'bright, silent birds'.

6   It also sets up a positive feedback mechanism in which conceptual impoverishment feeds ecological impoverishment, as Weston (1996) argues.

7   'No traditional Aboriginal myth was told without reference to the land, or to a specific stretch of country where the incidents it narrates were believed to have taken place. No myth is free-floating, without some local identification. Without their anchorages, they could be regarded as being simply "just so stories" (Berndt and Berndt, 1989, p5) The land was a communicating and participating land, and 'through the attention [Aboriginal people] give to their country, communication becomes two way' (Rose, 1996, p13). Another component of Aboriginal world views, according to anthropologist Deborah Bird Rose, is the idea that 'nothing is nothing...there is no alien world of mere things, or of things without meaning....For many Aboriginal people, everything in the world is alive: animals, trees, rain, sun moon, some rocks and hills, and people are all conscious' (Rose, 1996).

8   In those days, many non-indigenous people supposed that there was just one Aboriginal language and tribe.

9   Of course, power names do tend to become conventionalized, empty and irrelevant very quickly, which is another good reason for avoiding them. An exception might be highly rationalized and systematized power names, such as those of the Canberra suburbs commemorating prime ministers.

10   The bushwalking community has long contested these colonial power names, and has worked at its own renaming – on their maps names such as Mount Cloudmaker replace names such as Mount Renwick, which commemorates the survey office.

11   There is no single equivalent Aboriginal name for the area we know as Mount Brockman.

12   Some Aboriginal people of Arnhem land use the terms *binitj* for Aboriginal people and *balanda* for non-indigenous people.

13   Local councils, schools and community groups might set up literary contests to generate names and narratives, for example.

14   For a wonderful example of such cultural convergence in the field of narrative, see Craig San Roque (2000) 'The Sugarman Cycle', *PAN*, vol 1, pp42–64.

REFERENCES

Abram, D (1996) *The Spell of the Sensuous.* Pantheon, New York

Benhabib, S (1992) *Situating the Self.* Routledge, New York

Berndt, R M and Berndt, C H (1989) *The Speaking Land: Myth and Story in Aboriginal Australia.* Penguin Books, Melbourne

Beston, H (1928) *The Outermost House.* Ballantine, New York

Bolton, G (1981) *Spoils and Spoilers.* Allen and Unwin, Sydney

Callicott, J B and Nelson, M (eds) (1998) *The Great New Wilderness Debate.* University of Georgia Press, Athens, Georgia

Commonwealth of Australia (1996) *The Australian State of the Environment Report.* Canberra

Cronon, W (1983) *Changes in the Land: Indians, Colonists and the Ecology of New England.* Hill and Wang, New York

Cronon, W (1995) 'The Trouble with Wilderness: or, Getting Back to the Wrong Nature' in W Cronon (ed) *Uncommon Ground: Toward Reinventing Nature.* W W Norton and Co, New York, pp69–90

Crosby, A W (1986) *Ecological Imperialism: the Biological Expansion of Europe.* Cambridge University Press, Cambridge

de Beauvoir, S (1965) *The Second Sex.* Foursquare Books, London/New York

Deloria, V (1970) *We Talk, You Listen.* MacMillan, New York

Frye, M (1983) *The Politics of Reality.* Crossing Press, New York

Gare, A (1998) 'MacIntyre, Narratives and Environmental Ethics', *Environmental Ethics,* vol 20, no 2, pp3–18

Gomez-Pompa, A and Kraus, A (1992) 'Taming the Wilderness Myth', *BioScience,* vol 42, pp271–279

Harrison, R P (1992) *Forest: the Shadows of Civilization.* University of Chicago Press, Chicago

Hartsock, N (1990) 'Foucault on power: a theory for women?' in L Nicholson (ed) *Feminism/Postmodernism.* Routledge, New York

Langton, M (1993) *Well, I Heard It on the Radio and I Saw It on the Television.* Australian Film Commission, Sydney

Langton, M (1996) 'What Do We Mean by Wilderness? Wilderness and *terra nullius* in Australian Art', *The Sydney Papers,* vol 8 (1), pp10–31, The Sydney Institute

Lines, W J (1991) *Taming the Great South Land.* University of Georgia Press, Athens, Georgia

Mackey, B (1999) 'Regional Forest Agreements: Business as Usual in the Southern Region?' *National Parks Association Journal,* vol 43 (6), pp10–12

Marshall, A J (ed) (1966) *The Great Extermination.* Heinemann, Melbourne

Mazama, A (1994) 'The Relevance of Ngugi Wa Thiong'o for the African Quest', *The Western Journal of Black Studies,* vol 18 (4), pp211–218

Memmi, A (1965) *The Colonizer and the Colonized.* Orion Press, New York

Nawakadj Nganjmirra (1997) 'Kunjinkwu Spirit' in N McLeod (ed) *Gundjiehmi: Creation Stories from Western Arnhem Land.* Miegungah Press at Melbourne University Press, Melbourne, p172

Neidjie, B (1985) *Kakadu Man.* Mybrood, Canberra

Niedjie, B (1989) *Story About Feeling.* Magabala Books, Wyndham

Parry, B (1995) 'Problems in Current Theories of Colonial Discourse' in B Ashcroft et al (eds) *The Post-Colonial Studies Reader.* Routledge, London, pp36–44

Passmore, J (1974) *Man's Responsibility for Nature*. Duckworth, London

Plumwood, V (1990) 'Plato and the Bush: Philosophy and the Environment in Australia', *Meanjin*, vol 3, pp524–537

Plumwood, V (1993) *Feminism and the Mastery of Nature*. Routledge, London

Plumwood, V (1996) 'Anthrocentrism and Androcentrism: Parallels and Politics', *Ethics and the Environment*, vol 1 (2), University of Georgia, Fall, pp119–152

Plumwood, V (1998)'Wilderness Skepticism and Wilderness Dualism' in J B Callicott and M. Nelson (eds) *The Great New Wilderness Debate*. University of Georgia Press, Athens, Georgia, pp652–690

Plumwood, V (2000) 'Deep Ecology, Deep Pockets, and Deep Problems: a Feminist Eco-Socialist Analysis' in A Light, E Katz and D Rothenburg (eds) *Beneath the Surface: Critical Essays on Deep Ecology*. MIT Press, Cambridge MA, pp59–84

Plumwood, V (2002a) 'Feminism and the Logic of Alterity' in M Hass and R Joffe Falmagne (eds) *Representing Reason: Feminist Theory and Formal Logic*. Rowman and Littlefield, Totowa, New Jersey

Plumwood, V (2002b) *Environmental Culture: the Ecological Crisis of Reason*. Routledge, London

Polanyi, K (1974) *The Great Transformation*. Beacon Press, Boston

Preston, B J and Stannard, C (1994) 'The Re-creation of Wilderness: the Case for an Australian Ecological Reserve System' in W Barton (ed) *Wilderness – the Future*. Envirobook, Sydney, pp127–147

Read, P (2000) *Belonging*. Cambridge University Press, Melbourne

Robinson, P and Robinson, M (1994) 'Wilderness "After" Native Title' in W Barton (ed) *Wilderness – the Future*. Envirobook, Sydney, pp68–77

Rose, D B (1992) *Dingo Makes Us Human*. Cambridge University Press, Melbourne

Rose, D B (1996) *Nourishing Terrains*. Australian Heritage Commission, Canberra

Said, E (1978) *Orientalism*. Pantheon, New York

San Roque, C (2000) 'The Sugarman Cycle', *PAN*, vol 1, pp42–64

Sinclair, P (2001) *The Murray: the River and Its People*. Melbourne University Press, Melbourne

Soper, K (1994) *What is Nature?* Routledge, London

Spence, M D (1999) *Dispossessing the Wilderness: Indian Removal and the Making of the National Park*. Oxford, New York

Stanner, W E H (1979) *White Man Got No Dreaming*. Australian National University Press, Canberra

Stepan, N L (1993) 'Race and Gender: the Role of Analogy in Science' in S Harding (ed) *The Racial Economy of Science*. Indianapolis, Indiana University Press pp359–376

Thoreau, H D (1862) 'Walking' in *Walden and Other Writings* (edited by B Atkinson, 1992). Modern Library, New York

Turner, F (1986) *Beyond Geography*. Rutgers University Press, New Brunswick, New Jersey

Walls, L D (1995) *Seeing New Worlds*. University of Wisconsin Press, Wisconsin

Warren, K J (1990) 'The Power and Promise of Ecological Feminism', *Environmental Ethics*, vol 12, no 2, pp121–146

Weston, A (1996) 'Self-validating Reduction: Toward a Theory of Environmental Devaluation', *Environmental Ethics*, vol 18, pp115–132

Whitehouse, J F (1994) 'Legislative Protection for Wilderness in Australia' in W Barton (ed) *Wilderness – the Future*. Envirobooks, Sydney

Chapter 4

The 'wild', the market and the native: Indigenous people face new forms of global colonization

Marcia Langton

INTRODUCTION

Indigenous and traditional peoples worldwide are facing a crisis, one that supersedes that inflicted on indigenous peoples during the imperial age. Just as, during the last 500 years, imperialism caused the encapsulation of indigenous societies within the new settler nation states, their subjection to colonial political formations and their loss of territory and jurisdiction, so have the globalizing market and the post-industrial/technological complex brought about another phase of profound change for these societies. The further encapsulation of indigenous societies by the global complex, to which nation state formations are themselves subservient, has resulted in continuing loss of territory as a result of large-scale developments, urban post-colonial population expansion, and ongoing colonization of the natural world by the market. This last point is illustrated, for example, by the bioprospecting and patenting of life forms and biota by new genetic and chemical engineering industries. Coincidental with the new colonization is the crisis of biodiversity loss – a critical issue for indigenous peoples, particularly hunting and gathering societies. The massive loss of biota through extinction events, loss of territory and species habitats, and environmental degradation, together with conservationist limitation of indigenous harvesting, constitute significant threats to indigenous ways of life.

While Aboriginal rights to wildlife are restricted to 'non-commercial' use, the pressures increase for indigenous peoples to forge unique economic niches in order to maintain their ways of life. Of particular importance is the vexed issue of Aboriginal entitlements to commercial benefits from the utilization of wildlife arising both from developing standards of traditional resource rights and from customary proprietary interests.

IMPACT OF THE GLOBAL MARKET ON THE INDIGENOUS WORLD

The new threats to indigenous life-ways in the era of the globalizing market have been brought about by the increasing commodification of features of the natural world, putting at risk the very survival of ancient societies who are directly dependent upon the state of their natural environment. In June 1978, Inupiat leader Eben Hobson, then founding chairman of the Inuit Circumpolar Conference and spokesperson for the Alaska Whaling Commission, appealed to the London Press Corps for understanding and support in the legal recognition of Inuit rights: 'We Inuit are hunters. There aren't many subsistence hunting societies left in the world, but our Inuit Circumpolar community is one of them.'[1]

The dilemma for indigenous peoples is also a political one, especially for those groups encapsulated by settler states that oppose developing standards of rights for indigenous peoples. As well as the opposition by some governments seeking to appropriate indigenous lands and resources, conservationist organizations resist compromise on land-use issues because they believe that global biodiversity preservation goals take precedence over the needs of local people. In some instances, because of conflict between indigenous and conservationist groups, common biodiversity conservation goals, in locations where development projects have threatened environmental values, have not been achieved. In their feasibility study in the Torres Strait Islands region, Dews et al (1997, p48) explain that while indigenous concerns are often pressing and immediate, 'biodiversity defenders look to the distant future'. Of critical relevance here is their conclusion: ' in the final analysis, property rights and especially the management of common property resources, may become the focal issue for both camps'.

A number of cases of the suppression, or attempted suppression, of indigenous economic activity provide evidence of environmental racism. Conservationist lobbying at the International Whaling Commission to prevent Inuit hunting of the bowhead, narwhal and beluga whales is one infamous case among many.[2] By targeting small-scale indigenous groups in their campaigns against national and multinational environmental violations, conservation organizations privilege global commercialization of the natural world over ancient economic systems in their increasing demands for the suppression of traditional forms of wildlife exploitation. Thus, subsequent to the deteriorating environmental circumstances of small-scale hunting and gathering peoples is the further limitation of their territorial base and traditional economic means by environmental racism. The high dependence of marginalized native peoples upon wildlife resources for basic subsistence needs is typically ignored by conservationists whose goal of biodiversity conservation is not based upon local knowledge of particular small-scale societies that are co-located with species targeted by conservation campaigns. Little regard is paid to the actual impacts of local populations; instead, highly emotive claims are made about the presumed threats without substantial or rigorous scientific research to support such claims. With their minimal and often inaccurate understanding of indigenous societies, environmental scientists, planners and managers have the potential to cause great harm to native peoples. Capacity-building and developing enterprise and investment strategies may well contribute to conservation goals more directly than any purely conservationist strategy aimed at national goals. Indigenous societies face increasing hardships as governments, conservation campaigners and the private sector further marginalize them. Furze, de Lacey and Birckhead (1996, p3), referring to a range of international case studies, make the point that:

> *...many protected areas are at risk because of the hardship they place on local communities. The protection of biodiversity may therefore be seen to be one of the most pressing issues in development.*
>
> *With the recognition that conservation often fails to achieve its goals when local people are unsupportive, or are not meaningful partners, the question of local participation is now firmly on international conservation and sustainable development agendas. As a result, many people involved in the conservation, development and academic communities, as well as local people themselves, are involved in the search for sustainable futures.*

Posey and Dutfield (Posey, 1996; Posey and Dutfield, 1996) have offered comprehensive accounts of the nature of the rights of local traditional peoples in resources and cultural and intellectual property, and the protection of such rights in the context of sustainable traditional use of resources. They observe that environmental concerns increasingly focus upon the roles of indigenous peoples and local communities in enhancing and maintaining biological diversity. Detailing the provisions of each of the relevant conventions, statements and case laws that impact upon traditional peoples, they provide a wealth of knowledge for local groups wanting to pursue their rights. They must do so in the context, however, of an absence of effective measures. For instance, as Posey observes, 'The Convention on Biological Diversity (CBD) does not provide specific mechanisms to protect the rights of indigenous peoples and local communities to their genetic materials, knowledge and technologies' (1996, pxiii). As he points out, however, the CBD does recognize that 'knowledge, innovations and practices of indigenous and local communities embodying traditional lifestyles' are central to successful *in situ* conservation. Moreover, the fundamental importance of benefit-sharing and compensation for the peoples and communities providing traditional knowledge, innovations and practices is also acknowledged. Posey's approach is to present the concept of Traditional Resource Rights 'to guide the development of *sui generis* systems, premised on human rights principles' (1996a, pxiii). The concept of Traditional Resource Rights, he explains, is a process and a framework to develop multiple, locally appropriate systems and 'solutions' that reflect the diversity of contexts where *sui generis* systems are required.

The coincidence at the end of the second millennium of the remnant indigenous territories and high biodiversity values, the globalizing market, and the growing recognition of resource rights for traditional peoples requires special attention as a problem of biodiversity maintenance. This is evident in Australia where indigenous societies have lost 85 per cent of their traditional land base since British colonizers arrived in 1788. The remaining 15 per cent of the Australian landmass under various forms of title owned by Aboriginal groups is an exemplary locus of this predicament.

The impact of globalization upon the indigenous world brings with its threats and benefits a profound contradiction: the global market itself poses the end of ancient ways of human life. Yet, at the same time, it offers opportunities for accommodating these life-ways to the new market forces with benefits for all of human society. The central benefit is the maintenance of biodiversity typical of the last 10,000 years of human history and sustained throughout the imperial and industrial ages by local indigenous peoples. As the imperative for further commercialization of the natural world, by, for instance, wildlife harvesting, intrudes into the indigenous domains, there are opportunities for indigenous societies to maintain their fundamental ideas about, and relationships with, the natural world while exploring what may be offered by the application of ecologically sustainable development practices in their territories.[3]

THE ROLE OF INDIGENOUS PEOPLE IN BIODIVERSITY CONSERVATION

In spite of the unsubstantiated claims of some conservationist organizations, there is increasing recognition of the role of indigenous cultures in supporting biodiversity. For example, Nietschmann made this point eloquently (Nietschmann, 1992, p7):

> *The vast majority of the world's biological diversity is not in gene banks, zoos, national parks, or protected areas. Most biological diversity is in landscapes and seascapes inhabited and used by local peoples, mostly indigenous, whose great collective accomplishment is to have conserved the great variety of remaining life forms, using culture, the most powerful and valuable human resource, to do so.*

The critical role of indigenous peoples in biodiversity conservation is no less the case in Australia. Indigenous involvement is essential to the Australian project of land, water and biodiversity conservation for a number of reasons. Land and water subject to indigenous ownership and governance constitute a significant proportion of the Australian continent. Those lands and waters that constitute most of that area are not subject to high-density settlement, degradation of natural values by industries such as agriculture, forestry, fishing, pastoralism and tourism, and are high-integrity areas, both in terms of natural and cultural values. Much of the land and water within the indigenous domain remain subject to indigenous management systems that have persisted since the late Pleistocene and include, for instance, the wet tropics and the wet–dry tropics, parts of which are listed as world heritage areas and other International Union for the Conservation of Nature and Natural Resources (IUCN) categories.[4] In these regions, there have been few, or no, extinctions of native fauna and flora. This contrasts starkly with the southern settled areas of Australia where the majority of extinctions have occurred, placing the nation amongst the worst offenders, despite the small population and relatively short record of colonial settlement.

Within the indigenous domain, there are indigenous systems of governance, both customary and Australian, with significance for the conservation challenges of this area. These are discussed further below. One of the important aspects of indigenous governance is the existence of vast indigenous knowledge systems that are based upon the very long periods of living on the continent (currently understood to exceed 40,000 years), as well as the intimacy of indigenous social life with the physical world, the biota and its systems. The loss of these knowledge systems would constitute an irretrievable loss to human cultural diversity and, therefore, to our capacity to understand human relationships with the world, upon which our search for sustainable futures depends.

In Australia, the extant territory within the contemporary indigenous domain – especially the large land and marine estates remote from non-urban areas – is the result of a colonial history that, especially over the first 150 years following invasion, favoured occupation of coastal regions in the south and east of the continent. Non-Aboriginal land use in Australia proceeded from earliest colonial times by radically altering extant environments, through extensive land-clearing, water capture and other means. British settlers perceived their new environments as harsh and inhospitable and they actively supplanted these 'wild', uncultivated lands with familiar European land-use and management systems, which they believed they could control, regardless of whether or not these imported management regimes were suitable to local conditions. As a result, settlers engaged in wide-scale clearing of vegetation, suppression of fire, development of irrigation systems, widespread use of pesticides, and the attempted eradication of native animals such as dingoes.

Spinks (1999, pers comm) reports that 76 per cent of Australia's 20,000 or so species of plants are now extinct, while some 5000 others are considered to be rare or threatened (see, also, Spinks, 1999b). Significant proportions of native mammals, reptiles, amphibians, birds, freshwater fish and marsupials are also threatened or extinct. Land and water resources have been degraded: agricultural land is plagued by salination, caused by clearing and irrigation, while fish and other aquatic life are at risk in inland waterways from the effects of toxic algae, exotic competitors, inbreeding, and through the removal or degradation of some of their natural habitats. Introduced agricultural regimes were ill suited to the arid rangelands and deserts that cover most of Australia's landmass. Therefore, with some exceptions, the indigenous domain has tended to be concentrated in desert and wetland environments of little apparent use to the colonizers.

The biological integrity of the indigenous domain has suffered considerably less than that of the lands which have been radically altered to suit the imported management systems and understandings of the settler society. Of course, this pattern of remnant indigenous territory being located on the remote periphery of settler states is a worldwide phenomenon, and similar patterns of environmental degradation in the non-indigenous domains are evident in countries other than Australia. The indigenous knowledge systems that have shaped and governed the Australian continent and its natural systems survive in many areas. It is in those areas of Australia – where high levels of biological integrity coincide with indigenous customary governance and knowledge systems – that opportunities exist to maintain that biological integrity through a strategic process which includes indigenous management systems.

With the exception of relatively small-scale mining operations and low-capital settler pastoralism, which was highly dependent upon largely unpaid indigenous labour, it was not until the expansion of large-scale resource extraction from the 1950s that this indigenous domain came under significant threat. This expansion into indigenous lands by large-scale extractive industries, together with substantial technological changes within the pastoral industry, has coincided with an upsurge in the assertiveness of re-politicized indigenous peoples and moves away from protectionism and assimilation that previously characterized Australian colonialism. One of the consequences of this history has been the development, in more recent times, of relationships between indigenous and non-indigenous people in land, sea and resource management, based upon an acknowledgement of the special knowledge and practices that indigenous people bring to the task.

Few people seriously doubt any longer that Aboriginal people *manage* their lands and seas. Aboriginal management of their land and sea estates is understood as being based upon their detailed knowledge of all of its features. Much of that knowledge is embedded in religious beliefs and practices, and is inextricably linked to the system of land tenure. The question of whether the management is explicit and principled, or merely a consequence of practices recognized *post facto*, is, however, still sometimes raised.

James Kohen, an archaeologist, in his book *Aboriginal Environmental Impacts* (1995), makes a distinction between management and exploitation: 'Essentially, management involves the utilization of the landscape without any long-term deterioration, whereas exploitation involves long-term degradation to the detriment of the environment.' He identifies two main interrelated factors that determine whether land-use practices can be defined as management or exploitation. The first is the nature of the land-use strategy and the second is the human population density (Kohen, 1995, pp125–127). Both of these factors may seem intuitively obvious; but they need to be justified because of the implications for our understanding of traditional and contemporary Aboriginal societies and the nature of their impact upon the environment. Once land management practices were adopted by early human populations on the Australian continent to increase the productivity of the landscape, there were pressures on their communities to maintain the environments they had created in order to feed the growing population.

The environment that confronted Europeans in 1788 was certainly one that was managed. The biogeographical history of Australia determined the range of plant and animal species that would occur within the region; but, to some extent, the balance and distribution of species had been altered, not only by climate change, but also by Aboriginal impacts. Most significant of these was the human use of fire as a management tool in a fire-prone continent, resulting in seasonal mosaic patterns across landscapes that prevented destructive, hot wildfires.

Such Holocene-period land management practices continue in the indigenous domain today, and Aboriginal leaders advocate that environmental protection and wildlife management depend upon the protection of indigenous cultural values and lifestyles because of the co-dependency of the natural world and indigenous use and management. Aboriginal strategies include local and regional multiple-use management planning for sustainable terrestrial, marine and coastal resources. To achieve conservation objectives, traditional practices alone are no match for the rapid population and development of indigenous territories by the settler state. Indigenous people and their local and regional bodies require collaborative relationships with other individuals and organizations in order to meet particular, identified challenges. Success in such collaboration depends upon highly qualified and experienced collaborators with a high level of commitment to the integrity of indigenous laws.

As an example, we can look at strategies needed to control outbreaks of invasive weeds such as *Mimosa pigra* and *Salvinia spp*. Because mechanical and chemical controls are limited in their capacity to prevent such outbreaks, regional multiple land-use planning and inter-agency coordination and sharing of resources are required for long-term control. Indigenous people have developed regional plans, particularly at the catchment level, in coastal northern Australia. Examples of such exercises include the projects of the Dhimurru Land Management Corporation in north-east Arnhem Land, the Arafura Catchment Management Plan in central Arnhem Land, and the Alice–Mitchell Basin management plan developed by the Kowanyama community in western Cape York Peninsula.

It is also in these biodiversity-rich areas of Australia that Australian governments are permitting commercial harvesting of wildlife. A number of large and small corporations are presently carrying out bioprospecting activities for commercial gain on indigenous land in Australia. While some of these activities are subject to satisfactory agreements, most are not. Commercial utilization of wildlife is also gaining increasing support from governments that have established licence regimes for commercial harvesters. Except where indigenous people have established their own wildlife harvesting enterprises or negotiated agreements with bioprospecting companies, they receive no benefits from the industry. Their involvement in any capacity is minimal, and the notion that indigenous groups may have customary proprietary interests in these wild resources has not been considered. Such appropriation of natural resources from the indigenous domain is a new form of dispossession.

ARGUMENTS ABOUT SUSTAINABILITY AND INDIGENOUS USE OF WILDLIFE

Indigenous people are subjected to highly political demands from an uninformed public to cease customary hunting and gathering based upon conjecture regarding indigenous contributions to population declines of some species, such as dugong and turtle. That such declines are more likely to be attributed to large-scale commercial, agricultural and industrial activities (particularly pollution of seabed grasses by run-off of agricultural chemicals) than to small-scale customary use has only recently become the subject of research in plant and animal population studies. Emotive public campaigns (notably by extremist animal-rights lobby groups) threaten legislative and structural reforms that are necessary to develop viable enterprises; such campaigns can only be countered by sound scientific evidence regarding the sustainable use of any particular species.

Scientific and government responses to the use of wildlife by indigenous peoples, and popular concern over its possible impact upon the conservation of wildlife, have led to demands for planning and regulation. Such regulation and planning severely limit Aboriginal hunting in Australia, particularly when indigenous hunting-and-gathering practices have been targeted as being the principle threat to endangered species. A specific objection that is often raised is that traditional hunters should not be permitted to use modern technology, such as vehicles and guns. However, such views can be best understood as settler-state cultural hangovers from a frontier society who almost achieved the extinction of Aboriginal peoples on the Australian continent. The primitivist conception of Aboriginal life as a remnant 'Stone Age' is a powerful cultural force in Australian life and is typically expressed in highly contradictory ways. For instance, on the one hand, there is the insistent demand that Aboriginal people should assimilate (or 'become like white people') according to the white supremacist premise that white settler ways of life are better. On the other hand, the use of vehicles or guns by Aboriginal people is highly unpopular in the electorate because of the clash with the primitivist ideals that Aboriginal people are required to fulfil. The result is that most governments in Australia have effectively banned traditional hunting and gathering.

Conservationist objections to Aboriginal life, when rationally analysed, are also cultural in the sense that the objections are often aesthetic in nature, inferring a contempt for 'distasteful' aspects of Aboriginal economic life, particularly hunting practices. The contribution of such practices to conservation aims is consequently ignored. A good example of this cultural blindness is a report prepared for the Australian Bureau of Resource Sciences by Bomford and Caughley (1996). The stated aim of this work was to assess 'the appropriateness of planned wildlife use in terms of benefits to Aboriginal peoples and Torres Strait Islanders, and the sustainability of wildlife use, and of the land, waters and other components of the natural systems they are part of'. The authors propose various forms of social engineering in order to achieve sustainable levels of wildlife resource use, as defined by environmental managers. The euphemistic use of language to discuss highly contentious issues such as Aboriginal use of firearms is exemplified in the following recommendation:

> *...a process to address community concerns over the use of modern technology in traditional hunting practices and a recognition and integration of indigenous and non-indigenous cultural perceptions and aspirations concerning the sustainability of indigenous wildlife use* (Bomford and Caughley, 1996, p1).

The authors further speculate about 'possible overexploitation of resources through subsistence hunting due to the loss of traditional regulatory mechanisms caused by societal changes and the interface of this with cash-based economies'. Contrary to all available rigorous research in the field, these environmental 'experts' recommend for indigenous people 'an analysis of the need for access to a cash income to underwrite an indigenous subsistence lifestyle'. Yet, despite offering uninformed speculation about Aboriginal use of guns and the impact of this on biota, the authors admit that there is a need for 'more data on the ecological factors that affect the sustainability of wildlife harvests. Data on many wildlife species is lacking and is required to fit complex harvest models' (Bomford and Caughley, 1996, p2) The authors also admit that there is a need for:

> *...case studies where wildlife use is an important component of the culture of Australian indigenous peoples. This includes the need for data on harvesting and its relevance to the communities concerned, as well as the legal constraints in the management of the resource* (Bomford and Caughley 1996, p2).

The report advocates that government agencies should respond to requests by indigenous peoples for increased funding to manage their natural resources by considering, as part their decision-making processes, 'a complex array of scientific, economic and social issues'. The recommendations of this report fail to acknowledge traditional resource rights and ignore indigenous rights in favour of conservation objectives for wildlife protection without regard to indigenous cultural relationships with, and dependence upon, 'wildlife'. In studies such as this, indigenous people are marginalized to the extent that their own aspirations for their futures are diminished. It is assumed in this report, and many others like it, that settler society aspirations should take precedence over all other life-ways. Thus, the authors believe it is sufficient to emphasize the need for protocols for consultations with indigenous people as if they were mere 'stakeholders' like other settler-state stakeholders in the wildlife-use planning processes.

At the same time, commercial exploitation of wild plant and animal products is widespread in Australia in industries such as commercial fishing; pharmaceutical bioprospecting; gardening and horticultural enterprises; edible plant and animal marketing; skin, hide and other animal product marketing; the pet food industry; the timber and sylviculture industries; and others. The indigenous participation in these industries is minuscule. Moreover, government-sponsored culling of native species such as kangaroos, emus and koalas goes without comment. Such inconsistencies between the actual situation and public perceptions raise the problem of environmental racism. This chapter draws attention to this issue because of its contribution to perpetuating social and economic inequity and injustice for indigenous peoples.

In contrast to the speculation of such quasi-scientific reports as that commissioned by the Bureau of Resource Sciences, the policy and research programmes in which indigenous people have played a substantial role have produced quite different outcomes – outcomes that present the possibility of a viable future for indigenous life ways. For example, in response to the 1992 Convention on Biological Diversity (CBD), ratified by Australia in 1993, the Australian government consulted Aboriginal representatives in producing the *National Strategy for the Conservation of Australia's Biological Diversity* (Department of Environment, Sport and Territories (DEST), 1996). This recommends a framework in which governments, industry, community groups and individual land-owners can work cooperatively to 'bridge the gap between current efforts and the effective identification, conservation and management of Australia's biological diversity' (DEST, 1996, p3). The report acknowledges that Australian indigenous cultures 'maintain a lively interest in, practical knowledge of, and concern for the well-being of the land and natural systems' (DEST, 1996, p14). Moreover, the strategy recognizes that 'The maintenance of biological diversity…is a cornerstone of the well-being, identity, cultural heritage and economy of Aboriginal and Torres Strait Islander communities' (DEST, 1996, p14).

Objective 1.8 of the *National Strategy* is the recognition and maintenance of 'the contribution of the ethnobiological knowledge of Australia's indigenous peoples to the conservation of Australia's biological diversity' (DEST, 1996, p14). The strategy also acknowledges that indigenous law and cosmology establish intimate associations between land, people and other species and ensure the transmission of this knowledge across the generations (DEST, 1996, pp14–15). While the strategy notes that traditional Aboriginal and Torres Strait Islander management practices have already proved significant for the maintenance of biodiversity and should be incorporated within mainstream management programmes where appropriate, it also cautions that access to this specialist knowledge is not guaranteed:

> *Although Aboriginal and Torres Strait Islander peoples may be willing to share some of their cultural knowledge, aspects of that knowledge may be privileged and may not be available to the public domain* (DEST, 1996, p14).

The strategy recommends that governments provide resources for the conservation of traditional biological knowledge through cooperative ethnobiological programmes. It further proposes that because Aboriginal and Torres Strait Islander peoples have access to accurate information about biological diversity, they should be involved in research programmes relevant to the biological diversity and management of the lands and waters in which they have an interest. However, all collaborative agreements, the report insists, must recognize existing intellectual property rights of the indigenous people and establish royalty payments in line with relevant international standards. The use of biological knowledge in scientific, commercial and public domains should only proceed with the approval of the traditional owners of that knowledge, and the further 'collection' of such knowledge should deliver social and economic benefits to the knowledge owners. Recognizing that Aboriginal and Torres Strait Islander communities have an interest in the preservation of endangered and vulnerable species, the strategy also recommends cooperative strategies aimed at species recovery and habitat preservation, especially on Aboriginal lands. At the same time, it acknowledges that traditional harvesting of wildlife is important to both the cultural heritage and economy of indigenous communities; consequently, it supports the continuation of such harvesting practices. To safeguard the rights of indigenous communities, the strategy recommends that all arrangements aimed at fulfilling Australia's obligations under the CBD should also take into account the protocols developed by the United Nations Commission on Human Rights.

However, in practice, promising ethnobiological programmes have not been able to sustain government support. For example, the Northern Territory government has radically reduced funding to the very productive ethnobiology programme of the Northern Territory Parks and Wildlife Commission, in a region where the encyclopaedic wealth of the extant indigenous languages and knowledge systems is in danger of being lost as Aboriginal peoples are increasingly pressured to assimilate into the white settler society. Since the publication of the *National Strategy*, there has been no progress made towards achieving its recommendations that specifically concern Aboriginal and Torres Strait Islander peoples. The proposed new approaches to collaborative conservation programmes with indigenous peoples have been undermined by Australian governments that increasingly favour sectoral interests over the interests of indigenous communities, to the extent that the rights of indigenous people have been further reduced by statutory regulation.

RECONCEPTUALIZING INDIGENOUS RELATIONSHIPS
WITH THE NATURAL WORLD

The rubric of Western discourses of conservation can be misleading when examining indigenous capacity to respond to resource-use challenges. Basic terms in the conservation literature require some reconceptualizing in order to address the issues for Aboriginal engagement with sustainable management of wildlife, including the commercial use of wildlife. For instance, the term 'conservation' cannot be used in a presumed commonsense way without bringing within the ambit of the term some of the cultural differences often overlooked in the conservation literature. A typical example of the absence of the human dimensions when considering resource-use problems is the social and, often, statutory privilege granted to environmental impact assessment over social impact assessments. The pre-eminence given to scientifically adduced environmental questions over human issues is unfortunately unremarkable in the indigenous world, where human populations are regularly relocated and life-ways disrupted by major projects, such as dams, mines, roads, and pipelines.

Western conservationists are increasingly aware of the dilemmas for indigenous peoples; and, yet, considerations of equity and justice remain peripheral in the delivery of national and regional conservation programmes and resources. For example, the attention that conservation organizations devote within developing nations to the protection of non-human biota, including pets, is staggering when compared to the level of understanding displayed towards small hunter–gatherer populations. Conservation – as a general descriptor of human activities that are intended to mitigate against environmental degradation and biodiversity loss – refers primarily to human decision-making about the wise use of resources and the maintenance of the natural and cultural values of land, water and biota. How humans make decisions, however, depends upon their cultural, social, political and economic contexts. Aboriginal decision-making styles are of relevance to the development and design of conservation policy and planning; yet this is rarely acknowledged in the conservation literature. Furthermore, such literature ignores even more fundamental questions, such as how a resource is defined by different resource users and owners. A typical example of a cultural assumption in conservation thinking, especially in the science disciplines, is that a resource is defined simply as a physical commodity without regard to its human values and significance.

It was only during the 1980s and 1990s in Australia that the biota and human and technological resources have been studied, surveyed and understood as a result of regional studies by research bodies.[5] The ongoing accretion of scientific literature and data collection by a myriad of government agencies, statutory authorities, research institutions and universities has extended our knowledge of these issues. Researchers from a range of disciplines concerned with the natural world were attracted to the regions where high biodiversity values remain. However, the coincidence of these research areas with the indigenous domain was not a significant factor in the research design. As a result, much of the data was of little use to indigenous conservation managers, nor was it intended to help them. The value of the data for indigenous people has been further reduced by the apparent unwillingness of relevant bodies to return the information to indigenous land-owners in a form that can be accessed by people with low levels of Western education. It is not accidental that conservation policy and research that has been most useful to indigenous land-owners has usually been commissioned by indigenous representative bodies, such as local councils, land councils and regional resource-management groups. This reflects the differing priorities and economic, social and cultural frameworks employed by indigenous and non-indigenous interests.

As a subject for human decision-making, conservation cannot be deemed a discrete field because of the relevance of social, cultural, economic and political factors that must be taken into account by any group of decision-makers. In short, the problem is not one of conservation alone, or one of conservation versus development. There is a much more complex mix of conservation *and* subsistence and development issues. Furthermore, decision-making takes place in a range of situations. 'Traditional' institutions of indigenous societies – such as customary kin-based corporations – and indigenous jurisdictions provide just one context for decision-making. There are also indigenous organizations – such as community councils, socio-territorial associations, land councils, statutory bodies and other administrative and representative bodies – that constitute another significant context of decision-making. Such a diversity of institutional contexts demands an analytical approach that focuses on the overall goal of enhancing indigenous participation in conservation.

Other basic concepts in the conservation literature require special discussion to explain their use and relevance in explaining indigenous involvement in conservation activities. Key words in Aboriginal conservation and management include: 'traditional' or indigenous knowledge system, ' intellectual and cultural property', 'customary law', 'native title' and 'traditional resource rights'. These ought to be more widely understood among the community of scientists and planners involved in indigenous wildlife management projects.

The point is well made by Dews et al:

> ...*it is important to keep in mind that indigenous peoples and conservation organizations have overlapping interests, but their perceptions of what is at stake in managing resources for the future may be quite different* (Dews et al, 1997, p48).

These authors identify the conflicting values between indigenous peoples and conservationists with which environmental researchers must contend:

> *Conservation biologists commonly operate from ideological stances, which view nature as being significant apart from human involvement, while indigenous groups do not separate the two. Indigenous peoples must provision themselves*

> *from the natural environment, whereas conservation agencies are interested in protecting vanishing wilderness areas from human predation and excessive exploitation* (Dews et al, 1997, p48).

Issues of scale – especially in conservation planning and programme delivery for small-scale societies with traditional, as opposed to post-industrial, relations to land – assume a special significance. As Dews et al (1997) note, indigenous groups tend to operate from a local perspective, whereas conservation biologists and planners are concerned with large-scale, regional, if not hemispheric or global, processes, and believe they are acting on behalf of the planet as a whole. It is often the case, however, that the claims by conservationists to global outcomes are grossly overstated. Even the Convention on International Trade in Endangered Species of Wild Flora and Fauna (CITES) and the Convention on Biological Diversity (CBD), which are global agreements among countries, rely upon implementation within countries for their effectiveness. The CITES public material explains that effective conservation actions generally take place nationally and locally, and not at the global level. There are very few mechanisms to conserve species above the national level.

Most indigenous groups who are resident on their traditional territories are small scale; moreover, indigenous societies have been classified in the sociological literature as small scale on the basis not just of their population size, but of the types of institutions and decision-making styles that are typical in these societies. It is important, however, to emphasize that while traditional ecological knowledge is undeniably local, and specific to place and people (Rose, 1996, p32), it is nevertheless the case that some responses of indigenous groups to global pressures show that innovative, small-scale commercial valuation and monitoring of wildlife – which rely upon indigenous knowledge – can lead to sustainable management of species endemic to regions with even wider migration patterns. Such responses can deliver solutions that are far better than the 'solutions' advocated by remote and standardized national systems.

In Australian Aboriginal societies, there is an established body of indigenous laws that allocates rights and interests of particular people to features of the natural world. Aboriginal property relations are, as Nancy Williams (1998) has noted, 'a sacred endowment'. They derive from the sacred ancestral past that imbues the present, shaping and forming the world we inhabit with its distinctive features, and, notably, placing individual and group entities and polities in jural relationships (that is, bound by Aboriginal laws) with attendant rights and responsibilities, according to religious principles. These property relations are then expressed metaphorically in the Aboriginal discourse of possession and stewardship, symbolized in a variety of ways – particularly as iconic or totemic relationships with the species and features of the natural world.

Such ways of conceptualizing the world have been referred to throughout the indigenous literature that has emerged during the last few decades. For example, a conference held in Vancouver in February 2000 on Protecting

Knowledge: Traditional Resource Rights in the New Millennium issued 'The Spirit of the Conference Statement', which stated in part:

> *Indigenous Peoples' heritage is not a commodity, nor the property of the nation-state. The material and intellectual heritage of each Indigenous People is a sacred gift and a responsibility that must be honoured and held for the benefit of future generations.*[6]

Similarly, the foundation of Australian Aboriginal biogeography is this engagement with the non-human world through the lens of the *a priori* sacred landscape, peopled by spiritual Beings and imbued with the essence of both human and non-human beings. The appropriation of a landscape full of danger and serendipity by the geomantic reading of places imbued with spiritual Beings inscribes the landscape with the laws of ritual engagement with ancestors and spiritual Beings. This is a process overseen by a hierarchy of Elders, who have acquired the ritual knowledge and a system of property relations from those ancestors. The ancestral legacy is both the nature of our being and the nature of our relationship to places in the landscape.

Anthropologist Nancy Williams (1998, pp4–5) describes 'the relationship of Aboriginal Australians to their environment' as arising from 'the religious basis of their proprietary interests in land and the plants and animals that are a part of that environment'. From three decades of study with Yolngu people, she concludes that:

> *This relationship is expressed* inter alia *in terms that have been labelled 'traditional ecological knowledge'. Within that body of knowledge are embedded the principles and prescriptions for the management of the environment as well as their moral basis. Aboriginal people regard the environment as sentient and as communicating with them.*

Jean Christie (1996, p65) refers to the intellectual integrity of indigenous peoples:

> *For indigenous peoples, their lands and waters underpin who they are and are the foundation of their very survival as peoples. Over and over again, when reflecting on biodiversity or indigenous knowledge, indigenous people from all over the globe insist that living things cannot be separated from the land they grow on, and that peoples' knowledge and myriad uses of natural resources cannot be separated from their culture, and their survival as peoples on the land. This oneness – of land and the things that live in it, of people, their knowledge and their cultural connection with the land – is the only basis for meaningful consideration of biodiversity and indigenous knowledge about it. What is at stake is the intellectual integrity of peoples, not simply intellectual property.*

In his study of central Australian Aboriginal peoples' perceptions of land-management issues, Bruce Rose found that:

> *Aboriginal people see caring for country as an integral part of living on their land. Caring for country forms part of the relationship individuals have with each other and with the land. It is not seen as a separate activity which must be 'carried out'. From this perspective the most important issues are land-ownership and access to land so that Aboriginal people can care for their country* (Rose, 1995, pix).

When he questioned these people about 'European notions of conservation', Rose found that:

> *Aboriginal 'management' of the environment is understood through song and ceremony. It is seen to be more of an integrated process whereby knowledge of the natural world is gathered through personal experience and passed on through tradition and culture. Aboriginal management links people to their environment rather than giving them dominion over it. Aboriginal relationships to land are defined in terms of culture and site protection, land usage and harvesting of natural resources* (Rose, 1995, pxvii).

Extant indigenous cultures in Australia regard land not just as a physical resource, but as a social resource – as customary estates or landscapes shaped by *a priori* spiritual forces and imbued with spiritual power. Indigenous laws acknowledge that the world around us is constructed spiritually and socially. In Australian Aboriginal land-tenure systems, the basic nature of property as a thing is that it is transmissible across generations – it is a bequest or an endowment – and that the temporal dimension of endowment implies legitimacy derived from the authority of the past. The temporal dimension imbues an instance of property – an owned place – with a meaning beyond its fate of being already there: its meaning is social and institutionalized, and, above all, rule-governed or subject to law. The transmission of rights across generations involves applications of law relating to the nature of a bequest that is acceded to by other members of a society or group. The regulation of matters, such as who may inherit the property and under what conditions, constitutes law when it is acceded to as tradition and custom among members of a group.

Under Aboriginal law, permission to enter another person's territory and to use the resources of that place must be sought from the appropriate traditional owners. Upon granting their consent, these owners would perform particular rituals to ensure the spiritual safety of their guests during their visit to the estate. Entry to an Aboriginal estate, and access to its resources, are subject to Aboriginal laws. As Williams has further observed, in north-eastern Arnhem Land, Yolngu land-owning groups organize responsibility for managing their estates through a set of checks and balances expressed through links of kinship. A patrilineal group (a clan) holds title to an estate; but that group cannot unilaterally make decisions on important matters concerning the estate, whether the issue is deemed to be – in non-Aboriginal terms – religious or economic. Not only must individuals related through women to the land-owning group be consulted; they must concur in the decision. Within the title-holding group, authority determined by age prevails in decision-making related to the land of that group. The authority of elders, as knowledgeable persons capable of ensuring spiritual safety, is a fundamental feature of indigenous life. Such elders are not merely senior in age, although that is often the case. Such persons, by virtue of their knowledge and, typically, ritual status, hold jural positions based upon a range of personal, organizational and structural factors. These would include seniority in a particular kin-based group, religious responsibilities acquired through attention to ceremonial duties, and authority in matters of land tenure and local political and economic issues that affect the affairs of the group over which the elder has influence.

Although religious, social, economic and geographic understandings of the world are interwoven, to greater or lesser extents, in indigenous understandings of the phenomenal world, it is nevertheless important to draw some distinctions and conclusions from Aboriginal understandings of the natural world. The primary ethic expressed in indigenous relationships with the natural world is that of the responsibility of stewardship for the non-human species and habitats, with these responsibilities having the force of jural principles. These jural principles are expressed, for instance, in the so-called 'totemic' affiliations established by the ancestral beings whose adventures are recorded in religious mythology. Aboriginal beliefs about the place of humans in the natural world construct a different concept of personal identity from that which is conventionally understood in Western epistemology. The Aboriginal person – as the socialized cultural being – is conceived of as not merely as a body enclosing a singular conscious being. Rather, the person is conceived of as spatialized by virtue of totemic affiliations. Persons with inherited spiritual essence, in common with non-human beings, share the world of those beings – including their natural habitats – as a personal responsibility.

Aboriginal people hold, therefore, that the possibility of the extinction of a species, whether fauna or flora, or the destruction of what is called 'biodiversity' in environment-speak, is offensive to the nature of human existence. Aboriginal resistance to attempts to suppress their involvement with the natural world, by continuing to use fire according to tradition, for example, or by organizing with experts to sustain biodiversity through weed control, are expressions of these cultural values. They sit alongside, and interrogate, the initiatives taken in order to ensure the viability of Aboriginal culture through its incorporation within the global economy and related developments, such as the spread of technological infrastructure. The maintenance of Aboriginal culture, particularly social relationships with land conceived of in a supra-kinship discourse, is held in Aboriginal law to be fundamental to the well-being of human society and non-human society alike – the former bearing a special responsibility for wise and respectful use of the latter.

The Aboriginal cosmology poses a different set of relational values between humans and non-humans from the inherent (and often explicit) hierarchy of values attributed to biota, landscape features and other subjects of Western natural science, and the application of those values under the rubric of 'natural and cultural values'. In practical applications, such as in the privileging of environmental over social impact assessment, this Western hierarchy assumes that Aboriginal traditional relationships with the non-human environment are irrelevant to the capacity of fauna and flora populations to reproduce themselves. Biological research concerning early human populations and fire in tropical northern Australian regions in recent times shows that this assumption must be reconsidered for the traditional Aboriginal domain.

This is not to deny that the Aboriginal domain is changing because of population growth, increasing Aboriginal participation in the economy of rural Australia, changes in the biophysical environment, and changes in the political, social and legal climate. Nevertheless, the influence of Aboriginal customs and law remains significant, and this has global implications for conservation of biodiversity. The activities of Aboriginal land managers demonstrate that a materialist consideration is necessary to an understanding of human–nature relations in the indigenous domain; and those relations are, necessarily, economic, and have been so since the evolution of the human species. If we admit that Aboriginal people are fully sentient and intellectual beings, we can admit that they would engage with the effects of the global economy and information society, and that they would bring to these problems interesting and innovative approaches.

INDIGENOUS RESPONSES TO THE PRESSURES OF DEVELOPMENT

The pressures for developing the remote areas in which the indigenous domain is largely located are a persistent and dominant feature of national political life. The key industries in rural and remote Australia are mining, pastoralism and tourism – are all land based. Because of the primacy of these industries in the rural economy, the models of economic development currently available to indigenous communities require radical alteration at various scales of the land and water and the importation of conventional European management systems and expertise. This occurs also in protected areas, to one extent or another, because all national parks are subject to management plans, many of which marginalize indigenous land use and management.

In the context of their limited ability to resist incorporation within the global economy, increasing reliance upon Western technology and infrastructure, and facing a population explosion and increasing poverty and disadvantage, the challenge for indigenous groups is to develop economic niches to sustain their ways of life and to sustainably manage their environments. For Aboriginal groups considering their futures, wildlife harvesting is regarded as a high priority for further development because they already have the necessary skills and knowledge that flow, ironically, from a localized way of life. There are a number of indigenous enterprises that utilize wildlife. These include crocodile egg-harvesting for sale to hatcheries with royalty payments to traditional owners; harvesting of seed for regeneration of mine sites; harvesting of marine life, such as fish pearl shell, trochus and crayfish; supply of 'bush tucker' and bush condiments to the restaurant trade; the use of subsistence hunting by-products (such as feathers and bone) in craft products; the production of artefacts and art from bush materials; the harvesting of didgeridoo sticks; the semi-domestication of native honey-bag bees; *trepang*-harvesting and processing; the harvesting and production of bush medicines; and the propagation of trees and shrubs for regeneration and landscaping. Because industries based upon wildlife harvesting enable indigenous people to use their existing knowledge and skills, they offer opportunities for small-scale enterprises that create small but useful levels of income. Where the operation of these enterprises is a natural adjunct to life in their homelands, the levels of benefits derived could be significant given the marginal effort required.

Small-scale commercial use of natural resources presents options for developing Aboriginal approaches to the sustainable stewardship of their traditional land and water estates. The benefits include the expansion of appropriate levels of economic development under the control of traditional hunting-and-gathering groups whose ways of life are jeopardized by sedentarism. These economic activities are a suitable accompaniment to the practices of traditional hunting and gathering; importantly, they do not create cultural conflicts over potential breaches of Aboriginal law concerning totemic affiliation with the particular species. Appropriate senior clan members must authorize access to estates and any activities carried out on them, including traditional hunting and gathering and commercial harvesting of native and non-native species. Small-scale ventures are compatible with traditional law and culture because compliance is possible at this scale and non-compliance can be redressed according to tradition.

Initiatives taken in this area, so far, have been based, in part, upon the notion that commercial valuation of wildlife constitutes a fundamental protective measure for sustaining populations of species under threat from human impacts. The valuation itself accords the species a status as a potential non-renewable resource that must be managed sustainably. For example, in central Arnhem Land in the Northern Territory of Australia, an Aboriginal land management scheme operated by an association of traditional land-owners, Bawinanga, manages a crocodile (*Crocodylus porosus*) egg-harvesting venture. During the 1980s, commercial crocodile farms sought permission from the Northern Territory government to harvest crocodile eggs on Aboriginal land. The Yolngu response was to commence harvesting arrangements of their own in order to prevent the opening up of the resource to non-Aboriginal operators who might have been given the opportunity to exploit the resource unsustainably (*Crocodylus porosus* was almost hunted to extinction by commercial white hunters before bans were introduced in early 1971). Since 1990, *Djelk* rangers have gathered crocodile eggs from a number of central Arnhem Land river systems. The eggs are hatched and transported to a specialist agency in Darwin for sale to domestic and international markets (Webb et al, 1996).

The harvesting is monitored by experts and Aboriginal staff. Webb et al (1996, p181–182) report that following the recovery of the crocodile population after their protection in 1971, over 100,000 eggs and 6000 animals have been harvested in the Northern Territory by commercial operators until 1994. It is not easy to monitor the impacts of such harvesting; but the authors conclude, upon the basis of studies of hatchlings at monitoring locations, that 'recruitment into the older age classes is continuing and there is every reason to expect the harvest to be sustainable' (Webb et al, 1996, p182). However, in 1997, senior elders of the local Yolngu clans rejected a proposal for a trial harvest of adult saltwater crocodiles for the skin trade and local subsistence use of meat, reasoning that commercial harvesting of adults ran counter to the great respect accorded in customary beliefs to these creatures. The religious observance of the ancestral crocodile totemic being in ceremonial life is regionally important, uniting all human descendants and their reptilian cohorts in common interest.

The application of local indigenous laws and the concern of local traditional owners for high biodiversity values are critical to sustaining highly localized species populations in the indigenous domain. Gongorni leader from the Bawinanga association, Dean Yibarbuk, makes this point well about the impact of poorly managed fire in his homelands:

> *Today fire is not being well looked after. Some people, especially younger people who don't know better or who don't care, sometimes just chuck matches anywhere without thinking of the law and culture of respect that we have for fire. This is especially true for people just going for weekends away from the big settlement. Fire is being managed well around the outstations where people live all the time.*
>
> *The other big problem is large areas of country where no one is living permanently now. Where grasses and fuels are building up, sometimes over a couple of years, until one day someone's little hunting fire, or a cigarette chucked out of Toyota gets going and hundreds or thousands of kilometres are burned out in very hot fires.* (Yibarbuk, 1988, pp5–6)

It was Yibarbuk's attention to such environmental details that alerted environmental scientists to the problem of wildfires in the regions that had been vacated by Aboriginal people under the Australian government's assimilation programme of the 1950s. Yibarbuk and other men of the central Arnhem Land region have addressed this problem (which they identified in 1998) by taking traditional people to these areas and replicating, with some caution, the burning regimes that once protected the region from hot wildfires. They have obtained the cooperation and assistance of a number of agencies in their efforts.

As mentioned, Aboriginal communities are attracted to small-scale harvesting ventures because they are amenable to the traditional forms of governance; increasingly, throughout Arnhem Land and central Australia, such communities have collaborated with research bodies to undertake monitoring in order to guide their decisions regarding the sustainable harvesting of specific species and the protection of their habitats. There is, of course, an ancient tradition of wildlife trading within and between the indigenous nations in Australia and with our near Asian neighbours. Now it offers new opportunities for developing sustainable industries that are accessible to indigenous people. There is scope to develop industries that are appropriate in scale and in capital and technical requirements, and which are conducive to traditional practices regarding the management of natural and cultural environments.

RECOGNIZING TRADITIONAL RESOURCE RIGHTS AND SUSTAINABLE PRACTICES

The recognition of traditional resource rights, benefit-sharing, control of access and intellectual property, and the development of mechanisms to facilitate the commercial involvement of indigenous people in resource exploitation, are important for the success of indigenous peoples' lives in their homelands. However, there is a different starting point in terms of the resource rights of indigenous peoples in the jurisdictions of different settler states throughout the world. There is wide variation in both the rights of indigenous peoples and the extent to which they are able to enjoy those rights. As UN Special Rapporteur Madame Daes pointed out in a 1999 report to the UN Human Rights Commission, most countries where indigenous peoples live assert a power to extinguish the rights of those people 'most often without just compensation'. The doctrine of extinguishment, Madame Daes noted, is something that 'came into prominent use during the colonial period' (p12).

Australia is unique among the former British colonies in that no recognized treaty was ever concluded with any indigenous group. The indigenous peoples in Australia are in a comparable situation to the native peoples of South America and Asia, where there is a low standard of domestic recognition of civil and political rights, and, indeed, high levels of breaching human rights in general. Under the doctrine of *terra nullius*, Aboriginal traditional resource rights were believed to be wiped away by Crown sovereignty and possession for a period of 200 years. Even though some limited legal recognition of indigenous rights has emerged during the last 25 years, this has coincided with the advance of market forces into the indigenous domain. In recent years, these limited rights have been eroded by a resurgent white nationalist agenda pursued by the federal government and some of the states.

Traditional resource rights in Australia have been procured in two ways: by statutory recognition of rights under the 'grace and favour of the Crown' or by case law. Statutory recognition of resource rights has concerned, primarily, access rights to special forms of title over Aboriginal land for mineral, gas and oil exploration and extraction. Case law – following the Mabo No 2 decision of the High Court of Australia – has found, for limited areas, Aboriginal customary rights and entitlements in resources, including water. In the Mabo No 2 case, the judges found that native title (the land tenure system that pre-existed the arrival of British law) had survived the annexation of Australia to the Crown under particular circumstances, and that it could be recognized at common law. However, they also confirmed the power of the sovereign to extinguish native title.

Two recent cases have particular significance. Firstly, in supporting a native title claim by the Miriuwung and Gajerrong people in western Australia, the federal court ruled that they had the right to 'possess, occupy, use and enjoy' the land that they claimed and either use it as they saw fit or 'receive a portion of any resources taken by others'. Of particular significance is the fact that the judgement included the allocation and use of water rights, and it could lay the ground for a new configuration of jural, economic and social relationships between the indigenous and settler societies if it survives an appeal lodged by the government of western Australia and other parties. Secondly, the High Court of Australia recently upheld the right of Aboriginal activist Marandoo Yanner to hunt for crocodiles in the area where his people come from after he had initially been charged with killing a protected species under the Queensland Fauna Act. Yanner had succeeded in having the charges against him dismissed in a magistrates court before the magistrate's decision was overturned on appeal. In a majority decision, the judges of the High Court of Australia found that the magistrate had been right in ruling that the fauna act 'did not prohibit or restrict the appellant, as a native title holder, from hunting or fishing for the crocodiles he took for the purpose of satisfying personal, domestic or non-commercial communal needs'. Although this ruling imposes limits on Aboriginal resource rights (that is, for non-commercial use only), it was a breakthrough in recognizing Aboriginal rights in Australia.

In the US, by contrast, treaty rights have given the indigenous people stronger legal protection as long as the courts have been willing to support the intention of the treaties. Guerrero (1992) notes that treaties between governments and Indian peoples included the premise that water – like trees, grass and air – was integral to the concept of land dealt with under such treaties. Over the years, increasing development pressures have encouraged a variety of forces to seek to separate land and water rights; yet a number of significant decisions have resisted this separation. This is especially the case in relation to fishing rights, and Levy (1998) comments:

> In the US, the Supreme Court has expanded this right from a mere access right to a right to avoid licence fees, and to include a harvest share. In the United States v Washington (Phase I), Justice Boldt held that the Indians were entitled by the treaty to receive half of the harvestable fish to pass their fishing grounds.

Indian rights to water in the US are also supported by the Winter's Decision of 1908, which ruled that the doctrine of 'prior use' applied to the use of water (Guerrero, 1992, p192–193). Sixty years after this decision, the Umatilla Confederated Tribes in Oregon were able to cite the Winter's doctrine in a successful 1977 suit, in which they argued that the Army Corps of Engineers, in constructing the Chief Joseph Dam, had illegally interfered with the water flow necessary for the spawning of salmon and steelhead trout that were the basis of the Umatilla people's economy (Guerrero, 1992, p203).

At the same time, case law in the US has also resulted in the extinguishment or impairment of Indian rights. For example, in the case of the Tee-Hit-Ton Indians versus the US, the US Supreme Court extinguished the rights of the Tee-Hit-Ton peoples without compensation even though the US constitution explicitly states that the government may not take property without due process of law and just compensation (Daes, 1999). The legal doctrine created by this case has been widely invoked and, indeed, the US Congress relied upon it in 1971 when it voted to extinguish the land claims of nearly all of the 226 nations and tribes of Alaska under the Alaska Native Claims Settlement Act. This act transferred some of the land to profit-making corporations that the indigenous people were required to set up so that these same corporations could then sell the land at much less than the market value. The tribes themselves were paid no money at all, and the land that was not claimed by indigenous corporations was turned over to the state of Alaska or the federal government. Needless to say, the Alaskan tribes did not consent to this legislation.

In 1978 the Canadian Inupiat leader Eben Hobson said:

> *If we are to enjoy our Inuit hunting rights we must also be able to manage our land. With great care taken, our land can yield its subsurface wealth to the world; but we Inuit have the right to determine just how much care must be taken. Proceeding from our native hunting rights is the right to manage and protect our subsistence game habitat safe from harm. Our subsistence hunting rights must be the core of any successful Arctic resource management regime.*[7]

This followed the settlement of a pioneering land claim in the James Bay Northern Quebec Agreement (Editeur official du Quebec, 1976). This agreement has been followed by two other important land claim agreements affecting the Arctic region: the Inuvialuit Final Agreement (Anonymous, 1984) and the Nunavut Land Claims Agreement (Anonymous, 1993). These three agreements establish constitutionally protected access to resources. They establish rights, titles and interests in land and provide various degrees of land ownership, including access by non-beneficiaries. Surface and subsurface rights are detailed, as well as the establishment of co-management bodies with varying degrees of responsibility and funding for research and resource-use planning. The agreements allow for monetary compensation and environmental and social impact assessment processes. There is no ownership of wildlife under the agreements; rather, there are varying degrees of constitutionally protected priority access.

Even before these agreements came into effect there was a recognition that the Inuit people should have the right to hunt for whales, even though commercial whaling has been banned in Canada since 1972. This right was confirmed in 1996 by Dan Goodman of the Canadian Department of Fisheries and the Oceans when he said that Canadian policy on whaling accepted that 'whales are an important source of food for the Inuit and…whales and whaling are an important part of Inuit culture' (Goodman, 1996, p5). Eben Hobson put it rather more directly back in 1978 when he said: 'Our native hunting and whaling rights proceed directly from our basic right to eat.' (Hobson, 1978, p2). It should be noted that all three of the land claim agreements mentioned above list conservation as a core principle of community-based resource management.

The extinguishment doctrine has been applied in Canada just as it has in Australia and the US, with courts deciding that Aboriginal rights, including Aboriginal land title, are not absolute but may be ' infringed' by the federal or provincial governments when the infringement is 'justified' by the needs of the larger society. In a recent case, Chief Justice Lamer of the Supreme Court of Canada wrote:

> *In my opinion, the development of agriculture, forestry, mining, and hydroelectric power, the general economic development of the interior of British Columbia, protection of the environment or endangered species, the building of infrastructure and the settlement of foreign populations to support those aims, are the kinds of objectives that are consistent with this purpose and, in principle, can justify the infringement of aboriginal title* (cited by Daes, 1999, p13).

In New Zealand, resource rights ceded to the Maori under the Treaty of Waitangi have also been abrogated on numerous occasions. For example, in 1999, the Waitangi Tribunal released a report on a Maori claim to the Whanganui River, which found (with one dissenting opinion) that:

> *…in Maori terms, the Whanganui River is a water resource, a single and indivisible entity, which was owned in its entirety by Atihaunui in 1840. We have further found that the Treaty has been breached by the Crown in depriving Atihaunui of their possession and control of the Whanganui River and its tributaries and its failure to protect Atihaunui* rangatiratanga *in and over their river were and are contrary to the principles of the Treaty of Waitangi. Atihaunui have been and continue to be prejudiced as a consequence* (The Waitangi Tribunal, 1999, pxi).

This was a landmark decision, with the tribunal yet to rule on numerous other claims lodged with it.

However, while some national jurisdictions may offer limited protection of indigenous resource rights acknowledged under treaties, case laws or statutes, it is the international jurisdiction that constructs the regulatory space in which trade in wildlife is limited. The Convention on International Trade in Endangered Species of Wild Fauna and Flora (CITES) has been in effect since 1975, and the capacity of indigenous peoples to comply with the Convention has so far been proven to be at least as good as that of ratifying nation states. Specifically, CITES protects threatened species from all international commercial trade, regulates trade in species not threatened with extinction but which may become threatened if trade goes unregulated, and gives countries the option of listing native species that are already protected within their own borders. The convention embraces the view that trade in protected plant and animal species can be carried out on a sustainable basis, and its effectiveness is regularly reviewed at conferences and other forums where amendments can be proposed and adopted. CITES conferences allow for attendance of non-voting non-governmental organizations (NGOs) representing conservation, animal welfare, trade, zoological and scientific interests, and they frequently discuss traditional resource rights in the context of other political agendas. Indigenous spokespeople are generally marginalized by the aggressive and well-resourced delegations representing the member states and large international organizations.

The 'regulatory space' constructed by CITES and other international convention monitoring bodies has impacted on the indigenous world both beneficially and detrimentally. Traditional resource rights of indigenous peoples may be discussed more often; however, it is in the hegemonic discourses of such international bodies that local traditional and indigenous discourses become ensnared when global interests – whether corporate or regulatory – oppose the local populations and claim a regulatory authority over them. International law of previous centuries, which authorized or justified the colonization of indigenous peoples, constituted a hegemonic discourse with profound impacts. The powerful members of CITES are the very same nation states that systematically discriminated against the encapsulated indigenous populations, and they continue to appropriate indigenous property according to remnant imperial doctrines still held at law.

CONCLUSION

Sustainable use of biodiversity in remnant indigenous homelands provides both opportunities for maintaining indigenous cultures and ways of life and, at the same time, for developing an enduring indigenous economic base that would reduce social and economic inequity typical of most indigenous populations. Yet, for many indigenous peoples, the options for economic pathways to sustainability of ancient ways of life are hampered by the restriction of their harvesting rights to customary rights by both national and international regulation.

As we have seen, customary hunting and gathering is a contentious issue, and one can expect from the present antagonism to indigenous use of natural resources that indigenous commercial use of natural products might be even more contentious.

In these circumstances, the framework for developing *sui generis* options for protection and compensation for indigenous peoples from traditional resource use, as proposed by Posey (1996) and Posey and Dutfield (1996), has a special significance in the absence of protection of these rights by any convention and the vulnerability of such rights in domestic jurisdictions.

The injustice that this situation involves for indigenous peoples is not just a continuation of the long and terrible history of imperial dominion. There is more at stake, in general, than the impoverishment and dispossession of local small-scale societies, such as hunting-and-gathering peoples. The issue is one of a steadily advancing environmental crisis. Along with the potential or actual environmental degradation, the slowness of the advances, where there are any at all, in recognizing the contribution of indigenous peoples to maintaining biological diversity may contribute to the collapse of faunal and floral species that have been sustained by these groups for much of human history. Arguments and the accretion of evidence as to the contribution that indigenous peoples might make to sustaining biodiversity through cautious commercial harvesting in their local areas, where the global market persistently encroaches, thus become more urgent.

This survey of the vexed web of issues relating to sustainable environments in indigenous domains shows just how fragile the resource rights of indigenous peoples are, and this fragility itself emerges as a factor of great significance in the problem of thinking about indigenous futures. Hence, the issue of indigenous proprietary interests in the features of the natural world poses the potential for strategies for successful indigenous management of natural resources. If such proprietary interests were interpreted more widely than the fossilized post-colonial view of native peoples as having mere customary subsistence rights, the opportunities for rigorous assessment of non-subsistence harvesting might be elaborated beyond the rare instances we find, at present, on this subject.

NOTES

1   Eben Hobson (1922–1980) was an Inupiat (Northern Eskimo) leader, founder of the North Slope Borough (a county-like home rule municipal government serving the people of Alaska's vast 222,740-square kilometre Arctic Slope between Port Hope and the border of the Yukon Territory) and founder of the Inuit Circumpolar Conference. See *Hobson's Address to the London Press Corps*, 23 June 1978 at www.buchholdt.com/EbenHobson/papers/1978/London.html.

2   See the account by Eben Hobson in *Hobson's Address to the London Press Corps*, 23 June 1978 at www.buchholdt.com/EbenHobson/papers/1978/London.html and D Goodman (1996) 'Land Claim Agreements and the Management Of Whaling in the Canadian Arctic', Proceedings of the 11th International Symposium on Peoples and Cultures of the North. Hokkaido Museum of Northern Peoples, Abashiri, Japan, at www.highnorth.no/Library/Policies/National/la-cl-ag.htm.

3   The term ' indigenous domain' is used to refer to indigenous governance of
    territory, including title under settler or indigenous legal systems. This would include
    land and water, whether owned under Australian title or not, and in the latter case,
    whether or not under claim under native title or other legislation; and land and
    water under contemporary forms of indigenous governance, including local
    customary forms of governance, representative bodies, community councils, etc.
4   The IUCN is also known as the World Conservation Union.
5   Examples of such research include the reports of the Cape York Peninsula Land
    Use Strategy (see Cape York Regional Advisory Group, 1996), the Cooperative
    Research Centre for the Sustainable Development of Tropical Savannas (see
    Cooperative Research Centre for the Sustainable Use of Tropical Savannas, April
    1996), Wet Tropics Management Authority (see Wet Tropics Management
    Authority, 1992), the Great Barrier Reef Marine Park Authority (see Bergin, 1993),
    and, as well, the studies and inquiries conducted by the Resource Assessment
    Commission (see Resource Assessment Commission, Coastal Zone Inquiry, 1993),
    and the Australian Heritage Commission (see, for instance, Smyth, 1993;
    Sutherland, 1996; Department of Communications and the Arts; 1997).
6   *Protecting Knowledge: Traditional Resource Rights in the New Millennium*, Spirit of the
    Conference Statement, Espirtu de la Conferencia, Thursday, 24 February to
    Saturday, 26 February 2000, First Nations House of Learning and the UBC
    Museum of Anthropology, University of British Columbia (UBC), Vancouver,
    British Columbia, Canada, Hosted by the Union of BC Indian Chiefs. See statement
    at www.ubcic.bc.ca/protect.htm.
7   For information about Eben Hobson see endnote 1.

REFERENCES

Anonymous (1984) 'The Western Arctic Claim: The Inuvialuit Final Agreement', *Indian and Northern Affairs Canada*

Anonymous (1993) 'Agreement between the Inuit of the Nunavut Settlement Area and Her Majesty the Queen in Right of Canada', *Indian and Northern Affairs Canada and the Tungavik*

Australia International Council on Monuments and Sites (ICOMOS) (1997, revised version) *The Burra Charter* (The Australia ICOMOS charter on caring for places of cultural significance). Kingston, ACT

Bergin, A (1993) *Aboriginal and Torres Strait Islander Interests in the Great Barrier Reef Marine Park*. Great Barrier Reef Marine Park Authority (Research Publication No 31), Townsville, Queensland

Bomford, M and Caughley, J (1996) (eds) *Sustainable Use of Wildlife by Aboriginal Peoples and Torres Strait Islanders*. Bureau of Resource Sciences, Australian Government Publishing Service, Canberra

Cape York Regional Advisory Group (1996) *CYPLUS Draft Stage 2: A Strategy for Sustainable Land Use and Economic and Social Development*. Department of Local Government and Planning, Cairns, and Department of the Environment, Sport and Territories, Canberra

Christie, J (1996) 'Biodiversity and intellectual property rights: implications for indigenous peoples' in Sultan et al (eds) *Ecopolitics IX Conference; Perspectives on*

Indigenous Peoples Management of the Environmental Resources. Darwin 1995, Northern
    Land Council, Darwin
Cooperative Research Centre for the Sustainable Use of Tropical Savannas (1996)
    Draft Strategic Plan. Northern Territory University, Darwin
Daes, E-I A (Special Rapporteur) (1999) *Human Rights Of Indigenous Peoples: Indigenous
    people and their relationship to land.* Second progress report on the Working Paper
    Commission On Human Rights, Sub-Commission on Prevention of Discrimination
    and Protection of Minorities, /CN.4/Sub.2/1999/183, June 1999 at
    www.unhchr.ch/Huridocda/Huridocda.nsf/0811fcbd0b9f6bd58025667300306dea/
    154d71ebbbdc126a802567c4003502bf?OpenDocument#III.%20FRA, date
    accessed 19 September 2002
Department of Communications and the Arts (1997) *Heritage Places: Past, present and
    future* (Draft Guidelines for the Protection, Management and Use of Aboriginal and
    Torres Strait Islander Cultural Heritage Places). Department of Communications
    and the Arts, Canberra
Department of the Environment, Sport and Territories (DEST) (1996) *National Strategy
    for the Conservation of Australia's Biological Diversity.* DEST, Canberra
Dews, G, David, J, Cordell, J, Ponte, F and Torres Strait Island Coordinating Council
    (1997) *Indigenous Protected Area Feasibility Study.* Unpublished report prepared for
    Environment Australia and the Torres Strait Island Coordinating Council
Editeur officiel du Quebec (1976) *The James Bay and Northern Quebec Agreement.* Quebec
    National Library, Legal Deposit – 2nd Quarter
Furze, B, de Lacy, T and Birckhead, J (1996) *Culture, Conservation and Biodiversity: the
    social dimension of linking local level development and conservation through protected areas.* John
    Wiley and Sons, Chichester, UK
Goodman, D (1996) 'Land Claim Agreements and the Management Of Whaling in the
    Canadian Arctic', Proceedings of the 11th International Symposium on Peoples and
    Cultures of the North. Hokkaido Museum of Northern Peoples, Abashiri, Japan at
    www.highnorth.no/Library/Policies/National/la-cl-ag.htm, p5, date accessed 19
    September 2002
Gray, A (1997) 'The explosion of aboriginality: components of indigenous population
    growth, 1991–1996', Discussion Paper No 142. Centre for Aboriginal Economic
    Policy Research, ANU, Canberra
Guerrero, M (1992) 'American Indian Water Rights: The Blood of Life in Native
    North America' in A James (ed) *The State of Native America: Genocide, Colonization and
    Resistance.* South End Press, Boston, Massachusetts
Hobson, E (1978) *Hobson's Address to the London Press Corps,* 23 June 1978 at
    www.buchholdt.com/EbenHobson/papers/1978/London.html, date accessed 19
    September 2002
Janke, T (1997) *Our Culture, Our Future: Proposals for Recognition and Protection of Indigenous
    Cultural and Intellectual Property.* Australian Institute of Aboriginal and Torres Strait
    Islander Studies, Aboriginal and Torres Strait Islander Commission, Canberra, at
    www.icip.lawnet.com.au, date accessed 19 September 2002
Kohen, J (1995) *Aboriginal Environmental Impacts.* University of NSW Press, Sydney
Levy, R (1998/1999) 'Native Title and the Seas: The Croker Island Decision', *Indigenous
    Law Bulletin,* December/ January, p20–21
Nietschmann, B Q (1992) *The Interdependence of Biological and Cultural Diversity.* Centre
    for World Indigenous Studies, Occasional Paper 21, Kenmore, WA

Posey, D A (1996) *Traditional Resource Rights. International Instruments for Protection and Compensation for Indigenous Peoples and Local Communities.* IUCN, Gland, Switzerland, and Cambridge, UK

Posey, D A and Dutfield, G (1996) *Beyond Intellectual Property: Toward Traditional Resource Rights for Indigenous Peoples and Local Communities.* International Development Research Centre, Ottawa

Resource Assessment Commission (1993) *Final Report, Coastal Zone Inquiry.* Resource Assessment Commission, Canberra

Rose, B (1995) *Land Management Issues: Attitudes and Perceptions Amongst Aboriginal People of Central Australia,* CLC, Alice Springs

Rose, D B (1996) *Nourishing Terrains: Australian Aboriginal Views of Landscape and Wilderness.* Australian Heritage Commission, Canberra

Smyth, D (1993) *A Voice in all Places: Aboriginal and Torres Strait Islander Interests in Australia's Coastal Zone* (revised edition). Consultancy Report, Resource Assessment Commission: Coastal Zone Inquiry, Canberra

Spinks, P (1999a) Personal communication

Spinks, P (1999b) *Wizards of Oz: recent breakthroughs by Australian scientists.* Allen and Unwin, Sydney

Spirit of the Conference Statement, Espirtu de la Conferencia (1996) *Protecting Knowledge: Traditional Resource Rights in the New Millennium,* Thursday, 24 February to Saturday, 26 February 2000, First Nations House of Learning and the UBC Museum of Anthropology, University of British Columbia (UBC), Vancouver, British Columbia, Canada, Hosted by the Union of BC Indian Chiefs. See statement at www.ubcic.bc.ca/protect.htm, date accessed 19 September 2002

Stevens, S and de Lacey, T (eds) (1997) *Conservation Through Cultural Survival: Indigenous Peoples and Protected Areas.* Island Press, Washington, DC

Sutherland, J (1996) *Fisheries, Aquaculture and Aboriginal and Torres Strait Islander Peoples: Studies, Policies and Legislation.* Commissioned by the Department of Environment, Sport and Territories, Canberra

Taylor, J (1997) 'Changing numbers, changing needs? A preliminary assessment of indigenous population growth, 1991–1996', Discussion Paper No 42, Centre for Aboriginal Economic Policy Research, ANU, Canberra

The Waitangi Tribunal (1999) *Whanganui River Report,* 28 June, at www.knowledge-basket.co.nz/oldwaitangi/whanganui/Prelims.pdf, date accessed 19 September 2002

Webb, G, Missi, C and Cleary, M (1996) 'Sustainable Use of Crocodiles by Aboriginal People in the Northern Territory' in M Bomford and J Caughley (eds) *Sustainable Use of Wildlife by Aboriginal Peoples and Torres Strait Islanders.* Bureau of Resource Sciences, Australian Government Publishing Service, Canberra

Wet Tropics Management Authority (1992) *Wet Tropics Plan: Strategic Directions.* Wet Tropics Management Authority, Cairns

Williams, N (1998) *Intellectual Property and Aboriginal Environmental Knowledge.* Centre for Indigenous Natural and Cultural Resource Management, Northern Territory University, Darwin

Yibarbuk, D (1988) ' introductory Essay: Notes on the Traditional Use of Fire on Upper Caddell River' in M Langton (ed) *Burning Questions: Emerging Environmental Issues for Indigenous People in Northern Australia.* Centre for Indigenous Natural and Cultural Resource Management, Northern Territory University, Darwin, pp1–6

Chapter 5

Sharing South African National Parks: Community land and conservation in a democratic South Africa

Hector Magome and James Murombedzi

INTRODUCTION

Environmental policy initiatives in the recently democratized South Africa (since 1994) are attempting to strike a delicate balance between two urgent sets of political issues. The first are the pressing needs and aspirations of previously disenfranchized, but now politically powerful, majority of black people (90 per cent of the 44 million population).[1] The second are the requirements of the highly politicized but equally powerful global environment. Having been marginalized for nearly a century, the previously disenfranchized constituency now derives power from their vote or potential subversive actions, both of which can be used to unseat politicians. To avoid this, livelihoods must be improved as a matter of urgency. Already there is a plethora of appealing terms, such as 'black economic empowerment' and 'fast-tracking development', that act as constant reminders to politicians about the promises they made during elections. Indeed, the lesson of history in decolonized African states is that democratization must mean more that just creating new political institutions; increasingly, it must bring about the trickle-down of 'visible' economic benefits to the broader constituency. However, since the 'peaceful' transition to majority rule, South Africa has shed more jobs than it has created and the local currency has lost over 100 per cent of its value. This situation does not augur well for a country that is dependent on imports.

South Africa is expected to take action on its signature to Agenda 21 and its ratification of the Convention on Biological Diversity (CBD). The country is already feeling the dictates of global environmental issues, and it is hosting two major international meetings, the Rio Plus 10 Earth Summit in 2002 and the

World Parks Congress in 2003. Politicians are being pressured to deliver something quantifiable at these events. In terms of the number of endemic plant species, South Africa ranks among the top 'biodiversity hot-spots' in the world (Cowling and Hilton-Taylor, 1994; Johnson, 1995). The Cape Floral Kingdom, with some 8500 plant species, 6500 of which are endemic, is the 'hottest spot' and unequalled botanical reserve of global importance. However, with only 6 per cent (70,000km^2) of the land surface under state protected areas, the country is far from the 10 per cent goal set by the World Conservation Union (the International Union for the Conservation of Nature and Natural Resources – IUCN). To complete a system of national parks, over UK£300 million (US$480 million) will be required for land purchase.

The financial burden associated with expanding national parks must be traded off against social needs such as health care and other welfare services. In fact, the state is struggling to fund existing protected areas, and in some areas management borders on criminal neglect (Kumleben et al, 1998). Some neglected protected areas from nearly bankrupt provincial conservation agencies might be added to the portfolio of South African National Parks (SANParks) to curb widespread criticism that the country cannot adequately manage its conservation mandate. However, SANParks is also financially burdened and has laid off 1000 of its 4000 employees. To achieve the 10 per cent IUCN ideal, some 50,000km^2 of additional land (2.5 times the size of Scotland) must be acquired. Equally, to meet the imperatives of land restitution, the state must somehow provide land to the majority of its citizens, currently restricted to 15 per cent of the country's total land surface. This chapter analyses the South African state's difficulty in trying to combine land restitution for the disenfranchised majority of its citizens and in taking a lead in biodiversity conservation, particularly in the context of trans-frontier conservation areas.

LAND DISPOSSESSION

The history of land conquest in South Africa is well documented (Magome, 1996; Tordoff, 1997; Reader, 1998; Ross, 1999). Briefly, land dispossession in South Africa was based upon apartheid policy, a racially based separate development strategy that was designed by government to advance and benefit the interests of its minority white citizens at the expense of its majority black people. Although colonial influence in South Africa dates back to 1652, when the first European settlers arrived, the land conquest was institutionalized when the apartheid government passed the Natives' Land Acts of 1913 and 1936, which restricted land ownership by black people to just 13 per cent of the country's total land area.

The land set aside for black people consisted of fragments scattered in selected areas of the country, first called 'native reserves' and later 'homelands'. This land was, with few exceptions, infertile and thus agriculturally unproductive. This situation forced many black males into the migrant labour system of the gold mines. Black families were also forced to settle for cheap wages on maize farms. For this reason, these acts have been described as the product of the alliance of 'gold and maize' (Worden, 1995). Most forced removals took place between 1958 and 1988, over which period over 3.5 million black people were compelled to settle in unsuitable areas.

LAND REFORM

Apartheid officially ended on 27 April 1994, when a transition to democratic rule was made. However, its land conquest legacy still lives on. To redress this legacy, the government legislated its Restitution of Land Rights Act 22 of 1994, which is dominated by three factors (see Table 5.1). The first is the restitution of land rights, which aims to restore or compensate people for land rights lost because of racial laws passed since 19 June 1913. The limitation here is that emphasis is placed on restitution, not restoration. This applies a strict judicial procedure to what, in essence, is a political problem (Winberg and Weinberg, 1995). The second is land redistribution, which aims to provide the poor with land for residential and productive use in order to improve their livelihoods. The rationale is that it will be difficult for the poor to buy land on the open market without state assistance. The third is land tenure reform, which is supposed to restructure land rights. The dilemma is that the post-apartheid constitution protects the land rights of those unfairly privileged by the previous political order.

Table 5.1 *The key elements of the land reform process, South Africa, post-1994*

Factor	Key relevant issues to be addressed
Restitution	• Ensure that rural and urban claimants dispossessed of land after 1913 receive restitution in the form of land or other acceptable remedies. • Ensure that proper administrative and financial arrangements are developed and implemented in order to respond to claims in the time limit set.
Redistribution	• To respond to differing needs and aspirations for land in rural and urban areas in a manner that is equitable and affordable and, at the same, to time contribute to poverty alleviation and economic growth. • To address cases of landlessness that often results in land invasions.
Tenure reform	• To resolve the overlapping and competing tenure rights of people forcibly removed and resettled on land to which others had prior rights. • To strengthen the benefits of communal tenure systems and, at the same time, bring changes to practices, which have eroded tenure rights and the degradation of natural resources. • To extend security of tenure to the millions of people who live in insecure arrangements on land belonging to other people, especially the predominantly white farming areas.

Table 5.2 *Number of households reclaiming their land in South Africa, post-1994*

Province	Number moved	Number reclaiming land	Per cent reclaiming land
Eastern Cape	51,695	3061	6
Free State	1228	0	0
KwaZulu-Natal	8228	2697	33
Mpumalanga	11,995	1891	16
North West	22,373	2500	11
Northern Province	46,075	2252	5
Total	**141,594**	**12,401**	**9**

Source: South African Institute of Race Relations (1999)

Land claims must be validated through extensive research in order to ascertain whether people were removed under discriminatory legislation or practices, and whether restoration of land rights is feasible and, if not, what alternative compensation can be offered. Valid claims are subjected to the land claims courts, which follow bureaucratic procedures and require due processes of listening to conflicting testimony. However, that is the way democracy works, slowly, with painful attention to detail and substance, so that new forms of justice do not create new injustices (Winberg and Weinberg, 1995). This might explain why only 9 per cent of households removed have lodged land claims (see Table 5.2). Therefore, in practice, land reform is a cumbersome legal process (Murombedzi, 1999). Claimants must, as a matter of fact, balance the costs of a legal battle against the benefits of restitution because winning a court battle is only the first step on a rough road of economic development that might not be achieved in the lifetime of many claimants.

LAND CLAIMS IN NATIONAL PARKS

National parks are conventionally viewed as sacred in global conservation – places where human habitation is excluded, except for employees and paying tourists (see Chapter 2). Yellowstone National Park in the US, established in 1872 through forced removal of indigenous Indians, remains the icon and the model followed by many countries. Icons are rarely challenged; but in South Africa national parks are increasingly being targeted for land restitution objectives. Indeed, the White Paper on the *Conservation and Sustainable Use of South Africa's Biological Diversity* (Republic of South Africa, 1997) specifically states that:

> The government will through the Land Restitution Programme, and in accordance with the Constitution of South Africa and the Restitution of Land Rights Act 22 of 1994, facilitate the settlement of land claims, taking into account the intrinsic biodiversity value of the land, and seeking outcomes

> *which will combine the objectives of restitution with the conservation and*
> *sustainable use of biodiversity* (p34).

So far, there are two case studies where the land rights of local people have been restored in national parks. These land claims were, at the insistence of the state, resolved outside of the courts. In this climate, conflicting objectives between the claimants, often preoccupied with resource use, and SANParks, primarily concerned with non-use of resources, were harmonized using foreign models of joint management. Sadly, these models have not had extended implementation periods; but there are already mixed feelings within the conservation fraternity about their desirability. The concern is whether local people can be entrusted with co-management. In contrast, we question these co-management models.

The Richtersveld National Park

The Richtersveld National Park (Richtersveld), 1625 km^2 in extent, is situated in the north-western corner of the Northern Cape Province (Figure 5.1).[2] Richtersveld represents the unique arid mountain landscapes of the endemic succulent Karoo vegetation and wilderness features of the Namib Desert. The Orange River cuts between Richtersveld and Ai-Ais National Park in Namibia before draining into the Atlantic Ocean. Richtersveld evokes conflicting emotions because it captures the harshness of the desert and the endurance of the human spirit. Its diverse wild fauna and flora have adapted to an annual rainfall between 50mm and 300mm. Similarly, the Nama community has adapted to this hostile climate and has, for centuries, led a pastoral nomadic life.

In 1990, the communal land rights of the Nama in the planned national park were affirmed. The apartheid regime had wanted to 'protect' this landscape since the late 1960s; but it was only in 1991 that part of the land was proclaimed as a national park. The proclamation was made only after a successful court interdict by some 3000 affected Nama people. Indeed, the establishment of Richtersveld, as originally conceived, had met with strong opposition from the Nama, as they would have lost access to communal rights, such as grazing for livestock, firewood, medicinal plants and honey. SANParks (then the National Parks Board) conceded defeat and subsequently agreed to enter into negotiations with Nama representatives. At the time, the political climate favoured the Nama because it was during the dying days of the apartheid government and the rights of local people were being affirmed (Archer et al, 1996).

The outcome of the negotiations granted the Nama significant concessions, including:

- creating a contractual agreement that recognized the Nama as rightful landowners;
- a lease fee of UK£20,000 (US$32,000);[3]

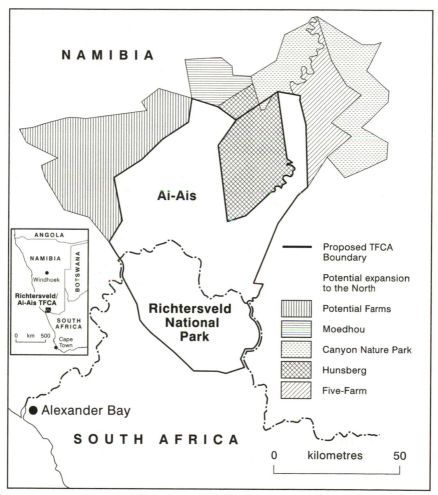

Figure 5.1 *Richtersveld National Park, South Africa*

- maintaining grazing rights for a total of 6600 livestock, mainly goats and sheep;
- reducing the duration of the lease of land for the proposed park from 99 to 30 years in order to allow renegotiation of Nama rights;
- reducing the size of the park from 2500 to 1625km^2 and providing 800km^2 additional grazing land;
- guaranteed job opportunities; and
- creating a Management Planning Committee between SANParks and the Nama, with the latter having more representation than the former; the chair of this committee alternates annually between SANParks and the Nama.

These concessions resulted in SANParks taking less and giving more as compensation for reduced grazing rights than they had originally proposed. All of the operational costs of managing Richtersveld are borne by SANParks.

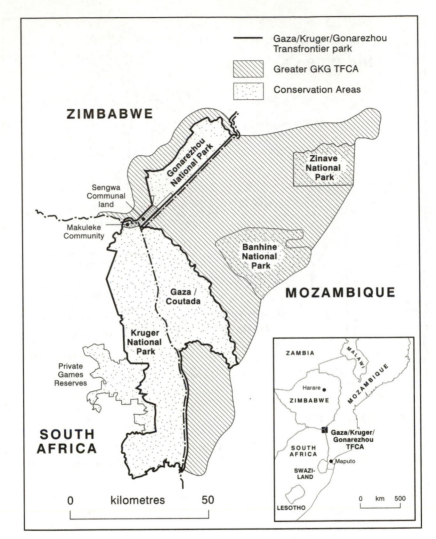

Figure 5.2 *Kruger National Park and the Makuleke land claim*

The Kruger National Park

The Kruger National Park (Kruger) covers 20,000km^2 of land – an area the size of Scotland or the state of Massachusetts (see Figure 5.2). Although the ecological importance of Kruger is now advanced as the key reason for its national park status, political agendas were at the core of its creation (Carruthers, 1995). Kruger was initially established as a game reserve in 1898 in order to rebuild wildlife numbers following overhunting in the area. Through forced removals of local people and the consolidation of various state game reserves, Kruger was consolidated to its current size during the 1970s. The reserve gained popularity as 'a hunting ground' for a limited number of privileged white South Africans; and when it gained the national park status, it became 'a playing ground' for local and international tourists. Black people were legally restricted from entering Kruger, which also acted as a military buffer area against the so-called terrorists from Mozambique, hence its shape. The forceful removal of 1500 Makuleke in 1969 is a recent act in the history of Kruger. Their previous residence is still demonstrated by vivid marks on a huge baobab tree (*Adansonia digitata*) and the remnants of demolished buildings.

In December 1995, the Makuleke lodged a land claim of about 250km^2 against the northern section of Kruger (see Figure 5.2). The claim was on the grounds that they were deprived of their land rights based upon discriminatory legislation, as they were forcibly removed with no adequate compensation offered for land and possessions lost. From the outset, the Makuleke land claim raised both hopes and fears (Steenkamp, 1998). Some saw it as a test of political commitment to the goals of biodiversity conservation and of land restitution. This sparked hopes of true community participation in the management of national parks. To others, particularly conservative officials of SANParks, the claim touched raw nerves. When the land restitution commission confirmed the validity of the claim, SANParks wanted to fight to the bitter end; but there was much political pressure to settle amicably. From this perspective, the settlement represented a 'worst fear come true' and a sure sign of impending disintegration of the national parks system (Steenkamp, 1998). However, to those sympathetic to the Makuleke, the claim symbolized the biblical fight between 'David and Goliath', and the Makuleke did win despite the odds being heavily stacked against them.

The state's precondition for restoring the land rights of the Makuleke was that the claimed land would continue in its current use of biodiversity conservation (De Villiers, 1999). The Makuleke agreed that their land would be used subject to the following conditions:

- No mining or prospecting may be undertaken and no part of the land may be used for agricultural purposes.
- No part of the land may be used for residential purposes other than for tourism, but these must meet the requirements of an environmental impact analysis.
- The land will be used solely for conservation and its related commercial activities.
- A servitude must be granted to SANParks to ensure that it can perform its obligations in terms of the agreement and the National Parks Act.
- No act shall be performed that is detrimental to the obligation of the state should the area be declared a Ramsar site.
- SANParks will be afforded the right of first refusal should the land be offered for sale.

Under these strict conditions, the Makuleke are only entitled to commercial developments on their land with limited harvesting of abundant wildlife species. Despite these restrictions, the Makuleke still agreed to have the land declared part of Kruger for 50 years provided that the agreement may be cancelled after 25 years. The Makuleke further agreed that even if the reclaimed land were to lose its status as national park, it would still be used for biodiversity conservation purposes. A joint management board, with equal representation from both parties (and its chair rotating annually), is supposed to be responsible for the day-to-day management of the reclaimed land; and decisions are also supposed to be taken by consensus. In reality, SANParks is the management authority because it has control over wildlife, the key resource that can make a difference to the lives of the Makuleke. Control over wildlife is, indeed, the greatest source of conflict between representatives of the Makuleke and of SANParks.

SIMILARITIES AND DIFFERENCES BETWEEN THE TWO CASE STUDIES

In South Africa, protected areas are fenced in, thereby limiting opportunities for local people to be involved in their management. As a result, there is a strong temptation to use case studies such as the Nama and the Makuleke as South African models of community-based natural resources management (CBNRM). We caution against this, for even though these case studies may, in time, evolve to mirror the rhetoric of CBNRM, currently they do not. South African CBNRM models in their 'true' form might exist in situations where traditional peoples such as the San have developed their own institutions (rules of the game) to try and approximate sustainability of resource use. In this context, state agencies and non-governmental organizations (NGOs) either 'accelerate' or 'decelerate' what is already in motion. In contrast, our two case studies can be termed conservation and development initiatives (CDIs) that are designed and operationalized by government agents or NGOs advancing a discourse that conservation and the development of rural people can be linked to mutual advantage (Magome, 2000).

The discourse on CDIs is often couched and packaged with the rhetoric of appealing terms, such as 'community participation and empowerment' or 'joint management', in order to disguise its main agenda of biodiversity conservation. CDIs offer the lure of a win–win solution to the human–wildlife conflict (Adams, 2001) and are often used as a 'tactic' to convince local people about the importance of wildlife conservation (Fabricius et al, 2001). Local people are expected to trade off their short-term livelihood needs against long-term survival of wildlife, to tolerate their conflict with wildlife, and, in the extreme form, to endorse Western conservation ideals. These crypto-conservation strategies partly explain why individuals who advance this discourse often rush to judge projects on the ground, and, invariably, conclude that results are 'mixed', or that linking conservation and rural development 'does not work' (Adams and Hulme, 2001). This begs the question: whose discourse is being advanced? We avoid this trap, preferring to highlight similarities and differences between the two case studies and drawing conclusions based upon the objectives of different actors involved in CDIs.

Similarities between the case studies

The similarities between these two case studies are mainly geographical. The Nama (Northern Cape) and the Makuleke (Northern Province, now renamed Limpopo Province) are located in the furthest and most neglected corners of South Africa's extremely poor provinces. Both communities are far away from the metropolitan areas of their provinces and must survive under extremely difficult situations. Unemployment levels in these provinces are high (40 per cent) and are matched by high proportions of adults without education (30 per cent). In the two case studies, unemployment is as high as 80 per cent, and livelihoods depend upon a mixture of livestock farming and cash income. For the Makuleke, some of their cash is derived from limited trophy hunting on their land, and from manufacturing industries located 200–500km away from their villages. In the Nama case, some cash is earned from concessions negotiated in Richtersveld; but most of it is derived from direct employment from a diamond mine located inside the national park. In both situations, limited employment opportunities are realizable from the national parks.

Richtersveld is a 'biodiversity hot-spot' that is complemented by the Ramsar site status of Orange River Mouth wetland.[4] In contrast, Kruger is not a biodiversity hot-spot, but to the privileged South Africans it is a model national park. The Makuleke land benefits from the Kruger brand – its huge size and 'big five' status, including lion, leopard, buffalo, rhino and elephant. The Makuleke land contains the unique floodplains and wetlands of the Limpopo and Levhuvu rivers, and the latter awaits the Ramsar site listing. Each of the two case studies attracts some 30,000 tourists a year; but these are 'extreme adventure-seeking' tourists, as the temperatures in these areas often climb as high as 40° Celsius.

Differences between the case studies

The differences in the two case studies are socio-political in nature. During the apartheid era, the Nama region was classified as a 'coloured reserve'.[5] This meant that the Nama were treated marginally better than black people in 'native reserves' or 'black homelands'. For instance, although the apartheid government wanted to declare both areas parts of national parks during the late 1960s, in the case of the Nama this was only achieved in the early 1990s. No forced removal took place, and the Nama gained significant control of their land. Other inhabitants, referred to as 'late arrivals', keep to different sections of Richtersveld. Therefore, the social structures and identity of the Nama have remained relatively intact, and they retained some of their traditional practices. However, Richtersveld is isolated from key economic hubs of the country, such as Johannesburg, Pretoria and Cape Town; as result, its inhabitants feel trapped.

In stark contrast, the apartheid government, using brutal military force, peremptorily removed the Makuleke in 1969. The Makuleke lost their identity, pride, history and access to a rich diversity of resources. They were dumped some 100km away from their original area and were made subject to a powerful ethnic group, the Mhinga. This destroyed most of their social structures, which had to be rebuilt through determination and good leadership. The Makuleke waited 30 years to get their land back. When they did, the settlement was seen as symbolic because it limited their ability to optimize use of the reclaimed land, and the concessions they won were relatively insignificant, making them appear as 'losers' and SANParks as 'winners'.

CONTRACT NATIONAL PARKS OR JOINT MANAGEMENT?

The Nama and the Makuleke experience of agreements with the state are particularly interesting in the light of a South African model of managing national parks in partnership with private landowners. Contractual national parks are becoming increasingly popular in South Africa as a model through which it is hoped that biodiversity conservation, social and development objectives can be met (Reid, 2001). This model evolved during the apartheid period, when the state, desirous of expanding national parks, entered into legal agreements with politically powerful private landowners. These were white farmers, and thus the state could not afford to upset them through land expropriation. The National Parks Act 57 of 1976 was amended to allow joining private land with national parks to mutual advantage. Such land was registered as a 'contract national park' and was reclassified as a 'schedule II' national park, denoting its lesser status compared to 'schedule I' national parks, which are strictly state owned.

In contract national parks, there is provision for landowners to generate income, primarily through tourism-related activities, including limited harvesting of surplus wild plants and animals. By entering into contract national park agreements, SANParks gains additional land for biodiversity conservation purposes, resulting in increased movement of wildlife over a larger system. The landowner retains title and undisputed management rights to his or her land, but must harmonize land-use practices with conservation. This often means giving up agriculture. However, agriculture in most areas adjacent to national parks is unprofitable, mainly due to marginal rainfall. Under a contract national park, the price of land can more than double in value because of the economic potential of conservation-related tourism activities.

Devised under the apartheid regime, the contract national park model was not meant for the disadvantaged majority of black people. Nor were contract national parks needed to mediate relations with black people: the government could, if it required their land for any purpose (including for a protected area), simply remove them. Those resettled had no legal recourse. Conservative officials of SANParks did not know how to handle cases in post-apartheid

South Africa involving communal land under the existing contract national park model. The notion of suddenly passing such a potential windfall to local people, who were typically treated by officers of SANParks with utter disdain and disrespect, was simply mind-boggling. The established approach to conservation was a classic one of 'fences and fines'. Officials of SANParks were regarded as 'police boys' and local people as 'poachers' (Carruthers, 1995). However, to local people, the contract national park model was attractive because it offered real business opportunities. Indeed, if a new joint venture between communal and state land could be given the same status as that between private and state land, this would be like winning at lotto.

The conservative officials of SANParks, desirous of changing the fences-and-fines approach to a 'fences-and-friends' approach, modelled communal contract national parks after those of the Aboriginal people of Australia. However in post-apartheid South Africa, black people are a major constituency and have political power in a way that the Australian Aboriginals do not. Therefore, the unequal treatment of private and communal landowners in their contracts with the state represents a new form of 'ecological apartheid' in the democratic South Africa. It perpetuates a dual tenure system (individual freehold for white farmers and communal tenure for black farmers; see Chapter 6 in this book). Furthermore, it fails to recognize the different political realities in South Africa and Australia. Therefore, the co-management agreements of the Richtersveld and Kruger National Parks are the result of unequal negotiation between relatively disadvantaged community representatives and sophisticated and advantaged officials of SANParks. They are like chefs with quite different ideas on menus, and different powers to cook them. There is a conflict between communities who favour consumptive use recipes (especially safari hunting), and SANParks, who insist on non-consumptive use or preservationist recipes. In this new imperialism, communities are prevented from reaching the full potential of possible resource utilization (Murombedzi, 1999). Indeed, co-management has seldom succeeded elsewhere in South Africa (Cock and Fig, 1999) and contract national parks are unlikely to be a panacea for all conservation and development problems (Reid, 2001). Local people are increasingly becoming aware of the problems associated with co-management. To circumvent these problems, the Nama and the Makuleke have adopted different strategies to ensure that the menu that is served fits their recipe.

The Nama strategy

The concessions that the Nama negotiated provide them with a 'guaranteed income in a highly variable environment' and that with 'no sweat' on their part. The lease fee paid into the community trust fund is not linked to either the management costs of Richtersveld or to the income generated by tourists. The 6600 Nama livestock allowed into Richtersveld have not been properly regulated, and the number has, on occasions, exceeded this limit (Hendriks, 2000). As already stated, the costs of managing Richtersveld are carried by

SANParks, and these include improving infrastructure. The Nama do nothing specific to improve the status of Richtersveld. They are, as a result, often seen by SANParks as presenting either a managerial dilemma, because they cannot be wished away, or a nightmare because the 'sweet dream' of biodiversity conservation cannot be enjoyed under what is interpreted as 'open-access regime' (with free exploitation of resources).

To the Nama, the big fuss about biodiversity, as exemplified by the interests of tourists in rare plant species, seems very strange. There is, therefore, blatant conflict of interest between long-term biodiversity goals and short-term livelihood strategies. Nama residents do not understand why tourists spend all of their money to see plants that are not 'pretty' and are totally useless to their livestock (Boonzaier, 1996). On the other side, the officials of SANParks, unable to implement their Western model of biodiversity conservation, assume that the donkeys and goats that the Nama keep in Richtersveld destroy nature. However, there is no evidence that livestock are incompatible with biodiversity conservation objectives (Hendricks, 2000). In fact, perceived incompatibility between livestock and biodiversity conservation is more often based upon taste, cultural ethics and value judgement than upon empirical evidence.

The main objective of the Nama is to maintain their livelihoods. To achieve this they have adopted a strategy that frustrates the objective of SANParks, which is to conserve biodiversity through non-use principles. The Nama have adopted a 'wait-and-see' attitude with SANParks. This has involved arriving late at meetings or not turning up at all, contributing little or nothing at all in meetings, and complaining about SANParks and its officials. Complaining about SANParks has, indeed, worked, because the managers of Richtersveld get worn out and are quickly transferred to other national parks. The Nama delayed the development of a management plan for Richtersveld and obtaining a title deed to their land. Any of these documents would have meant added responsibility and management costs on their part. However, these strategies are now starting to show serious limitations. The park management plan and the title deed are now much needed instruments in order to secure them a stake in the trans-frontier conservation area between South Africa and Namibia (discussed below). Their land title is still entrusted in the state, which has made its plans clear to the Nama about the urgency of establishing a trans-frontier conservation area. The Nama are concerned that the state might appropriate or modify their land rights to achieve the objectives of the trans-frontier conservation area.

The Makuleke strategy

The strategy of the Makuleke people with respect to Kruger is different. It fits the biblical analogy of 'David and Goliath', with the 'poor and weak' Makuleke against the 'powerful and strong' Kruger. Over time, Kruger has established itself as a world leader in wildlife conservation by re-establishing thriving populations of elephant (over 10,000), white rhino (4500) and black rhino (300). These charismatic mega-herbivores – the major lure to foreign tourists – were at one stage nearly extinct in the Kruger area. Recognizing the park's preservation achievements, the Makuleke made it very clear that they endorsed biodiversity conservation in much the same way as SANParks and the 'Green public' did. To demonstrate this, they planned to improve their livelihoods through developing their area for ecotourism – exactly what the Green public and SANParks wanted to hear – and this made the Makuleke 'a model community'.

Like David defeating Goliath, the Makuleke strategy had two well-executed elements: intensive home ground training and carefully targeted stones. The Makuleke leadership rallied their constituency, harmonizing differences and achieving coherence on the use of the claimed land. This involved frequent and well-planned community meetings and special formal education for the young Makuleke in tourism hospitality and conservation management. This is the stuff that appeals to donor agencies, and they poured in support, both technical and financial. The Makuleke also built a strong alliance with highly qualified and articulate white South African professionals in community development and planning of protected areas – 'the Friends of Makuleke'. The Friends of Makuleke took on the roles of coaches and mentors, and this dovetailed perfectly with the hunger for success that the Makuleke expressed. Unlike David's single lethal stone, the Makuleke have used a combination of approaches to make SANParks succumb. The arguments of the Friends of Makuleke matched the esoteric language of the officials of SANParks. The Makuleke, using lawyers, finally obtained title to control their land.

Two years after reclaiming their land, the Makuleke now find that the ecotourism bandwagon that they had jumped on has been very slow in reaching their remote area. Investors are not 'pouring in' with bags full of money. A feasibility study on the development options in their region concluded that their area was marginal for viable tourism activities, but that limited hunting could help the Makuleke bridge their financial hardship (Davies, 1999). In early 2000, the Makuleke, armed and informed by this study, proposed concessions for trophy hunting of two elephant and two buffalo bulls in order to raise UK£50,000 (US$80,000) for community projects. This initially met with strong objections from the management of Kruger, who argued that hunting should not take place in a national park. To this the Makuleke responded that it was appropriate in a contract national park. The hunt took place. In May 2001 the Makuleke earned a further UK£80,000 (US$130,000) from a second hunting quota.

TRANS-FRONTIER CONSERVATION AREAS

The experience of the Nama and the Makuleke at Richtersveld and Kruger National Parks are highly relevant to another major conservation initiative in southern Africa, the establishment of trans-frontier conservation areas (TFCAs). TFCAs are conceived of as relatively large areas of land within one or more protected areas that straddle boundaries between two or more countries and allow the protection of large-scale ecosystems. Although TFCAs have become fashionable, and something of a political bandwagon in conservation activities, they are not a new initiative. Albert Park, first established by the Belgian regime in 1925, spanned the colonial states of Ruanda-Urundi and the Congo (van der Linde et al, 2001). Following independence in the early 1960s, the Rwandan part became Parc des Volcans while the Congolese part became Virunga National Park (Wilkie et al, 2001). In 1932, Canada and the US jointly declared Waterton/Glacier as a 'peace park'. By 2001, the number of identified adjoining protected area complexes had more than doubled, since 1990, to 169 in 113 countries involving 667 individual protected areas (van der Linde et al, 2001). In Africa alone, there are 35 complexes involving 34 countries and 148 protected areas (Zbicz, 2001).

In most potential TFCAs, ecosystems have been fragmented by arbitrarily drawn political boundaries and fences have cut traditional migration routes (Hanks, 2000). A few functional trans-frontier protected areas still exist in Africa dating from the colonial eras. For instance, the world-renowned Serengeti-Mara ecosystem straddles the boundaries of Kenya and Tanzania, and migratory species such as wildebeest and zebra cross between the two countries with total disregard for political boundaries. However, common trans-boundary resources such as rivers are susceptible to overexploitation because users rarely bear the costs of abuse, typical of the 'tragedy of the commons' (Hardin, 1968). To avoid this, the Southern African Development Community (SADC) emphasizes that 'regional cooperation is not an optional extra; it is a matter of survival' (Southern African Development Community, 1994). A good example is the Zambesi River Basin, which alone spans eight countries in the SADC region (Chenje, 2000). Since virtually every country in the SADC region shares a major river basin with at least one other country, the management of rivers becomes central to economic growth and political stability (Katerere et al, 2001). Other important reasons for establishing TFCAs include improved biodiversity conservation (particularly, free movement of wildlife); increased political cooperation (leading to peace in the region); and economic growth based upon increased economies of scale (merging resources is now a major global phenomenon). The key step in establishing a TFCA is for the relevant governments to sign an agreement in which the principles of the TFCA are enshrined.

In April 1999, the presidents of Botswana and South Africa signed an international agreement to manage two adjacent national parks – Gemsbok (28,500km^2) in Botswana and Kalahari (9500km^2) in South Africa – as one single large ecological unit covering 38,000km^2 in extent. In May 2000, the presidents of the two countries officially opened the 'joined land', Kgalagadi Transfrontier Park (Kgalagadi), as Africa's first post-colonial TFCA. However, Kgalagadi was the easiest TFCA to establish. Wild animals have always moved freely between the two countries, and for the governments of Botswana and South Africa, this was a win–win situation. However, the San peoples of both countries were marginalized in the whole TFCA negotiation process. Consequently, those in South Africa are now pursuing legal action to entrench their rights.

The 'success' of Kgalagadi has encouraged reduced time frames for realising a further five new TFCAs by 2006 (see Figure 5.3). Two of these (the Richtersveld Ai-Ais and the Gaza-Kruger-Gonarezhou TFCAs) affect national parks and communities discussed in this chapter. The inventors of TFCAs, business people, politicians, ecologists and NGOs, eager to be counted as facilitators and 'dream-makers', are preoccupied with biodiversity conservation and promoting peace in the region under the banner of improved economic growth. However, they are often far removed from the realities on the ground, and cannot imagine the potential negative impacts that TFCAs can impose upon the lives of local people. In this case, the Gaza-Kruger-Gonarezhou and Richtersveld Ai-Ais TFCAs threaten the relative stability of the Makuleke and the Nama communities, who have just asserted their land rights and were beginning to enjoy the fruits of the decolonization of nature.

Gaza-Kruger-Gonarezhou

On 10 November 2000, the governments of Mozambique, South Africa and Zimbabwe signed an international agreement on the development of a second TFCA, Gaza-Kruger-Gonarezhou (GKG). Three adjoining cross border areas – 10,000km^2 of Gaza Province in Mozambique; Kruger National Park, 20,000km^2 (South Africa); and Gonarezhou National Park, 5000km^2 (Zimbabwe) – together form a 35,000km^2 reserve. The planners of the GKG

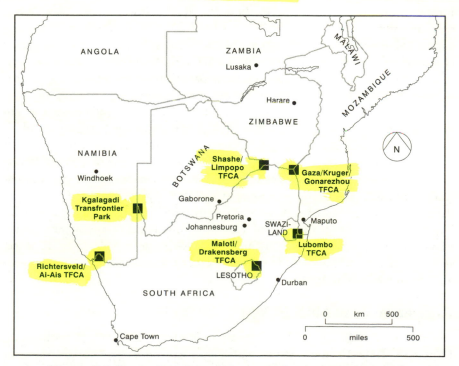

Figure 5.3 *Proposed southern African trans-frontier conservation parks*

TFCA, desirous of setting a new record, wanted to realize an area bigger than Portugal, where '4000 beds in one park are turned into 7000 beds in a bigger TFCA' (*Peace Parks News*, November 2000). The temptation to extend the TFCA to 100,000km², literally gobbling up nearly half of Mozambique, is irresistible (see Figure 5.2). The TFCA was launched in November 2001 and renamed Great Limpopo Trans-Frontier Park (GLTP), but neither Mozambique nor Zimbabwe was ready. Mozambique had requested that the opening ceremony be delayed to April 2002 in order to allow them to 'quickly' build a tourism lodge facility so that they can show the world 'something' on the opening day. Zimbabwe, meanwhile, had become preoccupied with its internal political unrest and had not benefited from donor funding to the same extent as Mozambique; local people resettled themselves to some 110km² of Gonarezhou National Park. There were also concerns that South Africa was 'rushing' the process and paying little attention to local people living inside the areas of Mozambique and Zimbabwe. There had been no mention of the effects of the proposed conservation area on the Makuleke. It was, in fact, common knowledge that South Africa was 'pushing very hard' and had, indeed, announced plans to start moving, in August 2001, 300 of 1100 elephants earmarked for Mozambique's protected area, now renamed Limpopo National Park.[6]

The Makuleke region of Kruger is part of the union of the GLTP. If, indeed, free movement between country borders will lure tourists, then the Makuleke land will become the tourism hot-spot of the economically depressed Limpopo Province (previously Northern Province). However, the Makuleke are not involved in the planning processes of the GLTP. The preparations and signing of the memorandum of understanding (MoU) between governments affected by the GLTP went ahead without attention being paid to the aspirations of the Makuleke. Equally, no attention was paid to the aspirations and concerns of affected local people in both Zimbabwe and Mozambique. The Makuleke are aware of the implications of a fully functional GLTP. They will be pressured to give up hunting concessions and any management practices that Western ideals consider distasteful in the core of a TFCA. After four years, only two investors look likely to build lodges on their land, and this is despite the Makuleke offering investors lucrative lease arrangements, such as 33 years with options to renew (compared to a 20-year lease elsewhere in the larger Kruger). Even if the developers were to start building lodges immediately, there is usually a time lag before the full benefits of tourism activities are realized (Magome et al, 2000; Magome, 2001). For tourism to benefit local people, a critical mass is required. It is the number of 'bodies in beds' that creates significant job opportunities and viable multiplier effects.

Richtersveld Ai-Ais TFCA

Enthusiasts for TFCAs, fully aware that the delayed opening of the Great Limpopo Trans-Frontier Park might start to raise questions about the practicality of TFCAs as a whole, increased pressure to move ahead with an 'easier' project, to precede or run in parallel with the GLTP. The two adjacent national parks, the South African Richtersveld National Park and Namibia's Ai-Ais National Park, became the next logical TFCA (see Figure 5.1). Richtersveld Ai-Ais will follow a different model from GLTP, in that land belonging to the community on the South African side will be joined to state land on the Namibian side. Planners are also talking about extending this TFCA to link up with the Huns National Park in Namibia and then, through the Namib Naukluft Park, Skeleton Coastal Park, and Commercial and Communal Conservancies in Namibia, to join, ultimately, the Iona National Park in Angola. If this proposed 'Three-Nations Namib Desert TFCA' is realized, it would, at 115,000km^2, be enormous. Planning for Richtersveld Ai-Ais TFCA is at an advanced stage; but signing the MoU was delayed when the Nama opposed what they saw as a crude 'cut and paste' of the Kgalagadi model. The negotiations between communities and the state in both cases are interesting.

KEY ACTORS IN TRANS-FRONTIER CONSERVATION AREAS

To understand negotiations about TFCAs, it is necessary to understand the behaviour of key actors. Debnam (1984) analyses the ability of actors to use sources of power in order to influence the actions of other actors, hence achieving their desired outcomes (see Figure 5.4). Interaction occurs in a dynamic continuum ranging from weak to strong power extremes, so that at any point in time actors with weak power can suddenly, as in a 'see-saw', acquire strong power, and vice versa. However, in situations where actors need buy-in or support from other actors in order to achieve favourable outcomes, compromises become imperative. As shown in Figure 5.4, the process can be dictated either by the desired outcomes or by the actors involved. In this analysis, we stretch the term 'community', despite its limitations, to cover all the communal landowners who are potential beneficiaries of TFCAs – in this case, the Nama and the Makuleke people. 'Government' here refers mainly to its agent SANParks, while NGOs are mainly the Peace Parks Foundation (interested in both Richtersveld Ai-Ais and Great Limpopo TFCAs) and Conservation International (CI) (only interested in Richtersveld Ai-Ais TFCA).

Government and NGO influence on TFCAs

The state and NGOs seek to establish TFCAs for a variety of popularized political reasons, such as 'promoting peace in the region', 'pooling resources to improve economies of scale', and the ecological principles of reserve design (for example, the single, large or several small – SLOSS – principle, which suggests that the prospects for biodiversity conservation are improved if reserves are large). The agenda is towards large reserves, with no limit of how large the system of protected areas should be. These promoters of TFCAs are energized by romantic ideals of recreating Eden, and the myth of wild Africa, where wildlife roams free and is supported by revenue from a 'Mecca of

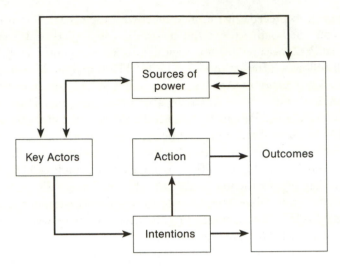

Figure 5.4 *The analysis of power in trans-frontier conservation areas*

tourism' that is free of immigration requirements. The power of the state is legislation and the discretion to exercise it, while NGOs derive their power from their technical expertise and the ability to fund TFCAs. In this context, NGOs sell grand ideas to the state, which, after buy-in, make these ideas government policy. As a result, these powerful NGOs are close to power holders and, therefore, powerfully influence decisions about TFCAs.

Community influence on TFCAs

The key intention of the community is to improve livelihoods, and it tends to favour smaller reserves. Communities are not certain how single, large reserves will benefit them, and they demand that the benefits are quantified. In fact, the number and range of stakeholders tend to be greatest in large-scale, multiple-tenure/land-use TFCA initiatives, involving many different levels (van der Linde et al, 2001). The 'single, large reserve' model can be problematic for communities. For instance, the San were completely ignored in all the planning and implementation phases of Kgalagadi. This was despite the fact that, on the South African side, they will have restitution to 500km^2 of the national park land. On the Botswana side, the government strongly contests the traditional rights of the San. The benefits that the community already enjoy in contract national parks, though somewhat limited, might be seriously threatened under TFCAs. Both the Nama and the Makuleke have lodged complaints about these TFCAs because they feel that their land is being recolonized. In the words of the Makuleke elders (in Steenkamp and Grossman, 2001): ' in 1969 John Vorster [then South African president] took our land away. In 1998 Mandela gave it back to us and in February 2000 SANParks tried to take it away.'

In Mozambique, concern is for the recently proclaimed Limpopo National Park, where some 20,000 people live in abject poverty, located around riverbeds, and eke out a subsistence living in the form of fishing, grazing livestock and limited agricultural production. What will happen to these people? Must they be displaced again? The first time displacement was caused by war – the second time it will be conservation (Mayoral-Phillips, 2000). Of the 20,000 affected Mozambicans, 6000 of them live in the core of area of Limpopo National Park and their fate appears sealed. They are most likely to be relocated elsewhere, while those living along the Limpopo River might be accommodated through zoning their location as a multiple-use area. The irony is that lodge operators are unwilling to invest in Limpopo National Park until the product (mainly wildlife and road infrastructure) is fully developed. In Zimbabwe, the Sengwe community, who are in the proposed corridor to link both Kruger and Gonarezhou National Parks, are also uncertain of their future. If, under the Communal Area Management Programme for Indigenous Resources (CAMPFIRE), their rights have not being devolved to the local level, why would politicians concerned with the GLTP behave otherwise?[7]

The Nama have effectively stopped the signing of the MoU of the Richtersveld-Ai-Ais TFCA, as originally scheduled. As the owners of the land, they argued that they had not given the government the mandate to sign the MoU on their behalf. The government and its supporting NGOs, unable to continue as planned, instituted a survey on the concerns of the Nama. The survey revealed that the major concern of the Nama was insecurity of tenure because they do not hold title to their land. Secure title to land is the *sine quo non* of power in state, private and community partnerships (Magome et al, 2000). Their title is still with the state, which may use its fullest discretion to impose new restrictions on the Nama. Even though the Nama have challenged this, the TFCA will happen with or without their full support. To understand this, we need to discuss the politics and potential benefits of managing community land in national parks, including TFCAs. The emerging pattern so far is that TFCAs are forcing rural local people into 'choiceless' partnerships with the state (Katerere et al, 2001). TFCAs attract huge foreign donor-funding, national prestige and international recognition, all of which are much needed in the southern Africa region. As a result, state agencies and NGOs view them as a quick fix to lack of development, particularly in remote rural areas. TFCAs are not a universal panacea for joint management of trans-boundary resource and will not succeed if internal natural resources management does not work (van der Linde et al, 2001).

POLITICS, COMMUNAL LAND AND NATIONAL PARKS

Linking biodiversity conservation to the development of local people is a political matter because conservation is a political issue. Therefore, the naive, idealized picture of apolitical conservation in Africa or anywhere else is absurd (Anderson and Grove, 1987). Indeed, in much of Africa, the key concern of the state has always been control over conservation and its associated benefits

(Gibson, 1999). To the community, insecure tenure – in land and its biodiversity resources – is perhaps one of the greatest obstacles to achieving their stated objectives. However, the call for vesting secure rights in local people is sometimes portrayed as dangerous because government might lose its power to protect wider societal interests. This creates conflict at three levels of scale.

Firstly, at the local level within the community itself, local politics spawn conflict. The Nama are an excellent example, and as stated by Archer et al (1996, p173):

> *Various factions and individual interests, antagonistic towards each other, compete for political power and economic advantages. Attempts to achieve community consensus on issues such as land management, local government structures, or development initiatives are intricate, time consuming, and often futile. Ethnic differences such as those between the indigenous Nama people and the more recently arrived Basters are responsible for only part of the complexity of competing interests.*

Local people often lack effective leadership required to harmonize and to harness competing interests to mutual advantage. Within their constituency, arrays of fuzzy entitlements abound, with all their members claiming rights to the same resource. With a high ratio of beneficiaries to available resources, conflict intensifies. In Richtersveld, the affected Nama people have difficulties excluding the 3000 recent arrivals. Similarly, the 10,000 people in Makuleke feel as entitled to benefits from the claimed land as do the 5000 that were actually affected by the removal. In this climate, the little benefits derived from contract national parks become a source of conflict.

Secondly, at the national level, the greater public feels entitled to some of the benefits accruing from natural resources located in the spheres of local people. As summarized by Murphree (1995, p47):

> *The mixed profile of success and failure in CBNRM [community-based natural resource management]...in the region owes much of its ambiguity to our strategic pragmatism in its implementation. We have placed policy and practice before politics and thus have encouraged the birth of CBNRM (in its 'modern' version) into a politico-legal environment, which, if not hostile, is hardly a nurturing one. In so doing we have put an ironic twist on the conventional approach to planned change.*

The political environment is still hostile to local people and this is unlikely to change, particularly as the pressure of globalization intensifies. Forced to take up a 'follow-the-stream role', rather than craft their own strategies, developing countries drag their constituencies along, including rural local people.

Thirdly, at the international level, global politics take the centre stage of conflict and, as stated by Peuhkuri and Jokinen (1999, pp133–134):

The complicated nature of the biodiversity issue makes it possible to emphasize its different aspects. In other words, different interests tend to own the problem of the loss of biodiversity and define it in their own terms. There are divisions, for example, between actors recognising or denying the problem, between property owners and groups without property rights, between anthropocentric and ecocentric values, and between local and global spheres of action.

These are issues of power and, where a global resource such as biodiversity is involved, conflict becomes intensified. This begs two key questions: Why is there such a discrepancy between theory and practice when it comes to achieving workable solutions in linking biodiversity conservation with the development of local people (Magome, 2000)? Are there cracks in the paradigm (Steenkamp and Grossman, 2001)? We argue that the idea of a joint management model might not be flawed, but that its assumptions or expectations are incongruent with reality. As a concept, biodiversity conservation means different things to different people and this alone creates management puzzles. The puzzles are constructed from different cultural backgrounds with false expectations of what the outcome should look like. The two pillars of biodiversity conservation, altruism and posterity, are human-devised puzzles that do not fit with reality (Hardin, 1977). Indeed, biodiversity conservation has an appeal, in terms of altruism, that the individual must constrain their own actions, to their own immediate detriment, for later benefit, or for the benefit of individuals of present and future generations (Bell, 1987; Mentis, 1989). However, many contemporary values, attitudes and institutions militate against altruism (Caldwell, 1990). The reality is that biodiversity conservation is a long-term strategy that conflicts with short-term individual interests, and this leads to resistance. Biodiversity conservation has serious implications on how people use land – a highly limited resource.

Most attempts to link biodiversity conservation to the development of local people are flawed for two reasons. The first flaw is the dogged belief by most policy-makers and practitioners that the 'community' exists and that it is the best vehicle for implementing biodiversity conservation programmes. The notion that a 'community' is a group of homogenous people, all with common interests and purpose, is false. Despite this, it is difficult to dispel this belief because it is already part of received wisdom that is conveyed by a durable narrative (Leach et al, 1999). The second flaw is a strong belief that the ancient rural past – prior to modernization – was compatible with nature and that it can be easily recreated. However, there can be no return to a harmonious state of nature. Hence, the pieces of the puzzles rarely fit because the issues surrounding biodiversity conservation continually present themselves as moving targets in a fierce battlefield of competing and conflicting interests (Magome, 2000). The right fit between local, national and international actors remains difficult to find. However, although the politics of biodiversity conservation creates unworkable puzzles when it comes to implementing models, the potentials that can be realised from cooperation between various actors encourage the quest for best practice. Let us now consider these potentials.

THE POTENTIAL FOR COOPERATION

Why does the contract national park model work well with private landowners? There might be a variety of reasons for this, but four are key. Firstly, the officials of SANParks treat private landowners with respect because private ownership is often perceived as superior to all other forms of ownership. In some extreme cases, they are feared because of their wealth and ability to use legal systems to defend their rights. Secondly, private landowners are registered individuals, conservancies (group of individual landowners) or corporate bodies. At any given time, SANParks know exactly whom they are dealing with. Thirdly, the private landowners share both the management costs of contract national parks and benefits accruing therefrom. Fourthly, and very importantly, private landowners often reside or conduct their daily business inside contract national parks; therefore, SANParks cannot afford to ignore or marginalize them.

In stark contrast, local people reclaim land in national parks in order to try and maximize tourism benefits (Hanekom, 1996). They are, from the start, expected to co-manage with veterans against their position of weakness, which is compounded by ignorance of the highly globalized tourism sector. In this cut-throat business, their ability to perform efficiently and effectively is severely limited by the constant need to harmonize differences within themselves and those arising between their veteran partners (the state and private sector). Therefore, to overcome problems related to an unequal power balance between communities and SANParks under contract national parks, the mode of conducting business might have to change. Critically, they need institutions with sufficient 'hardness' and solidity in order to manage their interests effectively (Steenkamp, 1998). The challenge facing local people in a contract national park model is to approximate successful attributes displayed by private landowners. To put it bluntly, hardness of institutions is, today, often linked to privatizing or outsourcing the management of assets. Indeed, despite the existence of successful communal tenure systems elsewhere, the increasingly globalized world accords more respect to private property rights than it does to other types of property regimes.

The central question is: do local people want to maximize returns on their investment or do they want symbolic rights? If they want to maximize returns, then they may have to use conventional business principles. We suggest that local people should privatize or commercialize the management of their equity in protected areas to competent individuals, companies or corporations that can match the sophisticated and complex business world of managing tourism-related activities. Privatizing in this context does not mean selling off, but outsourcing. If, and when, they do, two potentials from such an arrangement can be realised. Firstly, they can 'hire or fire' the privatized management based upon its ability to maximize returns on their investment. Secondly, they can afford to invest time in training their own people to be future managers of their investment.

CONCLUSION

The need to link biodiversity conservation to the development of local people is a critical issue in most developing countries. Post-colonial countries suffer from 'poverty of choices and of opportunities' (see World Bank Report, 2000). What local people can or cannot do with biodiversity resources is largely driven by available choices and opportunities. In most cases, they are helpless participants in biodiversity conservation processes over which they have little influence. Where national parks are concerned, the agenda, disguised or blatant, is that biodiversity conservation should assume top priority, and development paths based upon alternative uses of the land should receive a low priority (Magome, 2000). In southern Africa, trans-frontier conservation initiatives are a reality and the choices of affected local people appear limited (Katerere et al, 2001). The failure or success of various models that try to link local people to biodiversity management should be seen in the greater context of local, national and international politics. We conclude that if the dominant agenda is conventional biodiversity conservation, the political expediency that facilitated the decolonizing of nature at the national level will cause its re-colonization at the international level.

NOTES

1   The definition of black people in the democratic South Africa is politically extended to include Indians/Asians and 'coloured' people (see endnote 5), who form 12 per cent of the population. Black people, of African origin, only constitute 78 per cent of the population and white people constitute 10 per cent.
2   Thanks to Ian Agnew for redrawing the maps.
3   In 2001, it was UK£10,000 (US$16,000) due to currency devaluation.
4   The Convention on Wetlands, signed in Ramsar, Iran, in 1971, is an intergovernmental treaty that provides the framework for national action and international cooperation for the conservation and wise use of wetlands and their resources. There are currently 130 contracting parties to the convention, with 1129 wetland sites designated for inclusion in the Ramsar List of Wetlands of International Importance (www.ramsar.org).
5   'Coloured' refers to a mixed race resulting from interbreeding between white and black people. During the apartheid era, coloured people were treated marginally better than black people.
6   Limpopo National Park was proclaimed on 27 November 2001, following the launch of the Great Limpopo Trans-Frontier Park. During the launch, 30 elephants were released into Mozambique as a symbolic gesture, but 3 adult bulls have since homed back to Kruger National Park. There has also been a 'Limpopomania' because the Northern Province of South Africa was renamed, in February 2002, Limpopo Province.
7   The Zimbabwean National Parks and Wildlife Act (1975), amended in 1982, gives appropriate authority over wildlife to rural district councils, allowing communities to profit from safari-hunting revenues (see Chapter 6).

REFERENCES

Adams, W M (2001) *Green Development: Environment and Sustainability in the Third World*, second edition. Routledge, London

Adams, W M and Hulme, D (2001) 'If community conservation is the answer, what is the question?' *Oryx: The International Journal of Conservation*, vol 35(3), pp193–200

Anderson, D and Grove, R (eds) (1987) *Conservation in Africa: People, Politics and Practice*. Cambridge University Press, Cambridge

Archer, F, Turner, S and Venter, F (1996) 'Range management, livestock production and nature conservation: the Richtersveld National Park' in Centre for Development and Cooperation Services, Vrije Universiteit, Amsterdam, *Successful Natural Resource Management in Southern Africa*. Gamsberg, Macmillan Publishers, Namibia, pp173–195

Bell, R H V (1987) 'Conservation with a human face: conflict and reconciliation in African land use planning' in D Anderson and R Grove (eds) *Conservation in Africa: People, Politics and Practice*. Cambridge University Press, Cambridge, pp79–101

Boonzaier, E (1996) 'Local responses to conservation in the Richtersveld National Park, South Africa', *Biodiversity and Conservation*, vol 5, pp307–314

Caldwell, L K (1990) *Between Two Worlds: science, the environment movement, and policy choice*. Cambridge University Press, Cambridge

Carruthers, J (1995) *The Kruger National Park: a social and political history*. University of Natal Press, Pietermaritzburg

Chenje, M (ed) (2000) *State of the Environment Zambesi Basin 2000*. SADC/IUCN/ZRA/SARDC, Maseru, Lusaka, Harare

Cock, J and Fig, D (1999) *From Colonial to Community-Based Conservation: environmental justice and the national parks of South Africa*. Unpublished report

Cowling, R M and Hilton-Taylor, C (1994) 'Patterns of plant diversity and endemism in southern Africa: an overview', in B J Huntley (ed) *Botanical Diversity in South Africa*. *National Botanical Institute*, Pretoria pp31–52

Davies, R (1999) *Financial Overview and Development Options and Strategies for the Makuleke Region of the Kruger National Park*. GTZ, Pretoria

Debnam, G (1984) *The Analysis of Power: a Realist Approach*. MacMillan Press Ltd, London

De Villiers, B (1999) *Land Claims and National Parks: the Makuleke experience*. Human Sciences Research Council, Pretoria

Gibson, C C (1999) *Politician and Poachers: The Political Economy of Wildlife Policy in Africa*. Cambridge University Press, Cambridge

Fabricius, C, Koch, E and Magome, H (2001) 'Community wildlife management in southern Africa: challenging the assumptions of Eden', *Evaluating Eden Series No 6*, IIED, London

Hanekom, D (1996) 'Community approaches to wildlife management. Keynote address by Derek Hanekom, Minister of Land Affairs, South Africa' in *ODA: African wildlife policy consultation – final report of the consultation*. 18–19 April 1996, Civil Service College, Sunningdale Park, Berkshire, UK, Overseas Development Administration, London, pp13–22

Hanks, J (2000) 'The role of transfrontier conservation areas in southern Africa in the conservation of mammalian biodiversity' in A Entwistle and N Dunstone (eds)

Priorities for the Conservation of Mammalian Diversity: has the panda had its day?
Conservation Biology 3, Cambridge University Press, Cambridge, pp239–256

Hardin, G (1968) 'The tragedy of the commons', *Science*, vol 162, pp1243–1248

Hardin, G (1977) *The Limits of Altruism: an ecologist's view of survival.* Indiana University Press, Indiana

Hendricks H (2000) 'Reconciling the Perceived Incompatibilities of the Richtersveld' in *Towards Best Practice: Communities and Conservation*, Conference Proceedings, 15–19 May 2000, Berg en Dal, Kruger National Park, South Africa, South African National Parks, Social Ecology, pp90–92

Johnson, N (1995) *Biodiversity in the Balance: approaches to setting geographic conservation priorities.* Biodiversity Support Programme, USAID-Funded, WWF, The Nature Conservancy and World Resources Institute, Corporate Press, Inc, Landover, Maryland

Katerere, Y, Hill, R and Moyo, S (2001) 'A critique of transboundary natural resources management in Southern Africa', *Paper No 1, IUCN-ROSA Series on Transboundary Natural Resources Management*, IUCN Regional Office for Southern Africa, Harare

Kumleben, J, Sangweni, S S and Ledger, J A (1998) *Board of Investigation into the Institutional Arrangements for Nature Conservation in South Africa.* Government of South Africa, Pretoria

Leach, M, Mearns, R and Scoones, I (1999) 'Environmental Entitlements: Dynamics and Institutions in Community-Based Natural Resource Management', *World Development*, vol 27, pp225–247

Magome, H (1996) 'Land use conflicts and wildlife management in Southern Africa' in P Hirschoff, S Metcalfe and L Rihoy (eds) *Rural Development and Conservation in Africa: studies in community resource management.* Proceedings of a seminar tour, Africa Resources Trust, Zimbabwe, pp10–14

Magome, H (2000) 'Biodiversity Conservation, Development and Local People: Politics, Puzzles and Potentials' in *Towards Best Practice: Communities and Conservation*, Conference Proceedings, 15–19 May 2000, Berg en Dal, Kruger National Park, South Africa, South African National Parks, Social Ecology, pp14–18

Magome, H (2001) 'Biodiversity Conservation and Rural Livelihoods in Southern Africa', in *Community-based Conservation and Development in Southern Africa*, Africa Resources Trust, Lisbon, Portugal, pp11–15

Magome, H, Grossman, D, Fakir, S and Stowell, Y (2000) *Partnerships in Conservation: the state, private sector and the community at Madikwe Game Reserve, North-West Province, South Africa.* IIED, London

Mayoral-Phillips, A (2000) 'Transboundary Conservation Areas: a new approach to an old problem?' *Commons Southern Africa*, vol 2(2), November 2000

Mentis, M T (1989) 'Conservation: a controlled- versus free-market dialogue' in B J Huntley (ed) *Biotic Diversity in Southern Africa: concepts and conservation.* Oxford University Press, Oxford, pp80–92

Murombedzi, J C (1999) 'Land Expropriation, Communal Tenure and Common Property Resource Management in Southern Africa' in *The Common Property Resource Digest*, No 50. Quarterly publication of the International Association for the Study of Common Property, October 1999, pp1–4

Murphree, M W (1995) 'Optimal principles and pragmatic strategies: creating an enabling politico-legal environment for community based natural resources management (CBNRM)' in E Rihoy (ed) *The Commons Without the Tragedy: strategies for community based natural resources management in southern Africa.* Proceedings of the

Regional Natural Resources Management Programme Annual Conference, SADC Technical Coordinating Unit, Lilongwe, Malawi, pp47–52

Peace Parks Foundation (2000) *Peace Parks News*, second edition. Peace Parks Foundation, Stellenbosch, South Africa, November

Peuhkuri, T and Jokinen, P (1999) 'The role of knowledge and spatial contexts in biodiversity policies: a sociological perspective', *Biodiveristy and Conservation*, vol 8, pp133–147

Reader, J (1998) *Africa: a biography of the continent*. Penguin Books, UK

Reid, H. (2001) 'Contractual National Parks and the Makuleke Community', *Human Ecology*, vol 29(2), pp135–155

Republic of South Africa (1997) *Conservation and Sustainable Use of South Africa's Biological Diversity*. White paper, Government Gazette No 18163, vol 385, Republic of South Africa, Pretoria

Ross, R (1999) *A Concise History of South Africa*. Cambridge University Press, Cambridge

Southern African Development Community (1994) *SADC Policy and Strategy for Environment and Sustainable Development in Southern Africa*, SADC ELMS, Maseru, Lesotho

South African Institution of Race Relations (1999). *South Africa Survey 1999/2000, Millennium Edition* South African Institution of Race Relations, Johannesburg

Steenkamp, C (1998) 'The Makuleke Project – beyond the rhetoric of "community participation in conservation"' in D Holt-Biddle (ed) *Endangered Wildlife, Business, Ecotourism and the Environment: a vision*. Endangered Wildlife Trust, sixth annual, Johannesburg Zoological Gardens, pp70–75

Steenkamp, C and Grossman, D (2001) *People and Parks: Cracks in the Paradigm*. IUCN, South Africa Country Office

Tordoff, W (1997) *Government and politics in Africa*, third edition. MacMillan Press, London

van der Linde, H, Oglethorpe, J, Sandwith, T, Snelson, D and Tessema, Y (2001) *Beyond Boundaries: transboundary natural resources management in Sub-Saharan Africa*, Biodiversity Support Progamme, Washington, DC

Wilkie, D S, Hakizumwami, E, Gami, N and Difara, B (2001) *Beyond Boundaries: Regional Overview of Transboundary Natural Resources Management in Central Africa*, Biodiversity Support Programme, Washington, DC

Winberg, M and Weinberg, P (1995) *Back to the Land*. The Porcupine Press, Johannesburg

Worden, N (1995) *The Making of Modern South Africa*, second edition. Blackwell, London

World Bank (2000) *World Development Report 2000/2001: Attacking Poverty*. Oxford University Press, Oxford

Zbicz, D C (2001) 'Global list of internationally adjoining protected areas' in T S Sandwith, C Shine, L S Hamilton and D A Sheppard (eds) *Transboundary Protected Areas for Peace and Cooperation*. IUCN, Gland, Switzerland, and Cambridge, pp55–75

Chapter 6

Devolving the expropriation of nature: The 'devolution' of wildlife management in southern Africa

James Murombedzi

INTRODUCTION

The idea of integrating conservation with development is an important theme in debates about conservation in Africa. It offers the lure of a win–win solution to the problem of conflict between the interests of wildlife conservationists and rural people, and it fits the broader model of sustainable development (Adams, 2001). The idea of consumptive use of wild resources by communities themselves, community-based natural resource management (CBNRM), to provide both incomes to rural people and sustained populations of wildlife species is central to the notion that wildlife should pay its way (see, for example, Western et al, 1994; Hulme and Murphree, 2001). In southern Africa, debate about CBNRM centres on the experience of the Zimbabwean Communal Area Management Programme for Indigenous Resources (CAMPFIRE), and analagous policies in countries such as Namibia (Olthof, 1995; Hasler, 1996; Murombedzi, 1999; 2001; Jones, 2001; Bond, 2001).

However, the implementation of CBNRM policies in southern Africa cannot be understood except in the context of the broader politics of land. The post-independence political settlements of those southern African countries whose colonial histories are histories of settler expropriation (principally, Namibia, South Africa and Zimbabwe) are centrally concerned with protecting the property rights of the settler class. The state's capacity to implement meaningful land reform is severely constrained by the nature of these constitutional dispensations, as well as by the pressure brought on the state by the ' international community', through aid or the threat to withhold it, to respect the constitutions and the so-called 'rule of law' (that is, legal protection of colonial property relations). The Lancaster House Constitution, which defined the transition process from Rhodesia to Zimbabwe, made provision for a limited transfer of land from the settler colonial class on a market driven basis, while at the same time making it impossible for independence government to change that aspect of the constitution for the first ten years of its existence. Similarly, the independence constitution of Namibia, negotiated between the liberation movement in Namibia and the South African land and other property-owning classes, guaranteed the property rights of mostly white South Africans in Namibia. Section 25 (1) of the South Africa constitution is typical: 'No one may be deprived of property except in terms of the law of general application, and no law may permit arbitrary deprivation of property.'

Yet, the liberation struggles of these societies were also fought on the logic of freeing the land and restoring it to its rightful owners. The oral histories of most communities in these countries remain histories of the brutal force used by the colonial state to dispossess them and create new property rights for its citizens. Thus, the fighters in Zimbabwe's liberation war, for instance, were referred to as *Vana Vevhu* (children of the soil). The post-colonial state in southern Africa is, in effect, tasked with the responsibility of protecting and ensuring colonial property rights regardless of how these rights were acquired in the first place, and in direct contradiction to the ideals of the liberation movement, which brought this state into being. The denial of land and resource rights to the indigenous populations is the fundamental injustice of these post-colonial dispensations.

The post-colonial state has to control demands for land and other property rights by its ' indigenous' citizens – the erstwhile subjects of the colonial state – and to channel them into 'development' initiatives that do not threaten (and may sometimes even reinforce) colonial land divisions. This is a problem akin to the 'native question' that faced the colonial powers in the first place, and that was partially resolved through native administration (Mamdani, 1996). In dealing with this problem of controlling popular demand for an overhaul of colonial property rights, while at the same time extending some land and resource control to indigenous citizens, the post-liberation state has not sought to change the colonial dispensation. Rather, it has maintained, in some cases even perfected, colonial practices of resource control. While it has espoused the rhetoric of devolution, it has continued to strengthen colonial institutions, including traditional authority (as redefined by colonial indirect rule imperatives), as a way of exerting and increasing its own control over the countryside. Despite the discourses of 'communal tenure' and devolution to local communities, the state has also retained rights to and control over the so-called 'communal lands' of the region.

In this regard, devolved natural resources management, particularly through community-based natural resource management (CBNRM) programmes and projects, has become a convenient intervention. It gives the state the opportunity to extend its control over certain economically and financially valuable resources while, at the same time, appearing to be empowering local 'communities' regarding the control and use of these resources. Invented by well-meaning donor organizations, CBNRM in southern Africa has thus come to disguise the real dilemma faced by the state, which is powerless to resolve the contradictions of colonial property rights. At the same time, its centralizing tendencies lead the state to want to increase its control over the countryside (Murombedzi, 1994). Thus, CBNRM in this region basically means enabling the communities to acquire property rights on land to which they were assigned by colonial history, without questioning the legitimacy of such historical origin, or challenging the property rights of the colonial classes. CBNRM, in effect, acts to pre-empt such demand. The implementation of CBNRM tends to strengthen local government in the same way that native administration was strengthened by various colonial property laws that placed ownership of communal property rights in the hands of the 'Tribal Trusts'.

The CBNRM programmes of the region are articulated on a logic of poverty alleviation and development. Control over natural resources is devolved to local communities in order to create new opportunities so that communities can benefit economically from their exploitation. In practice, this means that these communities, particularly those involved in devolved wildlife management enterprises, enter into arrangements with private-sector safari operators to utilize these resources, usually through safari-hunting and related enterprises, in exchange for concession and other fees. In return, the communities guarantee unlimited access to these concessioned resources for the private operators. These guarantees are usually in the form of restricting all local contestations for access to the same resources, and usually involve increasing the policing by the communities of the use of the resources in question by individual community members. Thus, local game guards and committees are created to develop new forms of policing and to enforce regulations that secure the access of private operators to the 'communal' wildlife resource. The effect of this new arrangement is to increase the access of the private sector (typically representing white sectional interests) to the previously restricted 'communal' resources.

Three propositions are advanced in this chapter. Firstly, the devolution of 'rights' and control over natural resources in southern Africa, and the associated CBNRM projects and programmes, have the effect of extending and strengthening the state's control over the countryside through the strengthening of rural local government, the creation of new community institutions, and land-use planning. Secondly, the devolved natural resources management programmes function to strengthen and reinforce colonial racial and class patterns of access to, and use of, the natural resources in question. Thirdly, devolved natural-resources use has the effect of curtailing accumulation by individual households in the communities who gain new rights to natural resources, rather than promoting significant benefits for these households, as claimed. The Zimbabwean CAMPFIRE programme will be used as a case in point.[1]

THE COLONIAL STATE, LAND AND NATURAL RESOURCES

Southern Africa today, and especially Zimbabwe, South Africa and Namibia, is characterized by a distinctive dual land-tenure system, with individual freehold tenure for a 'modern', mostly white, farming sector and 'communal tenure' for the 'traditional', exclusively black, farming sector. The historical origins of this inequitable land division are well documented. From the 1890s, the power of the settler colonial state in southern Africa grew on the basis of the state's control of land use and land tenure. The central concern of the state was land distribution, with the aim of disenfranchising the indigenous population and creating a large pool of labour. Thus, the so called 'communal lands' of the region refer to those areas, formerly known as reserves and later as tribal trust lands, or *Bantustans*, that were created for the African population through colonial expropriation of lands for white settlers, and through subsequent policies aimed at creating reserves of African labour and at undermining African agricultural self-sufficiency (Phimister, 1986).

In this scheme, native administration developed with dual objectives. Firstly, it sought to limit accumulation by individuals through expropriation, taxation and other extra-economic forms of coercion, thereby forcing them into wage labour in settler-colonial enterprise. Secondly, native administration was a means of streamlining the administration of the reserves through the cooptation of existing institutional frameworks within the colonial administration through a system of indirect rule.

The colonial process of establishing state ownership and control over natural resources was, in essence, one of readjusting the power of the state with respect to local communities regarding the use and management of those resources. This consisted of the disempowerment of the local communities and the concentration of power in the state and its agencies. The loss of the communities' capacity to manage natural resources was therefore preceded by a capture of power over these same resources by the state. The disempowerment of local communities by the colonial state was achieved largely through the destruction of local institutional arrangements for natural resources management. In particular, local people's rights to natural resources were appropriated by the colonial state and vested largely with native administrators. Local institutions themselves atrophied through desuetude, largely because they became irrelevant due to their replacement by state institutions. At the same time, however, the colonial state did not necessarily develop the capacity to replace the existing local institutions, with the result that resource use increasingly occurred without management in the communal tenure regimes of the region. The resultant resource degradation contributed to driving the natives off the land and into wage labour; this could not have unduly concerned the native administrators, at least initially.

It is evident that even as the state sought to assume greater control over local natural resource use by local communities, this did not diminish the importance of these resources to the sustenance of local livelihoods. It has been demonstrated that where resources have been key to local production systems or livelihoods, local communities have invested in developing and implementing appropriate regimes for managing the use of these resources (Scoones and Wilson, 1989). While, in some instances, local people did respond to state control by devising new mechanisms to manage their own use of resources that were critical to their livelihoods, in most instances resource use continued without appropriate management.

THE POST-COLONIAL STATE AND LAND TENURE

The issue of land tenure (ownership, control, access and use of land), together with the extraction of surplus through extra-economic forms, are the most important aspects of the agrarian question in southern Africa today. These questions have their origins in the land appropriation strategies of colonialism, and the subsequent land policies adopted by successive colonial regimes, which involved the alienation of land from the indigenous populations and its concentration in the hands of settler farmers (or large companies). In most of southern Africa today, land distribution continues to demonstrate a distinctly dualistic nature, between so called 'modern' and 'traditional' sectors. The modern sector typically comprises land held under freehold or leasehold tenure, mostly by the white settler farmers, while the 'traditional' sector is primarily made up of the indigenous populations, supposedly engaging in subsistence agriculture. Thus, an enduring impact of settler colonialism has been the creation of racially based land-distribution and tenure systems.

Current concerns with land reform across post-independence Africa include land ownership, distribution and access; land-use patterns and policy options for optimizing sustainable land use; legal and institutional frameworks and processes governing land administration; land markets; and rural labour processes. There is considerable debate, particularly in Zimbabwe, concerning the exact nature and characteristics of the tenure system operating in the so-called communal areas today. According to Cheater (1989), the current definition of communal tenure is largely normative and based upon an ideological construct, starting in the colonial era, to rationalize the racial division of land. It was also designed to create an effective basis for the indirect control of land and natural resources by the colonial state through the chiefs, and was continued by the post-colonial state in order to justify continued state control over land. It has also been observed that the current idea of communal tenure resulted from the colonial usurpation of land, and power over land, from the traditional chiefs. This created a power vacuum that the state was not anxious to fill, thus leading to local and consensual systems of land allocation and use (Ranger, 1985; 1988).

The growing power of the colonial state from 1893 onwards was based upon state control of land use and land tenure in a process where land distribution was the state's central concern (Drinkwater, 1991). Bruce (1998) and Scoones and Wilson (1989) maintain that the current system of allocating land to 'communities' originated with the colonial government, rather than prior to it. In this view, the attachment of communities to a discrete piece of land was a function of the colonial system of indirect rule, which passed control over land to chiefs and headmen as a substitute for direct political power. Pre-colonial self-allocation of land (Bruce, 1990), significant and recurring inequalities in land-holding size among the indigenous African population (Ranger, 1985; 1988), and African readiness to purchase land in freehold areas (Bourdillon, 1987) are all cited as suggesting that the communal nature of land tenure in Zimbabwe's communal areas may have been overstated.

While this debate has continued, however, several programmes ostensibly designed to improve the management of 'communally held natural resources' for community benefit have been developed and implemented in the region. CBNRM in southern Africa has tended to focus upon the development of programmes that address the use of specific high-value natural resources, particularly wildlife and trees. These programmes have tended to secure income-earning opportunities for a new entrepreneurial class, with its origins in the colonial settler class, allowing them to earn income from opportunities in the former native areas. It also creates the context for coopting at least some sections of the traditional authority, as corrupted by colonialism, in the management of these opportunities.

Thus, CBNRM policies affirm colonial dispossession. Regarding wildlife, in particular, colonial game practice has largely been retained intact by the post-colonial state because it seems to make good economic sense. The rich populations of 'game' in southern African countries seemed to convince the inheritor governments that tourism was a worthwhile sector of the post-colonial economy. Post-colonial governments have been attracted to this sector because of its ability to earn foreign exchange. Consequently, little attention is paid to legislation that restricts social access to game and associated resources, with the result that the wildlife industry in southern Africa has remained a class issue. CBNRM is justified in terms of a decentralization-devolution ethic, which questions the centralizing interests of the state (both pre- and post-colonial). However, it does not question the property rights in which decentralization occurs.

Land reform and CBNRM

Land-tenure reform redistributes not land, but rights in land. Similarly, resource-tenure reform redistributes rights to resources. The reform process constitutes adjusting the relative powers and responsibilities among the state, communities and individuals. To the extent that the region's CBNRM programmes constitute adjustments of the rights of the state vis-à-vis local communities regarding certain natural resources, they are, in fact, tenure reform programmes that attempt to reform the historical property relations of colonialism. CBNRM constitutes an adjustment of the relationship between the state and society regarding valuable natural resources located in the erstwhile reserves and *Bantustans*.

Another major problem is the absence of any legal status for the communities. This is only partially addressed in the devolved natural-resources management programmes in the region. However, these programmes typically devolve proprietorship of natural resources to some level or other of local government, and stop short of recognizing community rights to natural resources.

There is a tendency among practitioners and proponents of CBNRM to look to traditional authority as a natural repository of the community's authority system over natural resources. However, as with the 'community', there remains no clear definition of what 'traditional authority' is. The historical role of the state in designing, inventing, creating and recreating traditional authority to play certain specific roles is problematic. Starting with the colonial project of indirect rule, traditional authority in southern Africa has been engineered and re-engineered so many times that it is hardly fair to refer to the contemporary authority structures as 'traditional' at all. The concept of 'tribe' was a particularly useful tool for colonial indirect rule, and was also the basis upon which various tribal authorities and customary laws were created and enforced. Most CBNRM initiatives profess an intention to further develop and enhance the capacity of these tribal authorities to regulate and manage natural resource use. In my view, what is required are approaches that, at least, problematize the position and implications of tribal authority before identifying it as the necessary solution to the authority problem for natural resource management.

Of concern, also, is the continued dual legal systems that recognize customary law as some kind of ancillary legal system to which the more 'traditional' members of our society (that is, the black rural communities) can have recourse when it suits them and the state. The migrant wage-labour system continues to negate the customary law because migrants become subject to a different jurisprudence, while in wage employment, and typically choose not to be subject to customary law when it suits them (Mamdani, 1996). A further legal and policy problem concerns tenure. By implication, CBNRM operates within communal tenure regimes. Yet, communal tenure is hardly secure, as most legal systems in southern Africa do not provide for adequate security of tenure. This was deliberately so, to allow for forced removals, privatization and other development initiatives in both the colonial and post-colonial eras.

CAMPFIRE AND RESOURCE-MANAGEMENT INSTITUTIONS

In Zimbabwe, the post-colonial Communal Lands Act of 1982, in effect, vests ownership of communal lands and resources with the state, and assigns to rural district councils the power to regulate land holding and land use in the communal areas under their jurisdiction. According to the act, access to communal land is in terms of the customary law relating to the allocation, occupation and use of land. Rural district councils (RDCs) regulate land use in terms of communal land by-laws produced by the ministry of local government, which provides for the planning and control of land use within council areas.

In some RDCs, the constituency also includes owners and occupiers of alienated lands, held under private freehold or leasehold tenure. In such cases, the RDC has a dynamically different relationship to these private land-holders. In particular, private land-holders have full control over the planning and use of the land to which they have title or which they lease. The role of the RDC, in this case, is to provide services. This contradiction has resulted in tensions between the RDC and its constituencies. In South Africa, as the integration of the former *Bantustans* into the post-liberation state continues, no solution has yet been agreed regarding the question of local governance. Tensions continue to exist, especially between the traditional authorities (more commonly referred to as 'tribal authorities'), 'modern' local municipalities (with their origins in the apartheid era) and the state's own local councils.

Natural resource management in southern Africa has been interpreted to mean the management of natural resources through some formal project or programme, rather than the everyday interactions between people and natural resources in their daily struggle for livelihoods. Thus, CBNRM, in particular, refers to programmes that are usually sponsored by outsiders and backed by the state, through policy or legislation, or both. Such programmes tend to be dominated by the wildlife management programmes – the Communal Area Management Programme for Indigenous Resources (CAMPFIRE) in Zimbabwe, Living in a Finite Environment (LIFE) in Namibia, and the various game lodge and tourism-based development projects of South Africa. In the Zimbabwe case, the National Parks and Wildlife Act of 1975, as amended in 1982, gives appropriate authority over wildlife to the RDCs for the communal areas, and to the land-owners for the private/leasehold tenure sector. Communal residents typically do not determine how wildlife is going to be 'produced' and how the 'benefits' generated are to be utilized. These decisions tend to be made by the RDC and other 'outsiders'. The level of benefit is thus affected by policy decisions over which the 'wildlife producers' themselves have little or no control.

Moreover, communities also have to pay a variety of taxes and charges to the RDC for managing 'their' wildlife. Communities do not have the right to use wildlife, only the right to benefit from the use of wildlife by others. Owners and occupiers of private lands on, the other hand, can decide on appropriate wildlife uses without any external influences and are free to appropriate all the benefits of use, or to share some of these benefits with their communal lands neighbours in the case of 'conservancies'. In practice, then, appropriate authority has come to represent the decentralization of authority and control over wildlife only to the statutory land authorities with jurisdiction over communal lands – the RDCs.

Because of the absence of *formal* resource-management institutions in most communities, a significant component of implementing CAMPFIRE has been an institutional development programme aimed at creating new forms of communal organization for wildlife management. In practice, this has been implemented through the creation of village, ward and district wildlife management committees in a process led by the Zimbabwe Trust, a local non-governmental organization (NGO) that has become the leading implementing agency for CAMPFIRE. The new committees are, in effect, subcommittees of the devolved local government units, the village development committee (VIDCO), the ward development committee (WADCO) and the RDC. As such, they get their legal authority over wildlife through both the Parks and Wildlife Act and the Rural District Councils Act.

While this evolving institutionalization of wildlife management at the local level defines some local legal authority over the resource, the institutional development process itself has not developed into a process of defining local rights over the wildlife resource. Management has, instead, tended to be based upon RDC control over wildlife. As such, wildlife management has been completely divorced from other local systems of rights to communal resources. The institutional development programme has not attempted to identify existing ways by which communities manage other communal resources, to which they have rights (for example, grazing or trees), or to define a place for wildlife management within this system of communal rights.

Partly because of this, evidence suggests that most local people still do not view themselves as the joint owners of wildlife; rather, they continue to see it as a resource belonging to either the government or the RDC (Murombedzi, 1994). Because institutional development in CAMPFIRE has taken the form of creating *new* 'formal' institutions, it has tended to completely ignore the preponderance of *existing* traditional institutions in most land and resource-management situations in many communities in Zimbabwe today. This is largely because, in the absence of clear rights to wildlife for the local communities, institutional development has tended to be defined outside of the communities themselves, rather than to be responsive to internal micro-political dynamics within these communities. As a result, a lack of regard for local resource-management decision-making mechanisms has contributed to the alienation of communities from the CAMPFIRE initiative.

Traditional authorities continue to play a leading role in managing and regulating the use of communal resources. It has been demonstrated that where resources are critical to the household economy, communities will invest in their management (Scoones and Wilson, 1989). Typically, such management is undertaken through the operation of diffuse systems of rights to these resources, adjudicated locally by traditional leaders and authorities. Lack of recognition from government and programmes such as CAMPFIRE has not compromised traditional leaders' authority, particularly over land and natural resources (Ahmed, 1998). 'Traditional leadership draws much of its legitimate authority from its embeddedness in the social and cultural life of rural communities, where discourses of "tradition" associated with cultural identity are still persuasive for many' (Cousins, 1998).

To the extent that institutional development in CAMPFIRE ignores local rights and knowledge systems completely, it is fundamentally informed by a centralizing and 'modernizing' ethic. This constitutes a huge contradiction in a programme that is supposedly a decentralization programme, creating community forms of resource ownership.

CAMPFIRE AND DEVOLUTION

Attempts are currently underway in CAMPFIRE to stimulate the further devolution of authority over wildlife from the RDCs to the 'producer communities' (*CAMPFIRE News*, 1998, p8). The Tenure Reform Commission of 1994, for instance, recognizes that communal land tenure in Zimbabwe, in effect, gives all rights to communal lands to the government, and recommends that new village assemblies are created as communal property associations with clear and unambiguous rights to communal lands and resources. The commission bases this recommendation upon the operation of the CAMPFIRE programme, and its demonstration of the capacity of communities to control and manage resources over which they have clearly defined rights. However, as the foregoing section has demonstrated, the CAMPFIRE programme would itself benefit from the implementation of this recommendation, to the extent that it will define more clearly rights for local communities to wildlife.

It would appear that that CAMPFIRE has not sufficiently devolved rights in wildlife to local communities to the extent that these communities can use these rights to gain an increased stake in wildlife utilization enterprises at their multiple levels of value. Thus, communities have little control over wildlife management, little or no equity in wildlife utilization, and very few opportunities to provide goods and services to the wildlife utilization industry. In this regard, community participation in CAMPFIRE can be seen as constituting little more than the receipt of handouts.

It has been observed that attempts to entice people's participation in conservation through the distribution of revenues from some forms of resource utilization will not necessarily improve local stewardship of resources (regardless of the extent of these revenues), unless, at the same time, rights to these resources are devolved to local people. In this view:

> ...such benefactions exacerbate the land-owners' belief that they do, as an aspect of common sense and natural justice, have a prior right to both use and benefit from the natural resources on their land. Further, such benefit is inseparable from the powers of decision regarding general use that go with ownership (Parker, 1993, p3).

Because of the weak tax base of most local authorities, wildlife has become the most taxable commodity. For this reason, and also because of the traditional mistrust of local people by local government staff, it has become increasingly difficult to further devolve proprietorship of wildlife to local communities. The taxation of wildlife by local authorities has significantly reduced the levels of local financial and economic benefit, while, at the same time, facilitating continued local authority control over wildlife management. The inevitable result has been that nowhere in CAMPFIRE has wildlife come to represent a viable mechanism for household level accumulation. Consequently, CAMPFIRE is seen as beneficial not to the extent that it contributes to household incomes, because this is an insignificant contribution, but to the extent that it subsidizes the local authorities.

In CAMPFIRE, then, wildlife management continues to be driven, in the main, by external policy interests rather than responding to local dynamics stimulated by proprietorship. The RDCs, with appropriate authority, use this authority to provide services to a broad range of wildlife resource users, as well as to control potentially negative local community activities, such as livestock grazing and arable expansion. RDCs also serve to mediate conflicts between local and other resource users, as well as to regulate the conditions under which outsiders actually access the wildlife resources. In addition, the mitigation of local contestations for access to the wildlife resource, expressed primarily through poaching, is a major function of the appropriate authority.

CAMPFIRE AND THE SAFARI BUSINESS

CAMPFIRE's focus upon financial benefits appears to emphasize wildlife management for the purpose of supplying the market demands for safari-hunting and tourism. Consequently, the management of other natural resources upon which household livelihoods depends, perhaps to an even greater degree than wildlife revenues, is ignored. Thus, the greatest beneficiaries of the wildlife management services provided through CAMPFIRE are the safari operators, who benefit through increased security of access to the wildlife, as well as protection from the negative local community threats to wildlife through agriculture, poaching and so on. Land reorganization and land-use planning also ensure reasonable long-term security for wildlife habitat. Yet, communities do not manage natural resources in isolation. Systems of rights that determine the management of natural resources are diffuse; however, CAMPFIRE attempts to introduce an exclusive wildlife management regime without reference to these diffuse and nested systems of rights and management.

Employment is often cited as one of the benefits of CAMPFIRE. Although there has been no attempt to document the number of jobs created in the different communities who participate in the programme, it is quite evident that the safari industry is capital intensive rather than labour intensive. Furthermore, the actual management of wildlife by communities is undertaken by elected committees, rather than by dedicated organizations employing staff to undertake routine tasks. Thus, most local people volunteer, rather than get employed, in wildlife management in the CAMPFIRE programme. Moreover, the actual methods of wildlife utilization under CAMPFIRE are patently racist, and obviously alienating and humiliating for the local populations. The safari operation industry continues to be dominated by whites, with very little participation of blacks in the skilled worker categories of these operations (hunters and guides). The majority of black employees in the safari industry are cooks and camp attendants. The success of most safari hunts depends upon the tracking skills and knowledge of local conditions and animal habits of the local trackers, who are an integral part of every safari operation. Yet, these trackers are treated as unskilled labourers, rather than being recognized as qualified guides. Besides constituting another instance of devaluing local environmental knowledge, this treatment of local trackers also demonstrates the contempt with which local people tend to be regarded by the white safari operators.

The historical reasons for the domination of the safari industry by whites originate in the appropriation of rights from the local population by the colonial state. The racist conditions under which the safari industry in Zimbabwe developed exist to this day almost unchanged. Furthermore, in their desire to perpetuate the myth of a wild, pristine African experience for their clients, most safari operations prohibit all local access into the safari-hunting camps, except as lowly paid labourers. Livestock and dogs are shot or otherwise harassed if they are seen as interfering with hunting operations (they indicate the presence of human life in the 'pristine' wilderness).

Individual safari operators also impose restrictions upon local activities in the hunting areas, ranging from total prohibition of any form of access to some forms of negotiated access. This can only be possible because of the lack of clarity regarding the nature of local rights to these resources in the CAMPFIRE programme. In the hunting operations themselves, where locals have insisted that members of the local communities should be attached to hunting operations for monitoring or training purposes, there is no evidence that the so-called training programmes have actually resulted in any skills acquisition by the local people. To date, not a single community trainee in any of the CAMPFIRE training programmes has qualified as a guide. Locals attached to monitor the hunting operations are typically left stranded in the village due to 'lack of space for them in the hunting trucks'; consequently, the communities remain suspicious about what actually goes on out in the bush. Where local guides and monitors participate in the hunt, the treatment they receive is absolutely deplorable – they are viewed more as a nuisance than as an aspect of cooperation between hunter and community.

CAMPFIRE AND POVERTY

The poverty crisis facing rural households in Africa has been generally well documented. What is not as well documented, however, are the differential impacts of poverty on different households. One determining factor of such differentiation is micro-climatic conditions. The CAMPFIRE programme postulates that wildlife management is probably the most productive form of land use in marginal ecosystems. CAMPFIRE is thus being implemented predominantly in these marginal ecosystems, where there continue to be viable wildlife populations, and where there are obvious climatic limitations to arable agriculture and pastoralism. In essence, if CAMPFIRE is to become a viable land use in such areas, it must offer a potential solution for the crisis of accumulation to the residents of these areas. Accumulation means assigning social and economic resources to improving the production process, and has both qualitative and quantitative aspects. Quantitatively, accumulation means more implements, more land for arable agriculture, more marketing points, more inputs, and so on. Qualitatively, accumulation means the adoption of new and more sophisticated production technologies (mechanization, improved seed varieties, fertilizers, etc), better land protection, and the allocation of land to more productive uses (Barker, 1989).

Viewed through the lens of household accumulation, the premise of CAMPFIRE is that it will foster accumulation by allocating land to more productive land use (wildlife utilization) and by ensuring that the benefits of such land use accrue directly to the individual household. Consequently, the success of CAMPFIRE in stimulating household accumulation in the marginal ecosystems has to be tested against this premise. Wildlife management in CAMPFIRE, at least for the communities involved, means local programmes to enable the RDCs and communities to control arable expansion of agriculture, grazing and livestock, through collaboration in land-use planning. In a few areas, such as in Masoka, land-use planning is itself devolved to the local community, although this alone has been insufficient to stop the expansion of arable agriculture.

Elsewhere, wildlife management appears to entail the imposition of limitations on quantitative accumulation. There is sufficient evidence from the investment of CAMPFIRE dividends to demonstrate that accumulation for most households in the CAMPFIRE wards continues to be seen as a function of expanding arable agriculture and investment in livestock. In most communal areas, this accumulation depends upon access to off farm incomes. Wildlife incomes, on average, are too insignificant to constitute a source of accumulation capital for most CAMPFIRE households. However, at the community level, wildlife revenues can constitute a source of capital for qualitative accumulation, mainly through the investment of revenues in providing agricultural services (marketing points, warehouses, sources of inputs and food processing technology).

In quantitative terms, available evidence suggests that CAMPFIRE implementation has actually constituted a constraint on the ability of households to accumulate through arable expansion or the acquisition of livestock. This has occurred through restrictions on the importation of cattle and donkeys (for draught power) into those CAMPFIRE districts that did not have them because of tsetse fly infestation, as well as through restrictions on arable agricultural expansion achieved through land-use planning. Wildlife revenues have tended to be used as a carrot to encourage individuals to conserve wildlife while land-use planning has been used as the stick to prevent the expansion of agriculture and to control domestic livestock.

CONCLUSIONS

In small, discrete and relatively homogenous communities with access to expansive wilderness, CAMPFIRE has been a phenomenal success in terms of stimulating people to demand more secure rights to the wildlife resources from local authorities. In such communities, it is evident that as community rights over resources become clearer, and control enhanced, communities also begin to exert considerable influence over the actual utilization of the resource itself. The cases of Mahenye and Masoka are especially instructive (Murombedzi, 2001; Murphree, 2001). According to Bond (1997), 'there are a relatively small number of wards in which benefit per household is very high and comparable with average household income figures for households in semi-arid communal lands'. In such cases, CAMPFIRE appears to have been particularly successful as a means for qualitative accumulation. Wildlife revenues have been invested in the development of agricultural infrastructure and equipment, which, in turn, are seeing as having the potential to improve the conditions for individual household quantitative accumulation.

In both respects, then, it would appear that local valuations of CAMPFIRE relate to the ways in which CAMPFIRE revenues become available for individual household accumulation. Bond (1997) further observes that ' in at least 50 per cent of the wards, the revenue earned from wildlife can at best only be considered supplementary to other sources of income'. In such cases, then, it is debatable whether, in fact, land-use allocation will be determined by local economic imperatives. It is more likely that the households in these wards are being constrained by RDC policies to participate in wildlife management, and that the CAMPFIRE programmes in such wards will be heavily contested.

It is doubtful that in situations where wildlife management only contributes marginally to the local and household economies, individuals will be motivated to manage the wildlife beyond a certain minimum threshold. That minimum threshold is determined by existing coercive measures exercised by the appropriate authority, rather than by individual commitment to the resource. In other words, where wildlife costs continue to be greater than the benefits, management of wildlife will continue to be top down, authoritarian and coercive, and communities are not likely to seek greater rights to the wildlife resource.

Given the nature of wildlife management programmes in southern Africa, as characterized by the development of the CAMPFIRE programme in Zimbabwe, it is evident that these programmes play a dual role for the post-liberation state. Firstly, they serve to re-channel the legitimate demands for land reform in the direction of secondary rights to natural resources, and thereby act to defer local struggles for land. Secondly, they also serve to provide local authorities with new sources of revenue. These are then applied to increasing the control of the state over local communal lands and natural resources through a process of creating new 'democratic' institutions that function to implement state programmes at the local level.

NOTES

1   The National Parks and Wildlife Act of 1975, amended in 1982, gives appropriate authority over wildlife to rural district councils, allowing communities to profit from safari hunting revenues.

REFERENCES

Adams, W M (2001) *Green Development: environment and sustainability in the Third World*, second edition. Routledge, London

Ahmed, M (1998) 'Urban and peri-urban land tenure in southern Lusophone Africa: lessons from post socialist countries' experiences' in *Proceedings of the International Conference on Land Tenure in the Developing World with a Focus on Southern Africa*, University of Cape Town, Cape Town, pp10–20

Barker, J (1989) *Rural Communities under Stress: Peasant Farmers and the State in Africa*. Cambridge University Press, Cambridge

Bond, I (1997) 'An assessment of the financial benefits to households from CAMPFIRE: The wildlife benefit-cost ratio', *CAMPFIRE News*, 15 May 1997, CAMPFIRE Association, Harare

Bond, I (2001) 'CAMPFIRE and the incentives for institutional change' in D Hulme and M Murphree (eds) *African Wildlife and Livelihoods*. James Currey, Oxford, pp227–243

Bourdillon, M F C (1987) *The Shona Peoples*. Mambo Press, Gweru

Bruce, J W (1990) 'Legal Issues in Land Use and Resettlement', Background Paper for the Agriculture Division, Southern Africa Department of the World Bank, Zimbabwe Agriculture Sector Memorandum

Bruce, J W (1998) 'Learning from the Comparative Experience with Agrarian Land Reform' in *Proceedings of the International Conference on Land Tenure in the Developing World with a Focus on Southern Africa*, University of Cape Town, Cape Town, pp39–48

CAMPFIRE News (1998) 'Further devolution needed', *CAMPFIRE News* 17, CAMPFIRE Association, Harare

Cheater, A P (1989) 'The ideology of "communal" land tenure in Zimbabwe: mythogenesis enacted', *Africa*, vol 60, pp188–206

Cousins, B (1998) 'How do rights become real? Formal and informal institutions in South Africa's tenure reform program' in *Proceedings of the International Conference on Land Tenure in the Developing World with a Focus on Southern Africa*, University of Cape Town, Cape Town, pp88–100

Derman, B W (1990) 'The Unsettling of the Zambezi Valley: an examination of the Mid-Zambezi Rural Development Project', CASS Working Paper, Centre for Applied Social Sciences, University of Zimbabwe, Harare

Drinkwater, M (1991) *The State and Agrarian Change in Zimbabwe's Communal Areas.*
   Macmillan Publishing, London
Dzingirai, V (1994) 'Politics and Ideology in Human Settlement: getting settled in the
   Sokomena Area of Chief Dobola', CASS Working Paper, Centre for Applied Social
   Sciences, University of Zimbabwe, Harare
Farquharson, L (1993) *Commercial Wildlife Utilization in Zimbabwe: are commercial farms the
   appropriate model for CAMPFIRE?*, unpublished Masters thesis, McGill University,
   Montreal
Hasler, R (1996) *Agriculture, Foraging and Wildlife Resource Use in Africa.* Kegan Paul
   International, New York
Hulme, D and Murphree, M (eds) (2001) *African Wildlife and Livelihoods: The Promise and
   Performance of Community Conservation.* James Currey, Oxford
Jones, B (2001) 'The evolution of community-based approaches to wildlife
   management in Kunene, Namibia' in D Hulme and M Murphree (eds) *African
   Wildlife and Livelihoods: The Promise and Performance of Community Conservation.* James
   Currey, Oxford, pp160–176
Mamdani, M (1996) *Citizen and Subject: Contemporary Africa and the Legacy of Late
   Colonialism*, Princeton University Press, Princeton, New Jersey
Martin, R B (1986) *Communal Areas Management Program for Indigenous Resources
   (CAMPFIRE).* Government of Zimbabwe, Department of National Parks and
   Wildlife Management, Branch of Terrestrial Ecology, Harare
Moyo, S K (1998) Speech by S K Moyo, Minister of Mines, Environment and Tourism,
   reproduced in *CAMPFIRE News*, No 17, March 1988, p8
Murombedzi, J C (1992) 'Decentralization or Recentralization? Implementing
   CAMPFIRE in the Omay Communal Lands of the Nyaminyami District', CASS
   Working Paper, Centre for Applied Social Sciences, University of Zimbabwe,
   Harare
Murombedzi, J C (1994) *The Dynamics of Conflict in Environmental Management Policy in the
   Context of the Communal Areas Management Programme for Indigenous Resources.*
   Unpublished PhD thesis, University of Zimbabwe, Centre for Applied Social
   Sciences, Harare
Murombedzi, J C (1999) 'Devolution and stewardship in Zimbabwe's CAMPFIRE
   Programme', *Journal of International Development*, vol 11, pp287–294
Murombedzi, J (2001) 'Why wildlife conservation has not economically benefited
   communities in Africa' in D Hulme and M Murphree (eds) *African Wildlife and
   Livelihoods: The Promise and Performance of Community Conservation.* James Currey,
   Oxford, pp208–226
Murphree, M W (1997) 'Congruent Objectives, Competing Interest and Strategic
   Compromise: Concept and Process in the Evolution of Zimbabwe's CAMPFIRE
   Programme', Paper presented to the Conference on Representing Communities:
   Histories and politics of Community-Based Resource Management, Helen, Georgia,
   June
Murphree, M W (2001) 'A case study of ecotourism development from Mahenye,
   Zimbabwe' in D Hulme and M Murphree (eds) *African Wildlife and Livelihoods: The
   Promise and Performance of Community Conservation*, James Currey, Oxford, pp177–194
Olthof, W (1995) 'Wildlife resources and local development: experiences from
   Zimbabwe's CAMPFIRE Programme' in J P M Breemer, C A van den Drijver, and
   L B Venema (eds) (1995) *Local Resource Management in Africa.* Wiley, Chichester

Parker, I (1993) 'Natural justice, ownership and the CAMPFIRE Programme',
unpublished essay, CASS Library, University of Zimbabwe, Harare

Phimister, I (1986) 'Discourse and the discipline of historical context: conservationism
and ideas about development in Southern Rhodesia', *Journal of Southern Africa Studies*,
vol 12, pp264–275

Ranger, T O (1985) *Peasant Consciousness and Guerrilla War in Zimbabwe*. James Currey,
London

Ranger, T O (1988) 'The Communal Areas of Zimbabwe', *Land in Agrarian Systems
Symposium*. University of Illinois, Urbana-Champaign

Scoones, I and Wilson, K (1989) 'Households, Lineage Groups and Ecological
Dynamics: issues for livestock development' in B Cousins (ed) *People, Land and
Livestock: proceedings of a workshop on the socio-economic dimensions of livestock production in
Zimbabwe's Communal Lands*. GTZ and Centre for Applied Social Sciences, University
of Zimbabwe, Harare

Western, D, White, R M and Strum, S C (eds) (1994) *Natural Connections: perspectives in
community-based conservation*. Island Press, Washington, DC

Chapter 7

Decolonizing Highland conservation

Mark Toogood

INTRODUCTION

For the last 35 years, ecologists and conservationists working for government organizations in Scotland, and in the Highlands and Islands of the north and west of the country, in particular, have been publicly criticized by sectors of society as diverse as nationalists, the hunting lobby and crofters. These criticisms are broadly of two interrelated types. On the one hand, there is criticism of how state conservation ' interferes' with, and exercises control over, other land uses and ways of life in the Highlands and Islands, especially with small-scale land uses, such as crofting, and the large, dominant sporting estates.[1,2] On the other hand, and more significantly, is the criticism of state conservation's own institutional culture, forms of scientific knowledge and assumptions about nature and society. The practices and ideology of this kind of conservation are widely regarded in Scotland as being at odds with widespread aspirations and advances towards rural development through land reform – a process that can be termed rural 'reconstructionism'.[3]

This chapter argues that these critiques of Scottish statutory conservation cannot be understood without reference to several interleaved dimensions of the politics of nature and land ownership in the Highlands.

Firstly, few issues in Scotland are as sensitive as land ownership and its management. This centrality of land represents a distinctive political awareness, rooted in collective memory of the formalization and concentration of land ownership in the Highlands and Islands that took place during the 18th and 19th centuries. Present-day political issues surrounding land ownership are thus directly linked to the historic shift from small communal settlement to large, private agricultural and sporting estates; the concurrent conversion of rural society and economy; and the subsequent transformation of nature, both literally and symbolically. This chapter examines this politicized imagination of the Highlands and, in particular, how it relates to three actors central to land reform politics:

- the estates – the most historically powerful land-owning group, who regard themselves arbiters of the present and future stewardship of the Highlands;
- the crofters, their supporters and Gaeltacht culture generally – increasingly regarded in Scotland as inherently the rightful guardians of the Highland environment;[4] and
- the state conservation system – regarded by many as a bureaucratic 'outsider'.

Secondly, the authority of statutory conservation in the Highlands and Islands cannot be examined without placing it within the context of the resurgence of cultural nationalism in Scotland during the last 20 years, and an attendant rush of new ideas and debate about land reform, the environment and its future management. The Scottish parliament, established in July 1999, has put in place legislation that emphasizes 'community' ownership and 'community-led planning' as the basis of rural development in the Highlands and Islands.[5] However, institutional state conservation, narrow minded in its expertise and burdened by a lack of reflexivity about its basic assumptions and practices, is frequently identified as a *barrier* to renewal – as more of an 'ecological despot' than a catalyst for reconstruction.

Thirdly, this chapter is also concerned with how state conservation as a modern, progressive social institution has, however unconsciously, established a rationalized, ecologically defined and frequently asocial construction of nature. This both reflects conservation's colonial legacy and, because of its narrow focus on 'science' and 'heritage', has, at the very least, side-stepped issues of power and justice connected with the land. At worst, it has reinforced the construction of the Highlands most closely associated with the large estates and their practices.

In particular, this chapter will examine the culture of state conservation as one that has frequently failed to engage meaningfully with people and organizations outside of scientific and official circles. This culture is exemplified by the official concept of 'value' being defined in technical and rationally defended terminology that often distances and devalues other forms of expression. Despite the recent efforts of the current state conservation body, Scottish Natural Heritage (SNH), to produce objectives and mission statements that suggest a more human-centred and participatory approach, conservationists, acculturated to bureaucratic and inflexible modes of thinking, are arguably still limited by assumptions and practices that fail to resonate with a dynamic Scottish civic culture.[6]

Before beginning a discussion of the above issues, it is necessary to specify how such concerns can be framed in terms of decolonization. As certain post-colonial writers have observed, the historical experience of countries such as Scotland and Ireland can be properly considered as one of colonization (Said,

1993; Williams and Chrisman, 1993). The term colonization in this sense relates to the Scottish experience of political, institutional and cultural authority by England. Many of the issues raised by post-colonial critiques of the structures of colonialism (language, resistance, nationalism, migrancy and diaspora) are directly relevant when considering how this experience shapes modern Scotland. Yet, post-colonialism offers a set of concepts too sweeping to use unproblematically in relation to Scotland. From one point of view, Scots may consider themselves a colonized people; yet, from another view, in other parts of the British Empire, Scots prospered under colonial regimes and had a significant role as a driving force of colonialism. It is therefore necessary to specify, at the outset, that the 'decolonizing frame' which this chapter is concerned with is contingent and relates specifically to the relationship between the key social groupings named above, their historic and symbolic relation to the Highlands, their material practices, and their bounded areas of social knowledge.

IMAGINING THE HIGHLANDS

For people around the world, as well as for the population of Britain and Scotland, the Highlands and Islands have long been symbolic of Scotland, as a whole. Historically, they have been imagined through the romantic arts, tourism, film and TV, and associated with a range of earnest and ironic ersatz representations and iconography that include Walter Scott's novels, the clan system, tartans, bagpipes and Highland games – and, not least, an apparently unique natural environment of glens, lochs and *beinns*, and the habitats given their common name by the hunting traditions of the large estates: deer forest, salmon rivers, grouse moor. This section delineates two distinctive constructs of the Highlands and Islands. It is valid to do this here because these arrays of symbols, beliefs and iconography are directly relevant to the politics of land, nature and society in the contemporary context.

The history of the Highlands is therefore briefly examined in terms of how that history relates both to the iconography of 18th-century 'Highlandism' and 19th-century 'Balmoralism'. These are processes that have, in many respects, come to be regarded as *the* Highlands, rather than as historically specific forms of discourse that naturalize the form of land ownership, landscapes and practices of the current sporting estate system. This section also explores the construction of the Highlands, associated with the material history and popular memory of clearance, the disenfranchisement associated with contemporary resistance to the estates, nationalism and the process of reformism.

To understand why the Highlands are materially and symbolically contested, it is necessary to sketch out briefly the history of ideas relating to it. From the mid 18th century, British attitudes to the people and landscape of the Highlands of Scotland began to be transformed so that, by the early 19th century, wider Scottish cultural identity came to be synonymous with the symbols and landscapes of the Highlands. Until this transformation, popular and elite society in Lowland Scotland and England alike had regarded the Highlands as alien and hostile. The people were judged inferior, backward and untrustworthy, and the landscape as barren, ugly and desolate. This change of attitudes is significant because it was immediately preceded by open conflict: the Jacobite rebellion of 1745 marked the last of a number of risings involving Highland clans against the British Crown.[7]

The absorption of Highland symbols, such as the kilt and tartans, and the elevation of its people and landscape to romantic icons was ' invented' by Lowland elites and the English upper classes as the foundation of a fresh Scottish identity (Womack, 1989). However, this process of 'Highlandism' was deeply ironic in that it:

> *...took off precisely at the same time that commercial landlordism, market pressures and clearances were destroying the old order in northern Scotland. Indeed...some of the main protagonists of this new and fashionable traditionalism were themselves Highland proprietors who had long ceased to be clan chiefs and were now becoming rapacious improving landowners* (Devine, 1999, p233).

During this period, Anglicized clan chiefs and new landlords and land-owners from Lowland Scotland and England, while laying claim to, and adapting, the symbols and culture of Highland life for their own ends, also exploited the rights that ownership gave them over their tenants. These customary powers were used to 'modernize' land use, destroying small-scale subsistence and communal land use in favour of profit-focused, privatized, ranch-style farming of sheep and cattle in order to take advantage of the market of industrializing cities in Lowland Scotland and northern England. The tenant farmers and land-holders affected were not protected by common law, or by state or wider public concern. They were subject to a system of feudal land rights, clan custom and duty to protect their chiefs' interests, a system controlled by the landlords themselves. This infamous period of rural social change in the Highlands is known as the Clearances – the injury and sorrow of which is still felt by many Scots, both in Britain and elsewhere in the world.[8]

It may be remarkable to some that areas of industrializing colonial countries in Europe were themselves affected by processes often associated only with colonized countries or internal frontier areas in countries such as the US. In the case of the Highlands, such colonial processes included the imposition of drastic agricultural change, minimal property rights for local inhabitants, social disenfranchisement and forced evictions, males beholden to military service, and the establishment of categories of land primarily for the use of elites. Craig (1990, p7) comments:

> *In the aftermath of [1745], the Highland chiefs evolved into landlords, bent on maximizing the income from their estates. Big sheep from the Lowlands,*

> *often managed by Lowland or English farmers and their shepherds, invaded a*
> *way of life in which families with small lands grew their own food and fattened*
> *black cattle for the market. The big sheep, caoraich mhòr, must winter on*
> *the best grass – the glen bottoms, lochside meadows and coastal machair where*
> *the villages had been... From the early 1800s onwards, peaking after 1815*
> *and again after the Potato Famine in 1846, the estate managers drove the*
> *families out by the thousand, serving eviction orders, using fire and force if*
> *need be, and they joined the influx to the industrial cities, the efflux to the*
> *New World and the Antipodes.*

The history of the estate system is one in which the large sheep estates that replaced the crofting townships through clearance were themselves, in turn, partly replaced by sporting estates. Their origin is situated in the process of the 'Balmoralization' of the Highlands from about 1840, when wealthy aristocrats and industrialists, following Queen Victoria, adopted the fashion of Highlandism and brought up the estates to create a world based upon hunting and their own version of Highland tradition.

During the era of Balmoralization, the fashion for the Highlands spread throughout the world, and travel to Highlands from this period, for Scots, English and for wealthy classes from overseas, can be regarded as producing one of the key effects of colonialism in the Highlands. 19th-century travel in pursuit of aesthetic experience, whether to the Highlands of Scotland, the African savanna or the Canadian north, is one of the principle discourses of imperialism by which peoples living in 'remote', 'wild', 'spiritually uplifting' places were ennobled and exoticized as uncorrupted peoples, repositories of tradition and value. This process made such places functionally 'unreal': they became places of escape for the estate owner, traveller and tourist; in so doing, they became effectively marginalized from the broader political and socio-economic realities that determined their existence and future (Pratt, 1992; Gilroy, 2000; MacDonald, 2001).

The historical legacy of this process in Scotland is that land ownership and, therefore, control of much of the Highland socio-economy are concentrated into relatively few estates. Crofting itself is a form of tenure that was established in the late 19th century after the enclosure of common land, and is widely regarded as a tardy response to clearances. In a recent survey, it was estimated that 343 people or bodies own more than half of all private rural land in Scotland, with 85 estates accounting for one third of the land area of the Highlands and Islands (Cahill, 2001).

The large estates, therefore, have a central position in the debate about current land use and land reform. They have been the subject of considerable criticism for a historical responsibility for the creation of an impoverished ecological community, and for feeding a myth of a backward and romanticized Highlands that has contributed to poor social and economic development in the region. The estates are also of key significance in this imagination of the Highlands because of their iconic status (Toogood, 1996; Darier, Tabara and

Toogood, 1999). This iconography has symbolic force in two ways. Firstly, the estates symbolize status nationally and internationally, and wealthy overseas owners are regularly attracted to the market in these estates as a form of power: 'our country remains the last place in Europe where a rich man can buy a large chunk of wilderness to act out his dreams of owning a kingdom' (Hunter, 1997). Secondly, they are symbolic in the sense that an elite group of people enact, reproduce and consume the Highland myth as explained above.

In the context of resistance to the estates, the Highland landscape and culture can be regarded, in one sense, as an 'ethnoscape': a mythic hybrid of nature and culture that contributes to a sense of the survival of 'Scottishness' during a period of 'Anglicization' of the landscape. This 'ethnoscape' has become essential to other ways of characterizing the land in that it gives shape to a sense of continuity in 'a manner that satisfies the drive for meaning by providing new identities that seem to be also very old, and restoring locations, social and territorial, that allegedly were the crucibles of those identities' (Smith, 1999, p62).

This examination of the history of the Highlands and Islands thus contributes a background to understanding the symbolically contested dimension of current social and land-use debates.

REFORMING THE LAND

The Scottish parliament is advancing legislation that promises to challenge the status of the sporting estate. The legislation makes provision to abolish the feudal law that endows land-owners with 'ancient' rights over tenants, and, perhaps more importantly, acknowledges the need for a shift from state-led planning towards encouragement of so-called community-based ownership and stewardship (Scottish Executive, 1999). Furthermore, a new Scottish Land Fund has been established to facilitate participation in land ownership and management.[9] The way to legislation has been paved by a succession of small rural communities running successful and often high-profile public campaigns to take control of land from landlords. Notable cases have included Borve and Annishadder crofting township on the Isle of Skye, North Assynt, the Isle of Eigg and Knoydart.

There has been widespread moral and financial support in Scotland for these community buy-outs. While the definition of the community in this context is often problematical and frequently romanticized, there is little doubt that these 'victories' would not have occurred without popular hostility to the recollection of clearance, discrimination and injury: 'The folk memory of this historical period is so strong that it engenders feelings of empathy, even solidarity, with any societal group appearing, however remotely and/or irrationally, to be attempting to redress these historical wrongs' (Rennie, 1998).

Andy Wightman in his book *Who Owns Scotland* (1996) describes the front line in the land debate. For reformers like him, the Highland sporting estate is a gratuitous indulgence that the term 'economy' ill fits because such estates are purely the extravagances of the wealthy. For such a system to be regarded as a rural economy is a misnomer that no rural development agency would consider as sensible or sustainable. This view of the estates tends to dominate both populist reports of the land-ownership debate in the media, as well as originating from those in positions of power within Scottish government. For example, James Hunter, the current chair of the Highlands and Islands Enterprise agency, has stated that 'there can be no future in Britain in the 21st century for a rural economy dependent on tweedy gentlemen coming from the south to slaughter our wildlife. That is not the way to run the Highlands and Islands' (reported in Wightman, 1996, p173).

On the other side of the divide, such sentiments have been countered by die-hard comments on behalf of land-owners who regard populist opinion as viewing the vast tracts of land under their ownership as some kind of natural paradise, relatively untouched by economic activity. They make the case that the traditional sporting estates offer a solution to many of the pressures that the Highlands face. They argue that the expensive management incurred by private land-owners should receive public support because if they were forced out, the public purse would be liable for such management (Wigan, 1998)

Some government-funded opinion, such as from the Community Land Unit, intimates that a prerequisite for sustainable rural community development could involve the break up of large estates (Highlands and Islands Enterprise, 2001). But if communities are to be handed a greater role in managing the land, then this also presents issues about the role of state institutions and bureaucracies, such as planning and, particularly, conservation expertise. The current situation is one that is evolving fairly rapidly, especially as Scottish government will have to attempt to resolve the contradiction that power cannot be handed to local communities 'without altering the fundamental rights of landowners to decide outcomes affecting communities' (Bryden and Hart, 2000, p115).

CONSERVATION, THE ESTATES AND CROFTING

Given that land is such a major issue in Scotland, it is to be expected that statutory conservation, concerned with 'heritage' and the management of wildlife, would have a role to play. This role, however, has generally been a very problematic one. State conservation in Scotland has a relatively poor relationship with both the sporting estates and with small-scale farmers and crofters. The estates have accused state conservation as interfering with private property rights and the hunting tradition, and, effectively, being a stalking horse for the further state control and public ownership of land. Conversely, state interference is also a complaint of crofters, who also regard state conservation as favouring large owners with conservation funding and advice. This section will examine both of these positions, turning first to statutory ecology and conservation's relationship with the estates.

State conservation in Great Britain and in Scotland, in particular, is based upon an accommodation with, rather than a challenge to, land-owners and managers. For example, from 1981, the legal designation of Sites of Special Scientific Interest (SSSIs) was based upon the principle that a land-owner should be compensated for profit foregone from any operation damaging to that interest, which they were proscribed from carrying out. This effectively provided an incentive for land-owners to threaten to carry out damaging operations. Other proposed designations did not make it as far as the statute book. At the time of the first UK government wildlife conservation legislation in 1949, there was a suggestion that national parks should be designated in Scotland as they were to be in England and Wales. The land-owning classes in Scotland were horrified that anything apparently so regulatory of their interests could be superimposed onto their Highlands. No national parks were declared. Instead, a particular view of the Highlands was advanced: that Highland Scotland was a picturesque wilderness, already benignly stewarded and maintained by the land-owners of the Highlands and therefore hardly in need of such designation.

A more recent example of how state ecology and conservation have been the subject of criticism is in respect of the estates' management of red deer (*Cervus elaphus*) and the restoration of 'native' habitats. The stalking of red deer stags is of primary importance to both the estate system and the ecology of the Highlands and Islands. Red deer ranges can cover several estates and red deer belong to nobody in law, only coming into possession once shot. Hence the estates' traditional management of deer has been to encourage them to build up hind numbers, thereby, according to received wisdom, maximizing the number of shootable stags.

Red deer numbers in the Highlands have doubled since 1960 (Scottish Natural Heritage, 1994). This is one of the primary reasons for a clash with nature conservation interests, as conservationists contend, based upon a sizeable amount of research, that red deer graze and destroy regenerating trees, cause soil erosion and generally overgraze the open hills. They have long proposed that red deer numbers should be drastically cut by increased culls. Speaking about pinewood habitat, Max Nicholson, director general of the Nature Conservancy – the first state conservation body – demonstrated in forceful terms, now unlikely to pass any state conservationist's lips, the desire of conservationists to regulate human activity and to approach nature through science, and a conception of 'health' that would involve the restoration of past Highland environments:

> *Ruthless overburning and overgrazing by successive generations have so destroyed [and] degraded these forests that only the most painstaking research in the surviving remnants can show what they were like and how; by working with nature, part, at least, of the Highlands may be restored to health and freed from the curses of erosion, soil impoverishment and the spread of bracken and other consequences of wrong land use and mistaken land management* (Nicholson, 1957, p133).

The regeneration of the Caledonian pine forest, a habitat popularly understood, rightly or wrongly, to have rapidly declined as a result of the establishment of Highland sheep and sporting estates, has remained a priority for state conservationists (Aldhous, 1995; Ramsay, 1996) The idea of a Caledonian forest has considerable symbolic appeal in the context of Highland reconstruction because it is an apparently 'native' habitat whose decline parallels the disenfranchisement of Highland people from their lands (Toogood, 1995).

For the estates, the land degradation and forest regeneration issue causes internal division. For some, it suggests a need for the estate system to divest itself of the short-term approach of ' international playboy' landlords who buy into and leave the Highland land market on a whim. Instead, estates should embrace a new 'land ethic' based upon rural development and more 'ecologically guided' management that would create wider forest cover through comprehensive culling of red deer (Lister-Kaye, 1994). However, for the majority of the estates, conservationist views on red deer are symbolic of the wider struggle to influence the future character of the Highlands and to take control of rural politics (Wigan, 1993; 1998). For such voices, the dispute over what constitutes habitat health, and the preoccupation by state nature conservationists with establishing scientific definitions of habitat damage and of ecological limits to grazing, are ' in truth, a political struggle. Private land-owners' rights are being dismantled to make way for state control. The Trojan Horse is conservation' (Wigan, 2000, p66).

The role of non-statutory conservation bodies in the Highlands also needs to be alluded to in this context. The restoration of Caledonian forest and 'wildland' has been supported by a range of traditional voluntary conservation bodies, such as the World Wide Fund for Nature and the National Trust for Scotland, as well as newer organizations, such as the John Muir Trust. Such actors have themselves become players in the Highland land market, purchasing estates for conservation objectives, frequently with financial support from the state National Heritage Memorial Fund (NHMF). This development has been regarded as, on the one hand, another form of state interference by the estates and, on the other, as state-sponsored landlordism by land-reform and crofting groups. To land reformers, such organizations are viewed in a comparable way to Scottish Natural Heritage (SNH) – as distant elites who tend to use local communities, and who ideologically reinforce the power structures that lie at the root of the problem of disenfranchisement of Highland people and communities from the land.

Land reformers point out the contradiction that NHMF, advised by SNH, has been content to support the purchase of land by fund-raising voluntary organizations. However, where power was to be shared with local people – as in the case of the purchase of the Isle of Eigg – funding was not secured: conservation seems more likely to be successful if it does not involve local people. Where local active participation is assured, this is regarded as being superficial and in name only (Wightman, 1997). The persistence of the concentration of land-holding is regarded as a sign of the failure by Scottish government, including statutory conservation, to tackle the issue of private power over land.

CROFTERS AND CONSERVATIONISTS

The success of popular campaigns to back crofting communities to purchase 'their' land from estates illustrates the growth of 'reconstructionism' in rural Scotland. This reconstructionism fuses together a collective belief in three things:

- indigenous links to the land through memory, language and tradition;
- feelings of injustice about the concentration of ownership of the land and resources in the hands of 'outsiders';
- a discourse conceiving a Scottish 'traditional belief' that humans and nature are an indivisible whole.

At the heart of this:

> *The crofting community is seen by many as a natural champion in this reconstructionism, despite the last 200 years of decline, retrenchment and marginalization from what is perceived as the 'mainstream' of rural society. This tentative, vaguely described and even more vaguely rationalized image of the 'typical' Highland community can be considered as a powerful 'cultural landscape'. This term effectively conjures up the mental picture, or stereotypical image, of a landscape which has been created and/or maintained by the activities of the human community living and working on that land, and which lies close the heart of the imagination of the nation* (Rennie, 1998).

Crofting, as previously described, has taken on a broad symbolic resonance in Scotland as a whole. In a mixture of romanticism and cultural politics, crofting finds meaning as a practical model of democratic sustainable land use and economy. Most of rural Scotland is dominated by capital-intensive farming, subsidized by the European Union Common Agricultural Policy (CAP); on average, Scottish farm holdings are five times the size of those in continental Europe. In contrast to intensive land use, crofts are held up as a 'model for integrating social and environmental values with agricultural activities' (A Raven, 1999, p129). This assigned role places high expectation on crofting, locating it both as a venerated way of life and a spring of moral significance in relation to the land.

The crofting position is one that contests both the positions of state conservation and the estates (MacDonald, 1998). While the 'crofting community' itself is fairly heterogeneous in terms of socio-economic status, its self-definition of itself is one of common history, culture and values. This identity is activated in reaction to other groups. It also has a common voice with respect to two issues. The first, as reported above, is about access to land and self-determination in managing resources. The second is the challenge to SNH as the beacon of good conservation practice in the Highlands.

There have been at least two decades of hostility by crofters to the designation of protected areas in the Highlands, as well as a general enmity towards state conservation's self-assured expertise, bureaucratic remoteness and ' interference' in the use of the land. This is sometimes framed simply in terms of environmental protection of nature, imposing extra costs on crofting activity. A fairly recent example were the extra costs the Assynt Crofters' Trust had to bear when planning a small-scale hydroelectric power unit because of SNH's concerns about the potential effects of the scheme on the breeding habitat of a pair of black-throated divers (*Gavia artica*).[10]

However, this critique runs deeper. In state conservation discourse, the traditional cultural use of land and the crofters' use of the land are considered a general threat to nature. This is particularly so in the legal designation of SSSIs, where deviations from prescribed activities are described as 'operations likely to damage' (OLD) the scientific interest.[11] While these constraints apply to land-owners and managers of SSSIs, wherever they are, what is significant is that for crofters they are regarded not only as official interference, but as betraying an outsider's ignorance of their role as a living society who had survived many assaults on its integrity. Conservation is therefore subject to a twofold criticism: firstly, that it is statutory scientism, legalism and bureaucracy; secondly, because of the ignorance and implicit lack of respect for crofting culture and tradition that is perceived as tacit within the approach of institutionalized conservation in Scotland. These criticisms are compounded by the reporting, in the media, of the former practice of state conservation agencies in compensating land-owners for profits foregone should they not be able to carry out an OLD. Well-organized large land-owners have, in the past, been able to claim huge financial recompense for refraining from felling an ancient woodland, or damming a loch, for example. The rhetoric in the pro-crofting media is, thus, of the 'aristocratic villain' sanctioned by 'state bureaucracy' to benefit from ruining the ' indigenous heritage'.

The issue of place is quite central to this decolonizing framing because, in the Gaelic culture of the Highlands and Islands, place and land are central to identity formation and reproduction. Place does not become a particular issue until powerful forces, such as the legal, technical discourse of institutional conservation, represent place as natural space through a process of survey evaluation and designation. The social content of these places is then disengaged from their location by scientific representations and designations. The scientific and partitioning approach of nature conservation, although underlain by a complex of motives that are non-scientific, can be contrasted with the Gaelic Highland tradition of poetry and song as being too self-aware, too distant from such heritage. The designation of space into ordered categories, such as SSSIs and National Nature Reserves (NNRs), and giving account of nature in conceptual terms such as biodiversity, sustainability and even conservation itself, lacks connection with the immediate experience of nature in the context of this culture.

This dissociation of understanding between crofters and state conservation can be taken further. Ecology and conservation are a particular form of knowledge and practice that bring together a complex set of scientific, aesthetic, progressive and legal ideas that interleave with each other. Its scientific framing of issues, classification of species and land, and so forth, is based upon the rational authority of science and also upon (national and European) legal frameworks. As such, this authority is a system that mediates between nature and people. It is a form of power over nature and society that is often naturalized. The 'neutral' pursuit of ecological knowledge and the definition of the limits of environmental systems, as well as the attribution of value to species and habitats are presented as a primary basis for what constitutes 'natural heritage'. As Fraser MacDonald argues, this form of natural heritage is then disseminated in conservation texts and communications as '*our* heritage', '*national* heritage' or even '*world* heritage', thereby linguistically distancing 'heritage' from its local meaning and geographical context (MacDonald, 1998, p240).

Conservation's representation of the Highlands and Islands is also ambivalent. The use, in conservation texts, of 'classic' Highland imagery is largely from a picturesque perspective. In this idiom, the land in which people live and work is rendered into a landscape: one that is *looked* at and visually consumed. The representation of the Highlands in conservation literature as habitat (often viewed from a distance, often from the air) – of mountains and Caledonian forest, for example – is a representation that eliminates local people from the scene, and renders the Highland landscape a depopulated 'wilderness'. As noted above, this way of representing and looking at people and landscape has concurrent processes of marginalization attached to them:

> *The importance of 'Scottish nature' and nature imagery is that it eases the appropriation of a local cultural resource and makes apparent the particular audience (Lowland urban Scotland) that conservation must court, in order to maintain its dominance of the Highland rural* (MacDonald, 1998, p242).

Part of the problem for SNH and its predecessors may be the dependence upon the scientific approach as a foundation of all that it does. This sees nature as a basis not only for its knowledge of the state of ecology, but as a basis for state conservation practice. Therefore, regardless of how sympathetic institutional conservation is to the crofting tradition as a producer of 'environmental goods' and 'benefits', and however much it trades on the landscapes produced by generations of crofting and farming practice, the historical and discursive framework upon which state conservation is based is arguably incompatible with a *social* model of conservation – which better relates to the self-definition of Highland culture and to political aspirations for community control and management. It is institutional conservation's static and abstract view of nature as 'ecology' or 'heritage' that lacks any resonance with the sense of place and relationship to nature that is inextricably bound up with the social interaction, identities and practices of Highland culture.

CONSERVATION'S COLONIAL INHERITANCE

This lack of reflexivity and flexibility in the institutional framework of state conservation in Scotland can be located in a legacy of colonialism. This contributes to making it inflexible and ill equipped to creatively react to locally led land ownership and control. In Chapter 2 of this book, Bill Adams set out some of the common features of the colonial legacy that can be used, here, to describe how certain assumptions of state conservation in Scotland flow, both directly and obliquely, from this context.

Firstly, in Scotland, scientific knowledge and classification in conservation are orientated towards formalization, analysis and theory and have been given priority over lay knowledge. Thus, in the Highlands and Islands, lay knowledge is often referenced to emotional traditions based upon the use of the local environment. It is implicitly assigned a lower value in conservation than knowledge-based experiment and universal verification. This tension is still significant in the contemporary Highlands and Islands, where there is dislocation between public understanding of nature in everyday life and official discourse of ecological science and sustainability. However, while this is a very real tension, it is not a clear-cut one because the notion of a homogenous Highland community sharing traditional knowledge and values is itself a particular discourse about that community, often one that the community itself generates in dealings with state bureaucracy.

Secondly, colonial constructs of nature position it as separate from culture, not formed as part of it. The process of conserving the Highlands and Islands involves survey, designation, classification and monitoring, paralleling the division and parcelling up of space in the British colonies. In this process, the land is mapped and redrawn according to scientific criteria – this is a process where scientific classifications of habitat importance, 'biochemical boundaries' or 'landscape character' (Usher, 1999), for example, overwrite local definitions. In the colonies this process often involved displacing local human settlement, as well as policing of traditional land uses. The extreme of colonial science – for example, the legislation in the late 19th century after the massive decline of many species because of the excesses of elitist hunting in South and East Africa (MacKenzie, 1988) – can be detected in the thinking of 'home' state conservation: to use science and legislation to control land; to simplify the environment into 'blocks' that are more easily policed.

Curiously, however, there was a period in Scottish conservation that demonstrates an appreciation by some conservationists that nature and society are related rather than separate realms. Their ideas seem to reflect a much more contingent case for conservation, and demonstrated greater awareness of the issues surrounding the 'Highland condition' of small, marginalized land users, depopulation and inadequate access to resources. The Scottish Wild Life Conservation Committee, established in 1945 to investigate how state conservation should function, advocated that the best form of conservation for Scotland would be to feature a range of designations and practices that were relatively innovative for the period. For example, one ill-fated designation that was suggested was the 'conservation area', reflected later in the holistic approach set out in Fraser Darling's *West Highland Survey* (1955). Although ignoring the politics of land ownership, this thinking suggested that, with proper technical knowledge principally based upon ecological knowledge, integrating with local knowledge of agro-ecosystems, the impoverished crofters of the Highlands would be able to develop natural resources in a sustainable way. The committee also suggested in its report that there should be an independent Biological Service of Scotland, based upon the notion that the situation, as well as the nature in the country, was distinct from the rest of the Great Britain. Unfortunately, perhaps, all of these ideas were eventually not given any space in the final report to government, and there was to be no separate scientific body or designations reflecting particular contingencies in Scotland.

Thirdly, bureaucratic control and standardization of nature have taken precedence over other forms of engagement with land. As environmental historians of colonialism have pointed out, ideas about the scientific study of nature and the application of that knowledge for the efficient management of 'resources' often were freely exchanged between colonized nations and Britain, with many concepts – such as categorization of animals and land for conservation purposes and the idea of 'rescuing' endangered species – founded in such bureaucracies (Philip, 1994; Grove, 1995; MacKenzie, 1990). The application of scientific knowledge to the designation and management of land had also achieved a large part of its development in the particular context of colonialism, which subsequently transferred into the shaping of territory and regulation that formed the basis for state institutions in the 'home' countries.

Fourthly, British bodies were also closely involved in 'post-colonial' management of nature outside of Scotland. For example, the Nature Conservancy had statutory responsibility for advising the British Colonial Office on nature conservation until 1961. The Nature Conservancy was also in the heart of negotiating post-colonial structures for conservation after British colonies in Africa achieved their independence during the late 1950s and 1960s. British conservationists promoted the idea that African nature was of global importance, therefore legitimating a regime of 'shared' international interests in the management of natural resources there. This approach was epitomized by International Union for the Conservation of Nature and Natural Resources (IUCN) national parks definitions and, later still, the biosphere reserves concept. The International Biological Programme (IBP), which ran from 1964 to 1974 (see Chapter 1 in this book) and was a significant neo-colonial treatment of 'global' nature, had a considerable amount of practical involvement from the Nature Conservancy. The headquarters of the IBP's 'Conservation Terrestrial' section was situated at the Nature Conservancy's London headquarters. Many

Nature Conservancy scientists and reserves in Scotland were involved in ongoing projects under the IBP.

The significance of noting these continuities and connections is that they form cultural processes that have established, in conservation, a distinctive set of commitments and symbolic meanings that are not subject to conscious recognition, but which underlie the policies and practice visible in contemporary Scotland.

CONCLUSION

State nature conservation in Scotland is a descendent of the colonial legacy of Britain, in as much that it is a bureaucracy based upon science and 'progressive' rationalized planning – and the roots of many such bodies lay in the colonial era. However, the Highlands and Islands are a context that throws this legacy into stark focus. They are a place where common lands and stewardship were transferred from common to private ownership; by the 20th century, they were turned into a playground for the wealthy and, in the pejorative terms of many conservationists, 'miles and miles of bugger all'. The Highlands were transformed through processes of clearance, modernization and Balmoralization, through the practices of hunting estates as well as travel and tourism, into a place romantically constructed as a Celtic and natural world separate from the world of the metropolitan cities and core economic areas.

This chapter has contended that nature conservation by the state in the Highlands and Islands of Scotland uses a particular construction of the Highland environment. It makes particular assumptions about the relationship between nature and society that can conflict with other groups – most notably, the land-owners and managers of Highland sporting estates, and crofters and their supporters. The conservationists' framework and approach are rooted in a colonial tradition: embodied in the designations and knowledge and, indeed, woven into the very identity of state conservation science and practice. In contrast, the other groups involved have their own distinctive identities, definitions and commitments that are also grounded in particular notions of the Highlands and their own sense of history. These different groups actively engage with each other, which makes these identities and commitments very real and negotiated in material interactions rather than being abstract, and something handed down in some disembodied sense (Macnaghten and Urry, 1998). For example, crofters' own ideas about the land, while drawing upon notions of their own relationship to the Highlands and nature, are not merely a legacy of their cultural traditions. They are constantly negotiated and renegotiated through interplay with other social groups, such as state conservation. State conservation itself has been shown to be an important social force because it controls land and ecological and other forms of scientific knowledge. It also possesses a very particular power in that the reliability of its practices and knowledge still largely conforms to government assumptions about nature conservation being properly based upon 'science', 'rationality' and 'neutrality'.

However, as already suggested, we need to be wary of purified definitions of these positions. The construction of real crofters in real locations as the collective 'crofting community' has become a double-edged sword for contemporary Highland reformers who seek to actively affect environmental management and control of land. To position Highland life, land use and tradition in this fashion runs the risk of reproducing the rhetoric of Highlandism:

> *The Gaeltacht becomes, in every sense, an ideal country, until even those who seek to uphold its interests against the core find that they are doing so in the glowing and reverent language that ratifies its oppression',* (Womack, 1989, quoted in MacDonald, 2001, p168)

We should also be wary of casting statutory conservation in the guise of an all-powerful behemoth empowered by the apparently universal reliability of 'value-neutral science' to protect 'scientific' and 'public interest', and 'national heritage'. In the first place, many nature conservationists are, at least, vaguely aware of the limitations of the inheritance they work within. This reflexivity, albeit thinly spread, makes it curious that conservation as a social institution is still largely oblivious of the need to openly consider its colonial legacy. Furthermore, as described in this chapter, the political and cultural tide for conservation in Scotland may have already turned. We can see signs that the new Scottish political masters of conservation are not comfortable with the heat of social criticism about particular aspects of conservation – especially the assumption that 'they know best'. In addition, within the intense debate in Scotland about state regulation giving way to land reform and community-based rural development, crofters and their version of the Highlands have been constructed as a reference point for conservation's future development.

This consideration of the politics of nature and society in the Highlands and Islands has contrasted, and reflected upon, how nature and social relationships are contested through history and culture, and how definition and material practices might be transformed in the future. The power of conservation to define the Highlands and Islands will, no doubt, be subject to a continuing and sustained critique for some time to come.

NOTES

1   Crofting is a way of life based upon small, low-intensity agricultural holdings (on average, 5ha in size), with intergenerational tenure guaranteed by legislation. Crofts currently account for about 20 per cent of the land use of the Highlands and Islands area of Scotland and number around 17,700 holdings, with a population of about 33,000 (A Raven, 1999). Crofting development and regulation are controlled by a

government agency called the Crofters' Commission: see www.crofters commission.org.uk.

2 The estate system has its roots in the Victorian obsession with hunting and the Highlands. The Highland estate is frequently regarded as a fantasy of pre-modern nature, actually based upon enormous legal and economic power arising from a historic process of depopulation, Anglicization and modernization. These estates form the single most concentrated form of land ownership in Europe. In 1872, 15 people owned half of the Highlands; in 1995, 484 owners owned a similar amount of land, with an average estate size of just over 7280 hectares (Wightman, 1996, pp21, 142). Land ownership in Scotland conveys enormous legal rights, and these estates have historically, and still do, wield considerable social and economic power.

3 Good overviews of the Scottish land-use debate can be found in Cramb (1997), Lambert (2001) and Cameron (2001). For a general history of Scotland, including crofting and the sporting estates, see Devine (1999). Descriptions of the role and range of activities of state agencies in the Highlands and Islands can be found in MacKinnon (2001).

4 The Gaeltacht is the Gaelic-speaking part of the Highlands and Islands.

5 The Scottish parliament, currently made up of around 130 elected Members of the Scottish Parliament (MSPs), exercises a range of legislative powers in areas such as the environment and education. The Scottish Executive has its own decision-making departments, in the present case most notably Scottish Executive Environment and Rural Affairs Department (SEERAD). These powers are *devolved* but not independent from the UK government in London. In many areas of policy and legislation, the Scottish parliament remains subordinate to Westminster. Thus, Scotland is in a condition of semi-autonomy rather than being a state in its own right.

6 Scottish conservation until 1990 was under the control of bodies covering all of Great Britain: the Nature Conservancy (1949–1976) and the Nature Conservancy Council (1976–1990). The Nature Conservancy Council for Scotland (1990–1992) was an interim forerunner of Scottish Natural Heritage, which has responsibility for nature conservation as well as landscape and amenity protection (see www.snh.org.uk).

7 Many Highland clans were loyal to the Catholic Stuart line of monarchs that had been overthrown by the 'Glorious Revolution' of 1688–1689, installing a Protestant monarchy. The aim of the supporters of the Stuarts – known as the Jacobites – was to mobilize a range of Catholic supporters, at the centre of which were key Highland clans, in a counter-revolution that would, if successful, displace the Hanoverian succession in Scotland and England to reinstate the Stuart dynasty to the throne of Great Britain.

8 The Clearances were not a single event, but a transformation that covered about a century, beginning in the latter decades of the 18th century. This was a period that reflected the decline in traditional social systems, land uses and patterns of settlement, not just in Scotland but in certain parts of Europe as modern, market-orientated land uses eroded away traditional settlement, knowledge and land husbandry. The rate of loss of those systems, and their relative persistence to this day, reflects differences between countries in relation to the extent poor rural people were lacking in, or ignorant of, statutory protection. Clearly, in different circumstances, this 'modernization' found parallel in the contemporary colonization of the countries of empire.

In the Highlands, people were removed from their homes both by the erosion of rights and by direct force. The Clearances were a major factor driving migration to the Lowland cities in search of work and also, of course, massive emigration abroad (see Devine, 1994; Hunter, 1976). A further factor compounding this was the Potato Famine of 1846–1847, when landlords 'aided' 17,000 tenants struck by failed crops to emigrate to Canada and Australia (Devine, 1999, p419). Another custom land-owners were able to exploit, especially when tenants' food production or incomes were inadequate, was an obligation for men to serve in their private armies, most of which were integrated within the Highland regiments of the British army founded during this period. Paradoxically, given that such men's families were not infrequently forced out of their homes in their absence, Highland regiments became a significant force in imperial pursuits in North America, Africa and Asia.

9 The fund amounts to UK£10 million at the time of writing (see www.hie.co.uk).
10 The black-throated diver is a nationally rare species of bird.
11 OLDs were formerly known as 'potentially damaging operations'. Crofters are often highly reliant on government support, notably through the Crofting Counties Agricultural Grants Scheme (CCAGS). If the land has a legal conservation designation affecting it, the grant may be objected to by SNH, and crofters are advised that even if the relevant land is not within an SSSI they may be refused funding if SNH or a SEERAD office consider a CCAGS proposal to have negative environmental effects.

REFERENCES

Aldous, J (ed) (1995) *Our Pinewood Heritage*. Conference proceedings, 20–22 October, Inverness Forestry Authority, Edinburgh

Bryden, J and Hart, K (2000) 'Land reform, planning and people: an issue of stewardship?' in G Holmes and R Crofts (eds) *Scotland's Environment: the future*. Tuckwell Press, East Linton, pp104–118

Cahill, K (2001) *Who Owns Britain: the hidden facts behind land ownership*. Canongate, Edinburgh

Cameron, E A (2001) 'Unfinished business: the land question and the Scottish Parliament', *Contemporary British History*, vol 15, pp83–114

Craig, D (1990) *On the Crofters' Trail: in search of the Clearance Highlanders*. Jonathan Cape, London

Cramb, A (1997) *Fragile Land: the state of the Scottish environment*. Polygon, Edinburgh

Darier, É, Tabara, D and Toogood, M (1999) 'The "natural" object of national identities: hybrids in Catalunya, Quebec and Scotland'. Paper presented at the Third Catalan Sociology Congress, Lleida, 20–21 March

Fraser Darling, F (1955) *West Highland Survey: An Essay in Human Ecology*, Oxford University Press, Oxford

Devine, T M (1994) *Clanship to Crofters War: the social transformation of the Scottish Highlands*. Manchester University Press, Manchester

Devine, T M (1999) *The Scottish Nation: 1700–2000*. Allen Lane, Penguin Press, London

Gilroy, A (ed) (2000) *Romantic Geographies*. Manchester University Press, Manchester

Grove, R (1995) *Green Imperialism: colonial expansion, tropical island Edens and the origins of environmentalism 1600–1860*. Cambridge University Press, Cambridge

Highlands and Islands Enterprise (2001) *Community Land Unit Action Framework 2001*. HIE, Inverness

Hunter, J (1976) *The Making of the Crofting Community*. John Donald, Edinburgh

Hunter, J (1997) 'Return of the natives? If Scotland's parliament has no stomach for land reform is it a parliament worth having?' *Scotland on Sunday*, 14 December, p16

Lambert, R A (2001) *Contested Mountains: nature, development and environment in the Cairngorms region of Scotland 1880–1980*. The White Horse Press, Cambridge

Lister-Kaye, J (1994) *Ill Fares The Land: a sustainable land ethic for the sporting estates of the Highlands and Islands of Scotland*. Barail Centre for Highlands and Islands Policy Studies, Sabhal Mòr Ostaig, Sleat, Isle of Skye

MacDonald, F (1998) 'Viewing Highland Scotland: ideology, representation and the 'natural heritage', *Area*, vol 30, pp237–244

MacDonald, F (2001) 'St Kilda and the sublime', *Ecumene*, vol 8, pp151–174

MacKenzie, J M (1988) *The Empire of Nature: hunting, conservation and British imperialism*. Manchester University Press, Manchester

MacKenzie, J M (ed) (1990) *Imperialism and the Natural World*. Manchester University Press, Manchester

MacKenzie, J M (1997) *Empires of Nature and the Nature of Empires: imperialism, Scotland and environment*. Tuckwell Press, East Linton

MacKinnon, D (2001) 'Regulating regional spaces: state agencies and the production of governance in the Scottish Highlands', *Environment and Planning A*, vol 33, pp823–844

Macnaghten, P and Urry, J (1998) *Contested Natures*. Sage, London

McVean, D N and Lockie, J D (1969) *Ecology and Land Use in Upland Scotland*. Edinburgh University Press, Edinburgh

Nicholson, E M (1957) *Britain's Nature Reserves*. Country Life, London

Philip, K (1994) *Imperial Science Rescues a Tree: global botanic networks, local knowledge and the transcontinental transplantation of Chincona*. The Nature of Science Studies, a workshop on the environment, science and politics, 15–17 April 1994, Department of Science and Technology Studies, Cornell University, Cornell

Pratt, M L (1992) *Imperial Eyes: travel writing and transculturation*. Routledge, London

Ramsay, P (1996) *Revival of the Land: Creag Meagaidh National Nature Reserve*. SNH, Edinburgh

Raven, A (1999) 'Agriculture, Forestry and Land Use' in E McDowell and J McCormick (eds) *Environment Scotland: prospects for sustainability*. Ashgate, Aldershot pp127-138

Raven, H (1999) 'Land Reform' in E McDowell and J McCormick (eds) *Environment Scotland: prospects for sustainability*. Ashgate, Aldershot, pp139–153

Rennie, F (1998) *Land, Culture and the Future of Rural Communities*. The Rural Lecture, Lews Castle College, Stornoway

Said, E W (1993) *Culture and Imperialism*. Vintage, London

Scottish Executive (1999) *Land Reform: proposals for legislation*. Scottish Executive, Edinburgh

Scottish Executive (2001) *The Nature of Scotland: a policy statement*. Scottish Executive, Edinburgh

Scottish Natural Heritage (1994) *Red Deer and the Natural Heritage*. SNH, Edinburgh

Scottish Office (1997) *Towards a Development Strategy for Rural Scotland: a discussion paper*. The Stationery Office, Edinburgh

Scottish Office (1998) *Nature and People: a new approach to SSSI designations in Scotland.* The Stationery Office, Edinburgh

Smith, A D (1999) *Myths and Memories of the Nation.* Oxford University Press, Oxford

Toogood, M D (1995) 'Representing ecology and Highland tradition', *Area*, vol 27, pp102–109

Toogood, M D (1996) 'Nature and Nation', *Scotlands*, vol 3, pp42–55

Usher, M B (ed) (1999) *Landscape Character: perspectives on management and change.* SNH Natural Heritage of Scotland, Book 8, The Stationery Office, Edinburgh

Wigan, M (1993) *Stag at Bay: the Scottish red deer crisis.* Swan Hill Press, Shrewsbury

Wigan, M (1998) *The Scottish Highland Estate.* Swan Hill Press, Shrewsbury (revised edition)

Wigan, M (2000) 'Should the state control wild deer?' *The Field*, August, pp64–67

Wightman, A (1996) *Who Owns Scotland.* Canongate, Edinburgh

Wightman, A (1997) 'Do we want Scotland's finest landscape controlled by a benign dictatorship?' *Scotland on Sunday*, 23 February, p14

Williams, P and Chrisman, L (eds) (1993) *Colonial Discourse and Post-Colonial Theory.* Harvester, London

Womack, P (1989) *Improvement and Romance: constructing the myth of the Highlands.* Macmillan, London

Chapter 8

Responding to place in a post-colonial era: An Australian perspective

John Cameron

INTRODUCTION

My thinking about conservation strategies has been heavily influenced by an experience of four years' full-time consulting with a leading Australian environmental conservation organization. As a result of producing several reports on a conservation-oriented forest policy (eg Cameron and Penna, 1988) and ecologically sustainable land management (Cameron and Elix, 1991), I became involved in vigorous environmental debates at conferences, in the media, in Parliament House and at local forest protests. I grew concerned about the depth of polarization between the protagonists, and the vested interest of the media and lobby groups themselves in highlighting conflict, apparently for its own sake.

There is no denying the necessity for the conservation movement to bring the worsening state of the environment to national attention through conflict with the forces of the status quo. The national government, led by Prime Minister Bob Hawke, that was in office during the time I was involved in this work, did struggle to find an appropriate response, with attempts ranging from negotiated settlement using an industrial dispute model to the establishment of new institutions, such as the Resource Assessment Commission and the Ecologically Sustainable Development Working Groups. However, so much time and energy were spent on conflict and its management that other ways of understanding what was happening in the forests, other voices of care for country, did not receive the attention that I felt they deserved.

At one of the many meetings in the dispute over logging in the Tantawangalo and Coolangubra forests of New South Wales, a local man with a farming and forestry background spoke of his deep affiliation with the forests and farms as working landscapes. While he deplored clear-felling for woodchip and sawlogs, he related primarily to the forest as producing valued timber for construction and furniture. He was eloquent about his feelings for the trees that he felled and the hardwood they yielded; and while he understood those who wanted the forests left untouched, he didn't share their views.

My conservationist colleagues nodded their approval of his opposition to woodchipping and frowned at his opposition to logging bans, while the timber industry supporters had the reverse reactions. A motion was proposed, debated and carried. No one responded to that man in the same relational terms that he was using. Subsequently, the disputed forests were either declared national parks, where no logging could take place, or gazetted as production forests for modified clear-felling. There was no room for either the way he wanted timber to be harvested or for his expressions of his 'sense' of the forest.

There were, of course, many conservationists who expressed great affiliation with places in nature as a primary motivation for their stance, and many of these expressions were used in local campaigns. However, I became interested in how place relationships tended to disappear from the discourse as the debate moved from the local to the state, and then the national level. I encountered other people involved in conflicts over urban development and agriculture whose voices of place attachment were marginalized because they didn't fully accord with the positions of the main protagonists – small-scale farmers, suburban women, indigenous people. Disheartened by what I saw as ritualized public combat over the fate of the forests, I left my position with the conservation movement to explore these matters more deeply in a university setting.

Within the field of social ecology, I have designed and taught three experientially oriented courses in aspects of sense of place, and I have also convened the Sense of Place Colloquium – a group of Australian scholars and writers who research, converse and gather periodically to write about and discuss the relevance of place attachment to contemporary Australian social and political life. I use the term 'sense of place' by building on Relph's definition: 'The word "place" is best applied to those fragments of human environments where meanings, activities and a specific landscape are all implicated and enfolded by each other' (Relph, 1992, p37). To put 'sense of' in front of a word is to bring attention to the individual experience, so that a sense of place refers to the ways in which people experience the intertwining of meanings, activities and a particular landscape, as well as to the felt sense of belonging to a place that emerges from those experiences. The word 'sense' does not refer simply to the physical senses, but to the felt sense of a place and the intuitive and imaginative sensing that is active when one is attuned to, and receptive towards, one's surroundings.

I am still as motivated by concern for the extinction of native species, the loss of forest cover and topsoil, and the salination of rivers as I was when I was actively working as a conservationist. Now, however, I have a different set of questions. For example, how possible is it to move people to change the way in which they dwell on Earth in ecologically desirable ways through the vehicle of their own daily experience, their love of place, rather than fear of eco-catastrophe, appeals to the moral rights of other species or to a vision of ecotopia? Are these options alternatives or complements? What is the role of formal education in such a process? What challenges does this present for the conservation movement? What are the opportunities and barriers to promoting place attachment in contemporary Australian society?

THE CONTEXT: AUSTRALIA IN THE CENTENARY OF FEDERATION

These questions, and my university teaching experience, need to be put in the broader context of what is happening in current Australian place relations. The year 2001, 100 years after the federation of formerly separate colonies to create the nation, was an obvious occasion for Australians to look back upon their colonial heritage and how they have managed to create an independent identity and role in the world after they ceased to belong to a collection of British colonies. Renowned Australian author David Malouf has written in fictional and non-fictional terms of the Australian post-colonial experience. In his 1998 Boyer lectures, he described the 'complex fate' of Australians of European origin as:

> ...*the paradoxical condition of having our lives simultaneously in two places, two hemispheres [that] may be just the thing which is most original and most interesting in us. I mean our uniqueness might lie just here, in the tension between environment and culture rather than in what we can salvage by insisting either on the one or the other* (Malouf, 1998, p33).

The tension between a European cultural and intellectual heritage and the physical realities of the continent in which we live lies at the heart of our constant reinventing ourselves as a continent and as a people. It manifests itself particularly acutely in the debate on the possibility of Australia becoming a republic, symbolically as much as practically severing ties with Europe and charting a different course in this new century. It is one of the underlying factors in the debate over Aboriginal land rights, which grows out of an equally profound tension between European and Aboriginal heritages. In another manifestation, it complicates the process of closer economic and political ties with Asia as the physical closeness of the continents belies the cultural distances between them.

Five contextual factors

In an introduction to a recent book on the subject, I identified five historical factors that have a major bearing on how Australians individually and collectively view their sense of place (Cameron, 2001).

The first is the growing importance of an Aboriginal sense of place in modern Australia. There has been an explosion of Aboriginal creative activity during the past few decades that is of international significance. Since the introduction of Western painting materials to some Central Desert people during the early 1970s, Aboriginal art of great quality and distinctiveness has moved into galleries, museums and the art market. The work of Emily Kngwarrey and Rover Thomas, in particular, has achieved a degree of international attention and acclaim that is matched by few, if any, white Australian contemporary painters. Aboriginal rock music bands such as Yothu Yindi have international audiences. This explosion is all the more remarkable for the general conditions of poverty, institutional neglect and, often, racism that have prevailed for most of these people in their daily lives.

Because of the inseparable link between person and country that many Aboriginal people speak of, much of this creative expression is an expression of Aboriginal sense of place, although I suspect this phrase has little currency amongst Aboriginal people. Many of Kngwarrey's paintings are simply entitled 'My Country'. Books about the deep connection between Aboriginal people and their country appear more frequently; two outstanding examples are *Yorro Yorro* by David Mowaljarlai and Jutta Malnic (1993) and *Dingo Makes Us Human* by Deborah Bird Rose (2000).

In some quarters of the Australian community at least, this expression of person/place/culture has been enthusiastically received. In fact, the strength of the reception has created its own problems. 'White man got no dreaming' was an early phrase uttered by Muta, a Murinbata man, and used as the title of Stanner's influential book (1979), which has come back to haunt both sides of the discussion. On the one hand, Aboriginal people have complained of the ultimate exploitation of spiritually barren 'whitefellers' appropriating Aboriginal spirituality as their own. On the other hand, it has led to calls for Australians of European extraction to examine the depths of their own cultural traditions in order to rediscover their own indigeneity (Tacey, 1995). Whatever the merits of the various cases, it is now true that any discussion of sense of place in Australia must take Aboriginal sense of place as a vital factor, something that was not recognized 30 years ago. This discussion will be taken further in subsequent sections of this chapter.

A second dimension has been less spectacular and arguably less recognized – the awareness that the Australian continent, like all distinct land masses, imposes a way of thinking and acting upon its human inhabitants by virtue of its particular combination of climate, landscape and ecology. It is perhaps best illustrated by Tim Flannery's book *The Future Eaters* (1994), which popularized the views of a growing number of ecologists that the nation could no longer afford to ignore the ecological limits to human activity on this fragile and dry continent.

The distinctiveness of Australia's landscape, flora and fauna has been evident, often painfully evident, right from the start of the British colonies. What has been less evident is the cost of using European agricultural methods and mindsets to 'develop' the interior. Massive irrigation schemes have diverted water onto sediments that contain high levels of salt, turning our largest river, the Murray, into a saline drain. Cattle and sheep have been grazed in large numbers on semi-arid soils which, unlike those in England, have a very thin and easily eroded topsoil, much of which has been washed and blown away to leave a bare, infertile remnant.

The contribution of the ecological perspective to an understanding of modern Australian sense of place is the sharp edge of the recognition that place is not the mere passive recipient of whatever humans decide they wish to do upon the face of it. The land is an active participant in a very physical sense. For example, inedible native bushes are turning vast tracts of inland Australia into so-called 'green deserts' in response to the ill treatment of a century of overgrazing, curtailment of fire and destruction of native grasslands. Sense of place is not simply the affective response to a particular place that people might have; it includes a growing sense of what the place demands of us in our attitudes and actions.

This viewpoint has echoes at a deeper level. Carl Jung, who was profoundly interested in the interplay between psyche and matter, was struck by the Australian Aboriginal perspective on spirits within the land:

> *Certain Australian Aborigines assert that one cannot conquer foreign soil, because in it there dwell strange ancestor-spirits who reincarnate themselves in the new-born. There is a great psychological truth in this. The foreign land assimilates its conqueror* (Jung, 1927, p49).

Psychic material inherent in the land and its indigenous inhabitants can rise up into the unconscious, the dreams and symbols and myths of the conquering people and, ultimately, take them over and make them in the shape of the new psychic patterns. Perhaps this process is starting to take place in Australia today. Paralleling the physical assertion of the land against the assaults of the European invaders, do we have a growing psychic assertion? If so, one place to look would be the work of those poets and novelists who are closely attuned to the national psyche.

Our leading commentators on Australian literature have devoted considerable attention to the contemporary literary response to the land. David Tacey is explicit about the emergence of a deeper response:

> *When I came back to Australia in 1984, I began searching our literature for examples of imaginal vision, for expressions of a dynamic relatedness to the land that could provide a new basis for creative and transformative living. I was heartened to discover that there was, indeed, a great deal of literary evidence to suggest that a new spiritual pact or bond with landscape was developing here* (Tacey, 1995, pp160–161).

Tacey describes how post-war poets such as Judith Wright and Les Murray have overcome the supposed separation between the poet as subject and the landscape as object.

David Malouf writes about overcoming the separation in a different way. He describes the work of the writer as taking the sensate world into his or her consciousness and giving the world a 'second life', a world that we inhabit imaginatively, as well as in fact. He points to Kenneth Slessor's poem 'South Country' as a breakthrough in which the landscape finally gets inside the psyche, so that it is both an internal and external landscape:

> *The poem, in fact, makes no distinction between the two and part of its beauty and pleasure is that it allows us to enter this state, too, in which all tension between inner and outer, environment and being, is miraculously resolved* (Malouf, 1998, p42).

The three factors I have mentioned so far – Aboriginal, ecological and literary – have all been quite directly concerned with an aspect of Australian sense of place. There are also some more general features of modern Australia that have major contextual significance. Although the percentage of the population in rural areas has declined steadily this century, it has accelerated in post-war years and seems to have crossed some kind of threshold in national attention. Beyond the physical decline in the number of farmers and the number of rural banks, there is the general perception that Australia no longer 'rides on the sheep's back', a widespread view during the 1950s (reflecting the economic importance of the sheep industry and the focus on the people working in it). Increasing urbanization has had a number of effects on modern sense of place. As more people have settled into our cities, there has been increased attention given to urban planning, suburban growth and the quality of life in urban places.

Many Australians who are now city dwellers did not come from rural Australia, but from overseas. Australia's massive post-war immigration programme has had profound effects in all areas of Australian life, including our sense of place. Four Australians in every ten were either born overseas, or their parents were. As Martin Krygier comments:

> *We now have over 100 ethnic groups and 80 languages here. The peaceful way in which all these 'aliens' have become citizens should be at the forefront of any account of immigration in Australia. This was a real social experiment which could have gone awfully wrong* (Krygier, 1997, p68).

In discussing this phenomenon, Krygier steers a middle course between zealous proponents of post-World War II immigration and anti-ethnics who extol the virtues of the 'old Australian' Anglo traditions at the expense of the New Australians. He also strikes a balance between pride at the success of the 'social experiment' of immigration and shame over the disgraceful treatment of the Aboriginal people over the past two centuries.

Meanwhile, the country, as a whole, has been propelled into a new era of globalization. Australia's place in the world is far more in the everyday consciousness of individual citizens than in previous generations. To many place writers, it is one of the forces that is threatening to destroy the distinctive character of local places. For them, globalization – through the agency of the World Trade Organization and the proposal for a Multilateral Agreement on Investment – represents the triumph of multinational corporate power over the sovereignty of national governments. Governments have less capacity to influence the terms of foreign trade and investment in their country or to set high environmental standards for particular projects. Neither Australian developers nor their foreign counterparts have shown great sensitivity to sense of place in suburban or tourist developments, or mining or industrial projects, in the past. On the other hand, aspects of globalization, such as the Internet, have provided a new connection to the world, allowing people who are not physically or financially able to travel to communicate with people in any country of the world at a number of different electronic levels. Through satellite television, world music and similar developments, the world and its cultures are now a real presence in the daily lives of many Australian people, arguably giving them a much-expanded sense of place in the world.

These contextual factors have combined to create great public interest in the subject of Australian sense of place. There have been three international conferences held in this country during the past two years with the subtitle 'sense of place'. Interestingly, George Seddon, who has been known for decades as Australia's 'sense of place man', has recently become cautious about the increasing popularity and uncritical use of the term: 'Sense of place has become a popular concept, heard at every turn, unanalysed, and this is, for me, a problem' (Seddon, 1997, p105). A key question for Seddon becomes: 'Whose sense of place are we talking about?'

THE DEBATE OVER PLACE AND BELONGING

With Aboriginal and non-Aboriginal Australians living uneasily together on this continent, whose sense of place are we talking about? A debate has recently emerged that brings together a number of the Australian contextual factors, and provides a reference point for discussion of my experience in teaching the 'Sense of Place' subject at the University of Western Sydney. Tom Griffiths introduced the topic in a review in *The Australian's Review of Books* by observing that 'it has been rare in Australian studies to extend to non-Aboriginal groups the analysis of emotional and spiritual attachments to places of work and habitation, but this work is beginning' (1998, p13). However, extending deep place affiliation to non-Aboriginal people immediately raises the question of how non-Aboriginal place affiliation relates to prior and, in many cases, ongoing Aboriginal connection with country. This discussion has been taken up by Peter Read in his book *Belonging: Australians, Place and Aboriginal Ownership* and by Val

Plumwood in her critique of Read's book entitled *Belonging, Naming and Decolonization*, both published in 2000.

Read explores the experiences of non-Aboriginal Australians as they articulate their sense of belonging to the land. He challenges the prevailing view of the spiritual barrenness of European Australians in comparison with Aboriginal people: 'I want to feel I belong here while respecting Aboriginality, neither appropriating it nor being absorbed by it' (Read, 2000, p15). He is seeking to contest the view that 'white man got no dreaming', while investigating how white Australians are grappling with the fact that the land they are so attached to is the same homeland that Aboriginal people loved and so often lost. He acknowledges that we have to understand the 'rivers of blood and tears' that have been shed before we can talk of belonging here, and wonders what the knowledge of Aboriginal history brings to a modern white Australian sense of belonging.

Read journeys into the poetry and songs of both cultures to see how they deal with issues of reconciliation and belonging to country. He interviews four historians, seeking out historical roots and possibilities for a shared future and sense of collective belonging. Their answers are equivocal, some of them pointing to what is held in common, but others articulating the depths of cultural difference. He presents the individual stories of a number of non-Aboriginal people who have developed a strong sense of place, expressed through rituals, art and writing. For some of them this has come about as a result of contact with Aboriginal people; for others, it has not. There is a wide range of attitudes and experiences about the difference between first settlers, second settlers and migrants, and an open question about the modern relevance of a spiritual concept of place.

In view of the complexities and differences in these stories, it is surprising that Read develops the notion of separate but respectful development of place attachments so strongly towards the end of the book:

> *Leave the spirits to the people who made them or were made by them. Let the rest of us find the confidence in our own physical and spiritual belonging in this land, respectful of Aboriginality but not necessarily close to it. Let's intuit our own attachments to country independently of Aboriginals. We can belong in the landscape on the landscape or irrelevantly to the landscape. We don't all have to belong to each other. To understand that is a step to belonging* (Read, 2000, p204).

There are two very strong statements in this paragraph. To urge the independent intuiting of place attachments is to maintain that it is not only possible, but desirable, to do so without relationship with Aboriginal people or their understandings. Secondly, to say that we can belong irrelevantly to the landscape might be read as a simple statement of the current condition of many urban-dwelling Australians; but to follow it with the statement that we don't all have to belong is to suggest that it is a perfectly acceptable state of affairs.

It is important to recognize that these words are being written by a man who has a deep and extensive understanding of Aboriginal history and has been a passionate advocate of Aboriginal land rights. The last chapter describes his journey of rediscovery of land dear to him in northern Sydney with Dennis Foley, a descendant of the local Gai-mariagal people. His stance of separation appears in odd juxtaposition with the depth of his relationship with Foley: 'Now Dennis and I, the one indigenous, the other native-born, each respecting the past and present cultures of the other, are together travelling the northern beaches of Gai-mariagal lands in search of the proper country' (Read 2000, p210). He advocates the placement of commemorative plaques in urban areas, reminding the residents and visitors of ever-present Aboriginality and the joint exploration of country in common, the way he and Foley did it. He ends on an evocative note: 'I need the Gai-mariagal [local Aboriginal] stories, I need to believe that the voices in the river will never be silent, that the land bears our mark now as well as theirs' (Read 2000, p223). This is scarcely a call for independent association with land.

Val Plumwood, an eco-feminist philosopher, takes issue with some of Peter Read's arguments in a way that not only sheds light on the nature of the debate over place and identity in Australia, but offers a way of thinking about the sort of teaching I am doing, and its role in moving towards a society more oriented towards conservation and care for country. Plumwood is interested in the prospects for Australia developing what she terms a 'place-sensitive society', in which a deep connection with place is an integral element of the culture, enabling us to live sustainably within the environment. I prefer the term 'place-responsive culture' because the word 'responsive' carries with it the impetus to act, to respond, not merely 'to be sensitive to'. The word 'sensitive' has many connotations in contemporary Australia, often negative, as in the epithet 'sensitive New Age male'.

The difficulty, as Plumwood sees it, is to explain 'why people from a settler culture, who make such claims to love their land, have been engaged in destroying so much of it. What is it that has given non-indigenous Australia some of the worst vegetation clearance, land degradation and biodiversity extinction rates in the world' (Plumwood, 2000, p90). Armed with this question, she takes issue with Read's focus on the stories of individual place relationships, which suggest that because many of the non-Aboriginal people in his chapters are able to forge deep connections with their piece of land, society, as a whole, is closer to that goal than it actually is. This approach fails to challenge the structural obstacles to a genuinely place-responsive culture – for example, an economic system that requires regular movement of employees regardless of place attachment, and which treats place in terms of private property and a potential for development linked ever more closely to the demands of global corporate capitalism.

In part, it is unfair to accuse Read of failing to address the structural elements of modern alienation from place; that is Plumwood's agenda, not his. His purpose was to understand, through example, how individuals are responding to the challenge offered by prior Aboriginal place relationships, and how this is reflected in cultural expressions such as song and poetry. It is also unfair to claim that Read ignores the structural factors in environmental decline. For example, in his interview with the historian Tom Griffiths, he describes how the pastoral properties that Tom visited in outback New South Wales 'displayed the social and historical forces still driving the pastoralists to mine rather than work the land' (Read, 2000, p180). At the same time, Plumwood does argue cogently that relationships with place are strongly affected by gender, race, class and colonial status; and that there is no escaping the interrelationships between individual experience and the structure of society.

Plumwood also takes issue with Read's notion of non-Aboriginal people taking an independent pathway to a spiritual relationship with the land. Independence, she claims:

> ...*ignore[s] all the more interesting options of interaction, including dialogue, learning, convergence and hybridization, dynamically evolving and adaptive forms that are quite distinct from static cultural imitation* (Plumwood, 2000, p93).

As we have already noted, Read himself has such ambivalence about his call for independence that his relationship with Dennis Foley comes across as an illustration of the sort of dialogical and communicative relationship between the cultures that Plumwood is advocating. For my purposes, the point is less to decide who has the more correct position than to look at what sort of individual and structural initiatives are most likely to promote cross-cultural dialogue and action regarding place.

As an example of action at the structural level that could stimulate a democratic cross-cultural engagement with place, Plumwood suggests the renaming of Australian places, many of which reflect the unthinking continuation of a colonial past (see Chapter 3 in this book). While detailed consideration of the merits of her specific proposal is beyond the purview of this chapter, it provides an illustration of the sort of structural initiative involved in moving towards a place-responsive society.

The view from Europe: A critique of place essentialism

Structures in society are not only important for those writers, such as Plumwood, who are advocating a future in which place relations will be very different. They are also significant for understanding the politics of current place relationships and the way in which society can privilege particular ways of constructing a sense of place. Doreen Massey, in her book *Space, Place and Gender* (1994), provides a perspective on place that emphasizes social relations. Although she is writing as part of a different debate, regarding the scope of locality studies in Europe, she writes in accessible and general terms about global and local senses of place. For Australians, this view from afar is important for the topic of post-colonial conservation strategies regarding place, especially when it comes from the old colonial centre.

Massey begins by questioning whether the loss of sense of place (which is part of the phenomenon of 'time–space compression' involving the speeding up of life and the shrinking of the globe) is a universal aspect of modern life. In a telling example, she considers the case of the jumbo jets that regularly fly over the Pacific Ocean, shrinking the globe dramatically for Australian tourists and Japanese businessmen, amongst others, and speeding up their lives (Massey, 1994, p148). The same jets have caused a major decline in ocean shipping and made it harder for the islanders, over whom the planes fly, to move around the Pacific. The same forces that have compressed space–time for a Singaporean computer consultant have expanded time and space for a Pitcairn islander – it all depends upon who is being considered. Whose sense of place are we talking about?

Massey goes beyond arguing against universalizing the experience of loss of place attachment to look at the power dynamics of the new mobility. Businessmen and tourists use space–time compression to their advantage, and can, to some extent, control the degree to which they engage in it. Third World refugees and displaced migrants are not in control of their largely unwanted increased mobility; they are victims of the compressive forces. Even within Western countries, it is not a general experience; the poor and elderly might be aware of the shrinking globe in terms of foreign food, music and merchandise available, but are not able to afford it, and they are less mobile because of the steady decline of public transport services. So, there's not just a widening gap between the new global citizen and those on the margins in terms of their experience, but also in terms of their capacity to do anything about it.

It starts to become clear why sense of place is regarded as a reactionary concept by many 'progressives', who see place advocates as attempting to escape from the real task of changing the modern world for the better. A reactionary notion of place, according to Massey, is based upon the idea that places have single and essential identities, and are marked with clear boundaries that define a community on the inside that derives its sense of belonging from association with the place, and in counterposition with 'Others' on the outside of the borders. Massey maintains that places have never had fixed identities or characteristics; these were always in a state of flux as groups moved in or out, as land use changed. The 'identity' of the place was always very different for women than men (a point also made by Plumwood), and different for field workers than town dwellers. Stable place identity means fixing it in a particular time and giving primacy to one set of power relations. Finally, some communities are not place-based at all, but linked by other factors such as religion. Even when a physical boundary can be drawn, it usually does not enclose a coherent social group who has a common sense of place.

Massey suggests an alternative, progressive or global sense of place 'formed out of the particular set of social relations which interact at a particular location' (Massey, 1994, p12), which is more open and provisional than the reactionary view she outlined. By linking it so closely with social relations, Massey achieves a more open sense of place because a proportion of these relationships will extend beyond any area. The identity of a place cannot be fixed because its constituent social relations are constantly changing, and are changing the sort of place it is, as a result. Rather than defining places from an introverted sense of enclosure and history, she describes an extroverted sense of place in which the identity of a place derives from the particular nature of its relations with 'the outside' (Massey, 1994, p13).

Massey's work puts the Australian debate over place and belonging within the global context and introduces the important notion of place essentialism. There is much in common with Plumwood's work in Massey's emphasis on the social construction of place and the importance of structural change, and with Read in not wanting any one cultural construction of place to gain ascendancy as the 'true' nature of the place. At the same time, there is a distinctly European quality to her writing on social relations that is a challenge to Australians' interest in relationships with the land itself. These three writers together provide a useful framework within which to examine my students' experiences of place.

TEACHING SENSE OF PLACE IN A UNIVERSITY SETTING

For many years, I have been teaching 'Sense of Place' as a postgraduate subject based upon experiential learning principles in the social ecology programme at the University of Western Sydney. Students combine weekly immersion in a place of their choosing with subsequent reflection on their experiences, engagement with literature and different modes of expression of their emerging place relationships. In workshops and a two-day field trip in a remote bush setting, I introduce the students to the process of deepening the person–place relationship.

Emphasizing the need to engage with place on many levels, I explore the different ways in which place can be sensed, and how each of the senses can be used in an identifying, discriminating way, or in a way that experiences phenomena without naming them. Together we construct the various stories that are contained in the place – the geological evolution of the rock strata; the formation of the topography and the soils; the type of flora and fauna that have evolved in this landscape; what is known about the history of Aboriginal occupation of the area and the 'Dreaming stories' of the place; the history of European invasion and settlement; and, finally, the different personal stories of how each of the students came to be sitting there that day. Moving beyond place literalism, I discuss various indirect ways in which a place can 'speak' to a person through natural features, animals, poetry, symbols and dream images. Students consider their associations with the place and the role of imagination in building a sense of place. In later workshops, both in the bush and in urban settings, I explore the use of the elements and archetypes in understanding the person–place relationship, how to express place through different creative media, as well as how to bring out the commonalities and differences between urban and wild place experiences.

Over the years, the several hundred students who have taken this course have chosen a wide variety of places to visit for many different reasons. Some have been interested in the interaction between designed and natural features and have visited urban parks. One visited an art gallery to experience the creation of a contemplative urban environment in which other places were often depicted on its walls. Others have researched the connection between the healing of degraded land and personal healing by visiting and working on polluted or degraded sites. Many spend each week in a national park, seeking out the stories of the place, developing their ecological literacy and discovering how little remains of the Aboriginal stories in most places. Several students have immersed themselves in the process of being attentive to neglected or unloved areas of land, such as the land on either side of major power lines or waste dumps. A number have been interested in marginal or border lands, exploring the sense of place in a paddock and adjacent forest, or a beach and an estuary, or a garden and the surrounding bushland. Others have been motivated by the spiritual or eco-psychological dimensions of place and have tended to choose the most wild and remote locations they could find.

Many students have been surprised and touched by the depth and transformative effect of spending one afternoon a week visiting the same place over four months while reading and reflecting on the person–place relationship. The surprise comes, in part, because of their initial resistance to the apparent artificiality of selecting a place and spending regular time in it, and concern about the outcome. As one student expressed it: 'Relationship with a place? Are these people for real? How can I have a relationship with a place when I can barely hold down relationships with other human beings... At first nothing seemed to happen. I would spend many restless hours trying to form a relationship with this ungrateful place.'

This student's breakthrough came when he realized that while he was watching nature, he was being watched – in particular, by hundreds of golden orb weaver spiders. As he read about the biology of spiders, he pondered their role in mythology and observed the fearful response of others to spiders. His scientific and symbolic understanding led him into a 'spider's eye view' of his place and, also, into a deeper appreciation of the need to release unfounded fears and prejudices on the way to sustainability.

Another student was initially 'afraid of becoming bored, of not having enough to do. I was afraid of going to a place to which I did not already feel some connection and which was just a patch of bush.' Her journey into place was, in part, an exploration of Merleau-Ponty's (1962) ideas of body-as-subject and of her own physical responses to nature, and she wrote:

> *The world has become more animate. I look up at the pale, green, smooth branches of the eucalypt spreading out and I feel a kind of mimicking action in my body. I have started from not so much a place of indifference but a place*

of wishing I could feel more... I censored the knowing that my body was bringing to me. In the course of this project I have felt this censorship lifting and I feel I am learning to speak a new language. I am learning to take my part in what Abram (1996, p53) called 'the improvized duet between my animal body and the fluid breathing landscape it inhabits'.

In the workshops during the semester and in email conversations, the students have canvassed a wide range of issues as a result of coming to terms with their specific sense of place project. Most of them, at some point, become concerned about the apparent lack of mutuality in their emerging place relationships. While valuing their place visits as occasions of respite and nurturance, they have raised questions around the campfire, such as 'I feel like I am taking so much from the place, but what am I giving back?' and 'Does the land respond to the love and care I feel for it?' These questions have sparked discussions of the significance of physical action, complemented by an attitude of care, and the different levels of caring for country.

The importance of childhood places in the students' perceptions of place and their sense of self has been striking. Although most students did not start their projects with this in mind, many discover the significance of the places they grew up in as they begin reflecting about their response to their chosen place. For some, merely spending this amount of time quietly outside takes them back to childhood (and to their deeper selves). For others, specific and detailed memories of significant places from their early life come back with such power that they see their life's journey in a different light. Often it is a matter of making unconscious patterns more conscious. One student noticed that she was unable to relate deeply to her chosen place in a quiet reflective mode, and could only 'allow it in' when she was doing physical maintenance work. She made more sense of this observation, and her life patterns more generally, when she thought about her early life on a farm.

Many of the students show a growing interest in the possibilities of a healing relationship with the land. In part, this was a matter of acknowledging the wounds – the visible scars in the land and the invisible polluting of the waters – as well as the psychological wounding that each person carries. Healing, for some, means the physical work of removing weeds or planting trees, and this is personally sustaining; for others, it is attitudinal, and involves renewed care and respect.

PLACE, INDIGENEITY AND ENVIRONMENTALISM

The experiences of the students confirm Read's general contention that powerful place attachments are made by non-indigenous people in Australia, often without direct experience of indigenous knowledge. Given the opportunity to spend half a day per week in the same place – in fact, being required to do so within a formal university setting – some students have reported experiences as deep as those expressed by Read's interviewees. These comments have sometimes come years later, and not only during the field trip, when it could be argued that students are merely saying what the lecturer wants to hear (despite my repeated injunction to be true to what they actually experience rather than what they consider they are supposed to think and feel). I regularly receive emails and letters from past students letting me know how taking the subject changed the course of their lives, or their university careers, or helped them to recover from illness, or led them to become more environmentally active.

However, these student reports are not saying quite the same thing as Read. He has contacted a diverse group of people who have expressed, through their writing, or songs, or way of living, that they already have a strong bond with their country. Some of my students have already been deeply immersed in place; but many of them indicate at the outset that what drew them towards this elective subject was the fact that they did not feel a strong sense of place. Indeed, they felt displaced or felt that they didn't really belong in Australia. The result that most of these students have ended up expressing a strong connection with place suggests not only that non-indigenous people can form deep place attachments, but that they can learn to do so, given the opportunity and some starting ideas.

Only a minority of my students have come to the project with direct experience of indigenous knowledge. The course readings contain accounts of indigenous relationships with country and include a chapter from Read's book. Indigeneity is a central topic in the seminars and workshops. However, when asked at the outset why they chose the subject, few students mention Aboriginality. Motivated, in part, by the readings and discussions, most of them attempt to find out the Aboriginal history of their chosen place, the myths and stories that might belong to it, and to contact the relevant Aboriginal land councils or descendants of local Aboriginal people. This attempt is illuminating in itself, even if it only leads to the recognition of how much knowledge has been lost. Some students write directly of the sense of loss of countless millennia of continuous care for country, and how that loss affects their understanding of their place. Some imaginatively fill in what has been lost historically. Others follow the way of thinking that Peter Read ascribes to Bill Insch:

> *Aboriginality? That cannot help him; the past is almost unknown, the people are gone from the valley, and the only attempt to re-people it was a fiasco... But modern Man, deprived of Aboriginalities, must make the best way he can* (Read, 2000, p102).

Making 'the best way they can' includes students engaging in creative activities, such as constructing installations, engaging in rituals, and producing paintings, poetry and photographs.

Not many students have been as blessed as Peter Read was by his friendship with Dennis Foley, although a handful have had similar experiences. There are too few to offer many general statements; suffice to say, these were really significant encounters during which the students concerned learned a great deal, not simply about history and stories, but about how to be in the bush; how to observe birds, animals and insects; how to find edible food where none appears to exist; and how to remain still in body and mind for long periods of time. These fortunate few learned what Read learned from Foley – that even close to urban areas, there are descendants of the local Aboriginal people who care for country, carry the history and know some of the hidden stories. They, and the places of which they are custodians, are usually not known to the general public and they prefer to keep it that way.

Do these relationships show any of 'the more interesting options of interaction' to which Plumwood refers? Clearly, the first two of the options Plumwood mentions – dialogue and learning – are operating with the students, as they were with Peter Read and Dennis Foley. If one form of relationship involves settlers and migrants learning history and stories from the first peoples then many of my students have experienced that relationship. Peter Read was primarily in this position with Dennis Foley, as were the participants of the Sense of Place Colloquium in Central Australia (Cameron and San Roque, 2002, in press). The first two days of that colloquium consisted of the visitors listening to the Aboriginal custodian of the local area telling us the outer layer of the stories of the local Dreaming, and being slowly introduced to country. It wasn't until the third day that we were ready to converse with others about our own place experiences. Perhaps Plumwood's options of interaction are sequential – basic learning about place needs to occur before meaningful dialogue is possible, and this precedes convergence and hybridity, which are higher-order relationships. To countenance the more complex forms without basic learning is to invite misunderstanding. Most non-indigenous Australians have much to learn from Aboriginal people, and spending time together in place is a better way to learn and engage in satisfying dialogue than a generalized conversation about reconciliation or Aboriginality. Only through more specific interactions, it seems to me, can convergent spiritualities or hybrid cultural expressions be soundly based.

At the same time, most of the students found deep place relationships independently of Aboriginal people, which might seem to confirm Read's call for independent intuiting of our attachments to country. However, the matter of choice is critical here. By and large, my students attempted to find local Aboriginal people who could tell them about their places, but most were unsuccessful. The few who succeeded found their connection with the land greatly enriched as a result. The contentious part of Read's call for independence is the suggestion that even when faced with a choice, white Australians should choose a separate pathway. Some of my students and the Central Australian Colloquium participants would have been the poorer for that choice.

Discussion about the place relationships between Aboriginal and non-Aboriginal people needs to be grounded in the recognition of great diversity on each side. Generalizations about Aboriginality can obscure the fact that there are many Aboriginalities. The Yolgnu of Arnhem Land in the Northern Territory, for example, had many centuries of trade with the Macassans, from what is now Indonesia, and differ greatly in intercultural history and language from the Pitjatjantjara of the Central Desert and from middle-class suburban people of Eora descent in Sydney. Generalizations about non-Aboriginality can conceal the great differences between first- and sixth-generation Australians, and between immigrants from England, southern Europe and South-East Asia.

The whole project of grounding students in their own experience of place is subject to Plumwood's critique of individualizing a structural problem. To some extent, I address this concern by providing readings from Plumwood and Massey and others who discuss structural issues. My subject is also offered in a university department in which there are other subjects – such as Social and Political Change Movements and Eco-feminism, offered by Ariel Salleh – that cover the structural dimensions of environmental problems. The value of Plumwood's critique is not so much that it champions the structural level over the individual, which can lead to a false dichotomy, but that it stimulates consideration of structural questions in order to complement individual awareness and action. I have observed a tendency amongst some students to take refuge in their chosen places, to derive personal comfort and significance from these visits, to revel in their newfound place attachment, and not to relate to the larger questions of sustainability, or cultural change, or control of economic power. It is a risk for educators that experiential learning can lead students so deeply into their internal experience that they are reluctant to emerge from it. Most of my students, however, cannot avoid the larger picture of economic, political and social structures because the imprint on the chosen place is clearly visible. Coastal development is rapidly encroaching upon the beach visited by one student, motivating him to investigate the environmental and local political history of the area. Another student tried to trace the source of the brown scum floating in the creek at her place, and ended up with a complex mix of effluent from sewage treatment and heavy manufacturing. Another looked at the social pressures and gender relations that led her and her friends to feel unsafe on their own in the bush.

Just as it is possible to ignore the structural issues by focusing exclusively upon individualized accounts, it is also possible to lose the individual engagement in exclusive engagement with structural issues. During my years with the conservation movement, I observed that some of the activists with whom I worked were preoccupied with environmental and corporate policy issues, and were impatient with my concern for local place. It's another aspect of the muting of the voice of place affiliation that I described in the fist section of this chapter.

A rather more nuanced view of the interplay between structural and individualized forces emerges from my experiences. People act out of their own experience; therefore, attention to the individual's place relationships, and providing opportunities for deepening place affiliation, are important. If people have a poorly developed sense of place, there will be a process of immersion into place that could lead to a lack of considering larger structural questions for some time. There is a risk that place immersion could remain an individualized phenomenon; but if my students are any indication, most people engage more energetically with institutionalized forces once they are aware of the effect such forces have on their local places.

Plumwood quite rightly argues for collective effort to overcome the structural barriers to a place-responsive society that, at present, only a privileged few can overcome by their own efforts (many people are caught in economic, employment and social situations that give them little choice). She proposes a project of renaming places as an example of collective effort; others that occur to me are community-mapping projects that include local Aboriginal people as key participants, and national park and reserve signage projects that bring together scientific, cultural and historical aspects of protected local places. Broadening formal education to include learning from place responsiveness as an explicit goal could be another such undertaking. At the moment, the subjective response to place is taken for granted: a background for poetic or artistic endeavours or a minor part of environmentally oriented field trips. Conscious and regular attention to local place relationships has proven to be an effective vehicle for personal and environmental learning at the postgraduate university level in the subjects I have taught. Whether that is the case, more generally, in schools, other universities and informal community education settings await further investigation.

Massey's work provides an interesting view from the outside for students of the Australian debate about place and identity. Although her critique of place essentialism has much in common with Plumwood's, particularly regarding the construction of place attachment by gender, race and class, she focuses upon urban place relationships, whereas Plumwood clearly has a deep affinity for wild nature. Massey takes the reader on a walk down Kilburn High Road in London, describing how there are depictions of, and references to, many other parts of the world – IRA slogans, life-size models of Indian women, reminders of the Persian Gulf War, the Middle East and Pakistan (Massey, 1994, pp152–153). By contrast, Plumwood writes of bushwalking in the Kakadu National Park in the Northern Territory, describing evocative figures weathered into the sandstone plateau, and the 'extraordinary qualities of beauty, power and prescience' in the land (Plumwood, 2000, p102).

Recently, my students have picked up on these differences in the course readings. One student who was investigating a city park in central Sydney commented with reference to Massey's work that 'a dynamic concept of place with its recognition of multiple meanings, changing identities, fluid boundaries and complex interconnections is a more useful and relevant way to understand place in the city' than many of the place readings based in wild nature. Another student, while visiting a park in Adelaide city, found that Massey raised important points to consider, whereas in 'the timeless landscape of the desert hills' of the Flinders Ranges several hundred kilometres north of Adelaide, the critique 'all seemed so irrelevant'.

However, discussions among the students during the semester have revealed complexities within the apparent divide between urban and bush experiences. For example, around the campfire in 2001, a student visiting a creek-side park in central Melbourne spoke of the startling power of the nocturnal appearance of an owl and a fox within several minutes of each other in terms normally used by students encountering wildlife in more remote locations. Another described the single swooping glide of a currawong into one side of a multilevel car park and out the other side with the language of a numinous event.

The student responses to Massey's writing, and the apparent differences between European and Australian place writing, raise difficult questions about place relationships in Australia. Massey critiques working-class communities in the Docklands of London resisting the encroachment of 'yuppies' into their area for putting forward an invalid 'claim for timeless authority' (1994, p122). She considers their claim to be invalid because a generation ago it was claimed to be, in essence, a white area (to resist the encroachment of Asian immigrants), and a couple of centuries ago it had been field and farmland – that is, an essentialist definition of place collapses in the face of historical understanding. Is this critique of place essentialism in urban England simply 'irrelevant' when transposed to outback Australia, as one student felt? This would imply that the critique itself is place and culture bound, relevant only for urban, possibly European, places and Western culture. If, as other students consider, it is more widely relevant (and Massey does use very general language about space, place and gender), then are not Aboriginal songlines, identified with very specific places and associated stories and rituals, 'a claim for timeless authenticity'?

In the Central Australian Colloquium, participants were introduced to the notion, held by local Aboriginal people and some local non-Aboriginals, of an interconnection between human consciousness and consciousness within the land (Cameron and San Roque, 2002, in press). Plumwood writes of the 'prescience' of Kakadu country, and the Australian poets I referred to above bestow the land with subjectivity. The question thus arises: is it physically true, as well as imaginatively and mythologically true, that the land contains consciousness and energies of its own? This is similar to Peter Read's question: 'Do people respond to forces in the country already, or is it humankind which sacralizes the country?' (2000, p203). Read receives several different answers to this question from his interviewees, and my students who have considered this fathomless question also come up with differing responses.

It is, indeed, a deep mystery – one that underlies the discussion of sense of place in Australia, but which is seldom articulated. It is not specific to Australia, as the existence of geomancy and feng-shui attests. However, the status in Australia of vast areas of country still under Aboriginal law and maintained by ritual and ceremony gives it a present reality that is muted, to say the least, in most Western countries. The only way I can understand it is that humanity, country and consciousness have co-evolved in Australia for at least 60,000 years, so that Peter Read's question is moot – all three are inseparable and have been throughout human history. As a non-Aboriginal Australian, I have had an occasional glimpse of power and presence in the land that has been vast beyond comprehension. My regular engagement with my local garden and bushland has been co-evolutionary in a more modest sense. As I have worked in the garden and regenerated the surrounding bushland, I have modified the place while it has changed me, physically and mentally (Cameron, 2001).

And what of conservation strategies? As mentioned, some students who take my subject are moved to take immediate action to protect 'their' places. A few who had expressed antipathy towards Green activists as being narrow or 'anti-humanity' have ended up joining, or in one case creating, environmental campaigns in order to save a piece of bush or coastline. Many more have expressed a changed attitude towards environmental issues – greater empathy with the passion of environmentalists, more understanding of the link between daily actions and environmental issues, more willingness to take a stand in local affairs. One wrote a magazine article entitled 'Spiders for Sustainability', based upon his experiences of the semester.

Environmental activists who have taken the subject have reported mixed reactions. For some, it provided much-needed regeneration after being burned out from years of campaigning. It was a time of deepening commitment or, perhaps, reorientation within an activist framework. Others, however, have found it a challenging and complex experience. Several have complained, somewhat tongue-in-cheek, that life used to be simple as a Greenie before they realized that farmers and loggers have a sense of place, too. A greater number have found the subject to be a means of entering into a more reflective phase of their life – a time in which they are looking more deeply at their motivations for the positions they have taken, and, in some cases, questioning their involvement in activism or even the whole activist 'project'. From a narrow Green perspective, this could be problematic because it removes eco-warriors from the frontline, at least temporarily. But there can be longer-term gains.

Thus, whether it is of environmental benefit for activists to pay closer attention to their sense of local place is partially dependent upon one's point of view. Becoming a more reflective environmentalist, if my students are any indication, may lead a person to a more sustainable form of environmental activism; but it may lead them to question some of the strategies and actions of the movement. The loss of some eco-warriors from the frontline might be offset by the addition of some more grounded campaigners, able to enter into deeper dialogue with those of opposing viewpoints and able to maintain the campaign over the long haul. Indeed, there are already some seasoned Green campaigners and Green politicians with these qualities who have been able to sustain their deep connection with their local places.

There is some indication of more sympathy for the diverse voices of place attachment within the conservation movement and beyond than there was 13 years ago when the polarized forestry meeting that I described in the first section of this chapter occurred. For example, there has been the recent publication of the book *The People's Forest* by Greg Borschmann (1999), an oral historian, writer and journalist associated with the conservation movement. This book is based upon a series of sympathetic interviews with, and photographs of, a wide range of people who have a deep affinity with forests – farmers, rural women, saw-millers, logging contractors, field botanists and seed collectors, as well as people who overtly identify themselves as forest conservationists. In the introduction to the collection, Borschmann pays tribute to the voices of place affiliation who have sometimes been marginalized in the environmental debate:

> *These stories, then, are but the beginning, a scratching of the surface. They contain the kernel of a Bush Dreaming, both old and new. Have we the patience and humility to listen to each others' stories? There is wisdom, memory and insight here that we are in danger of losing, as surely as we may yet lose even more of the forests, bushlands, grasslands and their great waterway arteries. How soon will we come to know that they are inseparable – the stories, the people and the forests?* (Borschmann, 1999, pviii).

The broader question for conservation strategies is whether it is possible to engender love of place as a means of achieving conservation objectives. If so, it could sit alongside the use of fear of the consequences of unsustainable economic activity, or exhortations to do the right thing with regard to other species, or offering a vision of environmental utopia, and alongside government departments' and schools' use of education about the environment. Love of place is generally considered a matter for the individual, not the domain of any group in society, except perhaps poets, place writers, painters and film-makers, as I have discussed above. But what if educators and conservationists saw it as their mandate to foster deeper place attachment among students and the general public?

The several hundred students who have taken the 'Sense of Place' course over the past eight years are a self-selected and unrepresentative sample of the Australian population; but they at least suggest that it is possible to facilitate greater place affiliation in a way that is personally fulfilling for those involved. Its success as a conservation strategy is harder to gauge. Some previously uninterested students have become environmentally active, others less so. Many are more able to connect large environmental issues with the fate of their local places. Some retreated into local places as a refuge, or for healing in an insular fashion. Perhaps this could be interpreted as part of the process of place engagement for those without a previously strong sense of place.

Plumwood cautions more generally that place attachment cannot always be considered to be of conservation benefit:

> *One has to consider the case, increasingly common in commodified and colonial land contexts, where one's land of attachment thrives at the expense of other land which is treated as sacrificial. In this case, land attachment does not necessarily lead to positive environmental outcomes* (Plumwood, 2000, p105).

I encourage in my students an inclusive sense of place, in which experiencing a deeper relationship with one place opens one up to a deeper affiliation with all places, rather than an exclusive sense of place of the type referred to by Plumwood. The latter is analogous to the essentialist approach to place, critiqued by Massey, that does not allow for others to have a different sense of that place, particularly others of different gender, race or class background.

Allowing multiple stories of place to be voiced not only fosters an inclusive sense of place among a group of people, it can also help to deal with entrenched environmental conflict. This, in turn, can lead to the adoption of conservation strategies that have wider support than regulatory or legal measures that alienate at least one of the parties concerned. I encountered an example of the power of the storied approach to place when I was approached by a member of a catchment management committee in Tasmania after I had given a talk in Hobart on sense of place. She described how the committee had been sharply divided between pro-development and conservationist members, and had not been able to agree on any course of action. Then the members went on a two-day tour of the catchment. As they arrived at particular places, each member was asked to mention to the rest of the group any experiences they had had in that place, or any knowledge they had of it. Informally, especially in the evening, people starting swapping stories of growing up in the area or moving into it. By the end of the trip, there was much more understanding of each member as a person, not simply a representative of an organization or ideology. The experience transformed the functioning of the committee – committee members now had the capacity to work together for the benefit of the catchment community as a whole. The potential for working with place stories is further discussed by Martin Mulligan in Chapter 12.

Conclusions: learning responsiveness to place

Developing a place-responsive culture is, as Plumwood (2000, p96) has noted, a revolutionary process. It involves changing institutions and practices that are barriers to enriching place relationships, such as treating place as an inanimate property to be traded, or a resource for exploitation, or living lives of increasing mobility and displacement. My own view is that this sort of radical change is best approached through the notion of learning our way towards the place-responsive society. It is analogous to the view propounded by Lester Milbrath (1989) regarding sustainability. As he says in his preface:

> *My first intention for this book was to present a vision of a sustainable society; that is still its major topic. As the book evolved, however, I returned again and again to the recognition that we must improve and hasten social learning as the major avenue to social change. So the central theme of the book became:* learning our way to a sustainable society *[emphasis in original]* (Milbrath, 1989, pxi).

Promoting some sort of desirable end state called a sustainable society and describing its characteristics sets up the barrier of 'We are nowhere near that state now, so how do we get there from here?' It can even cause paralysis because the perceived difference is so large. A better question to ask is 'What are the conditions that enable a society to learn its way towards sustainability' (Milbrath, 1989, p366)?

What I have been doing at the university is promoting the conditions that enable the students, and myself in the process, to learn our way towards a responsiveness to place. It is a different approach from mainstream environmental education, for example, which primarily aims to provide students with information about the environment. It is learner-centred, focused upon the learners themselves and their experiences (Kolb, 1982; Brookfield, 1986). In the 'sense of place' subject, the learning is through the experience of the weekly place visits informed by workshops and course readings. It is learning about how to develop ecological literacy, awareness of the more-than-human aspects of place, openness to other stories of place than one's own, and the capacity to bring one's previous place experiences into consciousness.

From the learning perspective, the question at the structural level is how to redesign institutions and structures so that they enable organizations to learn place responsiveness, rather than continue to encourage a denial of relatedness to place. For educational institutions, one of the ways to do this is to re-examine the specializations into arts and sciences that occur in schooling. Understanding how the natural elements of place interact is currently the domain of the sciences – botany, geology, ecology. The feeling response to place is the domain of the humanities – literature and the arts. The two have become cordoned off so that the real power of dawning ecological knowledge, working in concert with a poetic appreciation of place, is lost. As many of my students discover, a felt response to place without ecological understanding is as one-sided as scientific and historical knowledge of a place without any emotional engagement with it.

Both Massey and Plumwood urge that learning about responsiveness to place should include learning about the way our responses are conditioned by our class, race, gender and colonial status. We carry social conditioning with us so that we recapitulate our early place and social relationships unless we bring awareness of that conditioning and the desire to challenge it. This is where engagement with Aboriginal people within the landscape and with their stories of place can be so valuable. The students who were fortunate enough to find Aboriginal guides, and those of us involved with the Central Australian Colloquium, were required to not only listen and learn about the profundity of a world view in which trees, rock forms and creatures are kin, infused with consciousness and purpose, but also to learn of the limitations of our own culture, by contrast. It is a privilege to glimpse the power of 60,000-year-old Earth-based tradition, and a sorrow to experience in the flesh, on the land, the devastating economic, social and environmental impacts that European colonization has had.

With Read, we can say that it is possible to learn responsiveness to place without direct interaction with Aboriginal people. To say otherwise would be to deny opportunities for many Australians for whom such an experience is not likely. After all, the evidence of Aboriginal connections with country is everywhere in contemporary Australian society – in art, music, dance, theatre, newspaper articles, poetry and novels. With Plumwood, we can say that learning responsiveness to place is greatly enhanced by such interaction, and every collective effort should be made to increase the likelihood of it occurring.

When this sort of learning is taking place, in reconciliation circles, in Landcare groups, catchment-management committees, classrooms and conservation groups, then we can begin to ask the harder questions about a place-responsive culture. What forms of agriculture and pastoralism provide for collective learning about sustainability and greater place affiliation? How different would the experience of buying and selling land be if both parties were primarily concerned about the passing on of what had been learned about the place? Culture does not remain static, and there are many different cultures in Australia. With such diversity, how can we grapple meaningfully with the complexity of multicultural dialogue around sustainable futures and place relations, while contending with the rapidity of the changes wrought by modernization and globalization?

These questions become too large, too generalized and decontextualized without ongoing appreciation of our local places, and without ongoing conversation with other cultures in urban and wild places. Learning to pay closer attention to place relationships helps to sustain the individual, as well as the society and its environment. It becomes an imperative when a highly biodiverse continent and the oldest land-based culture on the globe are both facing multiple threats.

REFERENCES

Abram, D (1996) *The Spell of the Sensuous*. Vintage Books, New York

Borschmann, G (1999) *The People's Forest: A Living History of the Australian Bush*. The People's Forest Press, Blackheath

Brookfield, S (1986) *Understanding and Facilitating Adult Learning*. Jossey-Bass, San Francisco

Cameron, J (2001) *Changing Places: Reimagining Sense of Place in Australia*. University of Western Sydney, Richmond

Cameron, J and Elix, J (1991) *Recovering Ground: A Case Study Approach to Ecologically Sustainable Land Management*. Australian Conservation Foundation, Melbourne

Cameron, J and Penna, I (1988) *The Wood and the Trees: A Preliminary Economic Analysis of a Conservation-Oriented Forest Industry Strategy*. Australian Conservation Foundation, Melbourne

Cameron, J and San Roque, C (2002, in press) 'Coming into country: the catalysing process of social ecology', *Philosophy, Activism, Nature*, vol 2, Monash University, Melbourne

Flannery, T (1994) *The Future Eaters: An Ecological History of Australasia and its Peoples.* Reed Books, Port Melbourne

Griffiths, T (1998) 'Legend and lament', *The Australian Review of Books*, November, pp11–13

Jung, C (1927) 'Mind and Earth' in *Collected Works, Volume 10.* Routledge and Kegan Paul, London

Kolb, D (1982) *Experiential Learning: Experience as the Source of Learning and Development.* Prentice-Hall, Englewood Cliffs

Krygier, M (1997) *Between Fear and Hope: Hybrid Thoughts on Public Values.* ABC Books, Sydney

Malouf, D (1998) *A Spirit of Play: The Making of Australian Consciousness.* ABC Books, Sydney

Massey, D (1994) *Space, Place and Gender.* Polity, Cambridge

Merleau-Ponty, M (1962) *Phenomenology of Perception.* Routledge and Kegan Paul, London

Milbrath, L (1989) *Envisioning a Sustainable Society: Learning our Way Out.* SUNY Press, Albany

Mowaljarlai, D and Malnic, J (1993) *Yorro Yorro.* Inner Traditions Books, Rochester

Plumwood, V (2000) 'Belonging, naming and decolonization', *Ecopolitics: Thought and Action*, vol 1, no 1, pp90–106

Read, P (2000) *Belonging: Australians, Place and Aboriginal Ownership.* Cambridge University Press, Cambridge

Relph, E (1992) 'Modernity and the Reclamation of Place' in D Seamon (ed) *Dwelling, Seeing and Designing: Toward a Phenomenological Ecology.* State University of New York Press, New York

Rose, D B (2000) *Dingo Makes Us Human: Land and Life in an Australian Aboriginal Culture,* second edition. Cambridge University Press, Cambridge

Seddon, G (1997) *Landprints: Reflections on Place and Landscape.* Cambridge University Press, Cambridge

Stanner, W (1979) *White Man Got No Dreaming: Essays 1938–1973.* Australian National University Press, Canberra

Tacey, D (1995) *Edge of the Sacred: Transformation in Australia.* HarperCollins, Melbourne

Chapter 9

The changing face of nature conservation: Reflections on the Australian experience

Penelope Figgis

INTRODUCTION

For most of the 20th century, environmentalists thought that they knew the best way to safeguard landscapes, seascapes and wildlife. Certainly in Australia, it became the case that when the environment movement cried 'save' the Great Barrier Reef, South-West Tasmania, the Alps, Fraser Island, Myall Lakes or the Tarkine, both environmentalists and the general community knew it meant 'declare this area a national park'. The 'safest' we could make nature was to have it formally declared under legislation and managed by a government nature conservation authority.

After such declarations, the task became one of defending these sanctuaries from any compromise that would undermine their natural values. This approach was largely driven by a philosophy shaped by what John Dryzek (1997) has called the 'survivalist discourse'. This refers to the perspective articulated by the Club of Rome and environmental futurists such as Paul Erlich, Garrett Harden and Barry Commoner that the ecological limits of the Earth are fast approaching, and that human beings and their rapacious appetites for resources are the fundamental problem. Under this world view, national parks were refuges of a declining natural world and people were the enemy of nature. Consequently, all people – apart from those who loved and did not damage nature – should be kept out, especially those behind the economic interests that were blamed for generating the environmental 'crisis'. Essentially, the majority of the Australian environment movement holds firmly to variations of this analysis, maintaining that publicly owned parks, under a strict protection regime, are the best means of ensuring nature conservation (Prineas, 1998).

Given the ecological crisis facing our Earth and our country, the argument that nature needs such 'safe havens' is compelling. A 1996 *State of the Environment Report* confirmed that Australia's rich and distinct biodiversity is under multiple threats and still in decline (Commonwealth of Australia, 1996). The last official figures had only 7.8 per cent of the Australian landmass in any kind of formal protected area (Thackway, 1996a). Fortunately, during the last few years, Australia's protected areas have been expanding. The National Reserve System programme (NRS), which has been operating since 1997, aims to produce a comprehensive, adequate and representative (CAR) reserve system. It has bilateral political support at the national level and the support of all states and territories. Priorities for reserve selection are being determined within a major framework called the Interim Biogeographic Regionalization for Australia (IBRA), and the programme receives a substantial allocation of the national Natural Heritage Trust funds. In the marine area, the Interim Marine and Coastal Regionalization for Australia (IMCRA) is being used to identify and establish the National Representative System of Marine Protected Areas (NRSMPA). Significantly, additional areas are added to the conservation estate through the Indigenous Protected Areas (IPA) programme, which promotes the voluntary declaration of Aboriginal land as protected areas. A separate NRS programme for private protected areas provides 2:1 funding for private land purchased for conservation. In addition, the Regional Forest Agreement (RFA) process, for all its significant flaws, also contains a key component that has enhanced forest protected areas, albeit inadequately (Figgis, 1999).

All the processes mentioned above – IBRA, IMCRA and the RFA – have also added dramatically to our knowledge and understanding of terrestrial and marine conservation in Australia. In particular, there is now a much better idea of which ecosystems are well represented in reserves and which are poorly represented.

These programmes are undoubtedly leading to millions of additional hectares of land and sea being declared protected areas. Environment Australia estimates that it has brought into protection an additional 3.1 million hectares through the Indigenous Protected Areas programme (Forsyth, pers com, 2001). However, many trends are converging to suggest that the familiar model of the publicly owned sanctuary, which the environment movement has both promoted and defended, may be substantially different, or at least augmented by substantially different models, in the 21st century. There is also increasing recognition that nature conservation in Australia is not just a discussion of protected areas. New ideas and models are emerging to add tools to the vast toolbox that will be necessary in addressing the challenge of conservation in the new century. This chapter discusses new ideas and challenges under the headings of 'New drivers', 'New models' and 'New mechanisms'. While welcoming the expansion of the debate about appropriate conservation strategies, the chapter ends with a note of caution about what could be lost in the rush towards the new era.

NEW DRIVERS

The national parks and protected areas of the favoured conservation models in Australia emerged a bare century ago. In shaping such reserves, Australia followed the Western model of defined boundaries, legislative status, public ownership and exclusion of human commerce and extraction. Australian national parks were influenced by a political culture that felt little pressure from population size and growth, and showed little understanding of indigenous rights or interests. Increasingly, however, in the same way as economic paradigms in Australia have been strongly affected by international trends, protected area policies have been exposed to global thinking. The major international trends that are creating a climate for change in protected area policy are the trend for governments to reduce their areas of operation – the 'retreat of government' – and consequent efforts to build community involvement – 'constituency-building'. To these drivers can be added growing international interest in the notion of bioregionalism, and the growing recognition of indigenous rights. I have discussed these trends in detail elsewhere (Figgis, 1999), but will summarize this discussion below.

The retreat of government

The 'retreat of government' refers to the trend for modern governments to shed or share responsibilities that it believes others in the community can manage. It stems from the ideological victory of capitalism over socialism during the late 20th century. This victory has promoted a form of neo-capitalism that supports market-based allocation of resources, deregulation, competitiveness, smaller government and a powerful private sector. As a result of the ascendancy of this paradigm, what is perceived as the legitimate province of government is shrinking. In addition, within many public policy areas it has led to a preference for incentives and market-based mechanisms over legislative and regulatory 'command-and-control' systems. The breadth of this shift has meant that no sphere of government – even when it is focused upon an evident public interest such as conservation – is seen as immune. In general, the retreat of government has resulted in reduced funding, reduced staffing, a pressure for parks authorities to generate separate income, and the exploration of increasing roles for the community and private sector.

In Australia, the overall picture is patchy and accurate figures are elusive. Some agencies have, in fact, had increased budgets; but when set against large increases in areas for which they are responsible, they are still effectively suffering cuts. As a result, even when budgetary allocations have increased – as has been the case in New South Wales (NSW) and at national level – the dollars are often allocated, in part, to help government find partnerships in the private or community sector in order to achieve conservation goals.

The search for other players and partnerships (involving indigenous people, local government, private land-owners and resource-sector industries) to further conservation is generally depicted as 'constituency-building'. The general need to build constituencies for protected areas has been high on the agenda since the Fourth World Congress on National Parks and Protected Areas in Caracas, Venezuela, in 1992.

Organized by the World Conservation Union (IUCN) every ten years, these congresses have become vital international forums where new ideas are discussed and taken back to the participant countries by key decision-makers. Between congresses, the World Commission on Protected Areas (WCPA) – formerly known as the Commission on National Parks and Protected Areas (CNPPA) – is an informal network of protected area professionals and is a major player in debates through its publications, committees and meetings worldwide.

In the Caracas Action Plan (CAP) (IUCN, 1993), the principal strategy document to come out of the fourth congress, some of the key directions for current international debates were established. The principal objectives of the Caracas Action Plan were:

- Integrate protected areas into larger planning frameworks.
- Expand support for protected areas.
- Strengthen the capacity to manage protected areas.
- Expand international cooperation in the finance, development and management of protected areas.

The first two goals have particular relevance in Australia.

Bioregionalism

The first CAP objective (the integration of protected areas into the broader planning frameworks) has been reiterated many times and is now a consensus view internationally. It emerges from a strong scientific consensus that 'island' national parks and protected areas *alone* will not achieve the task of biodiversity conservation. The impacts of climate change also give a major impetus for greater connectivity and flexibility in conservation. We are therefore likely to see mosaic corridors of diverse ownership and tenure over broad landscapes managed for biodiversity conservation. Parks would be linked, and/or buffered, by a whole suite of conservation entities, such as biosphere reserves, Indigenous Protected Areas, private sanctuaries and land stewardship agreements on 'working lands'.

This 'islands to networks' (Shepphard, 1997) – or bioregional – approach builds upon the 1970s concept of Man and the Biosphere (MAB) reserves. The MAB model envisaged a strictly protected core area surrounded by buffer and then transition zones. The concept has now evolved into a broader vision of many such areas linked together into total networks, even creating corridors on a global scale. Internationally, 'Yosemite to Yukon' in North America and the

Atlantic rainforests of Brazil are two examples. A pioneer project of this model in Australia is Bookmark Biosphere Reserve in South Australia, which is discussed later.

The concept of turning protected area 'islands into networks' has broad agreement (WCPA, 1997). It undoubtedly has much merit and allows for creative tools to be developed in order to deal with the imposition of myriad human jurisdictions over natural systems. However, in policy terms it constitutes a substantial shift from the current national park model and could bring problems along with the gains. The winding out of the bioregional approach will mean the inclusion of multiple-use zones in designated protected areas. This, in turn, could fundamentally change the Australian public attitude that protected areas are commerce-free sanctuaries to one far more accepting of human commercial activities. The concept also envisages the use of non-legislative mechanisms that may provide for greater flexibility, but will not deliver security. It could mean that the management of such areas is subject to the prevailing political, economic and social pressures of the day.

The crux problem arises from the fact that, theoretically, these new models should build upon, and add to, the viability of strictly protected cores; but there are many forces that seem to be championing such models as a replacement for strict protection models. The reduction of emphasis on strict protection suits the many interests that promote the 'multiple-use' model. Conservative governments in Australia are attracted by the notion of parks that allow for other 'extractive' uses, especially tourism and mining. The current federal government has warmly embraced the concept, especially in the marine environment. This shift not only suits extractive industries that have long railed against 'locked-up' models, but also suits the emerging, virulent, outdoor recreation lobby.

New constituencies

The second key objective of the Caracas Action Plan (CAP) was to 'expand support for protected areas'. It is now a received wisdom that parks will not survive in either seas of ruined ecology or seas of human hostility, if new forms of support are not generated for them. Therefore, a key task is to build widespread support for parks by building different constituencies, with each having an interest in the success of one or more protected areas. IUCN calls the concept 'social sustainability', and has recently brought out a two-volume publication on achieving conservation outcomes in concert with people, rather than imposed upon them, called *Beyond Fences: Seeking Social Sustainability in Conservation* (IUCN, 1997).

Internationally, this debate has led to a considerable shift towards the idea of integrating development needs, especially those of indigenous people and local communities, within overall protected area management. Inevitably, seeking support from the broader community leads to an emphasis on quantifiable human benefits flowing from a multiple-use approach. Such an approach is at strong variance with the 'sanctuary' national parks model to which most Australian environmentalists are committed. They fear that making concessions to rural communities, access lobbies, tourism interests and other interests will inevitably undermine hard-won gains for nature.

However, the idea of introducing new players will not necessarily threaten the central concepts of nature conservation; indeed, there are potential gains for biodiversity. For example, there are farmers who may want to be certified as 'wildlife friendly' in order to get a market edge; tourism operators who see the market for unspoilt nature experiences growing; land-owners who see new possibilities for earning money from their native vegetation either through incentives or new markets; local governments who are beginning to see biodiversity as part of their public responsibilities under Agenda 21.

It is early days for this trend in Australia; but so far there is no evidence that the involvement of new players has fundamentally undermined the existing models. However, there is no doubt that the proliferation of conservation models gives policy-makers more choice, and the most uncompromising choice – strict protection – may become a less-chosen path because it can be difficult to sustain politically.

Recognition of indigenous rights

Another international driver of change is the growing recognition of the rights of indigenous people. The late 1980s saw a worldwide explosion in recognizing indigenous people as vital players in conservation programmes and sustainable development (Stevens, 1997). Smyth and Sutherland (1996) trace the evolution of this recognition in international treaties, law and policy. Common themes of these processes are the imperatives to recognize the morality of prior ownership; the value of the intimate ecological knowledge of indigenous people; the rights and the importance of indigenous people continuing to practice their culture; and the need for indigenous people to share the benefits of any use of their traditional resources.

Australia has reflected this fundamental shift in thinking about indigenous people, and increasingly indigenous rights are factored into land-management issues, including management of protected areas. Apart from the moral imperative for change, there are pragmatic realities that drive a need to recognize indigenous rights in nature conservation. Currently, title to an estimated 14 per cent of Australia – an area of more than 1 million square kilometres – has been restored to Aboriginal people. Significantly, this is over twice the area currently in protected areas (Boden and Breckwoldt, 1995). Furthermore, much of this land is located in areas less modified by European settlement, and it therefore retains high conservation value. It is widely recognized that any truly comprehensive reserve system would need to include components of these lands.

Over two decades, the search for conservation models that acknowledge indigenous rights has produced both Aboriginal-owned parks, such as Uluru and Kakadu, which are leased back to parks agencies, as well as joint management of existing parks, such as Mootwingee in New South Wales (Figgis, 1999). More recently, there has been an effort to find models that fit with high degrees of Aboriginal autonomy, such as the Indigenous Protected Areas programme, discussed below.

Inevitably, there are areas where the imperatives of nature conservation and indigenous rights may not fit comfortably together. In particular, issues arise in reconciling the multiple present and future needs of indigenous people with the uncompromising nature of strict protection. Some Aboriginal leaders have been clear that their priorities are culture and economic development. In a statement prepared at an Australian Nature Conservation Agency workshop in Alice Springs in 1994, launching the concept of indigenous protected areas, the delegates asserted their right to 'develop economic benefit from all Aboriginal and Torres Strait Islander lands'. Indigenous delegates also made a strong statement of their perspective:

> *Any conservation partnership must be based on the premise that indigenous cultural objectives of a conservation programme have priority over environmental issues* (Australian Nature Conservation Agency, 1995).

This approach produces unease among those groups and individuals most committed to nature conservation through sanctuary parks and the concept of wilderness. However, there is a spectrum of opinion within the environment movement, and many organizations and individuals have been giving a high priority to reconciling their respect for the rights of indigenous people and the rights of nature (Hill and Figgis, 1999).

Taken together, the trends outlined above constitute a shift to a much greater degree of complexity, both in the forms that conservation is likely to take and the people who are likely to be involved. In summary, the trend of modern nature conservation thinking is towards creating larger conservation entities or networks, integrating them more closely with human needs and involving more elements of the community in securing areas and managing them for biodiversity benefits.

NEW MODELS

The trends mentioned above have produced a very different conservation landscape from that of the 1960s and 1970s. New entities, which were quite unknown – such as bioregional models, Indigenous Protected Areas, large private reserves and fenced wildlife sanctuaries – have emerged. It is therefore important to identify the most significant new models.

The bioregional model

While the concept of bioregional, or 'whole of landscape', networks is broadly endorsed as an important direction for conservation, few examples exist to date.

The best-known Australian example is Bookmark Biosphere Reserve in South Australia's Riverland Region (Brunckhorst, 1999). It brings together 27 parcels of land covering some 6000 square kilometres, including formal protected areas, private lands and land owned by private conservation organizations. However, the reserve is not only composed of *de facto* nature reserves, but also game and forestry lands, as well as working properties and pastoral leases. It includes substantial areas of the floodplains of the Murray River that are listed wetlands under the Wetlands of International Importance (Ramsar Convention) for migratory species and waterfowl. It also helps to protect the largest area of mallee scrub in eastern Australia. The reserve is managed by the Bookmark Biosphere Trust, which has government, land-owner and community interests represented on it. The properties include a former pastoral lease called 'Calperum', Dangalli National Park, and a 50,000ha property called 'Gluepot', which was purchased to become a major sanctuary of endangered birds such as the black-eared minor by Birds Australia, Australia's major ornithological organization.

The concept of a biosphere reserve is one of reconciling communities and nature conservation through involvement in conservation across the landscape, both on and off reserves. Proponents of the concept see it as a prototype of genuine ecologically sustainable development, or a 'restorative economic model'. The Bookmark Biosphere Trust is pioneering work on new sustainable industries, such as horticulture based upon native species, oil production from mallees, aquaculture, tourism based around a new Aus$1.1 million environment centre at Renmark, and the development of community-based Bookmark guides. These are all at pilot or research stage of development. A diversified meat industry based upon feral goat and kangaroo culling has also been discussed.

While the bioregional model is attractive, it is significant that over a decade of discussion of its desirability has brought forward very few examples 'on the ground'. There are other modest proposals in the pipeline in Australia, such as a project called FATE, which stands for the Future of Australia's Threatened Ecosystems. Led by the Australian Museum, the project hopes to illustrate that sustainable industry, wildlife harvesting and biodiversity conservation are compatible in the New England region of New South Wales. However, the primary impediment remains the complexity of putting together different land tenures and gaining the cooperation of the many government departments and agencies, as well as coordinating the private and community input (Archer, 2002).

Multiple-use model

The retreat of government, the search for new conservation partners and the shift from regulatory systems have given impetus to the multiple-use model. As already mentioned, 'multiple use' has long been the catch cry of those opposed to the strictly protected sanctuary model for protecting nature. The argument is, essentially, a 'have your cake and eat it too' approach, which suggests that effective conservation can occur alongside other more extractive uses, such as forestry, mining or grazing.

Multiple use has been defined as:

> *...the premise that many or all possible uses may occur within the defined area provided that the collective impact of those uses does not exceed the ecologically sustainable capacity of the environment and natural resources*
> (Kenchington, 1996).

Kenchington was speaking about marine-protected areas, where the multiple-use paradigm has been paramount; but the principles are equally applicable to the terrestrial environment. Kenchington (1996) also identifies the crunch issue for the concept: 'The hard question begged by the concept of sustainability is that of identifying the boundary state in which a use passes from being sustainable to unsustainable.'

In Australia's federal political system there are around 60 categories of protected areas (Pittock, 1996). While some of these categories do allow for extractive uses, the majority of Australia's national parks preclude mining, grazing and other extractive uses. The major exception is in South Australia, where approximately half of the 20,957,928ha contained within national parks can be accessed for mining and grazing 'under controlled conditions' (Cresswell and Thomas, 1997). Despite the exceptions, there is a strong public expectation in Australia that a national park will be essentially a commerce- and industry-free zone. However, that expectation is being strongly challenged.

The Australian mining lobby has been a major advocate for multiple use. It has expressed particular concern that national parks 'sterilize' their resources and it has argued hard for a regime that allows for exploration and mining. The concept is also supported by land-owners who wish to use parks for seasonal or drought grazing, and in the marine environment by the petroleum and commercial fishing industries. The advocates of multiple use readily find favour with political parties and governments who put economic growth above any other imperative. Furthermore, as mentioned above, the conservative national government led by John Howard sought to implement this model in the marine environment, where the national government has a greater role vis-à-vis the states.

The Australian national government has been working jointly with state and territory governmental agencies to develop the National Representative System of Marine Protected Areas (NRSMPA). The aim of the NRSMPA is to conserve sample representative ecosystems in each biogeographic region. However, few, if any, of the new marine parks will actually be the marine equivalents of national parks if current trends persist. The NRSMPA process has endorsed the concept of protected areas being managed in a bioregional context, with the majority of the areas managed for multiple sustainable use – that is, the biosphere reserve approach. Thackway (1996b) states:

> *A comparatively recent development is the establishment of large multiple-objective marine-protected areas (MOMPAs), which are highly protected or core areas within an integrated system of management.*

In fact, most new marine-protected areas have few, if any, strict protection zones. The Howard government's approach to the marine environment was summed up in a speech made by Minister for the Environment Senator Robert Hill (1998) to the Australian Petroleum Production and Exploration Association's National Conference in March 1998, when he said:

> *You can expect an emphasis on multiple-use and sequential-use management in order that the national return on marine resources is maximized, without compromising the sustainability of the important environmental values and marine diversity.*

Supporters argue that the emphasis upon accommodating marine industries is simply realistic. In pointing out that the high degree of connectivity in the seas requires very large areas to be reserved to ensure that ecological systems and biodiversity will survive, they go on to argue that trying to completely exclude industries from large areas is not politically, socially or economically palatable, and that the only way ahead for marine conservation is working with the marine resources industries. Hence, it is argued, a large multiple-use conservation unit with some highly protected areas as sub-units is the appropriate model (Kenchington, 1996). Insistence on strict protection as the predominant approach is dismissed as unrealistic and likely to lead to isolated, small and possibly non-viable reserves. Government sources have suggested that 'no take', or strict protection, may still be part of multiple-objective marine-protected areas, but not in every case.

In a direct parallel with debates regarding the terrestrial environment, there is also an emphasis on cooperative partnerships and non-legislative options for the marine environment. Opponents of these trends, however, see them as a road to incremental compromise and decline. Some marine environmentalists claim that we have already had a long trial of multiple use with the Great Barrier Reef, and the model is not convincing. In 1998 the Australian Conservation Foundation (ACF) published a supplement to *Habitat* magazine entitled 'Sustainable Use or Multiple Abuse?' (Prideaux et al, 1998). This article assessed the Great Barrier Reef reserve as not delivering on either broad-scale sustainability or adequate strict protection. Fifteen years after declaration of a conservation strategy for the Great Barrier Reef, a mere 4.6 per cent of the area is protected in national park or strict *no take* zones. In the face of such experience, the article questioned the prevailing interpretation of multiple-use marine-protected areas:

> *Traditionally protected areas have ensured conservation through minimizing or completely excluding potentially destructive human activities. The 'no take' philosophy best expresses this philosophy. The problem for the environment is the type of uses contemplated under a multiple-use management approach. Often many destructive, habitat-altering activities such as exploration, mining and commercial fishing will be allowed. Are these activities consistent with the*

public's expectations of the role of protected areas? We need to consider with some urgency whether the current interpretation of multiple use can provide real conservation outcomes (Prideaux et al, 1998).

The following examples highlight the conservation compromises that are intrinsic to the 'multiple-use' concept.

- In April 1998 the Commonwealth established the 1,713,429ha Great Australian Bight Marine Park (GABMP); but crayfish pots are to be permitted in the protected zone and pelagic fishing has not been restricted or curtailed in any way. Extensive negotiation took place with the fishing interests in the area to arrive at this position. However, the Australian Conservation Foundation has criticized the arrangement as not constituting a 'park', calling it, instead, 'thinly disguised resource use as conservation' (ACF press release, 21 April 1998).
- The Sea Mounts of Tasmania constitute an extraordinary area of some 60 marine pinnacles that rise up to 2000m from the sea floor and provide habitat for a rich and unique flora and fauna. The Commonwealth government proclaimed the area a marine protected area in 1999. However the Plan of Management, gazetted in June 2002, has introduced a vertical zoning with only the seabed to 500m fully protected. The water column from 500m to the surface is IUCN protected area category six, which is the lowest protection zone and allow for 'sustainable use' of resources. As such it will allow commercial fishing to continue. The tuna industry fought hard against accepting any restrictions being placed on their access to the area, even though their target species, southern bluefin tuna, is critically endangered. Conservationists fear the precedent that is set when such an internationally significant environment has to be compromised to a demonstrably unsustainable industry.
- The Monte Bello Islands in Western Australia are a state marine-protected area surrounding the Monte Bello Islands, north-west of Exmouth and Ningaloo. The Commonwealth government is proposing an extension to this park based upon an agreement reached with an oil and gas industry interest in which the latter would be given responsibility for 'sustainably managing' most of the area in exchange for the establishment of specific strictly protected areas. Conservationists are concerned that the price for the cooperation of industry in protecting a community resource is guaranteed access and a *right* to the area. This, in turn, could lead to the onus of proof resting with conservationists to demonstrate the need for greater protection levels, rather than with the users to demonstrate that they will not cause harm (Prideaux, 1998, pers comm).

Indigenous Protected Areas

The Indigenous Protected Areas (IPA) programme is a national government initiative funded through the Natural Heritage Trust by Environment Australia. The programme is basically a mechanism to increase the representativeness of the National Reserve System (NRS) through the voluntary inclusion of indigenous estates. It supports the development of cooperative management arrangements. By mid 2001, 13 Indigenous Protected Areas had been declared on Aboriginal-owned land, covering more than 3.1 million hectares and adding significantly to the NRS. The IPA programme funds management plans and practical work to protect natural and cultural features and to contribute to conserving biological diversity. These Indigenous Protected Areas will operate in accordance with the internationally recognized IUCN 'Protected Areas Guidelines' and will be managed through stewardship agreements based upon negotiated environmental management plans for each property.

Some examples of this concept include the following:

- Nantawarrina, an Aboriginal-owned property in the northern Flinders Ranges of South Australia, was declared Australia's first Indigenous Protected Area at a formal launch ceremony in August 1998. Nantawarrina is a property of 58,000ha that was previously used for pastoral and mining activities. The area had a history of overgrazing and was further degraded by the impact of feral goats, rabbits and donkeys. Nantawarrina is located immediately adjacent to the Gammon Ranges National Park. The Nepabunna community, with the support of the South Australian Aboriginal Lands Trust and national park staff, is investing considerable time and resources into addressing the significant environmental problems affecting the natural and cultural values of the area. The community is committed to managing the area for biodiversity conservation and cultural values. Because of its location, this will considerably enhance the size and effectiveness of the existing protected areas in the region.
- The Yalata Indigenous Protected Area was declared in October 1999. The 456,300ha property at the head of the Great Australian Bight in South Australia is managed by Yalata Community Inc. Yalata's cliffs are best known as outstanding vantage points for watching whales migrate to mate and calve in the waters of the Great Australian Bight. The semi-arid ecological zone on the edge of the Nullabor Plain is rich in native birds, mammals and reptiles. The region is also of great cultural importance, with 'dreaming tracks' that cross continental Australia converging in this region.[1] Yalata is adjacent to other large reserves, which together form one of the world's largest contiguous areas of land and sea managed for biodiversity conservation.
- The Watarru and Walalkara Indigenous Protected Areas were declared in June 2000. Both areas lie in the Great Victorian Desert, the traditional lands of the Pitjantjatjara, Ngaanyatjarra and Yankunytjatjara Aboriginal peoples (locally known as Anangu), who have maintained a connection with the land for many thousands of years. Watarru IPA covers 1.28 million hectares, including part of the magnificent Birksgate Ranges, while Walalkara IPA

covers 700,000ha. Both Watarru and Walalkara are biologically significant areas. They contain one of the highest diversities of reptile species found anywhere in the world and support populations of rare and endangered species, including mallee fowl and the great desert skink.

The large-scale areas that can be involved with IPAs indicate their potential importance. However, their long-term effectiveness will depend upon continuing government commitment and, in particular, funding to enable indigenous people to develop the skills that they need for dealing with other organizations and interest groups.

Private sanctuary model

The impetus to involve more players and share the task of conservation has led to innovations involving the private sector. This is critically important as some 70 per cent of the Australian landmass is currently in private hands. In fact, many of the lands that are most crucial for achieving a comprehensive, adequate and representative reserve system are privately held. Australia has not had a tradition of privately owned parks in the South African game park model. Nor, until very recently, has it had private philanthropic trusts set up specifically to purchase and manage conservation lands. However, this is changing, with several groups now involved and likely to be given a major stimulus by government funding under the NRS. There is growing interest, in Canberra, in private conservation as a cost-effective way to meet biodiversity conservation targets.

The NRS programme has a community component called private protected areas. The Australian Commonwealth defines the concept as:

> *A private protected area is a protected area other than a formally gazetted status protected area, managed for nature conservation and protected by legal or other effective means* (Environment Australia, June 1998).

Under the programme, incorporated private community groups and non-governmental organizations (NGOs), such as the Australian Bush Heritage Fund, are able to put in bids for 2:1 funding for land acquisition and short-term management costs to alleviate immediate threats. Ongoing management costs must be borne by the land-holder, although funding is available in a separate government programme called Bushcare. The Commonwealth undertakes to secure the future conservation management of these lands through covenants and other legal means. The programme envisages that the private protected areas will be managed principally as IUCN categories I–IV. A proponent must enter into a Private Protected Area Establishment Agreement.

An example of a private protected area that was purchased under this programme is Carnarvon Station in central Queensland. The Commonwealth assisted the Australian Bush Heritage Fund to purchase the 59,000ha property, which has a vast and beautiful landscape representing 17 regional ecosystems of which 7 are endangered. It adjoins Carnavon National Park and thus creates a very large and important conservation complex.

The Australian Bush Heritage Fund is Australia's most prominent example of the independent trust model. It buys land to hold and manage as part of the conservation estate. Established by well-known conservationist and Green Party senator Bob Brown in 1990, it is an independent NGO that seeks donations from supporters. The fund has been very successful and, as of July 2001, owned 13 properties around Australia.

There are other models of private biodiversity conservation. An example is Earth Sanctuaries, which was set up by John Wamsley, a colourful character from South Australia. In 1969, Wamsley pioneered the concept of a privately owned substantial sanctuary: Warrawong in the Adelaide Hills. He believes feral animals are the cause of species extinction and decline and is disdainful of government-run protected areas for having failed to protect endangered Australian species. Wamsley believes that the only hope for conservation is the private sector. What distinguishes his operations is that he heavily fences his properties against cats, foxes and rabbits, eradicates all feral animals and reintroduces mammal species from elsewhere. In 2000, Wamsley surprised the business world by floating his company on the stock exchange. Earth Sanctuaries Ltd became a private company that owned land, funding acquisition and management with shareholder capital and tourism revenues. Earth Sanctuaries developed several much larger sanctuaries, and by 2001 it was managing ten properties, covering 92,000ha. However, in late 2001 the company announced that it was selling most of its assets. The modest tourism revenues could not sustain the high cost of purchase and fencing.

It is indicative of the strength of the concept of private land conservation that the Earth Sanctuaries properties have had strong interest. Six of the ten properties on offer had sold within six months and others were under negotiation. Four properties – Scotia, Yookamurra, Buckaringa and Dalantha – were sold to an emerging strong new group, the Australian Wildlife Conservancy (AWC). AWC is an independent non-profit organization with a Perth base, set up by businessman Martin Copley.

Individual land-owners are also establishing sanctuaries. Calga Springs, north of Sydney, which opened in early 2001, is a wildlife sanctuary owned by no less than the former national minister for the environment, Barry Cohen. The trend for private lands and private interests in conservation is clearly growing. At this stage, the policy implications of this for protected areas are not clear. The key concern if private land holdings became a major component of a future reserve system is the fact that while mining cannot occur on most publicly owned reserves, private lands would not be protected. Lack of long-term security is also an issue. The removal of protected status of a legislated national park is a complex process; the long-term security of the envisaged covenanting processes is less certain.

There is also a possibility that the development of private models may strengthen the push for the privatization of public parks. Wamsley has been a vitriolic critic of the public sector, the environment movement and national parks. He clearly intended to demonstrate that the private sector could manage land and achieve more for biodiversity, especially species conservation, than the public sector (Wamsley, 1996). However, in the main, conservation agencies and organizations welcome the addition of this sector as providing welcome additional funds and capacity in an era of overstretched governments. There is a fundamental recognition that governments alone simply cannot cover the vast task of conservation and that many such tools will become necessary.

Certainly, McNeeley (1996), in a sweeping assessment of the future of conservation, predicts that:

> *Protected areas will be managed increasingly by a wide range of different kind of institutions, including private landowners, non-governmental organizations, and even private-sector institutions such as tourist agencies.*

NEW MECHANISMS

While the examples above generally produce an entity resembling a traditional national park, the future is also likely to see a proliferation of other nature conservation tools generally applied on smaller parcels of land. The last decade has seen all states and territories produce a range of initiatives aimed at encouraging biodiversity conservation on private land. The suite of tools usually includes voluntary programmes, management agreements, covenants and compensation, and other incentives to encourage land-holders to conserve particular areas of native vegetation on their lands. A great deal of this activity was stimulated by a major publication on economic instruments and incentives for achieving biodiversity conservation, *Reimbursing the Future: An evaluation of motivational, voluntary, price-based, property-right, and regulatory incentives for the conservation of biodiversity* (Young et al, 1996).

Voluntary conservation agreements

Around Australia a wide range of voluntary, non-binding programmes are being developed to encourage land-holders to conserve particular areas of native vegetation on their lands (Young et al, 1996). While such agreements have a low degree of security, as most only bind the existing owner for a period of time, they are seen as an 'entry level' into private conservation where land-owners can try a scheme and perhaps move on to a more binding covenant arrangement.

One example is the Victorian Land for Wildlife scheme, which encourages land-owners to conserve their land and foster wildlife protection. The scheme is entirely voluntary and government simply provides a statewide coordinator and extension officers in order to offer advice. The scheme has been very successful, and by March 1997 4043 properties were involved, bringing at least 110,655ha of land under wildlife management. New South Wales (NSW) also has a Land for Wildlife scheme, where the agreement is with the owner. The agreement is generally for a specified time period; it needs to be renewed when the agreement expires or the land changes hands, and it relies on goodwill of the land-owner and personal contact. NSW also has a long-running scheme, the National Parks and Wildlife Service's Wildlife Refuges, where the property itself is gazetted as a refuge. Since 1948, 600 wildlife refuges have been established covering over 2 million hectares.

Most states have some equivalent programme. The Western Australian government, for example, is encouraging land-holders to enter into agreements with the Department of Land and Water Conservation to protect areas of their land identified as being of high conservation value. In one example, a pastoral family in Murchison in 2001 signed the first such agreement in relation to 7000ha of their 347,000ha property, Boolardy Station. The land will be fenced off, yet will remain part of the Boolardy pastoral lease and be managed in conjunction with the owners for the long-term conservation of native species.

In NSW, voluntary conservation agreements can be entered over private land or leasehold land. An agreement can apply to all or part of a property. The agreement is voluntary for both parties, but once entered into is registered on the title of the land, is legally enforceable and binds all future owners of the land. The terms of each agreement are negotiated between the land-holder and the National Parks and Wildlife Service, NSW, acting on behalf of the relevant government minister, and may vary according to specific conservation requirements of the land and the wishes of the land-holder. They may be restrictive, require the owner not to carry out certain activities or can include positive actions. A plan of management can be negotiated for an agreement that sets out an appropriate and more detailed management regime for the conservation area.

There is also a range of voluntary education schemes that encourage land-holder involvement in conservation, such as the Landcare movement and Farming for the Future programme in NSW. Most of these tend to be driven by the land-holders themselves and encourage mutual learning from each other. They are based upon spreading the message of sustainable land management and encouraging biodiversity conservation in agriculture. Most of these systems, however, are highly dependent upon some form of grants for fencing or replanting or feral animal control. It is doubtful if long-term conservation will occur unless there remains this critical support.

Revolving funds and covenants

'Revolving funds' work on a model of raising funds, investing the funds in a property with conservation value, placing a legally binding conservation covenant or easement on the property title and then reselling into the market to generate funds for the next purchase.

This model provides a conservation tool that is becoming more popular. The original model in Australia was The Trust for Nature (Victoria), a statutory authority established by the Victorian government. This organization has achieved 368 covenants and protected over 15,569ha. The trust fosters a stewardship programme of regular contact, advice and support for land-owners who accept covenants. The trust also purchases and holds some lands in its own right. According to 2001 figures, 50 properties covering 4500ha are owned and managed as conservation areas by local community groups, individuals and councils (Trust for Nature [Victoria], website).

The Trust for Nature (Victoria) was established under the Victorian Conservation Trust Act, 1972, and receives a grant from the state government, as well as donations and bequests (over Aus$250,000 in bequests in 1996). The trust's main strength is that it is perceived as being independent from government, and for this reason the public is more likely to donate funds or negotiate with the trust on land purchase. It has financial flexibility compared with government departments in that it can conduct fund-raising appeals, offer tax deductibility for donations, receive bequests, donations and gifts, hold and invest funds, have access to philanthropic sources and broker land purchases (Whelan, 2001, pers com). The trust also maintains a register of properties that it holds and interested purchasers can register their names with the trust.

This model is gaining in popularity and is being encouraged by both state and national governments. In 2001, NSW introduced its scheme by legislating for a New Conservation Trust. This new organization started operation in 2002 and will follow the 'revolving fund' model.

Conservation Management Networks

Conservation Management Networks (CMN) is a new model being introduced in Australia in an effort to address one of Australia's critical conservation problems: the conservation of fragmented ecological communities (Higginson, Prober and Thiele, 2001).

In the national work to produce a comprehensive, adequate and representative reserve system (CAR), the Interim Biogeographic Regionalization for Australia (IBRA) analysis highlighted what many people already knew: that our existing reserve system was strongly biased towards the less productive lands. National parks tended to be declared in lands that were more scenically spectacular, closer to the city or not needed for other purposes. The ecosystems or natural areas that were on productive soils tended to be less spectacular and more remote, and they have consequently been poorly represented in our reserve system. While considerable effort is being undertaken to identify and rectify this problem, it will be very difficult to redress this legacy. Agencies have limited acquisition budgets and lands in more productive areas have higher economic value. In many cases, even if dollars could be found, it is simply the case that very little of a particular ecosystem remains and what remains is highly fragmented.

Dangerous fragmentation is certainly the case for the productive grassy ecosystems of south-eastern Australia. From the millions of hectares that once existed, there are no substantial areas left that are suitable for reservation as a traditional national park. Researchers working specifically on the once-extensive Grassy Box Woodlands of New South Wales have developed the Conservation Management Networks model for conserving fragmented ecosystems. The concept involves incorporating scattered ecosystems remnants into a network. A CMN is defined as 'a network of remnants, their managers and other interested parties'. While remnants may be widely dispersed and under different land tenures, those involved in their management as a network can share information, share extension efforts, apply for grants as a network, label specific remnants as something of broader importance, and undertake a wide variety of other actions that can be done more effectively as a network than as isolated entities. The networks have both a biological aim of enhancing biodiversity conservation and a social objective of enhancing community ownership and involvement in conservation (Higginson, Prober and Thiele, 2001).

Membership of a CMN is voluntary and open to any site that is managed primarily or partly for conservation, and has been given some formal long-term protection by its manager. Ideally, a remnant that belongs to a CMN will have a legally binding covenant and a plan of management that covers day-to-day operations. Without implementing a plan of management, the most detailed covenant may not allow a remnant to flourish in the longer term. Conservation Management Networks offer a new way of tackling the difficult issue of conserving fragmented ecosystems in Australia, whether naturally fragmented or fragmented by human intervention.

Market mechanisms

While there are increasing incentives for biodiversity conservation in the form of fencing subsidies, tax and rate relief, there are still few actual payments available for maintaining an ecosystem. Victoria has just launched a three-year trial of stewardship payments called BushTender, where farmers will be paid to help protect the 1 million ha of native vegetation on private land in Victoria (Garbutt, 2001). The trial will commence shortly in the north-central region of the state. BushTender offers land-holders the opportunity to receive payment for entering into an agreement to provide management services that improve the quality or extent of native vegetation on their land. The price would form the basis for a bid, which would be compared with the bids from all other land-holders participating in the trial. Successful bids would offer the best value for money to the community. All bids would be assessed objectively upon the basis of the current conservation value of the site, the amount of service offered and the cost involved. Only actions by the land-holder that are over and above those required by current responsibilities under existing arrangements and legislation will be eligible for payment.

The 'brave new world' of creating markets, property rights, trading credits and stewardship payments is still ahead of us. New South Wales is trialing both carbon credits, by creating new forests, and biodiversity credits by restoring an endangered woodland – in both cases to offset carbon production by energy companies (Salvin, 2000). Carl Binning, a leading researcher from the Commonwealth Scientific and Industrial Research Organisation, sees a major future for biodiversity credits where beneficiaries pay the manager or owner of a natural area for the ecosystem services provided by protected nature (Binning, 2000). According to Binning, 'If we want to conserve nature, someone has to pay. National parks and reserves are not able to achieve all of our conservation objectives' (Binning, 2000).

Many agree that such market mechanisms will be a major feature of future conservation. David Farrier (1996), an academic from Wollongong University, has strongly supported the need for national parks to be augmented by biodiversity conservation on private lands. He sees a major role for stewardship payments, as well as some degree of regulation:

> *Instead of telling landholders that they are being compensated to keep their destructive hands off the land, the message is that they have a vital role to play, a role which the community regards as being sufficiently important that it is prepared to pay for it* (Farrier, 1996).

A BRAND NEW DAY?

Nature conservation is certainly going through a major transformation in Australia and internationally. The models are diversifying and the range of people who will be involved in conservation is also dramatically widening. Overall, this is a rational response to the complexity of threats facing our natural world. The toolbox needed augmenting with many, and perhaps more subtle, tools than the simple protected area model. Most mainstream environmentalists, including the author, support this diversification. The concept of large landscape-scale initiatives is exciting and almost certainly essential if we are even to stabilize our biodiversity losses, let alone begin the process of building back viable communities of endangered species. Indigenous Protected Areas (IPAs) are another critical tool given the very large tracts of Australia under indigenous title and care and the consequent need to find processes that are compatible with indigenous cultural priorities. The full range of private initiatives are also welcomed as useful methods to support more traditional conservation, while economic incentives may well save many of the critical conservation lands that are currently vulnerable remnants on private lands.

However, the key issue, which I have raised in many forums, is whether this proliferation of approaches will provide healthy *additional lands* to the core lands of national parks or, rather, become a fundamental challenge to that core concept. There is a real possibility that these new forms may create a Trojan horse for the many forces in society who are opposed to the idea of, as they see it, 'locking up' the land. The multiple-use component of bioregional models and, at least some IPAs, could strengthen the push for what national Minister for the Environment Senator Robert Hill (1998) endorsed as 'multiple and sequential use of lands'. Similarly, the increasing entry of private interests into conservation may make it easier to gradually introduce privatization into the management of national parks. Such a development is still opposed by environmentalists, based upon their belief that privatization would inevitably mean the domination of commercial imperatives over those of conservation.

One of the best recent articulations of why the sanctuary model of national parks remains a vital and legitimate component of any future conservation strategy was made by New South Wales Premier Bob Carr. In launching a fund-raising campaign for the Dunphy Wilderness Fund (Colong Foundation, 2001), Carr said:

> *So this is what is special about wilderness. It reminds us of the ancient life of this continent, there is an echo there of the life of the old people, the ancient people who inhabited this continent, there is a reminder of what is special of the plant and animal life and the land forms and geology of this old continent, and there is an urgent plea emerging form the valleys and the great forests to save, to protect part of this land in its wild condition.*

This is a timely reminder that wild places are an irreplaceable and essential part of nature conservation.

NOTES

1   The term 'dreaming tracks' refers to the creation stories of Aboriginal cosmology, in which powerful living creatures crossed the land, creating the land forms that are now evident.

REFERENCES

Archer, M (2002) 'Confronting crises in conservation: a talk on the wild side' in D Lunney and C Dickman (eds) *A Zoological Revolution*, a report of a forum for the Royal Zoological Society of NSW and the Australian Museum, Saturday 20 May 2000, published by the Royal Zoological Society of NSW and the Australian Museum, Sydney, NSW, pp12–52

Australian Conservation Foundation (1998) 'When is a park not a park?', press release, 21 April 1998

Australian Nature Conservation Agency (1995) *Minutes from the Working Group Meeting Investigating Conservation Partnerships: Voluntary Inclusion of Aboriginal and Torres Strait Islander Estates into a Nationally Representative System of Protected Areas*, Alice Springs 13–16 June 1995, ANCA, Canberra

Australian and New Zealand Environment and Conservation Council (1997) *Best Practice Initiatives for Nature Conservation on Private Land*. Report of the ANZECC Working Group on Nature Conservation on Private Land, ANZECC, Canberra

Binning, C (2000) 'Selling and Saving our Biodiversity', CSIRO Press Release, 20 September 2000

Boden, R and Breckwoldt, R (1995) *National Reserves System Cooperative Program Evaluation*. Australian Nature Conservation Agency, Canberra

Brunckhorst, D (1999) 'Models to Integrate Sustainable Conservation and Resource Use – Bioregional Reserves beyond Bookmark'. Paper presented to New Solutions for Sustainability Conference, 4–5 March 1999, Nature Conservation Council of NSW, Sydney, pp130–140

Colong Foundation (2001) 'The launch of the Dunphy Wilderness Fundraising Campaign', *Colong Bulletin*, vol 187, July 2001 pp8–10. Colong Foundation for Wilderness, Sydney

Commonwealth of Australia, State of the Environment Advisory Council (1996) *Australia: State of the Environment*. CSIRO, Australia

Commonwealth of Australia (2001) *Midterm Review of the Natural Heritage Trust*. Commonwealth Department of the Environment, Sport and Territories, Canberra, www.ea.gov.au/nht/review, p24

Cresswell, I D and Thomas, G M (eds) (1997) *Terrestrial and Marine Protected Areas in Australia, 1997*. Environment Australia Biodiversity Group, Canberra

Dryzek, J S (1997) *The Politics of the Earth: Environmental Discourses*. Oxford University Press, New York

Environment Australia (1998) www.environment.gov.au, June 1998

Farrier, D (1996) 'Implementing the In-Situ Conservation Provisions of the United Nations Convention on Biological Diversity in Australia: Questioning the Role of National Parks', *The Australasian Journal of Natural Resources Law and Policy*, vol 3, no1, pp1–24

Figgis, P (1999) *Australia's National Parks and Protected Areas*. Australian Committee for IUCN Occasional Paper No 8, ACIUCN, Sydney

Forsyth, D (2001) Pers comm. Head National Reserve System Programme, Environment Australia, July 2001

Garbutt, S (2001) 'Dollars For Farm Bush Protection Trial – Minister', press release, 22 June 2001, Melbourne

Higginson, E, Prober, S and Thiele, K (2001) 'Conservation Management Networks for the Conservation of Fragmented Ecological Communities'. Paper presented to Conservation Management Networks Workshop, Canberra, 5–6 March 2001

Hill, R (1998) Speech made by the Commonwealth Minister for the Environment, Senator Robert Hill, to the Australian Petroleum Production and Exploration Association's National Conference, Canberra Convention Centre, March 1998

Hill, R and Figgis, P (1999) 'A conservation initiative: ACF Wilderness and Indigenous Landscapes Policy', *Habitat Australia*, vol 27, no 1, February, Australian Conservation Foundation, Melbourne, pp8–9

IUCN (1993) *Parks for Life: Report of the Fourth World Congress on National Parks and Protected Areas – Caracas Venezuela*. IUCN–The World Conservation Union, Gland, Switzerland

IUCN (1994) *Guidelines for Protected Area Management Categories*. Commission on National Parks and Protected Areas with the assistance of the World Conservation Monitoring Centre, IUCN–The World Conservation Union, Gland, Switzerland, and Cambridge, UK

IUCN (1997) *Beyond Fences: Seeking Social Sustainability in Conservation*, vols I and II. IUCN–The World Conservation Union, Gland, Switzerland

Kenchington, R (1996) 'Outline of Background and Key Issues for Multiple Use in Marine Environments' in *Proceedings of the Workshop on Multiple Use in Marine*

Environments. Australian Petroleum Production and Exploration Association, Canberra

McNeeley, J (1996) 'Conservation and the Future: Trends and Options Toward the Year 2025'. Draft discussion paper, 25 February 1996, in National Parks and Wildlife Service (1998) *National Parks: Visions for the New Millenium: Trends Paper,* Conference held 16–19 July 1998, University of Sydney, National Parks and Wildlife Service, Sydney, pp1–66

Muir, K (1997) 'Aboriginal Reconciliation and Wilderness', *Colong Bulletin*, no162, May, Colong Foundation for Wilderness, Sydney, p8

Nutting, M (1994) 'Competing Interest or Common Ground: Aboriginal Participation in the Management of Protected Areas', *Habitat Australia*, vol 22, no 1, February, Australian Conservation Foundation, Melbourne, pp28–37

Pittock, J (1996) 'The State of the Australian Protected Areas System'. Paper presented at the IUCN Commission on National Parks and Protected Areas Regional Meeting, Sydney, 8–10 June 1996

Prideaux, M (1998) Pers comm. Marine Biodiversity Campaigner, Australian Conservation Foundation, July 1998

Prideaux, M, Emmett, J and Horstman, M (1998) 'Sustainable Use or Multiple Abuse?' *Habitat Australia*, vol 26, no 2, April, Australian Conservation Foundation, Melbourne, pp13–20

Prineas, P (ed) (1998) *National Parks: new visions for a new century'*. Proceedings of the National Parks: New Visions for a New Century Conference, 18–19 July 1997, the Nature Conservation Council of New South Wales and the National Parks Association, Nature Conservation Council, Sydney

Salvin, S (2000) 'Developing a Market in Biodiversity Credits'. New South Wales State Forests paper, Sydney

Sheppard, D (1997) 'The Road from Caracas'. Paper presented at the World Commission on Protected Areas Symposium, Albany, Western Australia, November 1997

Smyth, D and Sutherland, J (1996) *Indigenous Protected Areas*. Environment Australia, Canberra

Stevens, S (1997) *Conservation through Cultural Survival: Indigenous People and Protected Areas*. Island Press, Washington, DC

Szabo, S G (1996) ' indigenous Protected Areas: Managing Natural and Cultural Values – A Two-Way Street'. Paper presented at the IUCN Commission for National Parks and Protected Areas Regional Meeting, Sydney, 8–10 June 1996

Thackway, R (1996a) 'The National Reserve System: Towards a Representative System of Ecologically Based Reserves'. Paper presented at the IUCN Commission for National Parks and Protected Areas Regional Meeting, Sydney, 8–10 June 1996

Thackway, R (ed) (1996b) *Developing Australia's Representative System of Marine Protected Areas*. Proceedings of a technical meeting, South Australian Aquatic Sciences Centre, West Beach, Adelaide, 22–23 April 1996, Department of the Environment, Canberra

Trust for Nature (Victoria) www.tsn.org.au, accessed 4 June 2001

Wamsley, J (1996) 'Wildlife Management: The Work of Earth Sanctuaries Limited' in T Charters, M Gabriel and S Prasser (eds) *National Parks: Private Sector's Role*. University of Southern Queensland Press, Toowoomba

Wamsley, J (1998) 'Report to Shareholders', *Earth Sanctuaries News*, no 28, February 1999, p1

Whelan, B (2001) Personal communication. Former CEO, Trust for Nature (Victoria), current director, Australian Bush Heritage Fund, September 2001

Woenne-Green, S, Johnston, R, Sultan, R and Wallis, A (1994) *Competing Interests: Aboriginal Participation in National Parks and Conservation Reserves in Australia.* Australian Conservation Foundation, Melbourne

World Commission on Protected Areas (WCPA) (1997) *Protected Areas in the 21st Century: From Islands to Networks.* Report from the WCPA Albany Symposium, 24–29 November 1997, IUCN, Gland

Young M D, Gunningham, N, Elix, J, Lambert, J, Howard, B, Grabosky, P and McGrone, E (1996) *Reimbursing the Future: An Evaluation of Motivational, Voluntary, Price-Based, Property-Right, and Regulatory Incentives for the Conservation of Biodiversity,* 2 vols. Biodiversity Series, Paper no 9, Biodiversity Unit, Department of the Environment, Sport and Territories, Canberra

Chapter 10

When nature won't stay still: Conservation, equilibrium and control

William M Adams

FIELD WORK

Two memories suggest themselves to me. In the first, I am standing on the slope of a rounded limestone hill in southern England, looking south across a huge vista of woods and fields, the rolling lowlands of the Kentish Weald. Near at hand there is thin grass with the little bumps of ant hills, and on the hilltop the remains of a Bronze Age earthwork approximately 3500 years' old. One or two of my fellow students are on their hands and knees, peering excitedly through hand lenses at grasses and flowers, and uttering the shrill squeaks of the conservationist at play. To our right lies what looks like a battlefield, a sea of hawthorn stumps and the ash mounds that marked the sites of small, hot fires. We are on a National Nature Reserve (NNR), a Site of Special Scientific Interest (SSSI), and this was the result of careful scientific conservation management.[1]

The reserve was famous for its chalk grassland plants and insects; but this 'natural' diversity was, in fact, artificial. Chalk grassland, I was being told, was human-made, an 'anthropogenic ecosystem', 'semi-natural' vegetation. In the intense agricultural and urbanized landscape of south-east England, nothing remained of the mix of vegetation communities that must once have existed on the unoccupied chalk and clays left at the end of the last glacial maximum 10,000 years ago. As the climate shifted, and plants and animals and eventually people arrived, the landscape changed, and 'natural' vegetation was forced to change with it. Under tens of centuries of human management, plants and insects that could thrive on the nutrient-poor limestone of the chalk hills, and cope with the inexorable nibbling of countless generations of sheep, accumulated in wonderfully diverse assemblages in what ecologists during the 20th century came to call chalk grassland.

I was told that human action had destroyed the 'natural' post-glacial vegetation. However, in its place anthropogenic activity had created a diverse, new vegetation assemblage in which a multitude of plants and insects found a foothold. In time, this, too, began to disappear. People had long ago cleared and ploughed almost all the rest of the chalk downland in southern England (especially during the period since World War II), and the chalk grassland species, presumably once common, were now rare. As a result, the whole of a much wider heritage of natural diversity was invested in this fragment of human-created sward. That is why it was a nature reserve.

However, even in a nature reserve it seemed that nature could not be left to itself. In this environment, chalk grassland was not a stable equilibrium vegetation community. Left alone, this grassy paradise would slowly turn into a dull, species-poor scrubland and, eventually, woodland. The only way to keep the diversity of grassland species was to stop vegetation succession. Conservation management was needed in order to hold back the tendency of nature to restore the natural balance. Since World War II, chalkland sheep-grazing had become uneconomic, the grassland had become rougher, and the scrub moved in – hence, the need to cut and remove the scrub in order to reset the clock of ecological succession at the stage with maximum species richness.

A second memory occurs a couple of years later and far away. I am peering through the windscreen of a Land Rover in northern Nigeria at a patch of bare soil, surrounded by scrubby trees. The screech of acacia thorns against the body work has mercifully stopped, and we are in an area of totally bare land in a clearing in the grazing reserve through which we have been driving. It is long after the rains and blindingly hot. We get out to inspect vegetation and soil. At some time in the past, people have cleared and cultivated this land. The lines of the cultivation ridges are still visible, but the soil has sealed over and the surface is mirror hard. Nothing grows now, not even weeds. The acacia trees have failed to recolonize. The land seems irrevocably spoiled. My companion is kicking the toe of his shoe against the hard surface, muttering and shaking his head.

A few kilometres on, we stop again in a new clearing in the thin forest. This time we find a small stockade of cut thorn branches with a large white bull inside. It is part of a Fulani pastoralist camp; but there is nobody about. The bull is tall and rangy, but surprisingly sleek. A pile of green branches has been cut for fodder, for on the dry, grey earth there is only a faint suggestion of wispy grass stems. On the edge of the clearing, small, scrubby acacia trees have been half-cut through quite recently and their green leaves eaten; others have been cut to make the small stockade. This seems like the scene that must logically precede the one before, where the healthy forest is being cut by unwary people, eventually to be farmed and spoiled, and abandoned. We talk about the processes that seem to be going on, the probability that the grazing reserve is slowly being destroyed by overgrazing. We eventually drive away, the Land Rover still protesting at the thorns.

At the time, these experiences seemed to offer classic morality tales. On the chalk hills of England, careful conservation management was needed to maintain the diversity of nature against its own powers of deterioration. In Nigeria, on the edge of the Sahel, management was required to stop people from destroying the environment. There were too many people in the wrong place, trying to grow crops on degraded soil and exhausting the soil, or cutting trees to feed livestock because the grassland was overgrazed. At that time, in the aftermath of the 'Sahel drought' of the early 1970s, the problem of desertification was a hot topic of debate in seminar rooms and learned journals. To me, conditioned by the literature on drought and human-induced desertification in the Sahel, it was easy to build in my mind a scenario for the future of these places. It was one of environmental degradation, with the natural vegetation progressively transformed by people and their livestock, the natural productivity of the land destroyed by unsustainable land use, the balance of nature upset by human action. It did not occur to me that this interpretation might be wrong. It did not (at least, not then) occur to me to wait until the bull's owner returned to see what he thought was happening in that hot place.[2]

THE BALANCE OF NATURE

The balance of nature is a powerful symbol. It was the single 'Big Idea' that underpinned the environmental revolution that began during the 1960s in Europe and North America, and which progressed in various ways and at various speeds until the 1990s, when it was mainstreamed by the 1992 Earth Summit in Rio. There was a 'balance of nature' that humans had disrupted. This certainly seemed self-evident to me through my childhood (trekking to Alexandra Palace in London to see the National Nature Week exhibition in 1963, or watching television pictures of the oil tanker *Torrey Canyon*, aground and burning on Seven Stones Reef between Land's End and the Scilly Isles in March 1967, and being bombed by the navy and the air force, while leaking Kuwaiti oil onto the Cornish coast).[3] To a child, the evidence was plain: nature was precious and under threat, it had found its own balance and this was being upset. People, in their greed and technological arrogance, were disrupting the balance of nature. As a basic environmentalist route-map to the ills of the late 20th century, the idea of nature in balance served me well enough for a long while, providing the oxygen for more late evening conversations and arguments with friends than I care to remember.

These ideas are as deep as the history of environmentalism (Grove, 1992; 1995). One need look no further than George Perkins Marsh's *Man and Nature* (1864):

> *Nature, left undisturbed, so fashions her territory as to give it almost unchanging permanence of form, outline, and proportion.*

...whenever the Indian, in consequence of war or the exhaustion of the beasts of the chase, abandoned the narrow fields he had planted and the woods he had burned over, they speedily returned, by a succession of herbaceous, arborescent and arboreal growths, to their original state. Even a single generation sufficed to restore them almost to their primitive luxuriance of forest vegetation (Marsh 1864, pp 29, 30).

Marsh's theme was clear: nature established an equilibrium and humans disrupted it. This simple idea was still providing the take-home message of Rachel Carson's *Silent Spring*, the proof text of Western environmentalism and the sound bite of countless television documentaries and Walt Disney animal movies 100 years after Marsh's writing.[4] It reflects, too, ideas that ran through the science of ecology. When this was in its infancy, during the late 19th century, shortly after Marsh was writing, it took on board a powerful, organic metaphor of nature, a view of nature balanced and integrated and threatened by change from 'outside', from human action (Botkin, 1990; Livingstone, 1995).

The idea of a balance of nature continues to be seductive and to have a powerful appeal for environmentalists, in general, and conservationists, in particular. However, during the last decade of the 1990s, it began to be challenged by other ideas that suggest a more complex approach to understanding ecosystem change. These ideas allow nature much more dynamism and variability. No longer can the gendered image of rapacious human and passive equilibrial nature be accepted comfortably.[5] Using two case studies, this chapter describes the implications of this change for conservation in understanding nature. The first is the semi-arid lands of Africa, both the classic terrain of 'big nature' (the 'big five' and savanna national parks) and the home ground of African pastoral people. The second is the more domestic scale of small nature reserves in the densely packed and intensively managed rural landscape of the UK. Although, at one level, very different, common ideological currents run through conservationist thinking. In both cases, a challenge to the dominant mode of understanding nature as balanced and threatened offers radical and challenging opportunities for conservation action. First, however, let me explain what I mean by the 'ecology of equilibrium'.

THE ECOLOGY OF EQUILIBRIUM

During the first decades of this century, nature was portrayed by the emerging science of ecology as, essentially, rather static, an array of habitat fragments as natural objects. In this thinking, ecology drew (like conservation) on the strength of amateur natural history and the Victorian mania for collecting (Allen, 1976, Griffiths, 1996). The links between ecology and conservation in industrialized countries were very close. In *Research Methods in Ecology*, the American ecologist F E Clements provided a scientific basis for identifying vegetation 'types' (Clements, 1905; McIntosh, 1985). In the UK, Arthur Tansley drew on the work of amateur botanists to write the classic *Types of British Vegetation* (Tansley, 1911), and provided both a classification of vegetation and a framework for the first lists of proposed nature reserves in the UK (Sheail, 1976; Adams, 1996). When Clements developed ideas about plant succession, he suggested a process of continuous change towards a 'climatic climax'. He likened the 'vegetation formation' to a complex organism 'developing' through time. This way of understanding ecological change drew deliberate analogies with the growth of individual organisms (Clements, 1916).

These ideas of vegetation as organism were subsequently challenged by Harold Gleason and by Tansley; but ecology's dependence upon the organic metaphor survived. In 1920, Tansley argued against the idea that all aggregations of plants had the properties of organisms, and in 1935 he published a sharp critique of Clementsian thinking about the climatic climax (McIntosh, 1985). He suggested that succession involved complex patterns, with soils, physiography and human action all driving change in different (but specific) directions under different conditions. To capture this complexity he framed the new concept of the ecosystem (Tansley, 1935; 1939; Sheail, 1987). In time this, too, came to be understood as a balanced system whose components meshed and integrated to create equilibrium through negative feedback.

The development of increasingly sophisticated theoretical and experimental approaches to ecology eventually led to a more mechanistic framework of analysis. This was based upon Tansley's concept of the ecosystem, to which the analysis of ecological energetics and, subsequently, systems analysis were applied (Tansley, 1935; Lindemann, 1942; McIntosh, 1985; Botkin, 1990). However, although the science of ecology developed in scope and sophistication, historians of ecology argue that the fundamental notion that ecosystems tended towards equilibrium endured (McIntosh, 1985; Worster, 1994). The classic 'equilibrium paradigm' in ecology dominated ecology until the 1970s (Steward et al, 1992). Ecological systems were closed, and ecosystems were self-regulating so that, if disturbed, they would tend to return towards an equilibrium state. This paradigm, in turn, fed ideas in the wider environmental movement, underpinning the notion that there was a balance of nature easily upset by inappropriate human action.

During the second half of the 20th century, when both ecosystem management, development planning and conservation were all becoming established in government planning, ecologists mostly portrayed nature as a kind of homeostatic machine (Pahl-Wostl, 1995). Nature was seen as a system whose state was maintained by processes of internal feedback; but it was also susceptible to external control. In fact, ecosystems were analysed as if they were '19th-century machines, full of gears and wheels, for which our managerial goal, like that of any traditional engineer, is steady-state operation' (Botkin, 1990, p12). Human action could upset the delicate working of the machine; but, fortunately, the ecologist could diagnose the problem and (potentially, at least) work out how to put the balance right. Ecological science could therefore be used to generate technocratic recipes for managing nature. Ecologists coined words and concepts drawn from thermodynamics and engineering (such as system, energetics, equilibrium, feedback, balance and control) to describe nature. Conservationists, schooled in ecology, saw themselves in some senses as 'engineers of nature' (Livingstone, 1995, p368).

Ecological science also offered a series of 'natural' subdivisions of nature. This is the fruit of a desperate desire to classify, dating back to the origins of taxonomy (see Chapter 2 in this book). The arbitrary distinction between species and subspecies are universally accepted, although modern genetic techniques may prove to have some surprises for those conservationists whose programmes are dependent upon these categories. Attempts to provide a taxonomy at larger scales (habitat, ecosystem or vegetation community) are graced by convention, but are less satisfactory. These 'natural' units are quite clearly social constructs, whether or not they carry the *imprimatur* of Two-Way Indicator Species Analysis (TWINSPAN) (Hill, 1979) and the reliable algebra of the National Vegetation Classification (Rodwell, 1991).[6] The attempt to classify the turbulent diversity of nature is based upon assumptions of equilibrium. Only if nature stays still can science get a long enough look at it to provide a usable classification. In that nature is *not* still, science has to work as if it is. Nature is therefore treated as dynamic, but tending to equilibrium – diverse, but open to simple classification that is robust enough to be useful.

CONSERVATION AND EQUILIBRIUM

Ideas of ecosystem equilibrium have been highly influential for conservation in the temperate environment of the UK. For British conservationists, it was for almost all of the 20th-century axiomatic that nature not only had to be reserved, but also managed within those reserves. Ecological ideas about ecosystem succession demonstrated nature's own capacity to change in undesirable ways. Awareness grew of the capacity of nature itself to cause change that could bring about the loss of valued features of a reserve (for example, a rare species), particularly through ecosystem succession. As nature conservation became an accepted form of land use in the UK, after the end of World War II, conservationists had to establish rules for reserve management, and for this it drew upon ecological science.

Conservation needed science, and science needed conservation. It was believed that effective reserve management demanded 'deep scientific knowledge' of ecosystems: 'paradoxically, we can ensure the survival of wild places of Britain only by finding out what happens when we interfere with them' (Nicholson, 1957, pp26, 19). In 1964, Pearsall argued that ecological research required large nature reserves for experiments 'large enough to allow [for] repeatable assessments of the systems or processes under investigation' (Pearsall, 1964, p8). Some ecologists were reluctant to accept that wildlife communities might need to be managed (Duffey and Watt, 1970); but conservation demanded an interventionist approach in order to control nature.

Conservation adopted ecology's language (system, equilibrium, balance, succession, competition, climax), and drew upon it to explain vegetation succession and to prescribe management treatments. In due course, 'management by interference' (Nicholson, 1957, p19) became the standard model and also, arguably, the distinguishing feature of British conservation (Henderson, 1992).

Woodwalton Fen in Cambridgeshire provides one example of the emerging need for intervention management. Until the mid 19th century, Woodwalton Fen was undrained, lying adjacent to the open water of Whittlesey Mere. In 1851, this last fenland mere was drained and reclaimed, Woodwalton Fen peat was dug and parts were cultivated. In 1910, it was purchased by a wealthy visionary, the banker Charles Rothschild, as a nature reserve. This purchase, of course, did nothing to stop the rapid plant succession taking place (Nicholson, 1970). By 1959, when the reserve was leased to the Nature Conservancy, about 90 per cent of it was covered with birch or sallow scrub. Many of the species for which it was originally famous had died out, or were close to doing so. The wetland had become a wood, standing like turf on a beach – a tuft of wet woodland, stranded by the drainage of the surrounding farmland that stretched as flat as a pancake away to the level line of the horizon, far away to the north-east.

Conservation of the fen's fauna and flora seemed to demand decisive intervention. Ecological knowledge directed conservation action to control ecosystem succession, and a programme of clearance, followed by cattle grazing, was begun. It was argued that 'detailed ecological knowledge' would be required to maintain the vegetation in the forms that gave the fen its conservation interest (Duffey, 1970, p595).

Although the basic principles of managing wildlife habitat are, today, widely known and taught (see, for example, Green, 1981; Sutherland and Hill, 1995), when conservation was established institutionally during the 1940s, little research had been done. Knowledge of either the need for ecosystem management, or of how and when to intervene in order to maintain the desired characteristics of 'seral, plagio or sub-climax ecosystems' (Green, 1981, p178), was rudimentary, at best (Sheail, 1995). New knowledge and skills were required to manage National Nature Reserves. Neither contemporary agriculture (already obsessed with technical and economic 'efficiency' through intensification) nor forestry (focused since the end of World War I upon developing skills in tree-farming with exotic conifers, often in exposed upland sites) provided adequate models for very many of the new tasks of conservation.

New methods were required to manage less modified ecosystems for conservation, rather than production. These methods were progressively developed. Some involved the recovery of former rural management practices, such as cutting reed on wetlands, coppicing woodland or laying hedgerows. Some adapted farming systems, such as livestock grazing, but substituted a concern for altering grass swards (by resowing and fertilizing) to maximize production with a concern for maximizing plant or insect species diversity (through minimizing fertility and adjusting stock type and stocking density). After 200 years of animal breeding for production, conservationists rediscovered less improved breeds and 'rare breeds' of livestock; and even lowland fields and fens began to be grazed by Highland cattle, Hebridean sheep and Konik horses. Other techniques were more novel, including the use of mechanized cutters, manipulation of water levels or the selective use of herbicides (Green, 1981; Sutherland and Hill, 1995; Wallis DeVries et al, 2001). These skills were adapted and institutionalized into new and standardized regimes of management. They were shared within groups of often urban-based volunteers (for example, the British Trust for Conservation Volunteers) and became elements in formal college-taught courses.

ECOLOGY, CONSERVATION AND DISEQUILIBRIUM

New ideas of 'non-equilibrium' ecology call into question the tradition of intensive conservation management in places such as the UK that assumes that nature is (and should be) in equilibrium, and seeks to control 'natural' processes. The abundance and distribution of organisms, as well as the appearance of the landscape, are controlled by natural physical processes. One of the most important sources of disturbance in ecosystems is the working of physical processes in the landscape, particularly processes of erosion and deposition (Werrity et al, 1994). Some landscapes, such as sand dunes, beaches or river floodplains, are highly dynamic. Physical processes also drive environmental change elsewhere – for example, in woodlands affected by storms that cause trees to fall, or on mountain tops affected by freeze-thaw processes.

Standard approaches to sand dune management are based upon the control of ecological change and dune stabilization. This kind of intensive management is ineffective since it also leads to loss of early successional stages in dune ecosystems. You cannot 'preserve' such ecosystems by 'managing' them any more than you can by putting a fence around them and declaring them 'protected'. Their biodiversity depends directly upon natural patterns of disturbance, driven by climate change. Indeed, their very existence depends upon such natural change, and in such environments disturbance must be seen as part of the 'nature' with which conservation is concerned. What you can do, of course, is to protect them, both from direct human exploitation (for example, quarrying of sand or shingle in the case of sand dunes) and from indirect human-induced change (for example, offshore dredging, or starvation of sediment by inappropriate coastal defence works). However, conservation then becomes not a matter of trying to dictate through management the exact form that nature takes, but of protecting *processes* of natural change from incompatible changes in economy and technology (Worster, 1994).

Ecologists have increasingly acknowledged the scientific challenge to old equilibrial ideas and have begun to consider the instabilities in landscapes, particularly the problem of disturbance, and different scales in space and time.

As the historian Donald Worster put it, 'nature, we are told now, should be regarded as a landscape of patches of all sizes, textures, and colours, changing continually through time and space, responding to an unceasing barrage of perturbations' (Worster, 1994). A 'non-equilibrium paradigm' in ecology emphasizes the openness of natural systems, and the need to understand them in the context of their surroundings, as well as the past events and disturbances that have affected them. Non-equilibrium ecology recognizes that the factors that are important in explaining how things change will depend upon the length of time and the area over which change is analysed (Steward et al, 1992). Ecology has undergone a profound shift from the notion that nature is a well-behaved, deterministic system towards a view in which equilibrium states are relatively unusual (Zoest, 1992).

Ideas about the fractal geometry of nature, and the idea that we should think of ecosystems as exhibiting the maths of chaos rather than the more comfortable dynamics of equilibrium, allow ecologists to begin to explore the ways in which different processes determine landscape pattern at different scales. Disturbances come in many shapes and sizes, from annual river floods or seasonal droughts to disease outbreaks. Ecologists suggest that in any given landscape, disturbances tend to occur at a characteristic scale, frequency and intensity that is determined by climate, weather, topography, geology and the species present. In river channels and floodplains, characteristic species and communities are maintained within different parts of the channel and the floodplain by processes of erosion and deposition, and by patterns of overbank flooding and groundwater recharge. If those processes are altered, ecological changes are likely to follow (Hughes, 1999; 2001).

Increasingly, during the last two centuries, there has been a human dimension to many 'natural' disturbances, and humans themselves have been major originators of disturbance (from local engineering activity to the release of carbon dioxide or ozone-depleting chemicals into the atmosphere). Ecologists can no longer work on the assumption that terrestrial ecosystems simply respond to climate changes and internal processes of competition. The scale and intensity of human activity is such that ecosystem change, driven by human action, can itself potentially drive climatic change. Ecology has to be able to shift scales in pursuit of explanation, reaching down to the molecular level and up to the global scale (May, 1989).

Conservationists should no longer conceive of nature in equilibrium, and therefore portray human-induced changes in those ecosystems as somehow 'unnatural'. Nature is dynamic and highly variable. Its patterns at one particular place and time are contingent upon preceding events; its trajectory through time is open ended and does not tend towards an equilibrial point. Human actions are part of the web of influences on ecological change, not external equilibrium-disturbing impacts. The implication of this is that science cannot tell conservationists what nature 'ought' to be like, and it may not always even be able to describe what it used to be like, and how and why it has changed. Conservationists will very often need ecology, but their science gives them no privileged insight into the way nature should be. They will have to work that out the same way everyone else does, by thinking and talking about it.

EQUILIBRIUM IN THE DRYLANDS

The idea that ecosystems have a 'natural' equilibrium state has also had significant impacts upon people, ecosystems and conservation in Africa. As in the case of conservation, pastoral policy has both needed and, in its turn, aided the growth of ecological science during the second half of the 20th century. In Africa, and in the US, from where the science mostly came, rangeland science drew upon wider advances in ecology, and provided clear evidence of ecology's usefulness (see Chapter 2 in this book). Throughout the 20th century, most analyses of ecological change in the drylands of Africa were based upon this view of the ways in which ecosystems respond to human action – and upon rather sweeping assumptions about the ways in which people use land. From most perspectives (certainly those of pastoralists, although, by and large, nobody asked them), the impacts of equilibrium thinking have been negative.

The conventional scientific view of rangeland management and mis-management has been built around ideas of range condition class and carrying capacity. Scientific research has established that there is a general relationship between rainfall and biomass of herbivores, whether these are wild or domesticated (Coe et al, 1976). The conventional logic is that the environment is capable of supporting a certain fixed number of livestock (or biomass of herbivores) that for any given ecosystem can be calculated primarily as a function of rainfall. It can then be argued that at stocking levels lower than this carrying capacity, pasture resources are being underused, and that at higher stocking levels resources are being overused. In an unmanaged grazing system, such overgrazing would be likely to lead to ecological change that would reduce its productivity (for example, by causing the extinction of palatable species and the eventually loss of vegetation cover), leading to loss of condition in grazing animals and, eventually, to a reduction in their numbers.

Pastoralist overgrazing was widely seen by scientists and policy-makers in the 1970s as a principal cause of desertification. The Sahel drought of 1972–1974, and the longer period of reduced rainfall that began in 1968, led some observers to believe that climate was undergoing permanent change. A range of hypotheses suggested that rainfall reduction could result from overgrazing – for example, through the loss of green vegetation cover from the savanna and increased surface albedo, or increased levels of dust at high altitude, both of them leading to stable air masses and dry conditions (Adams, 2001). Rising human and livestock population densities were blamed for reductions in vegetation cover and enhanced soil erosion, and these, in turn, were blamed for producing 'a new state of self-perpetuating drought' (Sinclair and Fryxell, 1985, p992).

Rangeland scientists have applied exactly the same logic to human-managed grazing systems. Studies of pastoral people in Africa (and elsewhere) suggested that they lacked an understanding of the ecological impacts of high stock densities, and lacked institutions for controlling livestock numbers, or controlling who had access to grazing land. Ecological studies of pasture change seemed to confirm this. Superficial accounts of decision-making by stock-keepers (often made by Northern researchers arguing from 'first principles', rather than by anthropologists who might actually have discussed the question with local people, or by or indigenous people themselves) suggested that a 'tragedy of the commons' (the phrase coined by Hardin, 1968) was inevitable.

The concepts of overgrazing and carrying capacity condemned nomadic pastoralists because of their apparently feckless management of seemingly fragile rangelands (Swift, 1982; Horowitz and Little, 1987). In addition to the apparent scientific rationale for such strategies, governments also tended to distrust people who are mobile and difficult to locate, tax, educate and provide with services. Typical government pastoral policies had several components. They were aimed, for example, at adjusting grazing intensity to available grazing resources and, thus, at improving stock health and weight. This was done by reducing stock numbers through compulsory de-stocking, controlling stock distribution though fencing, and providing evenly distributed watering points and improvement of range condition through bush clearance, pasture reseeding and controlled burning. Projects also typically sought to persuade stock-keepers to sell their cattle commercially, and to promote breed improvement (by importing European or North American stock and breeding them) and disease control, all with the hope of instilling a proper regard for the weight and health of each animal. None of these strategies fitted with nomadic or semi-nomadic subsistence livestock production; therefore, government pastoral policy also emphasized fixed settlements, formal land tenure (freehold or leasehold) and capitalist production.

In conservation terms, this approach to pastoralism essentially achieved two things, neither of them helpful. Firstly, it failed to recognize, or allow for, the historical tolerance of pastoralists for wildlife (Homewood and Rodgers, 1991; Homewood and Brockington, 1999). In doing so, it forced a conceptual and practical separation of areas managed for wildlife – protected areas (PAs) – and those managed for people and 'development'. It defined conservation as something done in spite of, against the interests of, and in the face of the opposition of pastoral people. Wherever pastoral management became more intensive (for example, where ranching systems were adopted), wildlife became increasingly unwelcome, a reservoir of disease (rinderpest, foot and mouth, bovine pleuropneumonia and sleeping sickness). Until the rise of game farming for safari hunting in southern Africa from the 1980s, and the growth of game-watching safari tourism, livestock grazing and wildlife were seen as mutually inimical activities.

The second result of this view of pastoralists as degrading the environment was the rigorous exclusion of pastoral people from protected areas: if nature ought to be in equilibrium, and humans and their livestock disrupted that equilibrium, then 'natural' areas had to be rid of people and their animals. And they were: most of the famous savanna national parks and reserves in eastern Africa were established on former pastoralist land (admittedly, sometimes on land whose users had been decimated by warfare and famine following the introduction of rinderpest and various other disasters; see Waller, 1988; Anderson and Johnson, 1988). In many parks (for example, at Amboseli National Park and Maasai Mara Game Reserve in Kenya; in the Serengeti National Park and Ngorogoro Conservation Area, Arusha National Park and the Mkomazi Game Reserve in Tanzania), people were evicted, or restricted in their use of land and resources. Access has been, in some instances, the subject of long-running and bitter dispute (Lindsay, 1987; Homewood and Rodgers, 1991; Brockington and Homewood, 1996; Neumann, 1998; Brockington 2002). This notion that people can and should be excluded from protected areas because they are places for 'wild' nature reflects the broader Western enthusiasm for wilderness (see Chapter 2). The portrayal of African savannas as 'wilderness', untouched, until recently, by human hand, is, of course, fundamentally flawed, as it is elsewhere – for example, Australia (see Chapters 3 and 4)

Researchers have increasingly expressed reservations about the universal applicability of the concept of overgrazing and with the unreflective links drawn between it and desertification (Sandford, 1983; Horowitz and Little, 1987; Mace, 1991). It has been argued that overstocking or overgrazing are rarely defined, and that judgements about carrying capacity are subjective, although that subjectivity is rarely admitted (Hogg, 1983; Homewood and Rodgers, 1984; 1987). They have become both entrenched and self-reinforcing

It is now recognized that there are wide gaps between pastoral policy prescriptions and the ways in which pastoral people actually manage their herds and rangelands. Pastoral development planning tends to focus upon commercial cattle production for slaughter for the production of meat and hides, whereas indigenous production systems tend to emphasize the production of products from live animals (milk or blood). Commercial production systems also typically focus upon a single species (usually cattle of an improved variety), whereas indigenous production systems tend to mix different kinds of livestock in their herds (cattle and camels and goats, for example, among the Turkana in northern Kenya; Coughenour et al, 1985). Moreover, poorer pastoral households will hold different a range of stock from wealthy ones. Mixed flocks and herds allow flexible use of land, water and vegetation resources in space and time. Unlike commercial ranching systems, indigenous pastoral ecosystems seem well adapted to exploit the spatial and temporal variability in biological production. Such systems offer a relatively low output compared to modern capitalist systems, such as ranching. However, they are remarkably robust in terms of providing a predictable, if limited, livelihood. Standardized assumptions about herd management, and formulaic prescriptions of carrying capacity are a poor guide to what happens on the ground.

DISEQUILIBRIUM AND DRYLAND ENVIRONMENTS

Despite massive research and a multitude of publications on the subject of desertification, which began with the Sahel drought of the 1970s and has been maintained in the face of persistent low rainfall in Africa ever since, it has slowly come to be recognized that the data necessary to assess 'long-term degradation' of vegetation or desertification, in most cases, simply does not exist (Warren, 1996; Swift, 1996; Adams, 2001). While it is clear that dryland rainfall in Africa varies from year to year (and in the timing and consistency of rainfall within years), this is not now blamed on farmers and pastoralists. Today, explanations emphasize the larger-scale links to global ocean–atmosphere circulation, particularly sea surface temperatures in the southern Atlantic and Indian oceans (Hulme, 1996; 2001).

Conventional thinking about carrying capacity and overgrazing began to be challenged during the 1980s and 1990s by so-called 'new range ecology' (Behnke and Scoones, 1991). New ideas hold that pastoral strategies are designed to track environmental variation (taking advantage of wet years, and coping with dry ones), rather than being conservative (seeking a steady-state equilibrial output). This awareness of the non-equilibrial nature of savanna ecosystem dynamics reflects a wider understanding of the importance of non-linear processes in ecology, as a whole (see, for example, Botkin, 1990; Pahl-Wostl, 1995). Much of what appeared to be perversity or conservatism on the part of pastoralists is revealed to be highly adaptive (Behnke and Scoones, 1991; Behnke et al, 1993).

The productivity of semi-arid rangelands varies a great deal both seasonally and between years. The primary cause of this variation is rainfall, which is now acknowledged to be highly variable in space and time in sub-Saharan Africa, particularly in drier rangelands. Here, ecosystems exhibit non-equilibrial behaviour, and ecosystem state and productivity are largely driven externally. The varied influences of fire, soil fertility and groundwater add to the complexity of rangeland productivity and its capacity to support grazing at particular places and times. There is no automatic ecological succession under grazing pressure towards an overgrazed state; instead, there are complex patterns of ecological change in response to exogenous conditions (especially rainfall) and stock numbers and management. Such ecological changes can take many forms, not all of them serious, and they can proceed by diverse routes, some of which can be reversed more easily than others, and some of which are more sensitive to particular management than others. Arguably, there are no 'naturally' stable points in semi-arid ecosystems that can usefully be taken to define an 'equilibrial' state.

Studies of the responses of vegetation to different stocking levels, or of livestock numbers, tend to take no account of seasonal or annual variations in fodder availability, and tend to be built upon estimates of regional stocking rates. Such estimates are notoriously unreliable because livestock are difficult and expensive to count, particularly if their owners do not want you to do so. Studies identifying overgrazing also tend to concentrate on absolute numbers of livestock and not on densities, rarely consider spatial mobility, and fail to take account of spatial and temporal variations. Conventional ideas about the overstocking of rangelands also typically fail to take account of the ways in which indigenous pastoralists understand the environment and adapt to it – particularly the skill with which they move stock around in response to seasonal environmental change in drier and wetter years, and the importance of institutions for the exchange and recovery of stock through kinship networks. Indigenous pastoralists can manage herds, and grazing land, in detailed, complex and often effective ways.

The attempt to define a single carrying capacity for an ecosystem with great annual variation in primary productivity is problematic (Homewood and Rodgers, 1987). The attempt to do so implies that the ecosystem has an optimal equilibrium state. If that equilibrium is illusory (because of the variability and resilience of the ecosystem), the concept of carrying capacity can only be relevant as a social or economic, rather than an ecological, concept – a judgement about the density of animals and plants that allows managers to get what they want out of the ecosystem (Homewood and Rodgers, 1987). The goals of a subsistence pastoralist, a rancher and a conservationist are likely to be very different. The pastoralist might wish to maintain herd size as capital and exchange value, as well as yields of milk and blood. The rancher needs to ensure profitable returns of capital through disease-free meat off-take. The conservationist seeks to maintain the 'naturalness' of the ecosystem and, like the rancher, probably wishes to fix the changing ecosystem in what is assumed to be its 'natural' state.

It may therefore be perfectly rational for the pastoralist to run a larger biomass of livestock than the rancher would, or than the conservationist would wish to do. Many African systems do, indeed, have a subsistence stocking rate that is higher than commercial ranchers would adopt, giving low rates of production per animal but high output per unit area (Homewood and Rodgers, 1987). This is not a mistake; it reflects people managing their assets in response to a different set of needs and different kinds of social arrangements and market signals.

It is now widely accepted that pastoral ecosystems should not be thought of as having a specific carrying capacity, equating to the density of livestock that can be supported at equilibrium, particularly if that density has been calculated for a commercial meat extraction system. Actual stocking levels can exceed such a standardized carrying capacity in a number of years successively (Behnke and Scoones, 1991). The critical point is that there is a constantly changing balance of grazing pressure and range resources. In wetter years, stock numbers rise (and animal condition and disease status improves). In dry years, stock lose condition and health. Severe drought years first reduce the condition of stock and then (through disease, death and destitution-forced sales) reduce stock numbers. When good rains follow, they allow pastures to recover, resulting in a lagged recovery of herd numbers as pastoralists track environmental conditions. Livestock numbers, like the ecosystem more generally, boom and bust with the rainfall.

To survive *without* degrading the environment, herd managers not only need their extensive knowledge of environmental conditions and opportunities in different areas open to them, but require access to those areas. Prevention of access because of government schemes for irrigation of large-scale agriculture (Hogg, 1983; Lane, 1992), or because of the establishment of protected areas (Brockington and Homewood, 1996; Homewood and Brockington, 1999; Brockington, 2002), can be a disaster.

Nature in the dry grasslands of Africa is not in equilibrium at all. Strategies to support environmental and social sustainability need to foster indigenous capacity in order to track rainfall and maintain social and economic networks, rather than demand a shift to a static, equilibrial capitalist form of production. Conservation need not automatically sign up to a policy of excluding people and their livestock. There is evidence that livestock and wildlife can run together without disaster at a wide range of densities; where they are incompatible, it is often livestock that suffer because of their susceptibility to disease (Homewood and Rodgers, 1991). Even in protected areas where pastoralist evictions are recent (for example, the Mkomazi Game Reserve in northern Tanzania, cleared in 1988), evidence of environmental degradation due to human occupation can be inconclusive or inadequate (Homewood and Brockington, 1999; Brockington, 2002)

Conservation planning in pastoral areas needs to ask more careful questions about people's role in the ways in which the environment is changing. Firstly, the long historical role of people in savanna ecosystems needs to be acknowledged, and any discussion of naturalness must be based upon clear historical and palaeo-environmental research. Secondly, arguments about the incompatibility of human occupation and biodiversity need to be based upon clear and specific research, and not upon general assumptions founded on unproved hypotheses about the equilibrial state of ecosystems and the risk of 'overgrazing'. Thirdly, conservation visions need to take specific account of the ideas that local residents have about nature – what is the area like, how is it changing, and which aspects of that change are acceptable and which not? Fourthly, in drylands, as everywhere else, conservation needs to learn to move forward in collaboration with local land users, instead of trying to bulldoze them aside.

NATURALNESS AND THE CONTROL OF NATURE

The idea that nature can be thought of as a set of ecosystems that tend to exist in equilibrium has led to an intrusive, and sometimes destructive, approach to conservation and to thinking about human use and degradation of natural resources. This seems to be so in contexts as widely divergent as the petite nature reserves of the UK and the expanses of African savannas. Of course, in many ways, these environments are not far apart at all; they are linked by the developing discipline of ecology and the colonial networks of science and ideology (see Chapters 2 and 7 in this book). Both of these reflect the scientific

Table 10.1 *Contrasting dimensions within conservation*

	Conservation as control	Conservation of wildness
Intellectual basis	Rationalist	Aesthetic
Priority values	Use values of nature	Cultural values of nature; intrinsic values
Response	Manage nature	Celebrate wildness of nature
Method	Control nature	Continued 'wildness' of nature
Objective	Predictability of natural systems	Unpredictability of nature

rationalization of nature that is characteristic of 20th-century colonial ideas (see Chapter 3). Nature conservation can be seen as a social practice that regulates (or seeks to regulate) relations between humans and non-human nature. It operates both within certain terrains or spaces (such as protected areas) and through a generalized moral discourse. That discourse often revolves around, and is developed through, specific conserved (or 'threatened') spaces.

The history of conservation practice reveals two contrasting dimensions (see Table 10.1). The first is what I would call 'the conservation of wildness'. This arises from a concern for wild nature, naturalness and unaltered 'non-human' nature. Robert Elliot (1997) points out in *Faking Nature* the importance of the view that 'wild nature' has intrinsic value. This wildness of nature comprises the basis for the cultural values of nature that have come to dominate conservation in the industrialized world. It explains one fundamental reason why people in countries such as the UK value nature (Adams, 1996).[7] The historical dimensions of this enthusiasm for notions of 'the wild' are discussed in Chapter 2 of this book

The second dimension of conservation is very different, and I have called it 'conservation as control' (see Table 10.1). This is conservation as the *technical practice* of the control of nature. It has become the characteristic approach to conservation in the UK and in places that have adopted British conservation ideas. The science of ecology, the techniques of habitat management and the bureaucratic/planning procedures of nature reserve management all represented an attempt to define and control the forms that non-human nature took (Adams, 1997). Reserves and other defined terrain were designated because of the 'wildness' or 'naturalness' of nature; but once established, they were mostly closely managed in order to keep nature within fixed bounds. Indeed, ecological research told conservation planners what nature ought to look like. Nature reserves were places where non-human nature could be maintained as it ought to be – its naturalness preserved and sometimes recreated (for example, this occurred when myxamatosis wiped out rabbits and chalk grasslands became hawthorn scrub, or when shallow water bodies became wet woodland habitats).

The tight management regimes of British nature reserves are one obvious context for this tradition of conservation as control, but the principle is more widely applicable. In the language of Birch (1990), any attempt to bound and protect 'nature' effectively put wildness in prison. He suggests that wilderness preservation (the US's defining contribution to global conservation; Henderson, 1992), is 'another stanza in the same old imperialist song of Western civilization' (Henderson, 1992, p4). His argument is an interesting one. He suggests that by the very act of designating 'wilderness' reserves for wild nature, the 'otherness' of wild land is itself locked up. Such reservation limits what humans can do to specified pieces of nature, and keeps people who might destroy wildness out; but it also allows humanity to contain and control the wild completely. Such 'wilderness' exists at the whim of legislators and government policy. Furthermore, such wilderness reservations can be (and are) managed in various ways, even if that management is disguised to hide it from human visitors' eyes. Thus, the wildness of nature is subjugated to a specified regime of human planning, bringing the outcomes of natural processes within a range acceptable to society. Birch comments: 'the imperium [the supreme or imperial power of Western civilization] has the power to manage, invade, declassify, abolish, de-sanctify the legal wildland entities it has created, and the creation of such entities on its terms does little to diminish this power' (Birch, 1990, p22).

The tension between the values attached to 'wild' nature and the need to control that wildness is much more broadly relevant than simply wildlife conservation. Perhaps the clearest example lies in the way river floods are understood and managed. For centuries, river management has tended to follow the 'rational use' element within conservation, informed by the need to control floods and bring the benefits of water (irrigation, water meadows, water supply and, latterly, hydroelectric power) to society.

This has demanded control of rivers and their waters: the dominant metaphors of river engineering are damming, harnessing, taming the mighty river, or bringing the desert to bloom. These ideologies were central to the American West as Donald Worster's *Rivers of Empire* (1985) and Mark Reisner's *Cadillac Desert* (1986) make clear, just as they were to imperial dreams in the Sahara (see Chapter 2) and colonial and post-colonial engineers who dammed Africa's major rivers (the Nile, Zambezi, Volta and Niger; Adams, 1992). Dams personified the 'can-do' of engineering, the capacity to out-think and control nature, to tame the wild. They create a macho world of concrete, steel and human endeavour.

Of course, in the UK things have been less butch; but the family resemblance to colonial ideologies of controlling nature is clear. One might consider the urge for developing the Scottish hydropower schemes of the 1930s (Sheail, 1981), the creation of Lake Efyrnwy and the flooding of the Elan Valley during the late 19th century to supply Birmingham with water, or the development of hydropower in north Wales (Gruffudd, 1990). The spirit of control is beautifully captured by the character of 'Mr Galvanic', fictional employee of the British Electricity Authority in the Clough Williams-Ellises' book *Headlong Down the Years*: 'If I had my way, this disgusting water would soon know its place! The place for water is behind dams and in pipes – all under control' (Gruffudd, 1990, p165, quoting Amabel and Clough Williams-Ellis, 1951)

Conservationists have frequently been opposed to dam construction, along with the wider environmental movement. One could think of the classic dispute over a dam in the Hetch Hetchy Valley in the US Yosemite National Park between the romantic preservationist John Muir and the gritty utilitarian conservationist Gifford Pinchot; Edward Abbey's book *The Monkey Wrench Gang* (1975), whose heroes are obsessed with the destruction of the Glen Canyon Dam on the Colorado River; or the work of Dan Brouwer and the Sierra Club (Brouwer was quoted as saying: 'I hate all dams, large and small'; Finkhouse and Crawford, 1991). Outside the US, the protests of local people and Indian environmentalists against the Sardar Sarovar Dam on the Narmada River comprise one example of the strength and diversity of environmentalist opposition to large dams (Adams, 2001).

RESTORING NATURE

The attraction of dams to their builders, and the issue behind the specific fears of their opponents, is the question of control over 'wild' nature. In the UK, flood control and the 'reclamation' of land liable to flood for urban development and agriculture have a long history. There is a dominant paradigm of 'flood control' that involves the defence of society and its capital and infrastructure against the incursions of wild nature. Institutionally, it has been inspired by the power of particular events, such as the great East Anglian floods of the 1950s, although the engineering is much older and the urge is ancient. Flood control (under Internal Drainage Boards and the Water Authorities, now the Environment Agency) has almost exclusively involved 'hard-engineering' solutions to the problems of flooding: changing the course, cross-section and regime of rivers with concrete banks, flood channels and culverts, as well as dams and barrages. The impact on riparian and aquatic ecosystems, wildlife and landscape has been vast and negative. During the 20th century, British rivers have become steadily less natural and less diverse.

Recently, there have been shifts in the control paradigm that has dominated river management (RSPB, 1994). Successive pieces of legislation have strengthened the requirements on river managers to have regard for conservation. This is all part of a wider shift towards 'soft engineering', rooted, for example, in the landscape design ideas of Ian McHarg's *Design with Nature* (1969).

One major fruit of the new river management paradigm is the growing interest in river restoration (Boon et al, 1992; Brookes and Shields, 1996). A great deal of energy in conservation and environmental planning in industrialized countries is now going into ecological restoration (Jordan et al, 1987a; Perrow and Davy, 2002). It is a new science, but has its own learned society and academic journal (*Restoration Ecology*).[8] The idea of ecological restoration nicely captures the tension between conservation's concern for the naturalness of nature and its confidence in its ability to predict, control and create nature.

River restoration typically involves replacing relatively small physical and biological elements of floodplains and channels. Most work is in low-energy floodplains, where created or recreated physical features tend to stay where they are put. The prime example of such work in the UK is probably the work of the River Restoration Project. Of their restoration work on the small lowland River Cole, one journalist remarked that 'engineers spent 900 years taming the River Cole in Oxfordshire by straightening it and deepening its bed to provide power for mills and to avoid floods – and then decided it was a mistake. During the past two years they have spent UK£150,000 reversing the process and recreating the river as it must have looked in the 16th century by putting the kinks back in' (Brown, 1997, p11).

Is restoration a science? Not exactly. Turner (1987) argues that it is neither a science nor a technology, for its goal is not product but process: 'one could say that the biological machine the restorer produces has no function but its own ordered reproduction' (Turner, 1987, p48). Turner argues that restoration is, in fact, an art: 'The attempt to reproduce accurately the functions of nature forces the artist not only to increasingly close observation, but beyond, to increasingly stringent experimental tests of ideas. This labour, so understood, is not merely analytical, but creative, and its natural reward is beauty' (Turner, 1987, p50).

Science is, however, central to the practice of restoration, and restoration is central to the science of ecology: 'the business of restoration and management [is] not just the acid test of its ideas, but [is] the very source of many of them as well' (Jordan and Packard, 1989, p26). The key to restoration is understanding the assembly rules by which species accumulate into assemblages (Keddy, 1999). With an inanimate object such as a clock, an ability to assemble it from pieces and adjust it properly suggests that 'perhaps we can claim to understand it' (Jordan et al, 1987b, p16). The restored ecosystem is a copy, of course. An analogy might be the work of a vintage car repairer. Nature is a machine, and if the vintage parts are reassembled, or modern facsimiles made, it will run much as before, although adjustments may have been made so that it can use modern petrol or meet safety standards. To all but the most hardened purist, a few modern components are hardly worth objecting to in the context of the wider achievements of the project.

The capacity of ecologists to predict and control nature is central to the restoration project: 'The essential idea is control – the ability to restore quickly but to restore at will, controlling speed, decelerating change, as well as accelerating it, reversing it, altering its course, *steering* it, even preventing it entirely (which, of course, is actually a frequent objective of the ecological manager)' (Jordan et al, 1987b, p17). Restoration is, therefore, at one level, restoration of naturalness. At another, however, it is the reverse, since the whole science of restoration is based upon the ability to predict outcomes and compare them to some template. Keddy stresses the importance of ecological indicators in restoration projects, emphasizing 'the ability to evaluate whether manipulation has produced the desired change' (Keddy, 1999, p718).

However, in ecological restoration, a distinction can be drawn between restoring form and restoring form-creating processes – for example, between replanting a wood and simply allowing woodland to develop by leaving a patch of grassland alone. Living systems self-repair, and restoration may involve 'bringing in certain key "ingredients", then letting nature take its course in shaping the result' (Jordan et al, 1987b, p16). In floodplains, this involves more than putting pieces of habitat 'back'; it entails linking them hydrologically, and in terms of sediment flux and geochemistry, with each other and the river channel and allowing ecosystems to evolve (Hughes, 2001). Johan van Zoest (1992) urges the 'management of processes rather than patterns' in sand dunes. He advocates the relaxation of control over the processes active in dunes, a process he calls 'gambling with nature'. He suggests that conservationists should think of managing nature as a game, not as tending a machine. Rather than trying to control nature, management is best done by thinking like a player in a game. Conservation should not manipulate populations and communities in order to achieve defined outcomes, but should expect complex and unexpected effects of human actions. Managers therefore should willingly play a game with nature, even if they have (or think they have) deep scientific understanding of the ecological rules of play and the role of chance processes.

RESTORATION AND THE CONTROL OF NATURE

Most ecological restoration, however, is less open spirited than this. Particularly in ecosystems with the capacity to cause damage to human interests (for example, rivers that flood), those proposing restoration must feel confident of being able to predict the outcome of the restoration process, or at least of specifying the range of conditions within which it will lie. Either way, restoration, in practice, demands prediction and the control of outcomes, and restoration projects in environments such as rivers will, in practice, usually be small in scale and limited in imagination. Restoration is almost always, therefore, creating naturalness within fixed bounds. How are these bounds fixed? Remarkably, there is increasing capacity to do without physical boundaries for nature.

Restoration work within river channels has made use of the last 20 years of fluvial geomorphology and the understanding it offers of how rivers behave. However, studies of river geomorphology are shifting. The dominant approach since the 1950s has been largely empirical, involving the statistical analysis of the physical shape of river channels, such as channel width and depth and meander wavelength, and the measurement of surrogates for the variables that control them (particularly river discharge). This approach implied that river channels were equilibrial at the scale of the reach. However, numerical generalizations no longer satisfy river scientists. Research is increasingly moving to a smaller scale, and to the intensive measurement of the ways in which channels respond to changes in discharge, sediment supply and other factors in small reaches of rivers over short time periods (Lane and Richards, 1997). Studies of real rivers are now being combined with studies of virtual rivers through laboratory experimentation and computer modelling. It turns out that (as with ecosystems) short-term, small-scale events have significance at a larger scale: rivers may behave as non-linear systems. The key to understanding them is to see them as dynamic systems; research must integrate work within and outside of nature, ' in the field, the flume and the computer' (Lane and Richards, 1997, p258).

New technologies of surveillance using micro-chip technology yield vast volumes of data about river behaviour. Computer models allow such data to be run through models of river behaviour. Nature can be described with an intensity and level of detail never previously known, and nature's agency – its capacity to act – is predicted with a precision never previously known. As uncertainty falls, management confidence rises. This is essentially why river managers have been willing to consider ecological restoration. The science behind them allows them to move safely away from their traditional (and highly expensive) approach of confining rivers within artificial channels and behind barrages in order to 'control' floods. In 'restoring' the river, river managers can cut nature more slack because they think that they know what will happen when they take the concrete and the dams away.

Greater knowledge of rivers, therefore, creates more confident management. Managers no longer fear the power of the 'natural' river – they do not need to control it because they understand it. The conservation turn of river management represents a greater openness to the 'natural' attributes of rivers. Restoration meets the new conservation objectives. However, control is not lost: it is simply that physical restraint is exchanged for knowledge-based ability in order to predict how nature will work.

In this sense, restoration ('the ultimate test for ecology') is a logical development of the rationalizing project of control. As conservation tries to move away from a concern for particular 'equilibrial' forms of ecosystems, by concentrating on the regimes of processes that give rise to those forms, we are, perhaps, not escaping the ideology of control as completely as we might like to believe. Our scientific and technical skills allow us to intensify our attempts to control nature under the guise of conservation. The abandonment of old equilibrial thinking may, therefore, not usher in a new era of egalitarian engagement between people and non-human nature, but a new regime of control. We may no longer need to intervene in the detailed way in which we did in conservation management; in a sense, science and technology, and new theories of ecosystem behaviour, allow us to achieve more control than ever before. We have control not by controlling nature's every move, but, more cost effectively, by thinking nature's thoughts.

CONCLUSIONS

This chapter has tried to argue that our beliefs in the innate equilibrial behaviour of nature have a number of significant implications for the way in which we approach the management or conservation of nature. A number of these might well make us uncomfortable. Formal policies for land management in the pastoral drylands of Africa have not only been unsuccessful but also, in many instances, unhelpful or even harmful for pastoralists. Conservationists have shared the standardized ecological understanding of savanna dynamics and have, perhaps, been slower than livestock planners to admit that the science needs a very thorough second look, and that they need to rethink their ideas about what is 'natural' and what is 'sustainable'.

In the UK, these same ecological themes have resulted in a wonderfully intricate practice of conservation management. Using these skills, conservation has maintained astonishing proportions of Britain's rather impoverished fauna and flora on a tiny proportion of the land surface – small isolated islands of semi-natural habitat marooned in a sea of chemical agriculture, roads and houses. This is a wonderful achievement; but this approach to conservation leaves nature trussed up, delivered with something like the same factory-like precision as the agricultural crops and industrial products that have so widely supplanted it. Even in conservation, the obsession has been to control nature, to ensure that its biodiversity is sustained, to provide it with special places – but, at the same time, to keep its wildness under control.

Ideas about ecological restoration challenge established ideas about conservation, and ideas about the restoration of natural processes, rather than simply natural features, challenge them further. These initiatives are exciting (and are discussed further in Chapter 11); but even in this enthusiasm for restoration, the human need for control rears its head. I have suggested that where (as in the case of rivers) we have been willing to take the concrete out and allow natural features back in, we seem to need to retain control, even if it is only exercised through our computer models.

There are, therefore, two challenges that lend themselves to a form of conservation based upon the idea that nature is non-equilibrial. The first starts from the premise of business as usual, where conservation does, and should, involve a large measure of human agency and control. The question is simple: who should decide about the form that nature takes? This is relevant in the UK (where river planners, conservation planners and local residents might have very different views about the desirability of letting a river flood). It is even more relevant in places such as Africa, where conservationists (and development planners) still tend to come into rural communities, from capital cities and foreign consultancies, donor organizations and non-governmental organizations (NGOs), with their agendas pre-formed. As Chapters 4, 5 and 6 all show, conservation is still not a very inclusive discourse. Conservation can make some heavy demands on people who live in biodiverse places, demands that they sometimes find inexplicable and unfair. Who should get to forge conservation policy? How should local needs and wider conservation interests be balanced? How can locally diverse ideas of nature be reconciled with national and global priorities for conservation? These are widely recognized issues.

The second challenge for conservation that arises from recognizing non-equilibrial ecology relates to a point made in several places in this book. It concerns the idea that nature is, by definition, wild: that which is unknown, uncontrolled. Can we imagine a conservation that recognizes and allows nature to be wild? Or is conservation, in Thomas Birch's words (1990, p8) 'just another move in the imperial resource allocation game?[9]

NOTES

1 National Nature Reserves (NNRs) and Sites of Special Scientific Interest (SSSIs) are statutory government conservation designations by English Nature. They originated under the Nature Conservancy, established in 1949 (Adams, 1996).
2 I still use the photographs I took of these places in lectures, although the stories I tell about them have changed over time.
3 See www.davidaxford.free-online.co.uk/torreycn.htm, 30 July 2001.
4 Rachel Carson (1963) *Silent Spring*.
5 Marsh expresses this gendered discourse clearly: 'The ravages committed by man subvert the relations and destroy the balance which nature had established between her organized and her inorganic creations' (Marsh, 1864, p42).
6 I am grateful to John Rodwell for this observation.
7 Note that this is the case regardless of the fact that UK nature is substantially human made ('semi-natural', to use Arthur Tansley's phrase). Most targets of conservation action are hybrids of human agency and non-human agency (for example, heathlands, chalk grasslands, ancient woodlands). Only a few 'natural formations' do not bear in their formation the obvious imprint of deliberate human agency (exceptions include some Scottish peat bogs and alpine plant communities, a few cliff forest understorey fragments or other communities on remote cliffs, and the vegetation of ephemeral environments, such as river banks and islands, or salt marshes or sand dunes).
8 See www.blackwell-science.com.
9 I would like to thank Martin Mulligan, Dan Brockington and Francine Hughes for their comments on this chapter.

REFERENCES

Abbey, E (1975) *The Monkey Wrench Gang*. J B Lippincott, New York
Adams, W M (1992) *Wasting the Rain: rivers, people and planning in Africa*. Minnesota University Press, Minneapolis, Minnesota
Adams, W M (1996) *Future Nature: a vision for conservation*. Earthscan, London
Adams, W M (1997) 'Rationalization and conservation: ecology and the management of nature in the United Kingdom', *Transactions of the Institute of British Geographers NS*, vol 22, pp277–291
Adams, W M (2001) *Green Development: Environment and Sustainability in the Third World*, second edition. Routledge, London
Allen, D E (1976) *The Naturalist in Britain*. Penguin, Harmondsworth, UK

Anderson, D M and Johnson, D H (1988) 'Ecology and society in north-east African history' in D Johnson and D M Anderson (eds) *The Ecology of Survival: case studies from North-East African history*. Lester Crook, London, pp1–26

Behnke, R H and Scoones, I (1991) *Rethinking Range Ecology: implications for range management in Africa*. ODI/IIED, London

Behnke, R H Jr, Scoones, I and Kerven, C (1993) *Range Ecology at Disequilibrium: new models of natural variability and pastoral adaptation in African savannas*. Overseas Development Institute, London

Birch, T H (1990) 'The incarceration of wildness: wilderness areas as prisons', *Environmental Ethics*, vol 12(1), pp3–26

Boon, P J, Calow, P and Petts, G E (eds) (1992) *River Conservation and Management*, Wiley, Chichester

Botkin, D B (1990) *Discordant Harmonies: a new ecology for the twenty-first century*. Oxford University Press, New York

Brockington, D (2002) *Fortress Conservation: the preservation of the Mkomazi Game Reserve*. James Currey, Oxford

Brockington, D and Homewood, K (1996) 'Wildlife, pastoralists and science: debates concerning Mkomazi Game Reserve, Tanzania' in M Leach and R Mearns (eds) *The Lie of the Land*. James Currey, Oxford, pp91–104

Brookes, A and Shields, F (eds) (1996) *River Channel Restoration: guiding principles for sustainable projects*. John Wiley and Sons Ltd, Chichester

Brown, P (1997) 'Tailored river gets back its bends', *Guardian*, Friday, 17 September 1997, p11

Carson, R (1963) *Silent Spring*, Hamilton, London

Clements, F E (1905) *Research Methods in Ecology*. University Publishing Company, Lincoln, Nebraska

Clements, F E (1916) *Plant Succession: an analysis of the development of vegetation*. Carnegie Institute, Washington, D C, Publication 290

Coe, M J, Cummings, D H and Phillipson, J (1976) 'Biomass and production of large African herbivores in relation to rainfall and primary production', *Oecologia*, vol 22, pp341–354

Coughenour, M B, Ellis, J E, Swift, D M, Coppock, D L, Galvin, K, McCabe, J T and Hart, T C (1985) 'Energy extraction and use in a nomadic pastoral ecosystem', *Nature*, vol 230, pp619–625

Duffey, E (1970) 'The management of Woodwalton Fen: a multidisciplinary approach' in E Duffey and A S Watt (eds) *The Scientific Management of Animal and Plant Communities for Conservation*. Blackwell, Oxford, pp581–597

Duffey, E and Watt, A S (eds) (1970) *The Scientific Management of Animal and Plant Communities for Conservation*. Blackwell, Oxford

Elliot, R (1997) *Faking Nature: the ethics of environmental restoration*. Routledge, London

Finkhouse, J and Crawford, M (eds) (1991) *A River Too Far: the past and future of the Arid West*. University of Nevada Press, Reno

Gleason, H A (1926) 'The individualistic concept of the plant association', *Bulletin of the Torrey Botanical Club*, vol 53, pp7–26

Green, B (1981) *Countryside Conservation*. Allen and Unwin, London

Griffiths, T (1996) *Hunters and Collectors: The Antiquarian Imagination in Australia*. Cambridge University Press, Cambridge

Grove, R H (1992) 'Origins of western environmentalism', *Scientific American*, vol 267, pp42–47

Grove, R H (1995) *Green Imperialism: colonial expansion, tropical island Edens and the origins of environmentalism, 1600–1800*. Cambridge University Press, Cambridge

Gruffudd, P (1990) 'Uncivil engineering: nature, nationalism and hydro-electrics in north Wales' in D Cosgrove and G Petts (eds) *Water, Engineering and Landscape: water control and landscape transformation in the modern period*. Belhaven Press, London, pp159–173

Hardin, G (1968) 'The tragedy of the commons', *Science*, vol 1628, pp1243–1248

Henderson, N (1992) 'Wilderness and the nature conservation ideal: Britain, Canada and the United States contrasted', *Ambio*, vol 21, pp394–399

Hill, M O (1979) *TWINSPAN – a FORTRAN Program for Arranging Multivariate Data in an Ordered Two-Way Table by Classification of the Individuals and Attributes*. Cornell University, Ithaca, New York

Hogg, R (1983) 'Irrigation agriculture and pastoral development: a lesson from Kenya', *Development and Change*, vol 14, pp577–591

Homewood, K and Brockington, D (1999) 'Biodiversity, conservation and development in Mkomazi Game Reserve, Tanzania', *Global Ecology and Biodiversity*, vol 8, pp301–313

Homewood, K and Rodgers, W A (1984) 'Pastoralism and conservation', *Human Ecology*, vol 12, pp431–441

Homewood, K and Rodgers, W A (1987) 'Pastoralism, conservation and the overgrazing controversy', in D M Anderson and R H Grove (eds) *Conservation in Africa: people, policies and practice*. Cambridge University Press, Cambridge, pp111–128

Homewood, K and Rodgers, W A (1991) *Masailand Ecology*. Cambridge University Press, Cambridge

Horowitz, M M and Little, P D (1987) 'African pastoralism and poverty: some implications for drought and famine' in M Glantz (ed) *Drought and Hunger in Africa: denying famine a future*. Cambridge University Press, Cambridge, pp59–82

Hughes, F M R (1999) 'Floodplain biogeomorphology', *Progress in Physical Geography*, vol 21, pp501–529

Hughes, F M R (2001) 'Floodplains' in A Warren and J R French (eds) *Habitat Conservation: managing the physical environment*. J Wiley and Sons, Chichester, pp103–121

Hulme, M (1996) Climate change within the period of meteorological records' in W M Adams, A S Goudie and A R Orme (eds) (1996) *The Physical Geography of Africa*. Oxford University Press, Oxford, pp88–102

Hulme, M (2001) 'Climatic perspectives on Sahelian desiccation: 1973–1998', *Global Environmental Change*, vol 11, pp19–29

Huston, M A (1994) *Biological Diversity: the coexistence of species on changing landscapes*. Cambridge University Press, Cambridge

Jordan, W R III and Packard, S (1989) 'Just a few oddball species: restoration practice and ecological theory' in G P Buckely (ed) *Biological Habitat Reconstruction*. Belhaven Press, London, pp18–28

Jordan, W R III, Gilpin, M E and Aber, J D (eds) (1987a) *Restoration Ecology: A Synthetic Approach to Ecological Research*, Cambridge University Press, Cambridge

Jordan, W R III, Gilpin, M E and Aber, J D (1987b) 'Restoration ecology: restoration as a technique for basic research' in W R Jordan III, M E Gilpin and J D Aber (eds) *Restoration Ecology: A Synthetic Approach to Ecological Research*. Cambridge University Press, Cambridge, pp3–21

Keddy, P (1999) 'Wetland restoration: the potential for assembly rules in the service of conservation', *Wetlands*, vol 19, pp716–732

Lane, C (1992) 'The Barabaig Pastoralists of Tanzania: sustainable land use in jeopardy' in D Ghai and J M Vivian (eds) *Grassroots Environmental Action: people's participation in sustainable development*. Routledge, London, pp81–105

Lane, S N and Richards, K S R (1997) 'Linking river channel form and process: time, space and causality revisited', *Earth Surface Processes and Landforms*, vol 22, pp249–260

Lindemann R L (1942) 'The trophic-dynamic aspect of ecology', *Ecology*, vol 23, pp399–418

Lindsay, W K (1987) ' integrating parks and pastoralists: some lessons from Amboseli' in D M Anderson and R H Grove (eds) *Conservation in Africa: people, policies and practice*. Cambridge University Press, Cambridge, pp149–168

Livingstone, D N (1995) 'The polity of nature: representation, virtue, strategy', *Ecumene*, vol 2(4), pp353–377

Mace, R (1991) 'Overgrazing overstated', *Nature*, vol 349, pp280–281, 24 January

Marsh, G P (1864) *Man and Nature; or, physical geography as modified by human action*. Scribners, New York; Sampson Low, London (reprinted Harvard University Press, 1965)

May, R M (1989) 'Levels of organisation in ecology' in J M Cherrett (ed) *Ecological Concepts: the contribution of ecology to an understanding of the natural world*. Blackwell, Oxford (for the British Ecological Society), pp339–363

McHarg, I L (1969) *Design with Nature*. Natural History Press, Garden City, New York

McIntosh, R P (1985) *The Background of Ecology: concept and theory*. Cambridge University Press, Cambridge

Neumann, R P (1998) *Imposing Wilderness: struggles over livelihood and nature preservation in Africa*. University of California Press, Berkeley

Nicholson, E M (1957) *Britain's Nature Reserves*. Country Life Limited, London

Nicholson, E M (1970) *The Environmental Revolution: a guide to the new masters of the world*. Hodder and Stoughton, London (Penguin edition 1972)

Pahl-Wostl, C (1995) *The Dynamic Nature of Ecosystems: chaos and order intertwined*. Wiley, Chichester

Pearsall, W H (1964) 'The development of ecology in Britain', *Journal of Ecology*, vol 52, pp1–12

Perrow, M R and Davy, A J (2002) (eds) *Handbook of Ecological Restoration*. Cambridge University Press, Cambridge

Reisner, M (1986) *Cadillac Desert: the American West and its disappearing waters*. Peregrine Books, New York

Rodwell, J, S (ed) (1991) *British Plant Communities, volume 1: woodlands and scrub*. Cambridge University Press, Cambridge, for the Nature Conservancy Council

Royal Society for the Protection of Birds (RSPB) (1994) *The New Rivers and Wildlife Handbook*, second edition. Royal Society for the Protection of Birds, Sandy

Sandford, S (1983) *Management of Pastoral Development in the Third World*. Wiley, Chichester

Sheail, J (1976) *Nature in Trust: the history of nature conservation in Great Britain*. Blackie, Glasgow

Sheail, J (1981) *Rural Conservation in Inter-War Britain*. Clarendon Press, Oxford

Sheail, J (1987) *Seventy-Five Years of Ecology: the British Ecological Society*. Blackwell Scientific, Oxford

Sheail, J (1995) 'From aspiration to implementation – the establishment of the first national nature reserves in Britain', *Landscape Research*, vol 21(1), pp37–54

Sinclair, A R and Fryxell, J M (1985) 'The Sahel of Africa: ecology of a disaster',

Canadian Journal of Zoology, vol 63, pp987–994

Steward T A, Pickett, V, Parker, T and Feidler, P L (1992) 'The new paradigm in ecology: implications for conservation biology above the species level' in P L Feidler and S K Jain (eds) *Conservation Biology: the theory and practice of nature conservation, preservation and management*. Chapman and Hall, London, pp65–88

Sutherland, W J and Hill, D A (1995) *Managing Habitats for Conservation*, Cambridge University Press, Cambridge

Swift, J (1982) 'The future of African hunter-gatherer and pastoral people in Africa', *Development and Change*, vol 13, pp159-181

Swift, J (1996) 'Desertification narratives; winners and losers' in M Leach and R Mearns (eds) *The Lie of the Land: challenging received wisdom on the African environment*. James Currey Heinemann, London, pp73–90

Tansley A G (1911) *Types of British Vegetation*. Cambridge University Press, Cambridge

Tansley A G (1935) 'The use and abuse of vegetational terms', *Ecology*, vol 14(3), pp284–307

Tansley A G (1939) 'British ecology in the past quarter century: the plant community and the ecosystem', *Journal of Ecology*, vol 27, pp513–530

Turner, F (1987) 'The self-effacing art: restoration as imitation of nature' in W R Jordan III, M E Gilpin and J D Aber (eds) *Restoration Ecology: a synthetic approach to ecological research*. Cambridge University Press, Cambridge, pp47–50

Waller, R D (1988) '*Emutai*: crisis and response in Maasailand (1884–1904)', in D Johnson and D M Anderson (eds) *The Ecology of Survival*. Lester Crook, London, pp73–112

Wallis DeVries, M F, Bakker, J P and Van Wieren, S E (eds) (2001) *Grazing and Conservation Management*. Kluwer Academic Publishers, Dordrecht

Warren, A (1996) 'Desertification' in W M Adams, A S Goudie and A Orme (eds) *The Physical Geography of Africa*. Oxford University Press, Oxford, pp342–355

Werrity, A, McManus J, Brazier, V and Gordon, J (1994) 'Conserving our dynamic and static geomorphological heritage', *Earth Heritage*, vol 1, pp16–17

Williams-Ellis, A and Williams-Ellis, C (1951) *Headlong Down the Years: a tale of today*. Liverpool University Press, Liverpool

Worster, D (1985) *Rivers of Empire*. Norton and Co, New York

Worster, D (1994) 'Nature and the disorder of history', *Environmental History Review*, vol 18(2), pp1–16 (reprinted in M Soulé and G Lease (eds) (1995) *Reinventing Nature: responses to postmodern deconstruction*. Island Press, Washington, DC)

Zoest, J van (1992) 'Gambling with nature? A new paradigm of nature and its consequences for nature management strategy' in R W G Carter, T G F Curtis and M J Sheehy-Skeffington (eds) *Coastal Dunes*. Balkema, Rotterdam, pp503–514

Chapter 11

Beyond preservation: the challenge of ecological restoration

Adrian Colston

INTRODUCTION

Habitat loss has been acute in lowland England during the 20th century. It has been the chief focus of conservation action from the 19th century, when the two largest British voluntary conservation organizations were founded: the National Trust for Places of Historic Interest and Natural Beauty (the National Trust), and what became the Royal Society for the Protection of Birds (RSPB) (both during the 1890s; Sheail, 1976; Evans, 1992).[1] Habitat loss was particularly rapid during the second half of the 20th century. Agriculture caused massive changes in the British countryside, both during World War II (the fruit of the county agricultural committees and the wider spirit of the 'Dig for Britain' campaign) and from the 1950s onwards (as agricultural intensification took hold, with fewer, larger and better capitalized farms). The impacts of these changes in biodiversity were considerable, although, clearly, scientific records before the late 19th century are fragmentary. Some 3500 species are listed in national *Red Lists*; the number would be over 5000 if such studies were available for all taxonomic groups. Many species are declining in numbers or range. A number of species are confined to a very few sites where ecological conditions are suitable. They are hugely vulnerable to ecological change.[2]

Derek Ratcliffe notes that the effect of a human population of more than 50 million on a set of islands measuring less than 230,000 km^2 was to leave very little truly natural vegetation (Ratcliffe, 1984). Of the 1423 native British vascular plant species, one in ten suffered a decline of at least 20 per cent between 1930 and 1960. Of the 317 higher plant species listed as nationally rare in 1983, 37 per cent had suffered decline in distribution of at least one third since 1930.[3] Table 11.1 summarizes the loss of bird species in Bedfordshire, Cambridgeshire and Northamptonshire over the past 250 years.

Table 11.1 *Loss of bird species in Bedfordshire, Cambridgeshire and Northamptonshire*

Species of breeding bird now extinct		
Bedfordshire	Cambridgeshire	Northamptonshire
Red kite; corncrake; stone curlew; wryneck; wheatear; red-backed shrike; cirl bunting	Bittern; red kite; hen harrier; Montagu's harrier; corncrake; black tern; nightjar; wryneck; tree pipit; wheatear; wood warbler; red-backed shrike; raven; cirl bunting	Honey buzzard; spotted crake; corncrake; nightjar; wryneck; woodlark; wheatear; red-backed shrike; raven; cirl bunting

Source: adapted from Holloway, S (1996) *Historical Atlas of Breeding Birds 1875–1900*, Poyser

In lowland Britain, agricultural intensification during the second half of the 20th century, fuelled by UK and European government policy, produced a farmed landscape where areas of semi-natural habitat became highly fragmented and small in extent (Shoard, 1980; Rackham, 1986; Peterken and Hughes, 1990; Adams, 1996; Harvey, 1997). Fast-growing weeds such as nettle, hog-weed or cocksfoot have spread at the expense of a much wider variety of slower-growing species. Patches of different kinds of semi-natural habitat have become separated from each other, so that different habitats rarely occur alongside each other. Blocks of semi-natural vegetation have become smaller and increasingly isolated from one another, raising the threat that local extinctions will not be balanced by natural reintroductions. Corridors in the landscape, such as hedges or streams, have progressively been lost or degraded, further increasing habitat fragmentation. Areas of new habitats have been created, several with a specific eye to conservation (for example, farm woodlands), some as a side-product of industry (such as gravel pits). However, Peterken and Hughes (1990) argue that the diversity of these habitats will be limited by the impoverished nature of the landscape around them. Loss of habitats such as grasslands has been particularly serious (Fuller, 1987). By the late 1980s, only 4 per cent of British grassland remained unimproved. Much of the habitat that remains in lowland Britain has been degraded through the withdrawal of traditional management, eutrophication and other forms of pollution.

The rapid rate of rural change has meant that conservation in the lowland parts of the UK (where the vast majority of people live) focused upon the preservation of a series of tiny and often isolated areas of habitat. These have been identified and mapped by careful county-level surveys, and many of them have been designated as Sites of Special Scientific Interest (SSSIs), County Wildlife Sites and nature reserves of various kinds (Adams et al, 1992).[4] Many of these are theoretically protected in law, and highly intensive management regimes are required to try and keep the assemblages of plant and animal species intact (Sutherland and Hill, 1995). This interventionist approach to conservation management has been the most characteristic feature of British conservation (Henderson, 1992; Adams, 1997; see also Chapter 10 of this book). So little natural habitat has survived in part of lowland England that it has been termed the 'Black Hole' for conservation (Colston, 1997). Figure 11.1 shows this

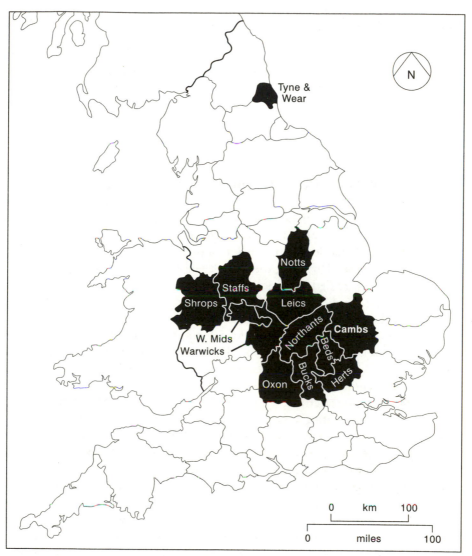

Figure 11.1 *The 'Black Hole'*

graphically, mapping all of the counties in England with less than half of the national average area of SSSIs. The counties of the 'Black Hole' have largely been bypassed by government countryside and conservation policies. The 'Black Hole' contains no National Parks or Areas of Outstanding Natural Beauty (AONBs) – both landscape conservation designations, originally introduced in 1949 – and no Environmentally Sensitive Areas (ESAs) – designated areas where grants are available to encourage environmentally friendly farming. There are no Heritage Coasts.[5]

This chapter discusses the challenge to nature conservation in the lowlands of the UK, using the Fens of East Anglia as an example. Fens are wetlands that receive nutrients and water from a catchment, as well as rainfall (Burgess et al, 1995). Wetlands globally have suffered extensive drainage, especially for agriculture (Dugan, 1990; 1993; Mitsch and Gosselink, 1993). British fens have been particularly susceptible to drainage for agriculture, and only tiny fragments remain of once extensive ecosystems (Williams, 1970; 1990; Peterken and Hughes, 1990). The chapter sets out a new approach to reversing these fortunes that is being pioneered by a British non-governmental conservation organization, the National Trust, at Wicken Fen in Cambridgeshire.[6]

NEW THINKING ABOUT CONSERVATION

The standard site-based approach to conservation has been remarkably successful, as the small number of species extinction in the UK in the 20th century attests (since 1900 the UK has lost 1 mammal, 6 birds, 2 fish, 144 invertebrates and 62 plants; Brown, 1994). However, there are a number of serious limitations to a conservation strategy that is so closely based upon small, isolated fragments of habitat. Firstly, it is expensive. Nature reserves have to be purchased or leased, a considerable burden on voluntary conservation organizations and an unpopular strategy to a government keen to off-load economically unproductive assets (as the British government was during the 1980s under Thatcherism, and as it has remained). If habitat is left in private hands (as it is in UK SSSIs), its conservation status is open to the whim of owners and the pressures of the market. By the 1980s, it had become clear that appropriate management of SSSIs needed to be paid for by compensating owners for the profits they could make through intensive agriculture. Policies have evolved; but SSSIs are still, primarily, protected by offering incentives to manage them appropriately. The costs of such a conservation strategy have been massive (Adams, 1993).

Secondly, it has become clear from the theory of island biogeography that small nature reserves will suffer from the local extinction of species, however well managed they are. MacArthur and Wilson (1967) showed that the number of breeding species on islands tends to stabilize at a level related to rates of immigration and extinction. These are controlled by isolation and island size: large islands close to a continental source tend to have more species than small, isolated islands. Subsequently, conservation biologists extended this idea to terrestrial habitats and isolated habitat fragments, and then to strategic questions about the selection of nature reserves. It was argued that reserves should be as large as possible; if small, they should be close together and connected by corridors of similar habitat (see, for example, Diamond, 1975; Simberlof and Abele, 1976; Margules et al, 1982). There is also growing interest in the connectivity of landscapes and in the extent to which landscape elements are linked to each other in a way that allows populations to interact and recolonize following local extinction (see, for example, Hobbs, 1990).

In the UK context, debate about reserve size has seemed somewhat academic. Reserve purchase has tended to be driven by threat of destruction and availability of funds, and the isolation of reserves is something that conservationists have become used to. However, the theory of island biogeography, along with the law of diminishing returns, has sadly now exposed this approach to nature conservation as unsustainable. Wildlife sites and nature reserves are too often viewed in isolation and not as part of a wider landscape or ecosystem. This is surprising, since systems thinking has been important to ecologists from Tansley's proposition of the ecosystem (Tansley, 1935), the rise of ecological energetics during the 1930s, and the development of systems ecology in the 1970s (McIntosh, 1985). The significance of systems thinking to conservation has been discussed in Chapter 10. Systems thinking, widely used in business management (see, for example, Senge, 1992), is holistic, treating all elements of the system as connected so that impact on one part of the system affects all the other parts, too. It is disappointing that so often nature conservationists in the UK, the vast majority of whom were trained as ecologists, seem to have abandoned systems thinking as an underpinning principle. This is especially true of those who operate in the lowlands, where there is so little habitat of conservation interest left.

The 1990s, however, saw substantial rethinking of traditional approaches in conservation (Bullock and Harvey, 1995; Adams, 1996). Many conservationists in the UK had become deeply frustrated with 'gardening' tiny sites in order to maintain species. The debate over the future of farming and rural livelihoods had intensified, with many people questioning the role of the Common Agricultural Policy (CAP) (and the huge cost of taxpayers' support for intensive agriculture), or fearing the impacts of the GATT on the profitability of farming (and its threat to agricultural protectionism).[7] The gearing back of agricultural support, the degradation of soils and competition for water have meant that high-investment, high-return agriculture (typical of the Fens, among other places) is no longer as widely profitable as it was. The stark clash between agricultural profits and wildlife was a major feature of public debate in the UK during the 1980s (Shoard, 1980). The public became less willing to accept the environmental costs of intensive farming. There has been a growing feeling that something needs to be done for the countryside and for conservation, and that the status quo cannot be maintained.

In particular, during the 1990s, British conservationists began to conceive of the idea of focusing conservation strategies on the restoration of habitat, and not simply on its protection. They turned from preventing habitat loss to thinking about habitat restoration and recreation (Harvey, 1995). There were many precedents for this seismic shift of thinking, and it reflected much broader developments in restoration ecology, and, in practice, in places such as the US (Jordan et al, 1987; Hobbs and Harris, 2001; Perrow and Davy, 2002; see also Chapter 10 in this book). It was recognized that conservation management decisions needed to be creative, subtle and sensitive to both the human-influenced past and the dynamics of natural change. Conservationists entertained ideas of abandoning land to ecological change, effectively 'creating wilderness' (Henderson, 1992; Potter et al, 1991; Green, 1995), and became involved in the restoration of environments such as rivers (Brookes, 1996) and the 'managed retreat' of soft coasts (Pye and French, 1983).[8] In 1994, the UK government produced an 'action plan' for biodiversity, from which different agencies developed specific action plans for threatened habitats and species. The 2001 Rural White Paper announced that the biodiversity strategy for England would set targets for the recreation and enhancement of such habitats (DETR, 2001).

Issues such as climate change offer new challenges to conventional conservation strategies. Sea-level rise and land lowering are facts of life in south-east England. The process of isostatic recovery from the weight of ice in the north-west of the UK at the last glacial maximum (10,000 years ago) is causing the land in the south east of the UK to sink by 1–3mm per annum. In addition to this, global warming may cause sea levels to rise by 20cm by 2030. The figure used by the Department for the Environment, Food and Rural Affairs (DEFRA) and the Environment Agency (EA) to accommodate sea-level rise and land lowering in flood-defence plans is currently 6mm per annum.[9] Sea-level rise is likely to inundate important wildlife areas along the east coast of England. Even with 'managed retreat' policies, nature reserves on the East Anglian coast, such as Cley, Titchwell, Blakeney, Holme and parts of Minsmere, will probably not maintain their current mix of habitats in their current state for more than 50 to 100 years.[10] Such threats suggest the desirability of habitat creation to compensate for their loss and to meet the targets in the *UK Biodiversity Action Plan* (HMSO, 1994) or the requirements of the European Habitats Directive.

Climate change also highlights a further limitation of a static and defensive approach to conservation, based upon the identification and protection of key sites. The scale of climate change across the UK is such that many reserves will probably cease to provide suitable habitat for the species that they currently support. Much more mobile and dynamic thinking is needed to allow ecosystems to change in response to changing climate. Nature reserves may need to be much larger, and less tightly managed, than they have been in the past.

This new thinking about the problems of conservation was also novel in its scale and ambition. During the late 1990s, the British public saw spectacular and expensive projects carried out in the arts (for example, the refurbishment of the National Opera House) and sport (such as the building of the Millennium Stadium in Wales), and began to feel that environmental projects should be of a similar scope. The White Paper noted growing recognition that 'our policies must be applied on a larger scale if they are to tackle the wider issues of habitat and species loss' (DETR, 2001, para10.3.8). During the 1990s, there were few examples of large-scale restoration projects in the UK. However, there was positive experience elsewhere – for example, in the Netherlands, where large tracts of intensively cultivated arable land have been turned into fen landscapes. Restoration projects such as Oostvadersplassen and Lauwersmeer (both exceeding 5000ha) on the Dutch coast demonstrate that fen communities can be recreated on a large scale within a few years and can be maintained as a rich patchwork of vegetation types through extensive grazing by large herbivores such as deer, wild horses and wild cattle.

The creation of the Heritage Lottery Fund (HLF) in the UK during the 1990s provided a possible means to turn these ideas into reality. It enabled conservationists to come up with large projects that are beginning to make a real difference (such as the Wildlife Trusts' UK£25-million project to restore all of their nationally important nature reserves). As a result, extensive discussions have been held with the HLF to determine their views on these large-scale visionary projects. The grant awarded to the National Trust for the Wicken project (discussed below) is a testament to their support.

THE FENS OF EAST ANGLIA

The Fens is a large coastal plain of around 4000 square kilometres, crossed by four main rivers, the Great Ouse, Nene, Welland and the Witham (see Figure 11.2). They lie in the counties of Cambridgeshire, Lincolnshire, west Norfolk and Suffolk. The Fens are recognized as a distinct natural area on the 'Countryside Character' map of the Countryside Agency, English Nature and English Heritage. The Fens were formed around 3500 years ago when sea levels rose, backing up the meandering rivers of the region. Extensive areas of forest were replaced by inland water bodies (meres) and huge tracts of shallow wetland habitats (reed beds, sedge beds, fens and carr woodland). Over the next 3000 years, the Fens were wild areas lightly inhabited by people, but teeming with wildlife. They provided a wide range of products, including wildfowl, grazing, peat and sedge for thatch. Around 2000 years ago, the Romans attempted to drain areas; but although some fenland was cultivated in Romano–British times, these projects were largely unsuccessful (Darby, 1940).

It was not until the 16th century that the Dutchman Cornelius Vermuyden, employed by the fourth Earl of Bedford, began successfully to drain the Fens by re-routing the River Ouse into a specially designed drainage channel (now part of the vast winter flood reservoir known as the Ouse Washes; Darby, 1940). This massive engineering scheme enabled the Fens to be drained and its valuable silt and peat soils used for arable agriculture. Peat shrinkage and wind erosion forced a progressive intensification of drainage, first by wind, then by steam and diesel and electric pumps (Darby, 1983). The area is, on average, 1m below sea level as far as 48km inland. The economic cost of maintaining this artificial environment is considerable. This was justified, in the past, by the exceptional quality of fenland silt and peat soils, although as these erode, land quality is falling, and the economic logic of drainage is becoming less compelling.

As the pace of drainage accelerated, the area of semi-natural fenland habitat shrank (NCC, 1984). Today, only three areas of 'wild' fen survive in the entire East Anglian Fen Basin – representing less than 0.1 per cent of the original resource. Intensive agriculture has transformed the landscape, leaving the few

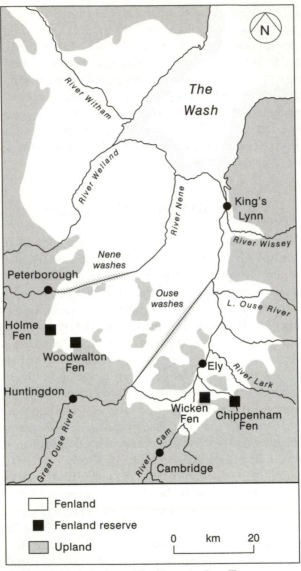

Figure 11.2 *The East Anglian Fens*

remaining fragments of semi-natural habitats as island nature reserves within a sea of arable cultivation. In Cambridgeshire, English Nature (the government nature conservation agency) identified less than 2.7 per cent of the county area (9239ha) to have sufficient wildlife interest in order to be declared an SSSI. By comparison, Cumbria (in upland England) has 159,902ha of SSSI, representing 23 per cent of the county. The average proportion of each county of SSSI quality in England is 6.8 per cent (see Figure 11.3). The average size of a SSSI in Cambridgeshire is 89.5ha, and the average size of a Wildlife Trust reserve in the county is only 16.4ha. Figure 11.4 graphically illustrates that the vast majority of

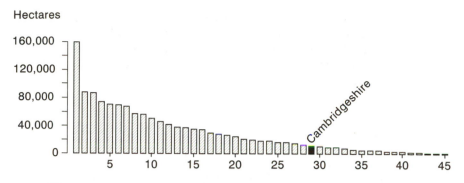

Figure 11.3 *Area of Sites of Special Scientific Interest in English counties*

nature reserves and protected areas in Cambridgeshire are very small – less than 100ha in extent.

By the end of the 1990s, the buoyant agriculture of the Fens was starting to decline. There were a series of linked problems. Firstly, soil fertility was falling due to soil erosion and shrinkage, and with it economic returns on agricultural investment. Secondly, the area shared the overall decline of agriculture in the UK due to patterns of agricultural support and more competitive international trade. Thirdly, these causes of economic decline made the costs of land drainage less acceptable. Flood defence works are largely the responsibility of the Environment Agency (EA), funded by central government, while most land drainage is carried out by the Internal Drainage Boards (IDB). The cost of these works will become economically non-viable in the future as income from some types of farming falls. Fourthly, catchments on the edge of the Fens (where Wicken lies) are very dependent upon summer irrigation. However, while winter drainage is a constant headache, summer water (from groundwater) is in short supply. Charges for irrigation water extraction in the past have been very low; but as charges rise to reflect the true economic value of water, irrigated farming

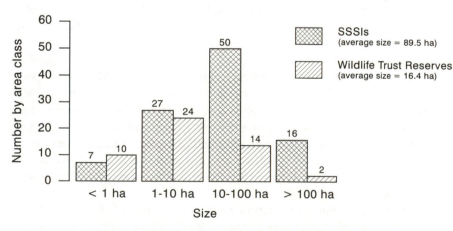

Figure 11.4 *Protected areas in Cambridgeshire by size*

becomes yet more unattractive. A fifth problem is future climate change. Climate change models suggest drier summers and wetter winters in eastern England, exactly the opposite of agriculture's needs. They also suggest that sea-level rise will be important. It is likely to become increasingly expensive to maintain the Fens in their drained state for intensive agriculture.

WICKEN FEN: CONSERVATION THROUGH RESTORATION

Wicken Fen is one of Britain's oldest nature reserves and celebrated its 100th anniversary in 1999 (Friday, 1997; Rowell, 1997).[11] The first 0.8ha strip was purchased on 1 May 1899 and donated to the National Trust. Fifty-five conveyances later, the reserve is over 320ha in size. Wicken Fen is the third largest reserve in Cambridgeshire, after the Ouse and Nene Washes. Nonetheless, it represents only a tiny fragment (0.08 per cent) of the thousands of square kilometres of fenland that existed before the great drainage projects of the 17th century.

Wicken Fen was established as a nature reserve because of the diversity of its invertebrates, and has also long been associated with studies of natural history and ecological research (Lock et al, 1997). Charles Darwin collected beetles on the Fen in the 1820s, and at the turn of the century the fathers of modern ecology and conservation, the Cambridge botanists Sir Harry Godwin and Arthur Tansley, carried out their pioneering work (Cameron, 1999). The Fen's long partnership with Cambridge University continues to the present day.

The Fen has been managed traditionally for centuries by sedge-cutting and peat-digging (Lock et al, 1997). This management has produced a unique fenland habitat rich in wildlife, particularly invertebrates. For example, there are 1000 species of moth and butterfly, 1000 species of beetle, and almost 2000 species of fly and 25 species of dragonfly. The Fen supports large numbers of *Red List* and 'nationally scarce' insect species (Corbett et al, 1997).[12] Over 7000 species have so far been identified on the Fen in all taxa (Friday and Harley, 2000), including more than 121 that are included in the *Red List* of rare invertebrates.

The value of the Fen is recognized by a host of designations, as a National Nature Reserve (NNR), a Site of Special Scientific Interest (SSSI) (both national designations), a Special Area of Conservation (SAC) (a European designation) and a Ramsar site (international wetland designation).[13] These designations have been principally made on account of the open fen habitats of sedge beds, reed communities and fen meadows. Aquatic habitats such as the dykes and pools are also very important. Drier grassland and woodland add diversity to the site; but in the case of woodland, its expansion has often been at the expense of more valuable open fen habitats.

Wicken Fen is unique in landscape terms. A remnant of the once massive Cambridgeshire Fens, it preserves a true sense of wetland wilderness. Standing in the middle of the reserve, nothing is visible other than wild habitats of fen, water and woodland. Outside the boundary is an expanse of carrot fields and intensive farmland; but within is an ancient landscape of great diversity and aesthetic appeal. The Fen also has deep social connections. Local villagers worked the Fen for peat and sedge from as early 1414. The National Trust has restored a fenman's cottage to highlight this social history of benign wetland use. The site also contains the last working wind pump in the Fen basin – originally used for draining peat trenches – and the remains of old brick pits and kilns also survive.

However, the population size of most of Wicken's resident species is comparatively small, and for some organisms, particularly the larger ones with greater demands for food and territory, numbers are dangerously near the limit for long-term survival. Local populations tend to fluctuate in size because of weather conditions, interactions with other species or catastrophes, such as fires or floods. The smaller the population, the more likely it is that the whole population will be destroyed by a single event, and its persistence in the long term may depend upon immigration from nearby populations. At Wicken, the replenishment of a diminishing or lost population now requires long journeys across a dry arable landscape, and is no longer possible for anything other than the most mobile plants and animals. Because of Wicken Fen's small area and isolation from other fens, it seems likely that, however well the reserve is managed, some of the species it currently sustains will die out.

Some of the local extinctions of species at Wicken Fen over the past 100 years are listed in Table 11.2. This shows that even for a site the size of Wicken Fen (over 300ha), extinction of species is a big problem. There are many specific reasons why species have become extinct at Wicken Fen. These include loss of open fen habitats as a result of scrub invasion; the loss of acid habitats as a result of the cessation of peat-cutting; and the lowering of water tables as a result of adjacent land drainage activities. However, the extent and scale of the reserve, along with its isolation from other similar habitat types, has also undoubtedly led to many of the problems. If the reserve was, today, the size that Burwell and Adventurers' fens were during the 1860s (more than 1000ha in extent), then local extinctions resulting from any of the above factors would have been made up for by immigration from other areas not directly affected by these factors. The situation can be compared to the Norfolk Broads, where similar communities of animals and plants occur. Reserves on the Broads are considerably more extensive – for example, the Norfolk Wildlife Trust's reserve at Hickling Broad covers 600ha and is adjacent to other similar habitats, such as the National Trust's property at Horsey Mere.

It was recognized during the 1990s that in order to secure the future of East Anglia's fenland flora and fauna, and to make the re-establishment of lost species viable, it would be necessary to think beyond the bounds of the existing tiny fragments of wetland (Colston, 1997). In 1996, the Wet Fens for the Future Project was launched collaboratively between a series of conservation organizations (Wet Fens for the Future, 1996). The idea that large artificial wetlands of great conservation value can be created is long established in the

Table 11.2 *Examples of species believed extinct at Wicken Fen*

Mammals	Water vole
Birds – examples only	Montagu's harrier; marsh warbler
Butterflies	Swallowtail; large copper; large tortoiseshell; dark green fritillary
Moths – examples only	Reed tussock; marsh dagger; the many-lined moth; gypsy moth
Beetles – examples only	*Dromius sigma*; *Pterostichus aterimus*; *Panagaeus crux-major*; *Lixus paraplecticus*
Dragonflies	Small red damselfly; common hawker; keeled skimmer; black darter; Norfolk hawker
Crustaceans	White-clawed crayfish
Vascular plants	Black bog-rush; bladder sedge; blue water speedwell; bog pimpernel; bottle sedge; bulbous rush; butterbur; common cotton-grass; fen orchid; field pepperwort; frog-bit; greater duckweed; greater water-parsnip; green-winged orchid; hairy rock-cress; heath grass; heath wood-rush; lesser bladderwort; lesser marshwort; marsh cinquefoil; marsh helleborine; marsh lousewort nodding bur-marigold; opposite-leaved pondweed; pale sedge; round-leaved sundew; trifid bur-marigold; various-leaved pondweed

fens. In Cambridgeshire, over 5060ha of SSSI have been created by human action (habitats such as flood washes, gravel pits, railway cuttings and reservoirs). This represents 54 per cent of the total area of SSSIs in the county. In Cambridgeshire, just two sites, the Ouse Washes and the Nene Washes (both created for drainage) represent over 41 per cent of the total SSSI area. Both are of international importance. Habitat creation projects have already improved the county for wildlife.

During the late 1990s, the National Trust identified the desirability and feasibility of extending the boundaries of Wicken Fen (see Figure 11.5). This would make it possible to maintain populations of fen flora and fauna over a wider area (thereby reducing the risk of individual species' extinctions and making possible migration between populations), allowing the area of peat, which is the fenland's most precious resource, to begin to grow after three centuries of loss (Friday and Moorhouse, 1999). It was concluded that the 3700ha of farmland to the south and east of Wicken Fen, formerly known as Swaffham and Burwell Fens, were topographically, geologically and hydrologically suitable for reclamation as fen. At present, water levels are held at about 2.5m below sea level (97.5m OD), and land levels lie between 1.5m below and 5m above sea level (98.5–105m OD). The National Trust proposed, therefore, to acquire up to 3700ha of farmland to the south of Wicken Fen over the next 100 years. This area includes most of the catchment supplying water to Wicken Fen.

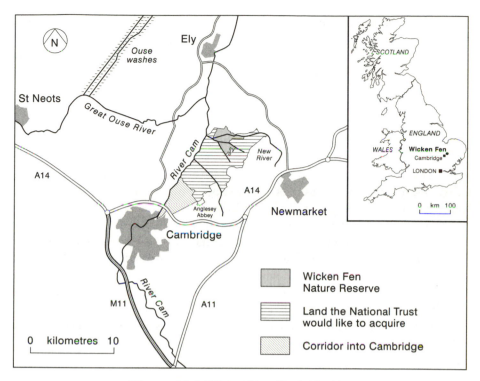

Figure 11.5 *Wicken Fen, Cambridgeshire*

The key to wetland restoration lies in the restoration of a suitable hydrological regime (Thompson and Finlayson, 2001). In the case of Wicken, calcium-rich groundwater, suitable for fen restoration, was available from the chalk uplands running along the southern boundary of the area. Rainwater, currently pumped out of the system, is likely to be sufficient to achieve rewetting to between 99.5m and 100.5m OD. The area lies over a sheet of boulder clay and is edged on the river margin by flood defence banks. Although the simplest solution would be to raise water levels over the entire area simultaneously, the area could possibly be rewetted in four sections (each section consisting of the land lying between the major waterways – 'lodes') if alternative means of pumping out water from the low-level drains into the high-level lodes and river could be provided for each area.[14] The area which is shown in Figure 11.5 is divided into a number of hydrological units by the lodes and drainage ditches, and therefore piecemeal restoration of the landscape to various types of habitat can occur without the need to own the entire area. The whole of the proposed enlarged reserve lies within the boundaries of the Swaffham Internal Drainage Board. The wetlands of the area would be restored by a combination of natural regeneration and the raising of water levels via a reduction in drainage pumping and the use of sluices.

Restoration of a fen system, with a patchwork of habitats ranging from open water through to scrub, according to topography, might be achieved within a decade or so once rewetting is achieved. Ongoing management would be very low input, using large grazing animals.

The scheme depends upon an extensive land acquisition policy. The area is a patchwork of holdings owned by around 120 individuals and acquisitions can only proceed with their approval – the National Trust has no powers of compulsory purchase. Few farmers would be prepared to consider selling land at present. However, they may consider selling land in the future should economic and political forces make arable agriculture less viable, and the difficulty of draining a shrinking land surface in the context of a rising sea level becomes ever greater. Any such acquisition policy would have to be on a time scale of several decades, for example, over the next 100 years or more. Land acquired piecemeal could be held on low-input agricultural tenancies in the short term in order to reduce the nutrient status of the soil and to generate income.

Much of the project involves the acquisition of land; but it is also possible that agreements with existing local land-owners, particularly around the fringes of the area, can be set up that will still enable the aims and objectives of the project to be met. It is also envisaged that an access–recreation corridor can be established at the southern end of the reserve in order to join the reserve to the centre of Cambridge, thus enabling the new area to become the 'green lung' for the city.

PUBLIC BENEFITS OF THE PROJECT

The project offers a broad range of potential public benefits. The economy of the county is widely acknowledged to be one of the fastest growing in the UK. There is a huge desire within the university, the city and the local councils to promote Cambridge as the high technological capital of Europe. As a result, there is a large amount of inward investment occurring, with many prestigious multinational firms locating to the area in order to utilize the highly skilled workforce and research potential of Cambridge.

Associated with this growth is the prediction that by 2025, 105,000 new houses will need to be built. There is currently a vigorous debate surrounding the publication of the regional planning guidance and the review of the Cambridgeshire County Structure Plan as to where these new houses should be located. There is much concern locally over the potential loss of the Cambridge Green Belt. However, the Green Belt currently is a rather passive spatial planning designation, dreamed up during the 1930s to stop suburban sprawl. It is not a designation that encourages access and enjoyment of the countryside – although in Cambridgeshire the partnership Green Belt Project has made much progress in developing this.[15] The Wicken Fen Vision offers a potential counterbalance to the inevitable housing development by providing areas of open countryside that are accessible to the public. The extended reserve could act as a 'green lung' for Cambridge and beyond, as well as dramatically improving the quality of life for local residents and users alike.

Access to the countryside around Cambridge is currently rather limited. There is an extensive public footpath network; but the area could not be described as 'good walking country' on account of the arable nature of the landscape. In addition, Cambridgeshire has as little common land as any county in England, and other than places such as Milton Country Park, the Devil's Dyke, the Gog Magog Hills and urban green space in the city centre there are few other areas of public open space. The Wicken project offers major opportunities to enhance the current provision through the creation of cycle paths, footpaths, horse trails and circular routes from the city centre to the countryside. It can provide a positive link between city and countryside. This potential new access needs to be carefully planned and discussed with local communities so that all needs are catered for in a sustainable fashion. In addition to quiet and informal recreation, it is possible that more intensive areas, such as a new country park, could be developed within the area in order to provide a gateway to the new reserve. There is also potential for the creation of new campsites.

It is essential that access to the new reserve does not rely upon car transport. The desired creation of the corridor at the southern end of the area into the centre of Cambridge offers huge potential for cycle, horse and foot access to the area. In addition, the railway station at Waterbeach and the possible new station at Chesterton also increase the access potentials. There is also a good bus service linking the Fen edge villages of Lode, Swaffham Bulbeck, Swaffham Prior, Reach and Burwell with Cambridge, again encouraging access to the area via public transport.

While the urban areas of Cambridgeshire are flourishing, economic development in the rural areas is depressed as a result of the current state of farming, even in the Fens. The new reserve has the possibility of providing additional jobs in the locality as a result of employment on the reserve. There is also the possibility of additional economic activity locally, resulting from visitors to the reserve – for example, there may be a requirement for additional accommodation in bed-and-breakfast accommodation, as well as meals at local pubs and cafés.

CULTURAL AND COMMUNITY INVOLVEMENT

For the new reserve to be successful and popular, it will need the full support of the local community and the business sector in Cambridge, along with a large number of voluntary and statutory organizations. The project has not been marketed as a plan that the National Trust is going to implement, but more as a possible vision over which we are seeking views and opinions, both within the organization and outside of it. Communicating and consulting with these interests has been a key issue for the National Trust, and as the project develops this will be integral to its progress. Media publicity, both regionally and nationally, has been given to the project, which has helped to encourage the debate.[16] The concept of creating a new large wetland in Cambridgeshire was debated at a citizen's jury in Ely in 1997 and was favourably received (Aldred, 1998). If this ambitious project is to proceed, the National Trust will have to work in partnership with many different and diverse organizations and individuals. Development of partnerships forms the centre-piece of the approach to implementing these ideas.

A community newsletter has been proposed, and a series of focus groups will be set up that enable us to involve all sectors of the local community. It is also hoped that in the near future, thanks to funding from the Heritage Lottery Fund, an officer can be appointed to address many of these issues, including developing community links, assessing local needs, identifying potential users, as well as addressing issues of social exclusion and education.

On the basis of the feasibility study (Friday and Moorhouse, 1999), the National Trust began to discuss the project more widely and to encourage support for the initiative. Following a series of meetings during 2000, the National Trust has approved the principle of implementing the 'Wicken Vision', and the project now forms part of the recently published *National Strategic Plan* (National Trust, 2001). The National Trust has sought views widely outside the organization in order to determine the feasibility and desirability of the project. Over 200 presentations have been given by the Wicken Vision Team, and, to date, the reception has been overwhelmingly positive. The project has been widely discussed and much useful advice has been received internally, ensuring that the Trust has adopted a holistic approach to the initiative, as opposed to viewing it simply as a nature conservation initiative.

The National Trust has contacted all of the land-owners in the project area, informing them of our ideas, and we have met over 70 in person. There has been a considerable amount of media coverage, both nationally and locally, in magazines, newspapers, on the television and on the radio, and this has helped considerably in generating interest in the project.

As a result of the media coverage, the National Trust has been approached by a number of land-owners who are willing to sell their land to assist with the project. The first area of land, Guinea Hall Farm (47ha in extent), was acquired in October 2000. This lies immediately adjacent to the east of the existing reserve. This was funded entirely from resources within the National Trust; but it is anticipated that all subsequent purchases will have to involve partnership funding. A second purchase of 168ha of Burwell Fen Farm was acquired in October 2001 for UK£1.7 million, including a grant of UK£933,500 from the Heritage Lottery Fund.

The challenges of funding have been discussed with a number of potential partners. The HLF, in particular, has been very positive about its potential future involvement. The HLF has already funded a revenue project (UK£322,000) in order to help enhance and develop the ancient fen at Wicken Fen. It describes Wicken Fen as an 'iconic' site and wishes to partner the National Trust in making the Wicken Vision a 'beacon' project.

Additional internal funding has allowed the employment of a part-time project officer to assist the Wicken Fen property manager and National Trust

Cambridgeshire area manager develop the project. Reports are currently being produced on a variety of different aspects of the project. These range from work on the tourism and public-access benefits, engineering reports on the potential impact of raising water levels on houses and other structures, a review of the historic and archaeological importance of the area, and production of the community newsletter for local circulation.

CONCLUSIONS

The scale and scope of the Wicken project, and the enthusiasm with which it has been received by both conservationists and the general public, suggest a considerable appetite for novel and creative solutions to long-established conservation problems in the UK. Past conservation policies achieved much in acquiring and attempting to protect the remaining fragments of semi-natural habitats. However, it is clear that these are not enough, especially in those lowland areas where habitat loss has been so extensive.

The Wicken project is an attempt to begin to put wildlife back into the countryside on a landscape scale. The project recognizes that to deliver this kind of conservation vision requires integrating the requirements of wildlife with the needs of local people, the economy and tourism. It is this holistic approach that has encouraged such widespread support. Perhaps Wicken will be an early example of a new era of nature conservation in the British lowlands, where habitats for wildlife can be restored and maintained without being divorced from the needs of local people.[17]

NOTES

1   For the National Trust, see www.nationaltrust.org/; for the RSPB, see www.rspb.org.uk.

2   G Wynne, M Avery, L Campbell, S Gubbay, S Hawkswell, T Juniper, M King, P Newbury, J Smart, C Steel, T Stones, A Stubbs, J Taylor, C Tydeman and R Wynde (1995) *Biodiversity Challenge: an agenda for conservation in the UK*, second edition. Butterfly Conservation, Friends of the Earth, Plantlife, the Wildlife Trusts Partnership, the Royal Society for the Protection of Birds and the World Wide Fund for Nature, Sandy

3   'Nationally rare' species are defined as occurring in 15 $10km^2$ grid squares or less: F H Perring and L Farrell (1983) *British Red Data Book 1. Vascular Plants.* RSNC, Lincoln

4   SSSIs are nationally designated and protected wildlife sites in the UK. In England, they are designated by the government wildlife conservation body, English Nature. County Wildlife Sites are identified by local government (county councils) and by Wildlife Trusts, local conservation non-governmental organizations (NGOs) that exist throughout the UK, mostly operating at county level.

5   These are all government national designations aimed at protecting the countryside and its wildlife. Heritage Coasts, AONBs and National Parks are designated in

England by the Countryside Agency (see www.countryside.gov.uk; formerly the Countryside Commission for England); ESAs are designated by the Department for the Environment, Food and Rural Affairs (DEFRA, formerly Ministry of Agriculture, Fisheries and Food; see www.defra.gov.uk).

6   The National Trust is Europe's largest conservation charity. It manages over 263,000ha of countryside and 200 country houses and gardens. It has 2.7 million members. See www.nationaltrust.org.uk

7   GATT is the General Agreement on Tariffs and Trade.

8   Instead of attempting to shore up artificial coastal defences at escalating cost and risk in the face of sea-level rise, managed retreat allows for the reversion of reclaimed land to provide natural coastal defences in the form of mudflats and salt marshes

9   DEFRA was created in 2001 following restructuring of responsibilities for rural affairs, agriculture and food in the wake of the foot-and-mouth disease outbreak in the UK.

10   Minsmere is owned by the Royal Society for the Protection of Birds (www.users.zetnet.co.uk/johnfirth/minsmere.html), while the rest are managed by the Norfolk Wildlife Trust (www.wildlifetrust.org.uk/norfolk/).

11   See www.wicken.org.uk.

12   The IUCN Species Survival Commission publishes the *IUCN Red List of Threatened Species*; see www.redlist.org/

13   NNRs and SSSIs are designated in England by the government conservation organization English Nature (www.english-nature.org.uk). A SAC is designated under the European Union's Habitats Directive, a Ramsar site under the Ramsar Convention on wetlands.

14   Of course, the raising of water levels in one area can only occur if it does not have a detrimental impact upon adjacent land or dwellings.

15   See www.sustainablecity.net/Resourceconservation/Wildlife/greenbelt.htm.

16   L F Friday and A Colston (1999) 'Wicken Fen – the restoration of a wetland nature reserve', *British Wildlife*, October 1999; J Theobald (2000) 'The Big Picture', *Guardian*, 12 January 2000 and BBC TV programme 'Matter of Fact: Wicken Fen: Nature in the Making', September 1999.

17   Thanks to Bill Adams and Francine Hughes for help in revising this chapter and to Ian Agnew for drawing the maps.

REFERENCES

Adams, W M (1993) 'Places for Nature: protected areas in British nature conservation' in A Warren and F B Goldsmith (eds) *Conservation in Progress*. J Wiley and Sons, Southampton, pp185–208

Adams, W M (1996) *Future Nature: a vision for conservation*. Earthscan, London

Adams, W M (1997) 'Rationalization and conservation: ecology and the management of nature in the United Kingdom', *Transactions of the Institute of British Geographers NS*, vol 22, pp277–291

Adams, W M, Hodge, I D and Bourn, N A D (1992) 'Conservation in the wider countryside: SSSIs and wildlife habitat in eastern England', *Land Use Policy*, vol 9(4), pp235–248

Aldred, J (1998) 'Land Use in the Fens: lessons from the Ely Citizen's Jury', *Ecos: A Review of Conservation*, vol 19(2), pp31–37

Brookes, A (1996) 'Floodplain restoration and rehabilitation' in M G Anderson, D E Walling and P D Bates (eds) *Floodplain Processes*. Wiley, Chichester, pp553–576

Brown, K (1994) 'Biodiversity' in D Pearce (ed) *Blueprint 3*. Earthscan, London, pp98–114

Bullock, D J and Harvey, H J (eds) (1995) *The National Trust and Nature Conservation: 100 years on*. The Linnean Society, London

Burgess, N, Ward, D, Hobbs, R and Bellamy, D (1995) 'Reedbeds' in W J Sutherland and D A Hill (eds) *Managing Habitats for Conservation*. Cambridge University Press, Cambridge, pp149–196

Cameron, L (1999) 'Histories of disturbance', *Radical History Review*, vol 74, pp2–24

Colston, A (1997) 'Conserving wildlife in a black hole', *Ecos: A Review of Conservation*, vol 18(1), pp61–67

Corbet, S A, Dempster, J P, Bennett, T J, Revell, R J, Smith, C C, Yeo, P F, Perry, I, Drane, A B and Moore, N W (1997) ' insects and their conservation' in L F Friday (ed) *Wicken Fen: the making of a wetland nature reserve*. Harley Books, Colchester, in association with Wicken Fen, pp123–143

Darby, H C (1940) *The Medieval Fenland*. Cambridge University Press, Cambridge

Darby, H C (1956) *The Draining of the Fens*. Cambridge University Press, Cambridge

Darby, H C (1983) *The Changing Fenland*. Cambridge University Press, Cambridge

Department of the Environment, Transport and the Regions (DETR) (2001) *Our Countryside: the Future*. DETR, London

Diamond, J M (1975) 'The island dilemma: lessons of modern biogeographic studies for the design of natural reserves', *Biological Conservation*, vol 7, pp129–145

Dugan, P J (1990) *Wetland Conservation: a review of current issues and required action*. IUCN, Gland, Switzerland

Dugan, P J (1993) (ed) *Wetlands in Danger*. Michell Beazley with the IUCN, London

Evans, D (1992) *A History of Nature Conservation in Britain*. Routledge, London

Friday, L F (1997) (ed) *Wicken Fen: the making of a wetland nature reserve*. Harley Books, Colchester, in association with Wicken Fen

Friday, L F and Harley, B H (2000) *Checklist of the Flora and Fauna of Wicken Fen*. Harley Books, Colchester, in association with Wicken Fen

Friday, L F and Moorhouse, T (1999) *The Wider Vision*. University of Cambridge, Cambridge

Fuller, R M (1987) 'The changing extent and conservation interest of lowland grasslands in England and Wales: a review of grassland surveys 1930–1984', *Biological Conservation*, vol 40, pp281–300

Green, B (1995) 'Plenty and wilderness? Let us make a new countryside', *Ecos: A Review of Conservation*, vol 16(2), pp3–9

Harvey, G (1997) *The Killing of the Countryside*. Jonathan Cape, London

Harvey, H J (1995) 'The National Trust and nature conservation: prospects for the future', *Biological Journal of the Linnean Society*, vol 56(Supplement), pp231–248

Henderson, N (1992) 'Wilderness and the nature conservation ideal: Britain, Canada and the United States contrasted', *Ambio*, vol 21, pp394–399

Her Majesty's Stationery Office (HMSO) (1994) *Biodiversity: the UK Action Plan*. HMSO, London

Hobbs, R J (1990) 'Nature conservation: the role of corridors', *Ambio*, vol 19(2), pp94–95

Hobbs, R J and Harris, J A (2001) 'Restoration ecology: repairing the earth's ecosystems in the New Millennium', *Restoration Ecology*, vol 9, pp239–246

Jordan, W R III, Gilpin, M E, Aber, J D (eds) (1987) *Restoration Ecology: a synthetic approach to ecological research*. Cambridge University Press, Cambridge

Lock, J M, Friday, L F and Bennett, T J (1997) 'The management of the Fen' in L F Friday (ed) *Wicken Fen: the making of a wetland nature reserve*. Harley Books, Colchester, in association with Wicken Fen, pp213–254

MacArthur, R H and Wilson, E O (1967) *The Theory of Island Biogeography*. Princeton University Press, Princeton

McIntosh, R P (1985) *The Background of Ecology: concept and theory*. Cambridge University Press, Cambridge

Margules, C, Higgs, A J and Rafe, R W (1982) 'Modern biogeographic theory: are there lessons for nature reserve design?' *Biological Conservation*, vol 24, pp115–128

Mitsch, W J and Gosselink, J G (1993) *Wetlands*, second edition. Van Nostrand Reinhold, New York

National Trust (2001) *National Strategic Plan: Summary. March 2001–February 2004*. The National Trust, London

NCC (1984) *Nature Conservation in Great Britain*, Nature Conservancy Council, Peterborough

Perrow, M R and Davy, A J (eds) (2002) *Handbook of Ecological Restoration*, Cambridge University Press, Cambridge, vols 1–2

Peterken, G F and Hughes, F M R (1990) 'The changing lowlands' in T P Bayliss-Smith and S Owens (eds) *Britain's Changing Environment from the Air*. Cambridge University Press, Cambridge, pp48–76

Potter, C, Burnham, P, Edwards, A, Gasson, R and Green, B (1991) *The Diversion of Land: conservation in a period of farming contraction*. Routledge, London

Pye, K and French, P W (1983) *Targets for Coastal Habitat Re-creation*. English Nature Science No 13, Peterborough

Rackham, O (1986) *The History of the Countryside*. Dent, London

Ratcliffe, D A (1984) 'Post-medieval and recent changes in British vegetation: the culmination of human influence', *New Phytologist*, vol 98, pp73–100

Rowell, T A (1997) 'The history of Wicken Fen' in L F Friday (ed) *Wicken Fen: the making of a wetland nature reserve*. Harley Books, Colchester, in association with Wicken Fen, pp187–212

Senge P M (1992) *The Fifth Discipline: the art and practise of the learning organization*. Century Business/Doubleday, London

Sheail, J (1976) *Nature in Trust: the history of nature conservation in Great Britain*. Blackie, Glasgow

Shoard M (1980) *The Theft of the Countryside*. Temple and Smith, London

Simberlof, D S and Abele, L G (1976) 'Island biogeographic theory and conservation practice', *Science*, vol 191, pp285–286

Sutherland, W J and Hill, D A (1995) *Managing Habitats for Conservation*. Cambridge University Press, Cambridge

Tansley, A G (1935) 'The use and abuse of vegetational terms', *Ecology*, vol 14(3), pp284–307

Thompson, J R and Finlayson, C M (2001) 'Freshwater wetlands' in A Warren and J R French (eds) *Habitat Conservation: managing the physical environment*. J Wiley and Sons, Chichester, pp147–178

Wet Fens for the Future (1996) *Wet Fens for the Future – the value of wetlands for people and wildlife in the Fens*, Sandy, Bedfordshire

Williams, M (1970) *The Draining of the Somerset Levels*. Cambridge University Press, Cambridge

Williams, M (1990) 'Protection and introspection' in M Williams (ed) *Wetlands*. Blackwell, Oxford, pp232–353

Chapter 12

Feet to the ground in storied landscapes: Disrupting the colonial legacy with a poetic politics

Martin Mulligan

WHITEFELLA FOLLY

The Gurindji people living in the Victoria River region of the Northern Territory are recognized as important pioneers of the 'modern' Aboriginal land rights movement in Australia. After walking off cattle stations where they were employed as stockmen and domestic workers over issues related to pay and working conditions in 1966, they squatted 'illegally' at a place long known to them as Daguragu, and known to white settlers as Wattie Creek. They sustained that occupation for nine years before winning some legal right to the land they claimed, and their action paved the way for new laws recognizing traditional Aboriginal rights to land in areas under the jurisdiction of the federal government. Their campsite at Daguragu was adjacent to a gorge where the bones of the dead had been stowed in caves for countless generations – where those killed by white vigilantes, pursuing Walbiri refugees of the infamous Coniston massacre of 1928, were also laid to rest. Central leaders of the walk-off had been born at Daguragu before it was annexed by a cattle station leased, in 1966, by the British food mogul Lord Vestey. Yet, when the land rights laws were enacted in 1976, the Gurindji still had to come up with some 'proof' that they had a traditional association with the land they claimed. Two white anthropologists – Patrick McConvell and Rod Hagen – were dispatched by the government-funded Northern (Aboriginal) Land Council to help the Gurindji prepare their case.

It was not a difficult assignment; evidence was plentiful. However, the Gurindji wanted McConvell and Hagen to include a story which, to them, questioned the legitimacy of the cattle station that had been established on their land in the first place, and McConvell and Hagen reported that when this story was told to them it was accompanied by much laughter directed at the white people who featured in it. The story is that when the first white settler – Nathaniel Buchanan – arrived in the area (in 1883), he claimed the land and built a homestead on the banks of the Victoria River. Very close to this spot was a hill with exposed strata of rock that displayed a wave-like pattern, and so Buchanan called his homestead Wave Hill. One funny aspect of the story is that Buchanan built his home adjacent to a river that floods on an annual basis – in the northern 'wet season' – and so the house had to be abandoned on a regular basis. Eventually, in 1924, it was washed away altogether. People who took over the cattle station from Buchanan realized his folly in locating the house so close to the river, so they built a new one on higher ground. However, they liked the name he had chosen and continued to use it. Twice more after that the homestead was relocated, and each time the name was relocated as well. As far as the Gurindji are concerned, the real punch line of this story is that the 'whitefellas' could even entertain the idea that a name could be taken from one place to another. For them, this was conclusive 'proof' that these interlopers had no serious connection with the land that they claimed. How ironic that the Gurindji were being asked to prove their 'ownership' of their 'country'.

I found this story in the report prepared by McConvell and Hagen that was in the file on the Gurindji land claim in the library of the Northern Land Council in Darwin. Since then I have used it widely in discussing the contrast between the way that indigenous Australians and those of European descent have perceived relationships between people and the land. And it's a story that students have often referred to when giving me feedback about what they have learned in my classes. It's a story that not only questions the legitimacy of the settlers' annexation of Aboriginal land – achieved by adopting the doctrine of *terra nullius*. It goes much further in making the claim of *terra nullius* seem ridiculous by looking at it from the perspective of the colonized, and it casts a shadow over the cultural values of people who move across the surface of the land – rootless and unaware. As in other parts of the world, the European colonizers in Australia tried to impose their visions of Arcadia upon landscapes that they did not understand, and the results were disastrous for the natural environments, as well as for attempts to create a new cultural identity. As Val Plumwood points out in Chapter 3 of this book, the naming practices adopted by Australian settler society reflected the colonizing mentality that has served us very poorly in our attempts to ground ourselves in this land.

As the Gurindji would remind us, we have totally failed to appreciate the uniqueness of every single place, preferring instead to create rather homogenized landscapes that we are always passing through on the way to 'somewhere else'. As Paul Carter has put it in his stimulating book *The Lie of the Land*:

> Our relationship to the ground is, culturally speaking, paradoxical: for we appreciate it only in so far as it bows down to our will.

> *We do not walk with the surface; we do not align our lives with its inclines, folds and pockets. We glide over it; and to do this, to render what is rough, smooth, passive, passable, we linearize it, conceptualizing the ground, indeed the civilized world, as an ideally flat space, whose billiard-table surface can be skated over in any direction, without hindrance* (Carter, 1996, p2).

The European colonization of Australia was built upon the desire to 'tame' the wild (see Lines, 1991) in order to make the landscapes both more 'productive' and more 'tidy'. And the practice continues. Rural townships compete fiercely for the prestigious Tidy Towns awards, and it was revealed in September 2001 that State Forests in New South Wales (NSW) employ a squad of workers to go through the forests to poison 'crooked, damaged and unhealthy native trees' in order to allow other trees to 'grow properly'.[1]

In the last section of *The Lie of the Land*, Carter borrowed the term 'drift lanes' from the writer Bill Harney (Carter, 1996, p356) to contrast the way in which the indigenous Australians moved across the land, compared to the corridor-like movement of the white settlers. Drift lanes, he suggested, might be thought of as anti-roads because they are more like a 'dialogue between foot and ground' than a passage to a destination (Carter, 1996, p360). Drift lanes are embedded in the land as intertwining tracks weaving through and over one another, and travel on drift lanes is a circular movement of deepening associations where 'home-coming' cannot be assured because travelling and remaining at home become the same thing.

FEET TO THE GROUND

As Carter also points out (Carter, 1996, p2), we settlers rarely come into direct contact with the land because we impose many layers between our bodies and the earth – shoe rubber, roads and paths, planted lawns. And the earth beneath all that has been moved about and 'displaced' anyway. We dwell above, and not in, the land. This reminds me of the way that Australia's great pioneering artist Russell Drysdale painted Aboriginal people in the 1950s. The trappings of white society were often evident in the way that they were dressed – in one case, dressed up to the hilt for a visit to the regional town of Cairns. But in all cases they were without shoes – even in the centre of Cairns. As one commentator put it, it gives the impression that the attempt to 'civilize' the indigenous people was imposed from the head down; yet it failed to disturb their connection to the land (Haynes, 1998).

A wonderful story attaches to one of Drysdale's paintings – called simply 'Man in a Landscape' – which depicts a strong-faced Aboriginal man in a red landscape, his arms draped over large boulders that he stands behind. This painting was given to Queen Elizabeth by the federal government on her visit to Australia in 1963 because it was seen as representative of the work of the country's most popular artist. Some time after the presentation had been made, the queen invited Drysdale to tea in Canberra and, at an 'appropriate' moment in the proceedings, she turned to the artist and asked loudly: 'Tell me, Mr Drysdale, what does your painting mean?' Drysdale replied, 'Ma'am, it is a painting of a man trying to hold onto his land.'

Of course, we can go too far in describing Western culture as being ungrounded, and in contrasting this to land-sensitive indigenous cultures around the world. In the introduction to his impressive work *Landscape and Memory* (1995), Simon Schama takes issue with environmental historians who have sought to pinpoint historical causes of the 'Western fall from grace' in environmental awareness and responsibility. In particular, he takes issue with Max Oeschlaeger for suggesting that we need 'new creation myths' to 'repair the damage done by our recklessly mechanical abuse of nature' (Schama, 1995, p13). Schama says that the mood of such historians is 'understandably penitential' and that he does not mean to 'deny the seriousness of our ecological predicament' by suggesting that there are plenty of old nature myths in Western cultures that remain alive and well 'if only we know where to look for them' (Schama, 1995, p13). For this particular book, Schama began his journey by physically returning to a place from which his ancestors came in a forested region between Poland and Lithuania, and he moved from his own experience to an exploration of the role this forest and its natural inhabitants played in the emergence of Polish and Lithuania literature. Even more impressive was his exploration of the strong role that forests played in the emergence of German culture, as reflected in art and literature (for both children and adults). Schama himself migrated for a period to the US and, in researching his book, he became fascinated by the encounter between the settlers and the giant trees of California. He seeks to demonstrate that people such as Henry David Thoreau and John Muir were products of a culture forged in the interplay between landscapes and people. National parks were eventually created as cultural shrines of the 'New World'.

Like many settlers in North America, it is also true in Australia that those who came to colonize the land were also fundamentally changed by what they encountered (see Mulligan and Hill, 2001). However, Schama's account of the role of landscapes in the development of diverse cultures around the world fails to acknowledge the damage that was done when attempts were made to impose the cultural myths forged in one part of the world on another. Nor does he provide an explanation for how the nature myths of old Europe eventually came to be marginalized in societies that became obsessed with the commercial exploitation of nature – especially when that exploitation could take place in lands that were far removed from the places they called home. In Australia, people of my grandparents' generation still often talked of England as 'home'. Perhaps this made it easier to turn a blind eye to the degradation being inflicted on the land they were living in.

THE VIEW FROM THE EDGE

No doubt, the experience of colonization is best understood by starting at the frontier. I was recently reminded of this when I flew from Australia to London, via Zimbabwe. Flying west from Sydney, the heavily modified landscapes of the coastal fringe eventually give way to a sparsely populated zone where the frontier of settlement is still very evident; this, in turn, gives way to a huge expanse of highly patterned desert – so impressive from the air – where the very notion of human control seems laughable. During a stopover in metropolitan Perth, we were herded into a hermetically sealed transit lounge that felt exactly like every other transit lounge at every other 'modern' airport in the world. However, on arrival at Harare, we walked down the stairs and across the tarmac, where strong, 'earthy' smells made me feel I had really *landed*.[2] Walking in dry bushland near the Hwange National Park felt quite a lot like walking in the Australian bush, except that my guide showed me the signs of a wildlife that is so dramatically different – the wildlife of so many children's books and so many nature programmes on television. Of course, unexpected encounters with animals that I had only previously seen in zoos could be dangerous; but the presence of danger made the 'wildness' feel more intense and, consequently, more exciting.

Immediately after arriving in London from Harare, I went for a walk in Kensington Gardens and Hyde Park and the culture shock was intense. Highly manicured gardens, with segregated flowers and neatly trimmed lawns, were such a contrast to the wildness and excitement of the African bush. Manifestly, this was a celebration of mastery over nature, and as I walked past the palaces and on to Westminster – past countless statues of admirals, generals and politicians of the 'glorious' colonial past – I became even more aware that the gardens were an integral part of a grand imperial museum. Captured 'exotic' plants from different parts of the world were sprinkled among domesticated species that had long been 'trained' to do their masters' bidding. It was all a celebration of power and control, a rejection of wildness.

No doubt, the culture shock was greater for the fact that I had so enjoyed my brief stay in Zimbabwe. Yet, on two occasions when I have spent some time in England, I have found myself feeling claustrophobic, hungering for a touch of the wild among the highly ordered landscapes. On the last occasion, I was taken to see an ancient forest near Cambridge that had recently been acquired by conservation authorities. Yet, even here the old trees were mainly in rows, reflecting the fact that it had once been a managed forest. Conservation volunteers showed me examples of native grasses that were apparently very rare; but to an Australian conservationist, European grasses all look like 'weeds', just as eucalypt trees are seen as weeds by conservationists in countries were they have been used for plantation timber. Again, I was reminded of the uniqueness of all places – conservation aesthetics being bound up with experience and a knowledge of what constitutes 'healthy' ecosystems.

Of course, Schama is right in saying that there is a neglected side of European culture that reflects a deep love of nature. For me, this emerged most strongly when I visited Ambleside in the Lake District of England and trod the paths once trodden by one of my favourite poets, William Wordsworth. Of course, Wordsworth was one who campaigned against the mentality of industrialization that accelerated the commercial exploitation of nature and, along with many others, he kept alive a tradition of sensitivity towards nature in English culture. Like Thoreau in Massachusetts, he was able to find inspiration in surprising encounters with wild nature, wherever he might be, and it was moving to sit in places where he must have sat, gazing at very similar scenes.

Like Schama, the place-sensitive Australian writer David Malouf has also warned against an overly critical view of the history of our settler society. He has pointed out that the Australian colonies were an unpredictable experiment in 'using the rejects of one society to create another'. Given opportunities they never would have had in the Old World – especially to own land – these 'vagabonds' proved to be extremely determined and creative, conjuring up all the 'amenities' of home with very few resources. They drew not only from English traditions, but from Europe more broadly and they:

> ...*displayed an inventiveness beyond the mere making do...a determination to create a world here that would be the old world in all its diversity, but in a new form – new because in these new conditions the old world would not fit* (Malouf, 1998, p3).

The 'vagabonds' and 'misfits' from Europe tried to create the Arcadian landscapes of their dreams; but they were also determined to create a more open and egalitarian society than the ones that had rejected most of them. The ancient and resistant landscapes colluded with this aspect of their dream because the difficult conditions undoubtedly had an equalizing effect on the settlers, particularly in the frontier regions. As the indigenous people had learned long before, the land demanded collaboration rather than competition, and the frontier experience created new cultural myths around stoicism and 'mateship' (see Mulligan and Hill, 2001). However, the important point to note here is that the settler society had to feel profoundly 'unsettled' in order to begin a process of meeting the land on its own terms. The Australian short story writer and poet Henry Lawson is probably best known for humorous stories that celebrate the mateship myth. Yet, what may have given him more enduring relevance was that he was one of the few writers of his generation who was prepared to confront the 'dark side' of settlement, reminding us of our vulnerability and fallibility. Lawson's stories are anything but a celebration of human mastery.

In a very interesting book called *Seeking the Centre: the Australian Desert in Art, Literature and Film*, Roslynn Haynes (1998) has pointed out that flat, arid land presented a particularly profound challenge to aesthetic sensibility of European settlers. Painters schooled in the 'picturesque' tradition of European landscape art could find no way of engaging with such 'god-forsaken' landscapes, and for a long time a large part of inland Australia was commonly referred to as the 'dead centre'. Eventually, there were artists – such as Sidney Nolan and Russell

Drysdale – and writers – such as Patrick White in the novel *Voss* – who were able to bring alive such landscapes in their work. Subsequently, white Australians began to see that they had much to learn from the Aborigines who had lived in these landscapes for so long. How extraordinary, Haynes (1998) notes, that the red desert has become a vibrant icon of Australian identity, much celebrated in literature, art and in the promotion of tourism. That which was deeply feared is now cherished, even if it is mostly experienced from the comfort of air-conditioned buses and motel rooms.

EMPATHETIC ENGAGEMENT

The Australian writer who has probably done more to unsettle Australian settler society than any other was poet Judith Wright – a great pioneer in the fields of literature, nature conservation work and reconciliation between white and indigenous Australians. Born into a family of the rural 'squattocracy', Wright spent much of her childhood outdoors exploring the landscapes of the New England district in north-eastern NSW. She often wondered what became of the indigenous people who had once lived in the same area – now evident only in 'fringe camps' outside some of the towns – and when her father once told her the dark secret of a place where early settlers had driven a large number of Aboriginal people to their deaths over a cliff, she wrote up the story in a poem contained in her first published volume.

In her early poems, Wright wrote of fondly of white farm workers like 'old Dan', for whom:

> *Seventy years of stories he clutches round his bones*
> *Seventy summers are hived in him like old honey*

(Wright, 1994, p20).

Yet, at the same time, she wrote with anger about the way that her own people had treated the land:

> *These hills my father's father stripped,*
> *And beggars to the wind*
> *They crouch like shoulders naked and whipped –*
> *Humble, abandoned, out of mind*

(Wright, 1994, p81).

During the 1960s, Wright formed a deep friendship with the Aboriginal poet Kath Walker (subsequently known by her Aboriginal name Oodgeroo Noonuncal), who helped Wright put faces to the stories that she knew were embedded in the land. In a very moving poem called 'Two Dreamtimes', Wright acknowledged that her friendship with Noonuncal was overshadowed by the grief over what the settlers had done to Noonuncal's people; but she ended the poem by saying:

The knife's between us now, I turn it round
the handle to your side,
the weapon made from your country's bones.
I have no right to take it.

But both of us die as our dreamtime dies.
I don't know what to give you
for your gay stories, your sad eyes,
but that, and a poem, sister

(Wright, 1994, p318).

Wright had an extraordinary empathy for those who were on the other side of the frontier of 'settlement', and her greatness probably lay in the fact that this empathy extended to both the indigenous people and the natural world that was also colonized. In an angry poem written in 1970 – the bicentennial of Captain Cook's arrival in the great south land – she began:

Die, wild country, like the eaglehawk
dangerous till the last breath's gone,
clawing and striking. Die
cursing your captor through a raging eye.

And ended:

I praise the scoring drought, the flying dust,
the drying creek, the furious animal,
that they oppose us still;
that we are ruined by the thing we kill

(Wright, 1994, pp287–288).

Wright, like the artist Russell Drysdale, was ahead of her time in seeing that white Australians could never be really settled in this land until they had looked at the experience of colonization from the other side of the frontier. The launching of the 'modern' Aboriginal land rights movement by the Gurindji and Yolngu people of the Northern Territory during the 1960s began a chain of events that culminated in a ruling of the Australian High Court in 1992 that finally abandoned the fiction of *terra nullius*.[3] The High Court's recognition of the existence of a 'native title' to land that existed prior to colonization stunned most non-indigenous Australians; yet, there also seemed to be a widespread relief that the nonsense of *terra nullius* had been finally put to rest. Environmentalists welcomed the decision not only because it was just, but also because the notion of native title challenged prevailing notions of land ownership. The pioneers of the Aboriginal land rights movement had made it very clear that their concept of land ownership was something of a reversal of the Western concept because they were convinced that people belonged to the land. Marcia Langton (1998) has made the point that Australian environmentalists inadvertently sustain the legacy of *terra nullius* when they use terms such as 'wilderness' in ways that deny Aboriginal occupation of the land. Furthermore, the necessary dialogue between white conservationists and Aboriginal custodians of the land has not always been easy. However, it is a dialogue that has great potential.

Aboriginal perspectives on the relationship between people and the land do not actually constitute a *reversal* of monological Western concepts of that relationship, but rather their replacement with a dialogical concept built on the notion of interactive responsibility. As the anthropologist Deborah Bird Rose has explained, Aboriginal people have long preferred the English word 'country' to a word such as 'landscape' precisely because it implies some kind of two-way relationship. Rose has written:

> *Country in Aboriginal English is not only a common noun but also a proper noun. People talk about country in the same way they would talk about a person: they speak to country, sing to country, visit country, worry about country, feel sorry for country, and long for country. People say that country knows, hears, smells, takes notice, takes care, is sorry or happy. Country is not a generalized or undifferentiated type of place, such as one might indicate with terms like 'spending a day in the country' or 'going up the country'. Rather, country is a living entity with a yesterday, today and tomorrow, with a consciousness, and a will toward life. Because of this richness, country is home, and peace; nourishment for body, mind, and spirit; heart's ease* (Rose, 1996, p7).

Later in the same work, Rose explained the dialogical nature of the relationship by saying:

> *A 'healthy' or 'good' country is one in which all the elements do their work. They all nourish each other because there is no site, no position, from which the interest of one can be disengaged from the interests of others* in the long term. *Self-interest and the interest of all the other living components of country…cannot exist independently of each other* in the long term.
>
> *The interdependence of all life within country constitutes a hard but essential lesson — those who destroy their country ultimately destroy themselves* (Rose, 1996, p10).

However, according to the 'land ethic' of the Aborigines, it is not enough to simply avoid damaging country because people are active agents with a responsibility to nurture the land that nurtures them. According to Rose, Aboriginal people think of 'wild country' as country that has not been cared for. She illustrated this point with a story of visiting some sites in the Victoria

River district in the Northern Territory that had been badly affected by soil erosion in the company of a local man called Daly Pulkara (Rose, 1996, p18). In Rose's account: 'I asked Daly what he called this country; he looked at it long and heavily before he said: "it's the wild. Just wild"' (Rose, 1996, p19). By contrast, Rose continued, Pulkara described as 'quiet country' 'the country in which all the care of generations of people is evident to those who know how to see it' (Rose, 1996, p19).

ON DWELLING, TRAVELLING AND NAMING

At the beginning of this chapter, I recounted a story that shows how Aboriginal people see every place as being unique. This uniqueness is captured in the fact that every place has a range of stories associated with it – stories that are preserved by the rightful custodians of the land in which that place exists. What we sometimes forget is that Aboriginal people travelled across considerable distances and communicated across even more vast distances. Their knowledge of places was certainly not confined to the local. The mythical beings responsible for the creation of landscapes – such as the Rainbow Serpent – were thought to have travelled across the lands of many people, and the stories associated with them were often captured in the form of songs that could be shared with neighbouring people (hence the notion of 'songlines' that is sometimes used to refer to the creation trails of these mythical creatures). Such 'songlines' could bring people of different language groups together for major ceremonies. At the same time, there were well-established trading 'routes' that moved tradable goods over large distances. I was told by Vai Stanton – a Larrakia woman from near Darwin – that she was once at a conference near Cairns when she heard some of the local people 'speaking language' that included words she knew. Particular words, it seems, had migrated between the 'Top End' and the east coast of the vast continent.

Although they sometimes travelled far, the indigenous Australians obviously moved more slowly than contemporary Australians and they were much more aware of the places they were traversing. A rather amusing story told by US nature poet Gary Snyder illustrates this point well.[4] On a visit to Central Australia in the mid 1980s, Snyder found himself on the back of a table-top truck with a Pintupi elder named Jimmy Tjungurrayi. As the truck approached Tjungurrayi's country, he pointed to a mountain and began to tell the story of a 'dreamtime' encounter between some Wallaby men and Lizard Girls that took place there. He gave a quick and condensed version of the story, and as soon as he finished it he began another, prompted by the sight of another landmark. Initially surprised by the rapid-fire delivery of his host, Snyder soon realized that he was being given a fast-forward version of stories that were designed to be told at walking pace. Stories that could be told as people walked past the relevant landmarks served as a kind of orientation map, always locating them within a broader regional framework. In part, they were a survival guide because they helped locate water, food and shelter. However, the stories also included strong messages about the responsibilities of the travellers to the places they were traversing. They spoke also of the country's needs.

Aboriginal people had a very different relationship to space than European settlers brought with them. Paul Carter has pointed out that it was not easy for white anthropologists to even translate Aboriginal conceptions of space into the English language; but several of them have reported that the Aboriginal conception of territory could not be abstracted in the form of a linear map, because the boundaries were more like a series of camp-sites that people would move between (Carter, 1988, p345). Citing the work of anthropologist R Moyle, who studied the Alyawarra people of Central Australia, Carter said that 'boundary sites' would often be centred on a water source, which, in turn, would be a local centre for other living things. Consequently, the Alyawarra saw boundary sites as the centre of things and not the periphery (a concept that is best represented in the world-famous 'dot paintings' of the Aboriginal desert communities). Carter went on to say that for Aboriginal people, the country came alive as they travelled, citing another anthropologist who worked with Central Australian communities who once recorded that 'all the way out from Willowra, the women sang the songs of the country as they travelled through it...they sang, danced and felt the country' (Carter, 1988, p346). Carter commented that 'Travelling and story-telling are inseparable from each other. The country is not the setting of stories, but the stories and songs themselves' (Carter, 1988, p346).

Clearly, we are not going to revert to walking as primary mode of transport. However, a knowledge of stories associated with places we pass through can help us to feel better oriented, more constantly 'connected'. A sense of belonging extends from the local to the regional and beyond, and a sense of belonging *can* lead to a stronger sense of responsibility.

We shouldn't underestimate the effort required to gather some sort of insight into the ways in which Aboriginal Australians have traditionally experienced 'country'. In 1975, I had the privilege of spending eight months travelling in Aboriginal Australia (from the settlements of central Queensland and Cape York across to Arnhem Land, and down to 'the centre') in the company of some good friends, including the Brisbane-based Aboriginal educator and artist Lilla Watson. I knew that I had crossed a frontier when we sat in a fringe camp near the central Queensland town where Lilla had grown up, listening to the stories of the ancient 'Queenie' Dodd (born in the 1880s), while a radio somewhere played the theme music introducing the ABC radio national news. I might have been sitting in traffic on the Sydney Harbour Bridge listening to that same news bulletin; but here I was in a place where time seemed to stand still, listening to stories of lives from another world in the same land. Travelling with Lilla, I learned the importance of spending time building relationships with the people we met, waiting patiently for appropriate moments to share stories, jokes and tears. I was again reminded of the necessary protocols when I went to Yirrkala in north-east Arnhem Land in 1997 to interview the artist and community leader Banduk

Marika for a book that would include the story of the birth of the 'modern' Aboriginal land rights movement.[5] It took several days for the appropriate moment to talk to arrive, and a turning point came when my companion and I sat with Banduk and her 'mob' to watch a game of 'footy'. Our patience was richly rewarded. The experienced Aboriginal community worker Julie Foster-Smith has frequently reminded me that Aboriginal people are understandably suspicious of white people asking questions; but if you are accepted into a relationship of trust, then that is a relationship that should last a lifetime even if contact becomes infrequent. Building new relationships with the land through intercultural dialogue with indigenous Australians involves building lasting relationships with people, as well.

When I was growing up in Australia, Aboriginal 'dreamtime stories' were seen as being 'quaint', appropriate only for books aimed at children. Perhaps that is still largely the case; but, increasingly, they are being referred to in tourist brochures and material produced by conservation agencies such as the National Parks and Wildlife Service. We are learning that stories that attribute lifelike qualities to the land itself tend to be evocative and memorable, and when I ask students if they know of any stories that have changed their feelings about particular places, they often cite Aboriginal stories that they have heard or read. One group of students doing a group presentation acted out a story from the mythology of the Bundjalung people of how a goanna became a headland on the north coast of NSW following a conflict with a snake that had been harassing an emu (see Stewart, 1988, p80). To white Australians, that headland is known as Evans Head, even though very few people would know how it got that name. The headland does, indeed, take the shape of a lizard with a very long tail, and the group concluded that renaming the landmark after the goanna would encourage people to think more deeply about the place and its past. What would add poignancy to this act of renaming is that the headland is known to be the site of a massacre during the 1840s of Bundjalung people trying to reclaim their land from white settlers (Stewart, 1988).

I had a similar feeling about the need to replace colonial place names with the much more colourful pre-colonial names when I visited Victoria Falls on the border between Zimbabwe and Zambia during the my visit to Africa. Why should such a place be named in honour of a remote English queen when it already had a name that translated into English as 'the valley that thunders'? The latter certainly captures something of the power of the mighty Zambezi River as it tumbles relentlessly into the deep chasm, throwing up a spray above the falls that can drench a visitor a hundred metres back from the edge of the chasm.

As impressive as that 'natural wonder of the world' is something else impressed me on my visit. This was a story about the creation of the hippopotamus taken from the mythology of the Shan people, which was incorporated in a display in the rather humble visitors' centre at Victoria Falls. Just prior to my visit there, I had been reading in a newspaper that more travellers in Zimbabwe are killed by accidents involving hippos than from any other cause, especially along the Zambezi River, downstream from the falls. Then I read from the interpretation of the Shan legend that when the hippopotamus was created, it had been so embarrassed about its appearance that it asked the creator if it could hide its body in the water by day and come out to feed at night. The creator had been concerned that the hippo would start eating the fish in the water; but an agreement was reached that the giant animal could have its wish provided it ate only grass and left its droppings on the land so that other animals could routinely inspect them to make sure that they contained no fishbones. The story is an amusing one that is easy to remember. It teaches us something about relationships between hippos and their environments. But what struck me that day was that humour and danger can be lurking in the same animal and in the same set of circumstances. The natural world is full of such contradictions that defy simple understanding. I had earlier been reminded that an appearance of tranquillity can be illusory when looking across an apparently calm stretch of the Zambezi, just metres before the water gathers speed for its thunderous plunge into the valley below.

POETICS AND POLITICS

How can we express and communicate the rather contradictory feelings that emerge from experiences with what David Abram (1996) has called the 'more-than-human' world? I'm very attracted by Paul Carter's suggestion that poiesis – the Western art of representation – offers ways of engaging with the irregular and unpredictable in a language of the emotions as much as the intellect. In Carter's view, colonialism was the creation of Europeans *after* they became 'rootless rationalists' because 'a people without a dreaming, without an attachment to the land, were machines for free movement' (1996, p364). From this perspective, we need to look beyond the rational to decolonize our mindsets, and such a decolonizing movement might be led by people with expertise in non-rational understandings of lived experience. In Australia, for example, landscape painters, poets, novelists, creators of children's literature, photographers and film-makers have all been engaged in an exploration of the dialogical interaction between people and the land that might enable the settler society to finally ground itself in Australian environments (see Mulligan and Hill, 2001). This has been a very difficult project that is far from reaching any kind of satisfactory resolution; but the artists and writers have frequently placed themselves at the forefront of a broader public discourse about land and identity. Of course, there is nothing inevitable about poiesis being part of a decolonizing of attitudes towards the natural world. As Carter points out, the arts of representation in a settler society can also serve a colonizing role in creating the images that people are working towards in manipulating landscapes – the imposition of 'regularity' on 'wilderness'. What we need, Carter continues, is an environmentally attuned poetics that is anti-colonial in its aims. It does not mean 'climbing to a commanding point in order to see further', but rather 'renouncing this nostalgia for horizons, focusing instead on the ground at our feet, beginning to pay attention to its folds and inclines' (1996, p14).

Australian historian/journalist and one-time political adviser Gregg Borschmann has suggested that oral history projects that aim to capture the richness of lived experience in the Australian landscape could create a kind of 'Bush Dreaming' that might fill a void in our relationship with the land. In an impressive labour of love, he put together a volume of essays and a travelling installation featuring images and voices of people talking about their experiences of the Australian bush in a project he called 'The People's Forest'. The collection of essays – lovingly put together, artistically presented and self-published – included contributions from one of Australia's leading poets, Mark O'Connor, the eco-feminist philosopher Val Plumwood, Aboriginal writer Mudrooroo, and a leading figure in forest economics and resource management, Neil Byron. Despite the diversity in their professional practice, the contributors shared a very deep love of Australian forests, and in his introduction to the essays, Borschmann was moved to suggest that his project might constitute a small step towards the creation of a 'whitefella dreaming'. This phrase refers, of course, to the use of the English word 'dreaming' as it was used to 'name' the rich cosmology of Aboriginal Australians and, as Borschmann conceded, 'To call our chequered relationship with the Australian bush a "whitefella dreaming" may offend some people' (Borschmann, 1999, pvii). However, he went on to say that in taking back an English word that had been enriched by its association with Aboriginal cosmology, we might, in fact, acknowledge 'the great tradition of story-telling, lore, ceremony, dance, song, ritual and immutable truth that the Aboriginal nations cultivated in this continent that we now also call home' (Borschmann, 1999, pvii). Our 'dreaming', such as it is, may not be 'as rich, all-embracing and unifying as an Aboriginal dreaming. But we can work on that' (Borschmann, 1999, pvii).

The call for building a 'whitefella dreaming' is timely because the Australian environmental movement has been going through a period of critical self-examination (see Mulligan, 2001). There has been a growing recognition that 'rational' appeals for nature conservation based upon technical forms of knowledge have a limited public appeal. Australian writer Roger McDonald put it well when he was cited as saying (Hawley, 2001):[6]

> *I worry that in the environmental debate raging about trees, we only seem to hear about the botanical and conservation side, with arguments about forest regrowth, acceptable species, trade-offs – it's all in political language.*
>
> *The poetry and mystery of trees, rich personal experiences of enjoyment and wonder, the private moments of revelation people can feel in forests, when something about trees touches their soul – this more imaginative and intimate side rarely gets a mention.*

Like Borschmann's opus, McDonald's non-fictional homage to people whom he has known, who have lived and worked with trees – *The Tree in Changing Light* (2001) – is a lovely example of the sort of story-telling that might enhance our 'whitefella dreaming'. As manifestations of landscapes that we move within native and introduced trees, McDonald suggests, 'give language to our existence' (McDonald, 2001).

Critics of eco-philosophies that emphasize a 'reconnection' with the 'more-than-human' world have often said that this constitutes a form of romantic ruralism that maintains an 'urban blind spot' (see Light, 2001) when most people live, and will continue to live, in cities. However, Paul Carter has provided an interesting response to this in the form of a story, which, he notes, was included in a newspaper article 'lamenting the loss of a creek – "it was consigned years ago to a barrel drain and tied up in a ribbon of freeway ashphalt"' (Carter, 1996, p15). The author of the article recalled childhood memories of the pre-paved creek when it appeared to him and his friends as 'our patch of wilderness'; in particular, he recalled a time when one of his friends, 'Ronny', had shot an arrow from a bow directly into the air above them. The author wrote: 'For me, Ronny's arrow will never land. It will always be spinning and shimmering in the sunlight, a kind of airborne talisman connecting me to the time before expediency robbed us all of something beyond value' (Carter, 1996, p15). Suggesting that the lasting memory was of 'a community between the lie of the land and the curvilinear laws of the arrow's flight', Carter also proposed that it reconceived 'ground' as 'not a surface but as manifold surfaces, their different amplitudes composing an environment that was uniquely local, which could not be transposed' (Carter, 1996, p15) – and, further, that such a 'plea for a "less paved time"' embodies both a politics and a poetics' (Carter, 1996, p15).

It is interesting that Andrew Light concluded his article about the 'urban blind spot' of prevailing environmental ethics by focusing upon the potential of nature restoration programmes in urban areas. In Australia, urban 'bush regeneration' projects have frequently focused upon 'liberating' creeks from concrete encasements and reviving bush-clad embankments on those waterways. Poetically, this might be seen as a revival of connecting threads that reach beyond the urban frontiers, both spatially and in terms of our understanding that the natural systems we want to 'regularize' continue to exist below, and above, the layers of regulatory concrete. Urban bush regeneration is both a political statement and a re-engagement with the aesthetics of the wild (a poetic gesture). A creek restoration project involving the Merri Creek in Melbourne was so successful that the beautiful sacred kingfishers were spotted again in an area that they had long ago abandoned. In celebration, the local human community began an annual Return of the Kingfisher Festival that is creating a new, local, story.

A volume of essays that is very different in its style and *gravitas* to Gregg Borschmann's *The People's Forest* is *Places in the Heart* (1997) in which award-winning travel writer Susan Kurosawa put together contributions from 30 prominent Australians on 'their special corners of the world'. While a majority of the contributors chose to talk of exotic places overseas, a surprising number chose to write about Australian places that either held special childhood memories or ongoing associations. Several contributors wrote very lovingly about urban landscapes, with my favourite being actor Graeme Blundell's rather poetic piece on Sydney's King's Cross, which carried the title 'Where the stars are lit by neon'. Light reading, perhaps; yet, it is interesting to read what comes out when people are invited to speak 'from the heart', and there is some confirmation in this volume of Borschmann's point about oral histories of lived experience contributing to the accumulation of a 'whitefella dreaming'. This notion has the potential to cut across the normal boundaries between urban, rural and 'wild' landscapes.

However, when we talk in Australia about the poetics of reconnecting with the 'more-than-human' world, we can't go past the work of Judith Wright, whose rich and influential life came to an end in July 2000. On her death, novelist Thomas Keneally said that all Australian writers were in her debt because:

> *At a time when it was every writer's sacred duty to be alienated by Australia – to be a European soul descended into this terrible place – she was unaffected. Instead she made her myths out of this place. The spaciousness of her spirit has always been so grand* (Stephens, 2000).

Wright's capacity to feel and express an empathy for a world that will always be beyond our cognitive powers was reflected in 11 volumes of poems published between 1946 and 1985. Perhaps this was never more evident than in a short poem called 'Rainforest' that appeared in the last of those volumes:

> *The forest drips and glows with green.*
> *The tree-frog croaks his far-off song.*
> *His voice is stillness, moss and rain*
> *drunk from the forest ages long.*
>
> *We cannot understand that call*
> *unless we move into his dream,*
> *where all is one and one is all*
> *and frog and python are the same.*
>
> *We with our quick dividing eyes*
> *measure, distinguish and are gone.*
> *The forest burns, the tree-frog dies,*
> *yet one is all and all are one*

(Wright, 1994, p412).

As already mentioned, Wright was a daughter of the landed gentry who frequently expressed deep remorse about what her forebears had done to both the pre-settlement landscapes and to the indigenous people. A poet who eventually inherited her mantle as the nation's best – Les Murray – has taken a much more charitable view of the activities of pioneer settlers who were his own forebears. Yet, he too has called for an act of atonement for the theft of the land from the original inhabitants (Murray, 1999a). In an interesting essay called ' in a Working Forest', he shows how stories related to the interactions between people and the forest – involving both Aborigines and white settlers – have created a powerful forest folklore that can give people who live nearby both a sense of belonging and of not belonging at the same time (Murray, 1999b)

STORY-MAKING AND STORY-TELLING

As Simon Schama has stressed, the cultural 'baggage' that European settlers in the 'New World' have carried with them has not always been a barrier to a deep appreciation of the landscapes that they have entered. Just as often, he argues, deep cultural memories – embodied in stories and legends that have been passed down through the generations in the 'Old World' – have sensitized such settlers to the role that nature can play in creating new cultural stories. Even if we wanted to, we could not ignore the cultural heritage that was forged in European landscapes, and what emerges when Europeans settled in the colonies was often an intriguing combination of the old and the new. However, as David Abram (1996) argues, Europeans have also developed languages that disguise our ancient engagements with the 'more-than-human'. Wherever we go, we recreate the frontier between the settled and the wild, and when we travel we are cocooned by our technologies. Even in our most dedicated efforts to 'get back to nature', we carry backpacks loaded with the 'necessities' for survival and we encase our feet in robust hiking boots. I am not suggesting that, at a physical level, we need to abandon safety considerations or even comfort zones; but we need to keep in mind the degree of our separation if we want to become more attentive and empathetic with the non-human world – with a world that may be beyond all human experience (as alluded to in Judith Wright's poem, cited above).

If we can enhance our skills in becoming attentive and empathetic, then we will once again rediscover that every single place in the world is unique in both human and non-human terms, and that every place has a 'magic' of its own. If we shift awareness from abstract spaces (a kind of *tabula rasa*) to unique places, we might be much less inclined to want to homogenize our environments (as reflected in the near-uniform design of things such as airports, shopping malls, hotels and, of course, Macdonald's restaurants all around the world). Consider what happens when people make a conscious decision to 'sink roots' in a particular place. They try to learn what they can of the local stories and legends, maybe some of the local history. On top of this, they begin to lay down their own personal stories, maybe extending these into family stories that deepen a sense of belonging. Some people might go as far as consulting geographical literature about landforms and natural systems, or scientific information about local ecosystems and geology. To invoke an archaeological metaphor, the effort might involve some patient digging to uncover stories that are most deeply embedded in the land; in the case of Australia, for example, considerable effort is needed to uncover the local Aboriginal stories that were never recorded in the history books of the colonizers.

I can imagine a reader wondering if this sort of effort is really worthwhile. Maybe not for all; but I am reminded of a story told by the Australian writer and polymath academic George Seddon (1997) about an experience he had of returning to Australia after a long period of living in England. Seddon had spent his formative years in rural Victoria, enjoying opportunities to fish and swim in the Murray River and to walk in the 'high country' of the Great Dividing Range. However, he returned to Australia to take up an academic post in Perth and was shocked to discover that the coastal plains around Perth were so dissimilar to what he had known in Victoria that he did not feel he had returned 'home' at all. However, instead of remaining alienated by what he found, he set out to deepen his knowledge of the area and its myriad stories, eventually feeling more at home in Perth than anywhere else. The point is that a 'deepening into' place, in the manner discussed by John Cameron in Chapter 8, takes effort, as well as attentiveness and empathy. It involves the building of skills that subsequently enable the practitioner to deepen into more than one place.

Furthermore, the skills we need to build a personal sense of place can also be used in the important work of environmental education. Experienced environmental educators know that one way to get people talking about what nature means to them is to ask them to share some childhood memories of encounters with the non-human (see, for example, Thomashow, 1996). The Australian folk-singer Judy Small has a song about a place, called Charlesworth Bay, that she liked to visit as a child, but which was subsequently 'ruined' by an ill-considered housing development. She likes to introduce the song by saying that everyone has their own Charlesworth Bay. As much as a sense of place can help us feel more connected to, and, hopefully, responsible for, places, grief over the loss of 'special' places can make us more determined to oppose further environmentally insensitive developments.

If you ask adults when and how they lost their childhood propensity to be enchanted by the non-human, they struggle for an answer. Yet, each of us, in our personal journeys, probably mirrors the evolution of Western culture in its journey from a reliance on intuitive knowledge to the dominance of the rational. In order to 're-enchant' nature conservation work, we might need to actively encourage a regression of that particular growth pattern. Collectively, there is an important place for story circles when people can sit together in a relaxed atmosphere to share stories of 'magical' experiences. The experience always seems to be enhanced when there is a campfire at the centre of the gathering because the warm focal point of the flickering flames seems to gather the circle into a reflective and sharing mood. When people of different ages are present, some important intergenerational learning can take place. The wisdom of the elders seems to gain *gravitas* in such circumstances.

We all know from experience that some people are much better than others at telling stories; but it is a skill we can all enhance. Perhaps it is not a skill that is adequately valued in Western cultures because it is probably seen as a hobby rather than a vocation. Not surprisingly, people who relied entirely upon spoken language did value story-keepers and story-tellers highly, and again we might learn from the experience of the indigenous Australians. A story told by a white man who worked closely with the Gagadju people on building the case for the declaration of the world famous Kakadu National Park in Australia's Northern Territory will illustrate the point.[7]

Allan Fox was employed by the National Parks and Wildlife Service when he was involved in developing the case for the Kadadu National Park, and one of his duties was to work with Gagadju elder Bill Neidjie to document the stories associated with particular sites in the area. While he was working with Neidjie on this project, various parties of politicians and bureaucrats visited the area in order to assess the claims that were being made. Fox always arranged to have them visit sites with Neidjie so that he could tell them some of the stories *in situ*. After this had happened a number of times, Fox began to notice that the old man had told different stories to different visiting parties and, concerned that this lack of consistency would damage their claims, he confronted Neidjie about the 'problem'. However, Neidjie patiently explained that as a designated story-keeper, he knew many stories about each place that they might visit and his responsibility and skill lay in selecting which story to share on any particular occasion. Commonly, the stories he might choose to share were but fragments of much longer stories that might only be shared with people who are willing and able to become living custodians of such places and their memories.

As indicated earlier, Aboriginal people do not think of places as pre-existing blank spaces, but rather as relationships that they enter each time that they are in their presence. For them, poiesis is integral to the act of travelling because they 'sing up' the stories embedded in the land as they travel. In comparing the Aboriginal conception of space to that of the European settlers, Paul Carter suggested that for Aborigines the 're-enactment of the country does not occur on a stage: it is what brings the country into being and keeps it alive' (Carter, 1988, p346).

DISRUPTING THE IMPOSITION OF REGULARITY

As Marcia Langton's contribution to this book in Chapter 4 makes clear, indigenous people around the world are being subjected to ever-new forms of expropriation and marginalization. Magome and Murombedzi, in Chapter 5, demonstrate that in southern Africa the creation of National Parks has done little more than create a different set of problems for the indigenous people, and this tends to echo the experience of jointly managed parks in Australia. The ongoing framework of colonization needs to be kept in mind when we talk about learning from the cultural practices of these indigenous people. That said, however, we should also keep in mind the potential for a kind of 'reverse colonization' of attitudes towards the land, and of ideas about natural resource 'management'. After more than 200 years of racist neglect, there is a growing recognition that we white Australians have much to learn from human cultures that have existed in this land for more than 50,000 years! In order that gestures towards an Aboriginal experience of 'country' are more than shallow and tokenistic, we have to work hard to set aside our own conceptions about relationships between people and nature. We must also be prepared to build mutually beneficial relationships with those who are able to guide us in such matters. We must be patient and open minded. However, the effort can be richly rewarded with a new and deep sense of belonging, not just to local landscapes, but to the land as a whole.

At the same time, we can draw deep insights from our own poetic traditions that enable us to contemplate the unpredictable, the irregular and the almost unimaginable. We can do this by creating and/or contemplating images and a rich language that can be interpreted in different ways by different people. The aim of poetics is to resonate and not convince. By seriously contemplating the wild and unpredictable, we might overcome our desire to impose regularity and predictability upon the world around us. We can move outside a linear sense of time and an abstract sense of space in order to experience the magic of a unique time–place and, consequently, move closer to building the 'place-responsive' society that John Cameron discussed in Chapter 8. We can consciously 'regress' to the magical experiences of childhood, when sensuous experiences of the world were probably more important than rational explanation and when we were more trusting of our intuitions. If we step outside the 'busyness' of our adult lives, we can learn that insights will arrive to those who wait patiently with an open mind and heart. In the process, we can enter new and more ethical relationships with other people and the land that holds us all.

We need to overcome the colonial legacy of 'mastery over', not only because it has been profoundly repressive towards subjugated people, but also because it has left us profoundly alienated from the natural world. Henry David Thoreau was a powerful prophet of the poetic politics that I have in mind, and his journals and books from the 1840s and 1850s remain a major source of inspiration. It is not difficult to conjure up a mental image of him strutting about the stage during one of his public lectures at the Lyceum in Concord, Massachusetts, thundering out his famous and timeless dictum: ' in wildness is the preservation of the world.'

NOTES

1   As revealed in an article by environment writer James Woodford in *The Sydney Morning Herald*, 27 September 2001, p5.

2   Subsequently, Harare airport has also constructed a bland passenger terminal in a rather desperate attempt to make tourists feel more 'comfortable'.

3   This ruling regarded a claim to traditional rights to land by a group of Torres Strait Islanders led by Eddie Koiki Mabo – hence, the case is often referred to as the Mabo case.
4   The story is recounted in the book by Abram (1996, p173).
5   This research was for the book *Ecological Pioneers: A social history of Australian ecological thought and action* by Martin Mulligan and Stuart Hill (2001), Cambridge University Press, Melbourne.
6   Author of the critically acclaimed novel *Mr Darwin's Shooter* (Random House, Sydney, 1998) and the more recent *The Tree in Changing Light* (Random House, Sydney, 2001).
7   This story was told by Allan Fox to a conference of the New South Wales Association of Environmental Education held at Port Stephens, NSW in 1997.

REFERENCES

Abram, D (1996) *The Spell of the Sensuous: Perception and Language in a More-than-Human World*. Vintage Books, New York

Borschmann, G (1999) *The People's Forest: A Living History of the Australian Bush*. The People's Forest Press, Blackheath, NSW

Carter, P (1988) *The Road to Botany Bay: An Exploration of Landscapes and History*, Knopf, New York

Carter, P (1996) *The Lie of the Land*. Faber and Faber, London

Hawley, J (2001) 'Confessions of a tree-hugger', *The Good Weekend*, 29 September, pp33–40

Haynes, R (1998) *Seeking the Centre: The Australian desert in art, literature and film*. Cambridge University Press, Melbourne

Kurosawa, S (ed) (1997) *Places in the Heart: Thirty prominent Australians reveal their special corners of the world*. Sceptre, Sydney

Langton, M (1998) *Burning Questions: emerging environmental issues for indigenous people in northern Australia*. Centre for Indigenous Natural and Cultural Resource Management, Northern Territory University, Darwin

Light, A (2001) 'The urban blind spot in environmental ethics', *Environmental Politics*, vol 10(1), pp7–35

Lines, W (1991) *Taming the Great South Land: A History of the Conquest of Nature in Australia*. Allen and Unwin, Sydney

Malouf, D (1998) *A Spirit of Play: The making of Australian consciousness*. ABC Books, Sydney

McConvell, P and Hagen, R (1981) *A Traditional Land Claim by the Gurindji to Dauragu Station*. Central Land Council, Alice Springs

McDonald, R (2001) *The Tree in Changing Light*. Random House, Sydney

Mulligan, M (2001) 'Re-enchanting nature conservation work: Reflections on the Australian experience', *Environmental Values*, vol 10, pp19–33

Mulligan, M and Hill, S (2001) *Ecological Pioneers: A Social History of Australian Ecological Thought and Action*. Cambridge University Press, Melbourne

Murray, L (1999a) 'Some religious stuff I know about Australia' in L Murray *The Quality of Sprawl: Thoughts about Australia*, Duffy and Snellgrove, Sydney, pp19–49

Murray, L (1999b) ' in a Working Forest' in *The Quality of Sprawl: Thoughts about Australia*. Duffy and Snellgrove, Sydney, pp91–120

Rose, D B (1996) *Nourishing Terrains: Australian Aboriginal Views of Landscape and Wilderness*. Australian Heritage Commission, Canberrra

Schama, S (1995) *Landscape and Memory*. Fontana Press, London

Seddon, G (1997) 'Sense of place' in *Landprints: Reflections on Place and Landscape*. Cambridge University Press, Melbourne, pp109–112

Stephens, T (2000) 'Conscience of the country lives on', *Sydney Morning Herald*, July 27, p13

Stewart, D (ed) (1988) *Burnum Burnum's Aboriginal Australia: A Traveller's Guide*. Angus and Robertson, Sydney

Thomashow, M (1996) *Ecological Identity: Becoming a Reflective Environmentalist*. MIT Press, Cambridge, Massachusetts

Wright, J (1994) *Judith Wright: Collected Poems*. Angus and Robertson, Sydney

Chapter 13

Conclusions

William M Adams and Martin Mulligan

SOME NEW STRATEGIES

Some of the contributions to this volume have been aimed primarily at understanding the depth and complexity of the colonial legacy with regard to conservation practice, while others have begun to suggest some new strategies and approaches for the future. Recommendations for rethinking and reorienting conservation practice range from an articulation of the need to create more 'space' for the rehabilitation of indigenous land management and 'wildlife' management practices, to an enthusiastic endorsement of the work of restoration ecology (as in the example of Wicken Fen, see Chapter 11). Penelope Figgis (Chapter 9) has provided a thorough review of the new challenges and conservation 'models' that Australian conservationists are grappling with. A similar range of choices and dilemmas is facing conservationists in many other countries. Val Plumwood (Chapter 3) calls for a new movement to decolonize place names in the former colonies, and John Cameron (Chapter 8) argues that efforts to nurture place responsiveness can challenge the prevailing dangerous alienation of people from the places in which they dwell. Martin Mulligan (Chapter 12) argues that one way to *re-enchant* nature conservation work is to show people how they can re-engage sensuously with landscapes that are full of stories – perhaps to revive the 'magical' experiences of childhood engagements with the non-human. This emphasizes the point that ethical engagement with the land can be driven as much by inspirational experiences and memories as by a sense of guilt about the colonial legacy of taming the wild.

In sharing experiences from three parts of the world, there have been important opportunities for a cross-fertilization of ideas and experiences (as is evident in the common ground between Chapters 4–7, written by Marcia Langton, Hector Magome and James Murombedzi, and Mark Toogood). Several contributors have suggested some ways in which a more meaningful dialogue might be nurtured between nature conservationists and indigenous communities, and emphasize the need for it (for example, Mark Toogood in Chapter 7). Martin Mulligan suggests that this difficult dialogue holds the promise of re-enchanting conservation work for non-indigenous people. As mentioned above, Mulligan also suggests some ways in which an engagement with 'storied landscapes' can broaden the appeal of conservation work. John Cameron, in Chapter 8, suggests some ways in which many more people could be enticed into exploring their relationships with their immediate environments, while Bill Adams (Chapter 10) shows that new ideas about the dynamic nature of ecosystem change are exciting and scary at the same time.

However, the size of the challenge we set out to tackle with this volume – as articulated in the introduction in Chapter 1 – makes it impossible to end with a simple summary of ideas and recommendations that have emerged. As several contributors have stressed, we have much work to do in engaging more deeply with the legacies of the past before we can find better ways of pursuing conservation aims into the future.

Difficult legacies

Both the terms *colonialism* and *decolonization* mask a great deal of complexity. Although it is convenient to talk in broad terms about European colonialism as a dominant force in global development from the 17th century onwards, the manifestations of this phenomenon changed over time in response to both the specific goals of the particular European power concerned and the responses of the colonized peoples and lands. Similarly, as resistance to colonialism grew into stronger decolonization movements during the 20th century, the forms and processes of decolonization have varied over time and according to diverse geopolitical conditions. Furthermore, as Marcia Langton's contribution to this book makes clear (Chapter 4), new forms of colonization have come into play alongside messy decolonization processes in the latter stages of the 20th century. Indeed, it is something of an illusion to suggest that we are in a 'post-colonial era'.

It is important to an understanding of contemporary engagements between humans and non-human nature to be able to trace some of the broad characteristics of European colonialism and the Eurocentric values that underpinned, and emerged from, it – as Val Plumwood has done in Chapter 3. Indeed, it would be very difficult to make any sense at all of global developments in understanding nature without some analysis of how and why European powers came to dominate the world, and what the enduring legacies of that domination have been. In this book, we have focused our attention upon the particular phenomenon of British colonialism and its legacy, and the conservation movements that, among other things, have sought to halt its drive to create neo-Europes in the landscapes of colonized lands. We have been interested in the complex dynamics of the relationships between people and the land in Britain as well as the colonies, and the interplay between the centre and periphery. This exploration of British colonialism has broad significance. It had become the dominant form of European colonial enterprise by the end of the 19th century, and the dominant imperial power of the 20th century – the US – was itself the product of an earlier phase of British colonialism.

Nature conservation movements that emerged in various parts of the world during the second half of the 19th century were partly a reaction against the mercantilist exploitation of nature being carried out by both the European powers and the settler societies they had initiated. At the same time, they also reflected some of the European 'enlightenment values' that constructed nature as a resource for human use and enjoyment. Furthermore, the global conservationist agendas that emerged so strongly during the latter part of the 20th century were both anti-imperial in their defence of local diversity and, at the same time, imperial in their advocacy of certain Western ideas and assumptions. Hence, the nature conservation movement, in its various manifestations, has reflected the complexity of the overlapping agendas of colonialism and decolonization. The history and future of nature conservation are both bound up with this complex legacy of European colonialism.

SOME GROUNDS FOR HOPE

We can, of course, be overwhelmed by the complexity and problematic colonial legacies of nature conservation. While 'enlightenment values' continue to underpin the dominant utilitarian attitudes towards non-human nature, we can take some heart from a series of facts. Firstly, these anthropocentric 'Western' values have been subjected to rigorous and sustained critique during the latter part of the 20th century. Secondly, colonized, indigenous peoples have largely been able to reassert their rejection of colonizing ideologies, and have given voice to alternative, more ecocentric, world views. Thirdly, nature conservation movements, which have had some success in preserving biodiversity, have begun to explore new ways of thinking and working.

As we enter the 21st century, we can say that the need for a deep dialogue between nature conservationists and indigenous peoples has never been greater. Clearly, the potential parties to this dialogue have strong overlapping aims in wanting to prevent the degradation of non-human nature. Furthermore, the limited recognition of indigenous rights achieved by decolonization movements (as in the belated recognition of 'native title' to land in Australia) has given indigenous communities a stronger basis from which to converse and negotiate with conservationists and conservation agencies. The dialogue has not been easy, to date, because non-indigenous conservationists in many parts of the world have been forced to recognize that their desire to preserve people-free wilderness areas has, in part, reflected the colonizing imperative to rupture the link between the indigenous peoples and their lands. Furthermore, as Marcia Langton's contribution to this book also demonstrates, the tensions continue to mount as indigenous people search for economic strategies within market economies that can guarantee their survival as communities. Nevertheless, the willingness on the part of conservationists to enter meaningful dialogues with indigenous peoples is beginning to match the need. This is manifested in the desire to better understand indigenous cosmologies and values. Indeed, the fact that a book with this title and content could find a publisher and a readership indicates that the desire for dialogue is growing.

Of course, this book can only be a small step in reviewing some of the dialogues that have already taken place, and in opening up spaces for such dialogues to be extended. Those who enter into such spaces need to be willing to be both frank and courageous, and, at the same time, show respect for others who are willing to enter such spaces with good intent. Certainly, indigenous people have much to teach non-indigenous conservationists about what a 'land ethic'[1] might really mean in practice, and indigenous communities need support of many kinds in order to negotiate survival strategies. Any successes in 'mainstreaming' a land ethic will create greater security for both the endangered indigenous communities and the endangered species of plants and animals that have been imprisoned in 'marginal' landscapes and 'island reserves'.

CRITICAL CHALLENGES

If the legacy of colonialism is as extensive and pervasive as we have argued in the introduction to this volume (see Chapter 1), how can we *begin* to decolonize our attitudes towards nature? One obvious place to start is in critically examining the language that is often used in conservation discourses (see Chapter 3). For example, indigenous people in both Australia and southern Africa (and even in Scotland; see Chapter 7) have questioned the use of terms such as 'wilderness' and 'pristine nature' because they fail to acknowledge the long history of association between people and the landscapes that have been described in such terms. An exploration of prevailing language can provide an entry point into a deeper exploration of underlying environmental values, and the extent to which they might reflect the 'enlightenment' values of the colonial era. This, in turn, can lead to a realization that if we cannot separate ourselves from nature, then we need to learn how to organize our relationships with the non-human world more effectively and more ethically. For example, the growing realization in Australia that the Aboriginal people made extensive use of controlled fires to manage their relationships with the landscapes that nurtured them has led to an awareness that the prevention of fire in 'wilderness areas' is another form of intervention. Fire prevention leads to such a build-up of combustible material that less frequent, but much more intense, 'wild' fires can have some devastating consequences (see Flannery, 1994; and Chapter 4 in this volume).

In this book, the argument has been made that discussions focused upon the necessary search for 'sustainability' must be broadened in order to embrace understandings of the colonial legacy, explorations of the contradictory experiences of decolonization, and a critical review of conservation language and discourses. We passionately believe that the discussions currently taking place in academic forums must be taken out of the academy and tested out in the hard-edged world of conservation policy and practice.

Of course, we acknowledge that the difficult search for sustainability is made even more difficult by the acceleration of human impacts resulting from population growth, rampant consumerism and global tensions over access to 'natural resources'. Beset by growing anxieties, many conservationists will question the need for a wide-ranging discourse about the past. However, the past is deeply embedded in present practices, ensuring that many of them are becoming increasingly irrelevant and ineffective. Those of us who care about 'nature' (however we conceive of it), and about conservation, must analyse the legacy of our past to equip ourselves much better for the future, no matter how urgent the immediate tasks might seem.

While debates about the conservation of nature are being held increasingly within a global context, experiences of working with the notion of sustainability in different parts of the world suggest that effective strategies need to be emergent, localized and diverse in order to be locally relevant in natural terms and culturally sustainable in human terms (Adams, 2001). In the face of large and pressing challenges, conservationists cannot afford to be either timid or complacent. At the same time, we have the opportunity for dynamic renewal at a rather crucial moment in world history. Paradoxically, the building of a conservation ethic could become the fulcrum for a radical impulse towards the affirmation of life, diversity and coexistence.

However, if we are to make the most of new opportunities, we must also be willing to be very frank about *both* the achievements and limitations of conservation practice to date, and a number of the contributions to this volume make, or repeat, some pretty tough criticisms of dominant conservation practices. We suggest that six important criticisms have been made either directly or implicitly:

The first is that, in general, conservationists have an ongoing problem with their relations with indigenous people. While some have largely romanticized the world views of indigenous people, and portrayed their impact on nature as qualitatively different from that of other people, others have argued that the impact of all people on 'nature' is sufficiently harmful that all humans should be excluded from protected areas. Nature needs to exist as 'wilderness'. There has been little exploration of a middle ground, and little systematic understanding of the form and extent of human tenure of land and engagement with nature even in remote and biodiverse areas. Indigenous people, and indeed poor rural people in general, are rarely able to exercise power or authority in discussions about conservation. Conservation is too often an alien idea descending from some remote expert, backed by state bureaucracy and, if necessary, coercive force.

Secondly, while they claim to speak for all humanity, conservationists have rarely engaged in dialogue with those remote from corporate or metropolitan power. In industrialized countries, conservationists have been distrustful of the 'ignorant' general public, and this has highlighted the perception that nature conservation is an elite activity. In non-industrialized countries, conservation has often been imposed by remote national and international organizations. Conservation is not, by and large, something people do, but something that is done *for* them (or, sometimes, *to* them and their land).

Thirdly, conservationists have largely failed to convince Third World sceptics that nature conservation demands (for example, to preserve the rainforest or Africa's more 'awkward' mega-fauna) are not hypocritical, in view of the First World's exploitation of the Third World's nature and wealth in order to pay for First World industrialization. Conservationists in First and Third Worlds have not adequately demonstrated that the nature conservation they advocate is an essential requirement for just and sustainable societies. In the Third World, conservation still appears too often to impose controls on economic opportunities for the poor in order to protect a playground for the rich.

Fourthly, conservationists have become rigid and formulaic in their thinking, especially as they panic about the rate of biodiversity loss. As a result, they are unable to participate fully in action-oriented discussions about relations between people and nature on the ground. These require innovation, compromise and lateral thinking. Conservation practice has become locked within government programmes and procedures, and its boundaries are patrolled by special-interest non-governmental organizations (NGOs). Despite the almost universal rhetoric of 'community conservation', conservationists tend to be staunch policy conservatives.

Fifthly, conservationists have largely pursued national strategies in the face of an increasingly globalized economy and its rapid and highly unequal consumption of 'natural resources'. Conservationists frequently target local problems and the impact upon nature of the resource demands of the rural poor; they are less good at addressing broader political and economic structures and their impacts. Conservationists mostly deal with symptoms within national boundaries, and do not address root causes in the machinations of the world economy,

Sixthly, conservationists have been obsessed with 'preservation' and removing human impacts upon nature. At is best, this determination has helped hold back the worst excesses of industrialization and consumption. At its worst, it has denied the possibility of positive outcomes for interactions between human and non-human nature, and restricted conservation to a narrow set of scientifically defined values. In particular, conservation theory is still based upon the time-honoured concepts of equilibrium ecology, although research is rapidly revealing the non-equilibrial characteristics of ecosystem change. These new scientific understandings challenge ideas about the 'naturalness' of particular states of ecosystems; but conservationists have been reluctant to consider the implications of this new thinking for their ideas about the interactions between people and nature. Driven by fear of extinction rates, conservationists think on short time scales – decades and not centuries or millennia. Therefore, they often appear to be excessively conservative and afraid of change. This makes it hard for them to be innovative, relaxed and exciting partners in thinking about new forms of engagement between people and non-human nature.

Some of these criticisms may be a little outdated as conservationists around the world grapple with new ways of moving forward. Others may seem a little harsh and prejudicial (aren't other social movements faced with similar challenges?). Yet, it is essential for the revitalization of conservation practice that we acknowledge that such criticisms have not only been stated, but sustained and explained (including within this volume). If we are unable to address such criticisms in some detail, we will remain mired in our problematic past.

This challenge can be put in more positive terms. Conservation thinking and practice needs to become more future oriented and more broadly appealing. Contributors to this book have suggested a number of strategies for doing just that. For example, it has been suggested that we can:

- Develop strategies that increase trans-national awareness and international collaboration with regard to conservation initiatives.
- Develop more flexible modes of thinking of what constitutes healthy ecosystems and healthy relationships between people and nature.
- Find ways of involving a much broader range of people in conservation work.
- Show people how they might turn their own sense of alienation from nature into proactive conservation work.
- Broaden the appeal of conservation work by demonstrating that it can engage the 'heart' as much as the mind.

Some conservationists would suggest that this kind of reformist agenda expects too much of them. Others might suggest that the challenges are much greater than this sort of agenda implies. There is a lot to discuss here, and this book is just one small contribution to this debate. Its framework has allowed us to bring together a diverse line-up of both scholars and practitioners who have set out some of the ideas circulating in academia that we wanted to bring to the attention of practitioners, and to reflect some of the insights emanating from the lived experiences of practitioners. Some people manage to be scholars and practitioners at the same time, and such double acts are not only impressive but precious.

It is only through reflexivity that conservationists can forge a new route forwards, securing a truly sustainable social base and an acceptable relationship with humanity's fellow travellers (that is, non-human life). Informed argument, to which we hope this book has contributed, is the first step in self-criticism and reflexive understanding.

ETHICAL ENGAGEMENT

Perhaps the key conclusion of this book is that conservationists need to move from preservationist ideologies to new forms of ethical engagement with the land. The challenge to make this shift has come, in part, from indigenous people (see, for example, Chapter 4) and from the literature on post-colonialism (see Chapters 2 and 3). It has also come from environmental historians and scientists who have reviewed the history of diverse relationships between people and non-human environments (see, for example, Flannery, 1994; Cronon, 1995). And it has also come from the shifts taking place in the way that the Western mind understands natural processes and the acceptance of the complexity and unpredictability of natural processes (see Chapter 10). From all of these sources, it has become increasingly apparent that non-engagement is simply not an option; but the questions remain: what constitutes an *ethical* form of engagement; and how can we 'negotiate' outcomes that respect the sometimes divergent needs of humans and non-humans?

Of course, there is no simple answer to these questions. And there is no answer that doesn't involve some forms of compromise or 'loss'. Certainly, indigenous peoples have commonly had countless generations of experience in managing their relationships with the non-human in order to inflict minimal damage and, sometimes, to ensure mutually beneficial outcomes. However, for a wide range of reasons, traditional ways of living have been, and will continue to be, compromised. Pre-colonial practices are only partially relevant. Furthermore, strictly local approaches to healing relationships between human and non-human have limited appeal because they fail to challenge dominant practices of consumerist Westernized societies, and because the environmental 'problems' have grown from the local to the global. As Hector Magome and James Murombedzi demonstrate in Chapter 5, nature conservation challenges quickly spread from the local to the trans-national, bringing into play local, regional, national and international social and political institutions. For conservationists, the 1970s slogan 'Think globally and act locally' needs to be replaced by a more discursive dictum such as 'Think and act locally, nationally, trans-nationally and globally all at the same time, and do so in an ethical way'.

Not surprisingly, many well-meaning individuals feel overwhelmed by the complexity of this task and pin their hopes on national governments and international agencies to 'solve' the problems. The history of the 20th century, in particular, offers no reason to have confidence in this hope and, at any rate, it should not be left to representative institutions to grapple with the complexities of ethical behaviour. For a 'land ethic' to become a reality, it must grow from the daily practice of the people who see a need to mount an effective challenge to prevailing attitudes and practices. In his book *How Are We To Live?* (1995), the controversial Australian ethicist and pioneer of 'animal liberation' Peter Singer offers hope to the overwhelmed by saying that an applied notion of ethics suggests that the best any of us can do is to *minimize* the harm that we might inflict on other humans and non-human life. To internalize such an 'applied' ethical code – so that ethical behaviour becomes almost intuitive – we need deep awareness of the kinds of impacts our actions can have, sometimes a very long way from where we live and work. We need deep understanding of the way in which ecological systems work; but, at the same time, we should abandon attempts at ethical purity that are based upon rigid and dogmatic patterns of thought.

A willingness to act on the basis of ethical compromise can also help conservationists in their complex dealings with people and organizations who may share only part of their conservation goals. As Penelope Figgis points out in Chapter 9, active conservationists are being faced with more complex options for furthering their conservation agendas, sometimes even 'supping with the devil' in order to achieve better negotiated outcomes. Of course, many writers have pointed out (see, for example, Beder, 2000) that compromises can easily reach the point where they undermine conservation goals and even strengthen anti-conservation forces. Again, it is a question of developing applied ethical codes that grow out of deep ecological understanding and experience with the complex political processes that are part of any negotiation across competing agendas.

So, we reach the end of a book that has probably raised more questions than answers. As editors, we started with some ambitious aims and we knew that the book could only address them partially. We have been both delighted and challenged by the way our contributors have developed their arguments; their independent contributions deserve to stand in their own right. Readers will surely detect differences of opinion and differences of emphasis between contributors. However, this is just as it should be, for the dialogue we are hoping to foster is difficult and complex. When we conceived this book we wanted to show how much work there is to be done in decolonizing attitudes towards both people and nature. Our contributors have demonstrated that this work is not only urgent and necessary, but also highly stimulating. The challenge of a colonial heritage is one that conservation movements must face. If we do so without flinching, and in a spirit of innovation, there is much strength conservationists can draw from the deep past in order to help in uncertain and challenging futures.

NOTES

1   The term 'land ethic' was coined by US conservation pioneer Aldo Leopold; but it seems very appropriate to our purposes here.

REFERENCES

Adams, W M (2001) *Green Development: environment and sustainability in the Third World.* Routledge, London

Beder, S (2000) *Global Spin: The Corporate Assault on Environmentalism*, second edition. Scribe Publications, Melbourne

Cronon, W (1995) 'The trouble with wilderness; or, getting back to the wrong nature' in W Cronon (ed) *Uncommon Ground: toward reinventing nature*. W W Norton and Co, New York, pp69–90

Flannery, T (1994) *The Future Eaters: An Ecological History of the Australasian Lands and People*. Reed Books, Melbourne

Singer, P (1995) *How Are We To Live? Ethics In An Age of Self-Interest*. Mandarin, Melbourne

Index